Jill Hedges has been Senior Analyst for Latin America at Oxford Analytica since 2001 and was formerly Editorial Manager of the business information service at Esmerk Argentina. She has a PhD in Latin American Studies from the University of Liverpool.

'Jill Hedges tells the story of Argentina clearly. There is considerable emphasis given to the careers and calculations of the ruling strata, particularly the political careers of Juan Domingo Perón and his wives Evita and Isabelita. This is a concise, well-informed, and highly readable one-volume history.'

Laurence Whitehead, Nuffield College, Oxford

'Jill Hedges here provides a fact-laden and accurate political history that will be helpful to students of contemporary Argentina. She covers all of the key political movements – Liberalism, Radicalism, Peronism – while shedding particularly useful light on such institutions as the Church and the military. Her explanations of the twists and turns in Argentine economic policy are thorough and clear.'

Matthew B. Karush, George Mason University

ARGENTINA

A MODERN
HISTORY

Jill Hedges

I.B. TAURIS

LONDON · NEW YORK

New paperback edition published in 2015 by
I.B.Tauris & Co Ltd
London • New York
www.ibtauris.com

First published in hardback in 2011 by I.B.Tauris & Co. Ltd

ISBN: 978 1 78453 106 5
eISBN: 978 0 85773 057 2

A full CIP record for this book is available from the British Library
A full CIP record is available from the Library of Congress

Library of Congress Catalog Card Number: available

Printed and bound by CPI Group (UK) Ltd, Croydon, CR04YY

Front Cover Images:
Flag: © Julydfg | Dreamstime.com
Bronzes of Juan & Eva Perón: Photo by Stephen St. John/
National Geographic/Getty Images
Cover Design: Jan Marshall

CONTENTS

Illustrations vii

Acknowledgements ix

Preface to the Paperback Edition xi

Preface xiii

Introduction 1

1 National Consolidation 1853–80 11

2 The 'Golden Age' 1880–1930 24

3 The Infamous 'Decade' 1930–43 46

4 Peronism: The Original Protagonists 61

5 The Rise of Perón, 1943–5 81

6 The 'Revolution' of 17 October 1945 98

7 Peronism in Power 1946–52: The First
   Presidency 116

8 The Death of Evita and the Fall of Perón 148

9 Peronism Proscribed 170

10 Descent into Chaos 198

11 Provincial Perspectives 220

12 Return to Democracy 245

13 Default and Disarray 269

Notes 295

Bibliography 302

Index 311

ILLUSTRATIONS

FIGURES

1. Map of Argentina (Courtesy University of Texas Library)   x
2. Former Presidents Bartolomé Mitre and Julio A. Roca at the inauguration of the monument to Garibaldi (Courtesy of the archive, *Diario La Nación*)   25
3. Funeral of one of those killed during the 'Tragic Week', January 1919 (Wikipedia)   38
4. President Hipólito Yrigoyen and US President-elect Herbert Hoover in Buenos Aires, 16 December 1928 (Courtesy of the archive, *Diario La Nación*)   42
5. Crowds in the Plaza de Mayo, cooling their feet in the fountain, 17 October 1945 (Wikipedia)   101
6. President Juan Domingo Perón and Eva Perón, November 1949 (Courtesy of the archive, *Diario La Nación*)   130
7. Eva Peron receiving a delegation of maritime workers from Mar del Plata (27 August 1951)   131
8. Perón and Evita, 17 October 1951 (Wikipedia, National Archive)   140
9. Funeral of Evita (Wikipedia, *Caras y Caretas*)   145
10. Crowds celebrating the victory of the coup d'etat in Argentina's *'Revolución Libertadora'* (Liberating Revolution) that overthrew Juan Perón (Wikipedia)   166
11. President Juan Domingo Perón and Vice-President María Estela Martínez de Perón receive Bolivian President Hugo Banzer (Courtesy of the archive, *Diario La Nación*)   206
12. A soldier cries at Juan Perón's funeral, 1974 (Wikipedia)   209
13. President María Estela Martínez de Perón (Isabelita), addressing the crowds on 1 May 1975 (to the left, Social Welfare Minister José López Rega) (courtesy of the archive, *Diario La Nación*)   210

14. General Jorge Videla, Admiral Emilio Massera and
    Brigadier Orlando Agosti, the junta that seized power on
    24 March 1976 (courtesy of the archive, *Diario La Nación*)   214
15. President Raúl Alfonsín receives the report of the National
    Commission on Disappeared Persons (CONADEP) from
    Ernesto Sabato (courtesy of the archive, *Diario La Nación*)   247
16. President Carlos Menem, 5 August 1997 (courtesy of the
    archive, *Diario La Nación*)   258
17. Inauguration of President Cristina Fernández de Kirchner,
    10 December 2007 (courtesy of the archive, *Diario La
    Nación*)   287

GRAPHS

1. Census results 1869–2010   xvi
2. Inflation   246
3. Unemployment   250
4. GDP   278

ACKNOWLEDGEMENTS

The list of those who deserve to be acknowledged for their help, patience, academic material and moral support is long, and the final result may or may not be considered worthy of their efforts. It is impossible to mention all those who have contributed in some way to the completion of this book, but their efforts are greatly appreciated. They include many in Buenos Aires and the rest of Argentina – academics, colleagues, politicians, bishops, archivists, friends and family – who have gone out of their way to help with searching out material and with suggestions and criticisms.

I owe special thanks to the late Tomás Eloy Martínez for his insightful comments on an earlier draft, and for his enthusiasm and encouragement in this project. Special thanks are also due to Sr. Ernesto Castrillón, the director of the archive of *Diario La Nación*, who kindly provided photos from the newspaper's extensive archive. The unpublished photo on page 131 was given to me some years ago by the daughter of a former photographer at the Peronist newspaper *Democracia*, whose generosity is also much appreciated.

Personally, I owe my deepest gratitude and affection to Andrés, Maggie, Gaucho and my beloved Tango for their patience and moral support, even when their patience must have worn very thin. The (undoubtedly) numerous errors, omissions and wrongful conclusion to be found in the final result are entirely the responsibility of the author.

Figure 1. Map of Argentina (Courtesy University of Texas Library)

PREFACE TO THE PAPERBACK EDITION

At the time of publication of the first edition of this book, President Cristina Fernández de Kirchner had yet to announce whether she would seek re-election in 2011 following the death of her husband, former President Néstor Kirchner, despite strong indications that she would do so in the absence of any evident successor. After seeing her approval rating fall to only around 26 per cent shortly before Kirchner's death in October 2010, a wave of public sympathy more than doubled her popularity within weeks and a year later she was re-elected with 54 per cent of the vote – more than 35 percentage points ahead of the second-placed Socialist candidate, Hermes Binner. Predictably, that wide margin encouraged the government to press ahead with 'deepening the model', despite rising economic difficulties – all of them attributed to the opposition – the global economic crisis, predatory foreign investors and the 'vulture funds' that refused to enter the debt restructurings in 2005 and 2010 and continued to seek full repayment of defaulted bond holdings through the US courts. (The latter, at least, offered a credible target, given both the amoral conduct of the funds and the widely criticised rulings issued by a US judge apparently unfamiliar with significant elements of the case, which blocked the Argentine government from making payments on performing debt and led to a new technical default in July 2014.) The president, dressed invariably in rigorous widow's black for several years after her husband's death, made all such economic announcements on national television (with private media under increasing pressure), always backed by an image of Eva Perón – smiling or with clenched fist, depending on the nature of the announcement.

Despite the damage to the domestic economy, the president's increasingly 'us versus the world' attitude gained popular support within the country while undermining prospects of increased investment or a return to international financial markets. The latter factor has represented a particular concern: after taking a number of economic decisions scarcely designed to boost investor confidence, such as the 2012 re-nationalisation of former state oil company YPF, other costly decisions such as an eventual and rather generous compensation to

Spanish Repsol for YPF's assets, a deal to repay Paris Club debt and an attempt to produce more credible inflation statistics had been taken precisely with a view to gaining access to credit. The intransigent attitude on the part of both government and vultures that produced the new default (a term the government rejects) put paid to new credit at least for the time being, leaving the country worryingly dependent on shrinking international reserves and on exports of genetically modified soya to China.

Even the 'economic miracle' so long touted by the authorities proved something illusory: a new GDP calculation resulted in a significant reduction in the growth racked up under the Kirchner administrations since 2003, while efforts to produce more accurate inflation figures were rapidly rolled back, leaving official estimates far below the calculations of private economists who put 2014 inflation above 40 per cent. Similarly, confusion over inflation data led to the suspension of official poverty data, although here too unofficial estimates of around a third of the population below the poverty line diverged sharply from an official rate under 10 per cent.

So far, so much the same. A relatively poor result in the mid-term legislative elections in 2013 put paid to any notion of reforming the constitution to allow Fernández de Kirchner to seek a third term in 2015, leaving the president's Victory Front faction of the Peronist party again without an obvious successor candidate, despite a proliferation of would-be heirs and a rise in opinion polls by a dissident Peronist, Sergio Massa, and the centre-right mayor of Buenos Aires, Mauricio Macri. The strongest of the potential allies, Buenos Aires Governor Daniel Scioli, is only a 'quasi-ally' distrusted by the president, and whose position as governor allows him little room to distance himself from her government. With the president looking set to leave office in a negative economic context, the 'heir' is likely to receive a complicated legacy – and indeed the president might prefer an opposition win on the theory that this would favour her return in 2019. What all this suggests is how little politics, and economic policy-making, have evolved in Argentina even since the 2001 collapse, and despite the decline of traditional political party support. The continuing personalism of politics, and the lack of solid programmatic party structures and platforms that can readily be accepted or rejected, suggests that the boom-bust cycle of politics and economics will continue, with Argentina still 'never missing an opportunity to miss an opportunity'.

PREFACE

Having become one of the world's most prosperous economies by the early part of the twentieth century, Argentina has since suffered a series of boom-and-bust cycles that have seen it fall below regional neighbours such as Chile on a number of economic indicators – most recently the spectacular growth of the 1990s that ended in the economic crash, and the biggest sovereign default in history, in 2001. At the same time Argentina, since independence, has proved unsuccessful in creating an overarching national identity for a country 'descended from ships', and its political and social history has been marked by frictions, violence, a 50-year series of military coups d'etat and a persistent tendency for Argentines to identify themselves primarily in opposition to others: 'federalists and unitarians', 'civilization and barbarity', 'Radicals and Conservatives', 'Peronists and anti-Peronists'. Such difficulty in defining and resolving a common past has increased the difficulties in resolving a national project for the present and the future. This difficulty comes despite the lack of significant ethnic or linguistic divisions: by 2004, some 86 per cent of the population was defined as of white European origin (mainly Italian and Spanish), with around another 8 per cent described as *mestizo*/mixed race, some 4 per cent as Arab or of East Asian descent and only 1.5 per cent – some 600,000 people – as indigenous, of whom the Mapuches in the south and the Tobas in the north formed the largest groups.[1]

Immigration would, of course, be key to the make-up of modern Argentina and its relatively homogeneous population. In the nineteenth century, immigration rose from under 21,000 arrivals in 1871 to a peak of some 261,000 in 1889, reaching a total of over 1.5 million people during that period. Between 1891 and 1914, the number of immigrants increased to over 4.3 million, peaking in the decade before the outbreak of the First World War. By 1914, there were over 1 million Italians and some 800,000 Spanish living in Argentina; Italy and Spain above all would continue to generate a flow of migrants to Argentina in the interwar period and, in the case of Spain, even until the 1960s (although flows of migrants who returned to their home countries were not inconsiderable). However, although the descendants of those immigrants defined the modern ethnic breakdown noted above, the impact of immigration was mixed. For one thing, immigrants were disproportionately concentrated in urban areas: by 1914, they formed a majority of the male population in large cities, but only around a third of the population in Buenos Aires province, a quarter in Córdoba and some 10 per cent in Tucumán, with far smaller proportions in other parts of the country, especially rural areas. Moreover, only a very small number of those who arrived in the nineteenth and early twentieth centuries became naturalized, with most opting against Argentine citizenship. On the face of it, citizenship brought few benefits to economic migrants – indeed, it carried with it the obligation to do military service – but the lack thereof ensured that large middling sections of the population were politically unorganized and unrepresented.

This identity deficit, highlighted by continuing frictions between Buenos Aires and the 'interior', is perhaps one factor explaining the enduring attraction of Peronism since its origins in the early 1940s: Peron's maxim, 'if I define, I exclude', provided for a broad form of identification covering a range of different regional, socio-economic and political experiences. However, this also provided the basis of an amorphous and ideologically vacuous political platform that has eluded a precise definition for 50 years, thus distorting the country's entire political spectrum.

This lack of an overarching national identity, since Argentina's inception as an independent country, is not altogether surprising, given the broad and divergent range of histories, cultures and experiences of its 23 provinces. As Nicolas Shumway notes, the Spanish American colonies were designed to service the Spanish economy rather than to be entities possessing a national identity; this lack, together with the dislocation caused by the colonization process, made the creation of any common past virtually impossible – not least given persistent disputes among postcolonial leaders over what that past (and future) should be.[2] Continuing centralization of power in Buenos Aires and the resentments this has caused have only contributed to this lack of cohesion: 'They are not two parties, they are two countries; they are not centralists and federalists, they are Buenos Aires and the provinces.'[3] So considerable are the divisions over how to interpret

Argentina's history that even diagnoses of its long-standing problems and characteristics differ wildly: while Jonathan Brown considers that the underlying problems of Argentina relate to the 'coincidence of political power and economic privilege' and to 'prejudice and rigid class structures', Felix Luna defines the society's key characteristics as 'tolerance and pluralism', saying that 'democracy and egalitarianism . . . are invariable vectors of our history'.[4]

In practice, both these definitions hold some truth. Argentina has historically suffered from social and economic divisions, and political power and economic privilege have tended to coincide – as is the case elsewhere. Prejudice and classism, however frequently denied, have also existed since colonial times. However, since the nineteenth century Argentine society has enjoyed a strong degree of egalitarianism at least insofar as this relates to those of immigrant origin as opposed to those of *mestizo* or indigenous appearance. Although, as noted above, most immigrants in the nineteenth and early twentieth centuries were disenfranchised and had limited political weight, many had aspirations – in particular, economic aspirations – that were more readily achievable than in their countries of origin. With the rise of state universities and an expanding public sector, the children of immigrants at least enjoyed realistic hopes of entering the middle class and the commercial or professional sphere. Also, since the cities of Argentina were relatively new and class structures remained fluid, it was possible to be less fixed to a given class, allowing for social upward mobility. The paradox, however, is that the lack of fixed class could also imply the risk of downward mobility, arguably the reason why the more precarious members of the middle class felt more threatened by the poor than the members of the elite who were unlikely to be taken for anything else (even though family fortunes fell as well as increased).

Although unlikely to be regarded as 'aristocracy' by the colonial elite in the provinces, many immigrants could enjoy economic, social and cultural privileges unavailable to many in Europe at the time. Given that most European immigrants were economic migrants, therefore, Argentine society perceived their country as wealthy and sophisticated in comparison with the southern European countries that produced so many impoverished migrants; at the same time, Argentines who travelled in Europe were, by definition, usually wealthy, and the term 'wealthy as an Argentine' came into vogue

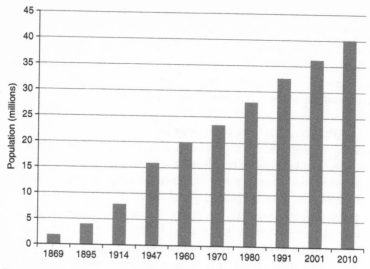

Graph 1. Census results 1869–2010

in Europe in the 1920s – many visitors famously brought not only their children's nurses, but also a cow to ensure good-quality milk. These somewhat unrealistic perceptions have likely contributed to Argentine feelings of insecurity with regard to Europe since the second half of the twentieth century; having viewed themselves as better educated and better off than their European counterparts, the decline of Argentina and the rise of southern European economies in recent decades has encouraged the illusion that Argentina has 'failed' its great promise and been overtaken by the countries it once patronized.

Nevertheless, neither these historical discrepancies nor the failure to attain early promise are unique to Argentina; indeed, relatively unsuccessful states are arguably far more common than successful ones, and some successes have been, at least in part, attributable to outside factors not present in Argentina. It is often argued that Argentina might reasonably have been expected to develop in the same pattern as Italy and Spain, the two countries that provided most of its immigrants and much of its culture. For example, Paul Lewis argues that Argentine capitalism might have developed along Italian lines had it not suffered constant state intervention.[5] However, it might be at least equally valid to argue that, in the absence of the much more dramatic interventions experienced by Italy and Spain – 40 years of Franco government, the Second World War and the Marshall Plan, and entry into the EU – either of those countries might have gone the same way as Argentina. At the same time, it could be argued that the perception of Argentina's failures has been exaggerated by the widespread feeling that the country is 'condemned to success', as former president Eduardo Duhalde put it; in 1929, José Ortega y Gasset noted that Argentines 'do not content themselves with being one nation among others: they hunger for an overarching destiny, they demand of themselves a proud future'.[6] Nevertheless, the persistence of the maxim that 'Argentina never misses an opportunity to miss an opportunity' is striking and needs to be explained.

While it would be teleological to contend that Argentina's roots condemn it to perpetual factionalism and disruption (and indeed its situation in that respect is not altogether unique), some continuing patterns can be traced throughout its modern history that have contributed to its patchy record as a nation. One of these is unquestionably the strongly-rooted tendency towards factionalism and opposition to an 'other' whose definitions change over time but whose general characteristics remain strikingly similar; tied to this is the persistent identification of interests as a zero-sum game in which some sectors must win and others lose. Another is the development of an economy that has depended, and continues to depend, on foreign markets, imports and capital, something that has exacerbated domestic economic boom-and-bust cycles as international market and investment climates fluctuate, as well as perpetuated deeply held suspicions of foreign interests and influences. The difficulty in reaching any broad degree of consensus and legitimacy has also led governments over the past century – Radicals, Peronists and military – to resort to heavy public spending as a means of satisfying and retaining their own client base; the resulting political difficulty in curbing spending, despite the fact that revenues have seldom covered outgoings, has led repeatedly to financing the deficit through printing money or increased debt-taking, leading to periodic inflation and payments crises.

Finally (though not exclusively), the weakness of institutions and lack of trust in them has been a constant throughout Argentina's modern history, as has the search for an individual capable of substituting for weak institutions. As early as 1829, General José de San

Martín observed that 'in effect, they seek a saviour,...who would save the country from the troubles that threaten it', recognizing, as his biographer John Lynch notes, the tendency 'to seek an imagined solution, not by changing institutions, where the real trouble lay, but by imposing strong government'.[7] He could well have been speaking 150 years later.

This book aims to provide a history of modern Argentina focusing on the period from the adoption of the 1853 constitution onward and, in particular, the continuing failure to create an overarching national identity or a relatively coherent economic model based on cooperation and effort rather than zero-sum principles:

- The book therefore proposes to start from the examination of how Argentina has functioned as a so-called federal system from 1853 onwards, although in practice federalism has proved largely a mechanism for party politics and clientelism – used by both provincial and national governments to retain power and to disguise the fact that both the nation and the provinces are politically weak and dependent. Thus, the concept of federalism has been used to paper over weaknesses in the union of disparate territorial entities, despite the fact that Argentina's highly centralized, presidentialist system has made federalism an empty concept, in particular since 1930.
- It will consider the implications of the large-scale agricultural model adopted from the 1870s in particular, the impact of massive immigration, the rise of an urban middle class and the increasing tensions between the traditional oligarchy and new socially mobile citizens that gave rise to the creation of the Radical Party, universal male suffrage and the expansion of public employment as a mechanism to dispense political patronage.
- It will also address how these tensions, and the economic impact of the Great Depression, led to civilian collusion in the 1930 coup d'état, and the political and economic effects of the policies adopted during the 'Infamous Decade', as well as the role played by other sectors of society (notably the Catholic Church and the labour movement).

The book will devote considerable space to the phenomenon of Peronism from 1943 to the present, in a bid to explain a historical movement which has successfully reinvented itself over time to represent the changing aspirations of large sectors of society. It will also take the premise that, while Peronism has usually been written about as an incomprehensible phenomenon or a form of Latin American fascism, it is in fact a more straightforward political movement than is usually supposed, and extremely explicable in the context of its (changing) times in Argentina. It will look at the movement from its beginnings in the early 1940s through its later version in the governments of Presidents Carlos Menem, Eduardo Duhalde and Nestor and Cristina Kirchner. Both Menem and the Kirchners could be said to have undermined their initial successes by failing to maintain this capacity for change and moving away from initial pragmatism to ideological rigidity.

Since the early 1940s, Peronism has seemingly metamorphosed into apparently irreconcilable factions on the far left and far right, into the neo-liberal 'Menemism' at the end of the twentieth century and into the supposed 'New Left' under Nestor and Cristina Kirchner. However, Peronism is not especially 'enigmatic', to use Robert Crassweller's word,[8] just as Argentina is not an especially 'enigmatic' country. Nevertheless, it is an unusually emotive phenomenon, and this book also hopes to explain the emotive, unscientific elements of Peronism to readers outside Argentina, whose recent history cannot be understood without an understanding of Peronism and the influences underlying it. In particular, this understanding is needed to put into context at least three of the most significant failures of recent years: the 'Dirty War' of the 1970s, the difficulty of constructing a culture of democracy post 1983 (as opposed to the institution of regular elections) and the 2001–2002 economic and political debacle and its aftermath. The difficulties in constructing a more transparent, coherent and representative political system will influence the direction of the post-crisis future and prospects for greater future stability.

INTRODUCTION

The area of South America that would eventually become the Argentine Republic was not immediately attractive to the Spanish who came to the continent seeking wealth. Despite the optimistic name given to the Río de la Plata (River of Silver), where the port of Buenos Aires would eventually be constructed, the river itself was a muddy estuary and silver and other precious metals were scarce in the region, unlike Alto Perú (now Bolivia), immediately to the north, where the silver mines of Potosí would become a key source of Spanish wealth in the seventeenth and eighteenth centuries. Nor was the area home to great indigenous cultures such as the Incas in Peru, whose own empire tailed off in the part of northwest Argentina that is now Catamarca and La Rioja. On the contrary, the area was sparsely populated by indigenous groups, roughly calculated to have numbered only around 700,000 people (similar to the number of Argentines identified as indigenous today) in an area some five times the size of France, who in the main were nomadic rather than settled populations dedicated to agriculture or the working of precious metals.

As such, in the sixteenth century the area offered little of interest to the Spanish in terms of wealth, a captive work force or even souls to be converted to Christianity. The latter point had a lasting effect on the Catholic Church's influence in Argentina: a relatively poor institution that found it difficult to attract priests, the Catholic Church has traditionally had less influence than in the rest of Latin America, which has often led the hierarchy to adopt a defensive position in the belief that the institution is under attack from 'anti-clerical' governments. (The one obvious exception to this generalized statement is the case of the Jesuits, who dominated academic life, in Córdoba province in particular, and also enjoyed substantial religious, political and economic weight through the missions established in the northeast until they were expelled from Spanish territories in 1767.)

Given the lack of immediately obvious attractions, the southern end of Spain's American colonies was slow to develop. In particular, it took many decades for the area around what is now Buenos Aires to become established as a permanent settlement, with little hint of its future dominant role in the later United Provinces of the Río de la Plata, the Argentine Confederation and the Argentine Republic. The coast where Buenos Aires now stands was explored by Juan de Solís as early as 1516, but his expedition ended in failure amid lethal Indian attacks. In 1536 Pedro de Mendoza attempted, again unsuccessfully, to found a settlement at the mouth of the estuary, but again the Spanish were routed by disease and hostile Indian attacks, leaving nothing but the cattle and horses that would form the initial basis of the wild herds that would later be found in the Pampas region. It was not until 1580 that Juan de Garay successfully founded a permanent settlement (Santa María del Buen Ayre) on the site of Mendoza's failed experiment, by which time permanent settlements had been in place for two or three decades in Tucumán and Cuyo (what is now Mendoza) and cities had already been founded in Santiago del Estero (1554), Tucumán (1565) and Córdoba (1573). Indeed, the first governorships were created in Tucumán and Paraguay-Río de la Plata in 1563, and the first diocese in the territory was created in Tucumán in 1570, a decade before Buenos Aires was successfully founded. However, the governorship of Tucumán, which included Córdoba, Santiago del Estero, Jujuy, Salta, La Rioja and Catamarca, as well as Tucumán itself, was far larger and more important than that of the Río de la Plata headquartered in Buenos Aires.

The rise of population centres in Tucumán and Córdoba (followed by Salta in 1582, La Rioja in 1591 and Jujuy in 1593) was attributable to their importance as commercial and agricultural centres serving the silver economy based in Potosí. The eventual decision to found the city of Buenos Aires was in response to the same cause: the need to create an Atlantic port to ship silver from Potosí to Spain and goods from Spain to the colonies, rather than continue to trade solely through the Pacific port of Lima. This was followed by the establishment of the cities of Santa Fe and Corrientes in the early seventeenth century in order to provide a river route from Buenos Aires to Alto Perú. However, Buenos Aires remained small, poor and struggling in its early decades, living off of contraband – primarily from Brazil – in order to meet local needs ignored by the Spanish, for whom trade through the port was devoted exclusively to shipments of silver from Potosí to Spain and of Spanish goods for the wealthier and more productive settlements in Alto Perú. Thus, from an early period, 'the *porteños* [residents of Buenos Aires] acquired the custom of evading the law: they knew that they could thus live in much better conditions'.[1] This has been argued to be the early origin of the *porteño* characteristic of finding ways around the law where the law is burdensome: '*hecha la ley, hecha la trampa*' ('where there's a law there's a loophole'). Contraband trade was increased following the 1703 alliance between Portugal and Great Britain, which boosted illegal trade with the British via Brazil.

Most contraband goods were paid for through the sale of hides from the wild cattle herds that had grown up on the Pampas grasslands since Pedro de Mendoza's luckless settlement; cattle round-ups (*vaquerías*) took place regularly to kill cattle for their hides, with the rest of the animal left where it fell, largely unusable before the advent of salting or chilling. Exports of hides rose to some 100,000 annually by the mid-seventeenth century and to around 700,000 by 1700. The *vaquerías* were eventually prohibited in 1715 as the herds were decimated by slaughter, risking the extinction of Buenos Aires's chief commodity. This coincided with the rise of an increasingly structured ranching sector well placed to capitalize on the trade; at the time the *vaquerías* were banned, 26 *estancias* (ranches) were already in place in the area surrounding Buenos Aires. This early consolidation of large-scale agricultural exploitation had several consequences for subsequent developments. Firstly, it squeezed out smaller producers, reducing prospects for the consolidation of a rural middle class in the province. Secondly, it cemented the dominance of an activity that was not labour-intensive, ensuring that the region remained sparsely populated and that the rural gaucho labour force was poor and nomadic. Thirdly, and related to the second point, it made Argentina a relatively small exploiter of slave labour, which was not needed for agricultural purposes; the majority of slaves were urban domestic servants rather than farm labourers. (The virtual disappearance of Buenos Aires's black population after the mid-nineteenth century has given rise to much speculation, and has been attributed to the disproportionate number of former slaves and their descendants who were involved in the armies of independence, Rosas's militias and the War of the Triple Alliance, as well as to the effects of periodic yellow fever outbreaks.)

Despite its economic marginality in the eighteenth century, Buenos Aires began to concentrate (if not greatly profit from) trade flows

with Spain, and became increasingly isolated from trends in its hinterland. While interior provinces increasingly began to specialize in
determined types of output, and made common alliances to defend
against Indian attacks, Buenos Aires did not, and contributed little to
the common good. This became a greater issue of contention from
1776, when the Viceroyalty of the Río de la Plata – the last viceroyalty
of the Spanish American empire – was created with Buenos Aires as its
capital. As a result, other governorships were subordinated to Buenos
Aires, exacerbating existing rivalries. These rivalries were worsened by
the establishment of free trade in 1778, which gave Buenos Aires a
virtual monopoly through the port, and by the disruptions to Spanish
trade arising from the US War of Independence and the Napoleonic
Wars. Diminished trade weakened Buenos Aires's key tie with Spain,
boosting its illicit trade with British and Dutch ships, as well as height-
ening resentment in the interior. With silver from Potosí now shipped
through Buenos Aires rather than Lima, *porteño* merchants were virtually the only group to benefit from the new realities, strengthening
a class whose influence was based on wealth rather than land, titles
or government posts. Moreover, events in Europe underscored Spain's
relative weakness, while the French Revolution encouraged the ques-
tioning of hitherto unquestioned assumptions over empire and the
rights of monarchy.

   In 1806 a British naval force invaded Buenos Aires, cementing the
decline of Spanish influence. While the Spanish Viceroy, the Marquis
de Sobremonte, and his military force abandoned the city, *porteños* led
by Santiago Liniers and the local militia defeated the invading force,
forcing out a second British invasion in 1807 using British weapons
captured in 1806. Although the Spanish authorities would later return, they did so with greatly diminished credibility and power, while
the *porteños'* own administrative and military power, as well as their
self-confidence and prestige, were significantly raised by the events.
However, authority over the interior was no better exercised by Buenos
Aires than by Spain, and corruption and bad practices remained endemic, while imports of cheaper goods from Britain and other sources
hit interior economies and products that had previously enjoyed a
degree of protection. Thus, while the resentments of the *porteños* were
concentrated on Spain, the resentments of the interior were concentrated on Buenos Aires.

   In 1810, with the French invasion of Spain, leaders of the Buenos
Aires militia called an open meeting (*cabildo abierto*), which on 25 May

voted to oust the viceroy and elected a representative governing body (the *Primera Junta*), which in turn designated a Triumvirate to lead Buenos Aires. However, the Junta pledged allegiance to the Spanish king, once he was freed by the French, rather than declaring outright independence. It nevertheless angered the interior – which wanted Spanish rule replaced by local government – by seeking to collect taxes, control foreign relations and name governors itself, in place of the Spanish authorities (and, logically, to its own benefit rather than that of the other provinces). The hero of the 1806 uprising, Santiago Liniers, was imprisoned and executed for his opposition to these moves. Moreover, the Junta was plagued by bitter splits and infighting; one of its key members – Mariano Moreno – who called for the proclamation of an independent republic, was ousted in 1811 and died at sea on his way to Europe. By 1812, when Congress declared the sovereignty of the so-called United Provinces, political power was concentrated largely on the Triumvirate's secretary, Bernardino Rivadavia, whose centralizing policies were seen as particularly nefarious for the interests of the interior, focusing on free trade and control of the port and customs by Buenos Aires.

Similarly, Buenos Aires – and Rivadavia in particular – gave only limited political and financial support to the independence struggles led by figures such as General Manuel Belgrano (leader of the Army of the North), Martín Guemes and his Salta gauchos and the Liberator, General José de San Martín, who, after commanding the Army of the North in 1814, created the Army of Cuyo and crossed the Andes from Mendoza to liberate Chile in 1817, before moving north to Peru. This, in turn, increased scepticism over the rule that could be expected from Buenos Aires, with San Martín taking the view that political strife in Buenos Aires represented a greater danger than Spanish domination. San Martín, born in Yapeyú, Corrientes, in 1778, was the son of a Spanish official and an Argentine mother. Brought up in Spain from an early age, he began his military career in the Spanish army at the age of 14. He returned to Argentina in 1814 to offer his services to the United Provinces in the wars of independence, where his prestige earned him some distrust on the part of political figures such as Rivadavia. A brilliant tactician, San Martín created a disciplined and successful military force largely out of volunteers (willing or reluctant) and slaves, despite the lack of solid support from Buenos Aires.

Independence was not declared until 9 July 1816, at the Congress of Tucumán, following San Martín's invasion of Chile, and Juan Martín de Pueyrredón was elected as the first director of the United Provinces of the Río de la Plata. However, the 1819 constitution generated protests and uprisings over the power it gave Buenos Aires over the interior (in particular, control over navigation), and Pueyrredón was deposed the same year after losing disputes with the federalist leaders of Santa Fe and Entre Ríos provinces, Estanislao López and Francisco Ramírez. His successor, José Rondeau, was defeated in 1820, after which the constitution was abrogated. San Martín thereafter resigned his post as commander of the army, on the basis that he had no authority now that the government that he served had disappeared.[2] The aftermath saw a new rise in conflicts between federalists in the interior and unitarians in Buenos Aires, the latter again led by Rivadavia, who became president of the United Provinces in 1826.

Even before that date, Rivadavia was responsible for key measures, including the establishment of the state University of Buenos Aires in 1821 and the taking of a 1 million pound loan from Barings of London in 1824 for the purpose of establishing a national bank to finance public spending. The onerous terms of the loan implied that only about half the amount was received, the remainder going on commissions, and the repayments would contribute to Argentina's first debt crisis. The first default on repayments came following the 1825–8 blockade of Buenos Aires by Brazil in the context of a war that saw Brazil annex Uruguay (which had already declared its independence from Buenos Aires in 1814 following a revolt by José Artigas premised on the abolition of slavery, egalitarian policies and land reform). Also, in 1824, a new electoral law was adopted, ostensibly providing for universal suffrage, although in practice it excluded large swathes of the population including servants, soldiers, the illiterate, those under 20 – and of course women. In 1825 the government signed a 'free trade and friendship treaty' with Great Britain, which gave Britain substantial commercial advantages that would be enjoyed for decades. Under the treaty, London guaranteed that British merchant ships would receive the same privileges as Argentina's (non-existent) merchant fleet, and that Buenos Aires would supply raw materials while purchasing manufactures from Britain.

In 1826, Rivadavia took two further key steps: the Law of Emphyteusis and the presentation of a new constitution. The Law of Emphyteusis, which was designed to raise revenues to pay off the Barings loan, envisaged the leasing of public lands to agricultural producers in order to boost output and 'settle' the lands around Buenos Aires. However, the law set no limits on the size of the holdings to be leased, and in practice favoured existing large landholders, cementing the structure of the agricultural sector as one based on huge extensions, minimizing the land available to small farmers. By 1830, some 538 lessees had received an estimated 8.6 million hectares, paying only a derisory 5,000 pesos in rents to the state.[3] Nor was the proposed new constitution a success. Under the 1825 Fundamental Law, provinces were allowed to be self-governing until such time as the new constitution was promulgated with the approval of all of the provincial governments. However, the constitution was rejected as a centralizing measure, and in 1827 Rivadavia resigned and the national government was dissolved, marking a return to provincial self-rule except in the area of foreign relations.

As governor of Buenos Aires province in 1827, Manuel Dorrego presided over the return to an Argentine Confederation, as opposed to the fictitious United Provinces, and also over the 1828 peace treaty with Brazil, which created the Oriental Republic of Uruguay. Dorrego also found himself saddled with a large public debt, an army at a loose end following the treaty with Brazil and inflationary pressures that led to moves to fix the prices of necessities such as bread and meat. Faced with a range of dissatisfied constituencies and a lack of funds to pay the returning troops, Dorrego quickly became the target of conspiracies and was ousted from power and executed by General Juan Lavalle, hitherto a prominent figure in the wars of independence.

In a context of increasing chaos and violence, Buenos Aires sought a figure capable of restoring a measure of order, and settled on Juan Manuel de Rosas (1793–1877), known as the Restorer of the Laws (though whether in practice there were pre-existing laws to restore is questionable). A relative of the Anchorena family, one of Argentina's wealthiest, Rosas was himself a large landowner, a successful rancher and the owner of one of the province's first meat-salting plants (*saladeros*). He was also known for his carefully cultivated rapport with the gauchos who worked for him, and respected for his authority; in 1820 he had led a gaucho militia in support of the federalist cause, which increasingly represented the country's most important economic interests, rather than the interior provinces. Rosas himself would note that most of the country's leaders were comfortable only with the educated classes, but had little knowledge of, or respect for, the poor. He was also consciously pragmatic, noting that 'they think that I am a federalist; no sir, I am of no party, but of the country'.[4]

In 1829 Rosas was elected governor of Buenos Aires, and, in alliance with the *caudillos* Estanislao López (Santa Fe) and Facundo Quiroga (La Rioja) in the Confederation of the Río de la Plata, successfully defeated unitarian resistance in Córdoba, Santa Fe and Entre Ríos. However, Rosas and Quiroga were in disagreement over the need to create a constitutional framework for the Confederation, with Quiroga in favour and Rosas opposed, on the grounds that existing conditions did not allow for such a national construct. In 1832, when his term ended, Rosas left office and led military campaigns against tribes in the south of the province, although his advances in securing a reduction in Indian attacks were due as much to patronage – payment of tribute to chiefs considered sympathetic – as to warfare. His successes in the Indian campaign increased his prestige among large landowners, not least because they expanded the lands available for exploitation. While he was out of office, his wife Doña Encarnación kept him advised of political developments, purportedly taking a hand in destabilizing his successors, and urged him to spare no effort or expense in maintaining the loyalty of the poor. Rosas himself professed to have withdrawn from political life. However, following the assassination of Quiroga and facing the rising risk of civil war, in 1835 provincial authorities again offered him the governorship, this time with 'the sum of public power'.

The period of Rosas's second governorship, which was to extend until 1852, was marked by the increasing authoritarianism that has coloured his historical image, although it is also fair to say that the repression was widely tolerated by those who found it preferable to the risk of anarchy (and, indeed, that his opponents also employed violence that could not readily have been met by more moderate means). Making use of his ties with both the army and the Catholic Church – which had greater influence in the interior than in Buenos Aires, where Rivadavia's supposed anti-clericalism had led provincial opponents to rally around the slogan of 'religion or death' – Rosas also created a more sinister force, known as the *Mazorca*, to coordinate espionage and mete out punishment to opponents. Informers routinely included servants, who reported any anti-government attitudes on the part of their employers, and those accused of opposition were often tortured or had their throats cut. Much of Rosas's intelligence network was purportedly managed by Doña Encarnación, who died in 1838 of apparent poisoning. At the same time, Rosas was careful to attend to the concerns of his supporters, both rich and poor, for whom his daughter Manuelita became a key conduit, receiving petitions and bringing them to her father in a manner not unlike the functioning of the Eva Perón Foundation a century later.

Although Rosas was the embodiment of federalism in the 1830s, and of the dichotomy between unitarians and federalists – all public documents had to include the heading 'Long life the Federation, death to the Unitarian savages' – his defence of federalism always put Buenos Aires's own interests first. (Rosas, like Facundo Quiroga, was also the embodiment of barbarism for Domingo Sarmiento, who defined Argentina as a clash between 'civilization and barbarism'.[5]) Nevertheless, moves such as the 1835 Customs Law, which boosted Buenos Aires's rights over the port and customs duties, also protected some regional products through the imposition of high customs duties. Rosas's tariffs also encouraged the French blockade of 1838, in support of the unitarians led by Lavalle and exiled in Uruguay, which was joined by Great Britain in 1845 despite a string of military victories by the federalists. Rosas himself successfully strengthened his own credentials as a defender of national interests through the blockades; San Martín would bequeath him his sword, believing him the only man able to defend Argentina from outside aggression. Nor did Rosas neglect his own interests and those of his supporters: suspending the Law of Emphyteusis, he gave land titles to public officials and military officers, many of which were sold on to increase the holdings of large-scale ranchers. Rosas himself had accumulated some 800,000 acres by the time he was overthrown.

Under Rosas, much of the intellectual and ideological opposition to his rule was crystallized in the so-called Generation of '37, a group of young members of the educated elite including Sarmiento, Esteban Echeverría, Bartolomé Mitre and Juan Bautista Alberdi, a native of Tucumán who would become the source of inspiration for the 1853 constitution. While identifying Rosas as one side of the civilization–barbarism schism, these Enlightenment-influenced thinkers also sought to define the ills of Argentina and the possible shape of a future republic. Although idealistic in nature, many of their ideas suggest that they would have preferred a different country altogether, defining Argentina's ills primarily as its large space, Spanish heritage and uncultured population, and its prospects for success dependent on the need to attract northern European settlers to create a stable and prosperous rural population. This brand of thought did nothing to lessen the rifts between the supposedly 'Europeanized' Buenos Aires and the interior, and indeed contributed to Rosas's position as representative of the 'genuine' Argentina. This division was also repeated at regular intervals in Argentine history.

Despite a considerable degree of support (or fear) for Rosas from other provinces during much of his tenure, by the early 1850s the effects of trade restrictions and the centralizing power of Buenos Aires were increasing provincial opposition to his government. A former supporter, Justo José de Urquiza of Entre Ríos, united opposition to Rosas, defeating the *Rosista* forces at the Battle of Caseros in February 1852. Rosas and Manuelita subsequently went into exile in Southampton, where he remained until his death in 1877. Urquiza, who became the new director of the United Provinces, called a convention in San Nicolás, Buenos Aires province, later that year to establish the basis for an eventual constitution. The San Nicolás accord, which proposed the creation of a strong central government, a public education system (propelled primarily by Sarmiento) and liberal trade policies, was ratified by all other provinces but soundly rejected by Buenos Aires, which remained aloof from the refounded Argentine Confederation put in place after Rosas's fall. This brought no small difficulties for the nascent country: although Great Britain recognized the Confederation in 1853 and others followed suit, the entity did not represent an attractive trading partner in the absence of Buenos Aires. Nevertheless, Urquiza, who was elected the first president of the Confederation, created a new capital in Concepción del Uruguay (Entre Ríos) and called a constitutional convention for 1853. Although Buenos Aires would continue to reject that constitution and to eschew incorporation into the new entity for the rest of the 1850s, the first serious steps towards nation-building were under way, despite the intransigent difficulties posed not only by Buenos Aires but by mutually exclusive provincial interests.

1 National Consolidation 1853–80

The rising importance of Buenos Aires vis-à-vis the other provinces of the newly constituted Argentina generated widespread resentments and cemented (or promoted) inequalities among the units that would eventually make up the country's 23 provinces.

Despite resistance by Buenos Aires to the San Nicolás accord and the threat of seeing its own assets 'nationalized' by Urquiza's project, the constitutional convention was held in Santa Fe, without delegates from Buenos Aires, from November 1852 and in May 1853 approved a constitution that remains substantially in place today. The constitution established Argentina as a federal republic with a division of executive, legislative and judicial powers, whose federal government 'sustains' the Catholic faith (until 1994, the president was required to be a Catholic). Liberal in social terms, the constitution abolished slavery and established equality before the law, with no rights arising from birth or title. It established a bicameral Congress to represent both the provinces and the population, giving it authority to impose limitations on executive power over customs and foreign policy issues previously handled at the discretion of Buenos Aires. However, despite giving Congress broad legislative powers and setting out a number of federal guarantees, such as the establishment of a federal capital and the right of provinces to adopt their own constitutions and elect their own authorities, the constitution also institutionalized the federal government's authority to intervene in provinces 'to guarantee the republican form of government' or to 're-establish public order', both vague concepts whose openness to interpretation provided the pretext for many politically motivated interventions designed to oust unfriendly governors, as discussed in Chapter 11. Federal intervention was exercised 132 times between 1880 and 1891 alone.

Much criticism has centred on the fact that the Argentine constitution was largely modelled on that of the United States and the ideas of the French Revolution, without taking into account the substantially different political and cultural circumstances prevailing, and indeed in many respects it may be seen more as an expression of ideals than a reflection of reality. Criticism has also focused on its stipulated intention of boosting immigration: the constitution both guarantees equal rights for the foreign-born and commits the government to 'foment European immigration' without restriction on those wishing to come to Argentina to work. These provisions reflected the views of the constitution's chief intellectual authors, notably Domingo Sarmiento and Juan Bautista Alberdi, whose view that 'to govern is to populate' was influenced by the belief that Argentina's ills arose in large part from its Spanish heritage and domestic population, and that they could be redressed by importing Northern European migrants able to bring a different cultural background. The view that European immigration and free trade would tip the balance towards civilization and away from barbarism was later attacked by revisionist historians, who argued that the constitution sought to negate Argentina's national identity and Spanish heritage. In any case, the dominant position of large landholders undermined the prospects for real success of this planned immigration policy, while the constitution itself was insufficient to impose 'the republican form of government'.

The tendency to equate 'Argentina' with 'Buenos Aires' has glossed over the regional diversities and divergences, making it still more difficult to understand the interests and influences (often dysfunctional) that both define and divide the country and its provinces as a whole. Those provinces range from highly developed to very poor, from industrial to rural, from long-established colonial societies to sparsely and recently populated spaces with little common history.

Federalism in Argentina was clearly based on the US model where, unlike the Argentine case, the western frontier was expanded and settled in the first instance, chiefly by established US citizens from the east, thus ensuring at least a certain basis for uniformity of national and cultural identity. The USA has been described as a form of 'centralizing federalism', while Argentina might be described as a sort of 'federalizing centralism', as the central government has tended to promote federal relations and decentralization to the provinces when it has suited its convenience. However, the US constitution devolves much greater powers to the states than does the Argentine constitution. Although under Article 104 of the constitution the provinces 'conserve all power not delegated by this constitution to the federal government', in practice this in fact limited the provinces' remit chiefly to the election of provincial authorities and the promotion of industry, immigration and transport with provincial funds. In cases of overlap or inconsistency between federal and provincial law (e.g., in areas such as labour and penal law, primary education and provincial judicial systems), the federal system will dominate.

The principal limitation on federal autonomy, contained in Article 6 of the 1853 constitution, is the right of the federal government to intervene in the executive, judicial or legislative power of any province at any time it is felt necessary 'to guarantee the republican form of government'. The mechanism has been distorted for the political convenience of the central government and its allies on repeated occasions since 1853, and has been refined to make it an even more useful political tool. The faculty of intervention to combat sedition or invasion was arguably a valid provision in 1853, when the country was far from being consolidated and uprisings and inter-provincial strife were frequent. Between 1860 and 1880 a number of federal interventions were carried out to support the elected authorities or for guaranteeing the electoral process, although this type of intervention largely disappeared after the intervention of Buenos Aires on the grounds that its government was in armed insurrection against the national administration. This intervention, which ended with the federalization of the city of Buenos Aires and terminated the civil war between Buenos Aires and the provinces, consolidated the federal government's dominance. Thereafter, however, the use of intervention increased. Julio Roca intervened in only one province (Santiago del Estero) during his presidency, but his successor Miguel Juárez Celman used the mechanism on a number of occasions (notably in Tucumán in 1887, where the only opposition governor in the country was elected). Hipólito Yrigoyen and Juan Domingo Perón were the main users of the mechanism: Yrigoyen made 13 interventions during his 1916–22 term alone.

The constitution was also intended to eliminate the dominance of provincial *caudillos* such as Rosas and Quiroga through the construction of a strong central state, although in practice, here too it failed to either satisfy provincial autonomies or establish a central authority capable of imposing its will on divisive provinces. Indeed, the federal system was more akin to the defensive alliances formed by medieval city states than to a state of national unity, given the lack of agreement on an overarching national identity, and reflected (then as now) the weakness of states rather than their strength. Nevertheless, the federalist tone of the constitution cemented resistance by Buenos Aires, which remained outside the Argentine Confederation although still theoretically a part of a putative Argentine Republic. That resistance was driven to a large degree by self-interest, and the unwillingness to hand over control over its revenues and its militias to a national government – and indeed, to part with a federalized city of Buenos Aires destined to become the national capital.

As a result of this posture, an uneasy de facto coexistence continued through the 1850s, with a Confederation comprising 13 provinces and both the executive (under Urquiza, as the Confederation's first president, and the 'forgotten' Santiago Derqui, from 1860 its second and last president) and Congress temporarily based in Paraná, Entre Ríos. This position seriously undermined the viability of the provinces, with much trade still forced to pass through Buenos Aires and foreign interest concentrated there. Access to the port became more crucial with the rise in wool exports during the 1850s. Buenos Aires by this time was well ahead of the Confederation in terms of wealth and progress: by 1853 it had a limited railway system – the 25-mile Western Railway out of the city – and by 1857 gas lighting, while the provinces struggled with a minimal income base. It also had a thriving cultural scene, with literary salons and performances of plays (both local and imported) and operas, often soon after their European debuts. The first permanent opera house, the original Teatro Colón, opened in 1857 with a performance of Verdi's *La Traviata*. However, Buenos Aires on its own also had limited viability as a stand-alone economy or a magnet for foreign interest: although economically dominant in the area, it was politically weakened by its stand-alone status, implying that over the longer term it was in the interests of neither party to maintain the status quo.

However, the road to eventual union was tortuous and still punctuated by military conflicts. In 1854, Urquiza was driven from Buenos Aires, but his forces won the Battle of Cepeda five years later, in October 1859, after which Buenos Aires accepted the Pact of San José de Flores, under which it promised to join (or at least subsidize) the Confederation in exchange for some reforms to the constitution. The following year, Bartolomé Mitre (who would be a prominent politician, military officer, historian, journalist and first president of the Republic, and who had led Uruguayan troops on Urquiza's side at the Battle of Caseros) became governor of Buenos Aires and sought a means to attain national unity on Buenos Aires' terms. At the Battle of Pavón in 1861, Mitre's militia successfully held off Urquiza's troops and then advanced as far as Rosario, where Urquiza, recognizing the practical need for an accord with Buenos Aires, capitulated and withdrew from public life. Thereafter, Buenos Aires ratified the 1853 constitution, under which the city itself became the nation's capital, although it continued to resist limitations on *porteño* power.

In 1862, Mitre (1821–1906) was elected president of the newly united Argentine Republic and began a series of reforms that formed the basis for consolidating the new country. Mitre established the national treasury and customs services, as well as the legal and tax systems; in 1864 a national army was created, followed by a civil code in 1870. Moreover, during his term, a railway linking Rosario and Córdoba was largely completed, mainly with British financing, thanks to substantial government concessions such as land grants, exemption from import duties on coal and a guaranteed 7 per cent annual return. In 1862, Congress authorized the contracting of European immigrants to settle isolated territories such as Chubut, although in practice this policy was only partially successful. From the 1850s efforts to settle European farming families in provinces such as Santa Fe, Entre Ríos, Corrientes and Córdoba, often with government subsidies, had met with some success, generating the basis of a rural middle class. Moreover, the rise in the wool (and eventually mutton) trade, aided in the 1860s by the impact of the US Civil War on the cotton trade, led to a sharp rise in sheep farming and attracted immigrants from Ireland and the Basque Country already experienced in this area. By 1859, wool exports accounted for about a third of total export revenues, and through the 1860s annual exports averaged some 50,000 tons. The need to fence lands previously occupied by cattle increased labour demand in sheep-producing areas, favouring immigration in those areas, as well as fomenting improvement in breeding techniques in order to improve the quality of wool (and eventually meat) available for export.

However, the concentration of land in few hands in Buenos Aires and the south, and outright *porteño* opposition to the establishment of farming colonies, militated against the success of this policy more broadly, and the number of migrants responded more to economic cycles in Europe than to Argentine immigration policy. Moreover, the rise in sheep farming shifted cattle production, as well as traditional activities such as tanning and the production of tallow or salted beef, to more marginal areas to the south of Buenos Aires. Immigration patterns would change only gradually, as the rise in Indian attacks in the post-Rosas period increased support for clearing new territory for settlement, and for the settlement of immigrants as a bulwark against the Indians. Nevertheless, average annual immigration would rise from some 5,000 in the 1850s to 50,000 in the 1880s, although most of those immigrants would swell Buenos Aires and other cities rather than populating the almost uninhabited hinterland.[1]

These early attempts at consolidation were insufficient to stamp out provincial uprisings, which continued under Mitre, led notably by Vicente 'Chacho' Peñaloza of La Rioja and his lieutenant Felipe Varela in 1867. The *caudillo* uprisings would not be largely defeated until around 1870, after a series of rebellions by Ricardo López Jordán in Entre Ríos that culminated in the murder of Urquiza in that year, and then to a considerable degree only by the rise of a central power, a national army and an infrastructure base as a result of the War of the Triple Alliance.

The impact of the 1865–1870 War of the Triple Alliance on the nation-building process was dramatic, although not without conflicts. The war itself was sparked initially, at least in part, by internal conflicts in Uruguay between rural (*blanco*) and urban (*colorado*) interests. Although Argentina and Brazil both supported the *colorados*, Paraguayan leader Francisco Solano López supported the *blancos*. At the same time, border disputes between Brazil and Paraguay had begun to increase. In late 1864 Paraguayan authorities captured a Brazilian gunboat on the Paraguay River, causing a Brazilian declaration of war. López thereupon decided to invade Brazil, and sent Paraguayan troops through the Argentine province of Corrientes for that purpose, provoking a declaration of war by Mitre. The war itself was catastrophic for Paraguay, which saw its population virtually halved (and its male population decimated) during the five years it continued and faced punitive reparations to the victorious Argentina and Brazil thereafter.

In Argentina, the war led to implementation of national conscription, with some 28,000 troops called up, which generated a surge in unity behind Mitre (who initially commanded the troops himself) and also resistance to the cost of the war – indeed, resistance reached such a pitch that Salta at one point threatened to secede. Nevertheless, the professionalization of a national army created new career opportunities for the middle classes in the officer corps, as well as a new mechanism for national unification and consolidation of central power. Much of the soldier class was made up of men of mixed or African origin, and the war is cited as one of the reasons for the virtual disappearance of Argentina's black population. At the same time, the need to feed and equip the army generated new opportunities for cattlemen, as demand for leather and beef increased. These opportunities were magnified by the parlous state of government finances as a result of the war, which led to the sale of large stretches of land – some 4 million hectares by 1871 in Buenos Aires alone.[2]

In 1868 Sarmiento (1811–88) succeeded Mitre as president for the period 1868–74, with the backing of the *Partido Autonomista*, a faction that split off from Mitre's *Partido Liberal*. A self-made, self-educated man from the interior province of San Juan, Sarmiento had spent much of his life abroad, notably in Chile, Europe and the USA, an experience that informed his strong admiration for the US political system and for the liberal currents of thought then prevalent on both sides of the Atlantic. However, this admiration often tended, as in the case of Alberdi, to translate as a rejection of many characteristics inherent in the Argentine system that could not readily be eliminated through either education or immigration.

As governor of San Juan during the early part of Mitre's presidential term, Sarmiento passed the first law making primary schooling mandatory; in particular after a three-year stint as ambassador to the United States (1865–68), he also became increasingly convinced of the need to modernize Argentina, moving from an agricultural economy to an urban one. Famed as the father of Argentina's education system, Sarmiento quadrupled education spending in a bid to make

primary education free and universal, opening 800 schools and increasing teacher training (notably for women) in the belief that citizens must be educated in order to exercise their citizenship – or, as
he said, 'the sovereign must be educated'. However, Sarmiento was
less concerned with higher education for the poorer classes, believing
that basic reading and writing skills were primarily what was needed
to make them more valuable as workers. Sarmiento also clearly believed that an educated population would be less susceptible to the
blandishments of *caudillos* such as Rosas, although in practice neither
he nor other modernizing influences were enthusiastic about universal political participation, fearing that the less enlightened classes
would represent a regressive rather than modernizing influence. Indeed, education was supposed to make them more useful to those in
government, rather than a class capable of self-government. Also, due
in part to his experiences in the United States, Sarmiento favoured increased separation of church and state, a position that implied greater
religious freedom and (it was hoped) greater encouragement for potential immigrants from Protestant northern Europe.

Sarmiento continued the efforts at modernization instituted under Mitre, undertaking the construction of nearly 1,000 kilometres
of railways and 5,000 kilometres of telegraph lines and improving
the postal system; before leaving office, he opened the first telegraph line linking Argentina with Europe. Following on from the
practice under Mitre, railways continued to be constructed solely to
bring goods from the provinces to the port of Buenos Aires and vice
versa, creating a hub-and-spoke system that forced all communications and trade to go via Buenos Aires, rather than creating connections among the provinces, a design that persists today. This system
continued to favour Buenos Aires to the detriment of the provinces,
and to favour imports to the detriment of many regional economies.
Sarmiento also conducted the first national census, which indicated
that, out of a population of some 1.8 million, 75 per cent lived in
poverty, 71 per cent were illiterate and 31 per cent lived in Buenos
Aires.

However, his government was not broadly popular; by the time
he took office, support for the costly Paraguayan war (in which
Sarmiento's own son died) had waned, while rising immigration
was blamed for an outbreak of yellow fever, which also began to
raise questions over the relative conditions enjoyed by immigrants.

Immigrants were not obliged to complete military service, and in general enjoyed at least limited social mobility, to a much greater degree than the native-born rural poor, who were largely consigned to menial occupations while immigrants were more likely to accede to positions as shopkeepers or tenant farmers. However, although immigration increased sharply during the period, its profile remained at variance with that imagined by Sarmiento and Alberdi – instead of attracting large numbers of northern European farmers, the bulk of migrants came from Southern Europe (mainly Spain and Italy) and from neighbouring countries. Sarmiento's term was marked by an economic crisis already brewing in the mid-1860s under Mitre; the end of the US Civil War brought a sharp fall in wool prices and a reduction in markets, which affected both producers and speculators who had bought up land during the wool boom; the fall in land prices hit not only buyers, but also the banks that supplied cheap credit to purchasers. The decline in wool also militated further against the development of smaller farming and in favour of large-scale cattle ranching in Buenos Aires in particular. Plans to create immigrant colonies of farmers similar to the successful experiment in the town of Chivilcoy came to nothing; an 1871 land law that aimed to settle farmers on 4 million hectares in the province was largely flouted, with the lands also falling into the hands of large ranchers.

At the same time, the efforts of Sarmiento to 'Europeanize' Argentina and to consign the 'barbarism' of the *caudillos* to oblivion generated their own cultural backlash, with a rise in 'gauchesque' literature that sought to paint the independent, long-suffering, honourable nature of the gaucho as defining the national character. Although not the first, the most famous of these works were the epic poems by José Hernández, *El gaucho Martín Fierro* (1872) and *La vuelta de Martín Fierro* (1879), of which the first is virtually the defining work of Argentine literature. This original work is a protest over Europeanization and the marginalization and ill-treatment of the gaucho at the hands of the landowner, the capitalist and 'progress'. However, the second volume takes a substantially different tone – instead of lauding the hero's capacity for resistance and upholding gaucho honour, the second volume sees Martín Fierro renouncing the struggle in favour of order and peace. The 'gauchesque' genre would remain popular in the twentieth century, notably in the works of Leopoldo Lugones and Ricardo Guiraldes, whose 1926 novel *Don Segundo Sombra* casts the title character as the quintessential strong, silent gaucho whose character imbues Argentine history and nature.

Outside events also affected other economic developments. The impact of the Franco-Prussian War in 1870–71, as well as the collapse of the railway boom in the USA, saw a sharp decline in both trade and investment, while foreign creditors began to insist on debt repayments rather than rollovers. The recession in Europe led to a severe drop in demand for Argentine exports such as wool and leather. As would occur on repeated occasions in the future, the government faced a situation of rising debt obligations and falling revenues, due not least to a decline in both export and import activity. Attempts to deal with this through domestic borrowing generated an internal banking crisis, a sharp rise in unemployment and bankruptcy and a political crisis. These events also led to an increase in nationalist sentiment in some quarters – in particular against the British, the main export market and the source of both investment and loans – and to a wider debate over the virtues of free trade as opposed to greater protectionism, as well as over the virtues of an agrarian market dependent on world demand as opposed to greater industrialization.

Although Sarmiento's term was not an unqualified success and failed to attract a large settled Anglo-Saxon population, the period was marked by a degree of constitutional regularity, institutionalization and a move away from absolute *porteño* dominance. This was to a large degree a first for the nascent republic, given that it had little past history of order to look back to or 'restore'. Elections still suffered from a high degree of fraud, with many voting according to the desires of their patron or other political pressures, others voting repeatedly in the same election and many others excluded from voting at all. Moreover, most immigrants did not vote or otherwise participate in politics, even after they had completed residency requirements, as a result of which their interests were little represented. Indeed, those interests often centred on economic improvement rather than citizenship, further reducing their appetite for local politics. Nor did the imposition of a more institutionalized legal system substantially alter the pervasive tendency to elude authority inherited from the colonial period. A frontier society in which different social groups and different provinces faced competing and often mutually exclusive interests, Argentina did not develop a strong culture of legality or civic responsibility; the old colonial maxim of 'I obey but do not fulfil' persisted (crystallized in the more modern Argentine concept, *'hecha la ley, hecha la trampa'*). This was despite the fact that disrespect for the law no longer reflected disrespect for a foreign power, but rather a government supposedly representative of the local population. At the same time, greater prosperity did little to bolster investment, with the government's financial problems encouraging speculation and distrust in the banking system; the lack of a solid domestic capital and investment base continued to deepen dependency on foreign capital, often lent or invested on onerous and unfavourable terms.

Nevertheless, after decades of virtual anarchy, violent and rapid turnover of political authorities and the long Rosas dictatorship, from 1862 national elections began to be held according to regular cycles, and a series of presidents completed their constitutionally mandated six-year terms and handed over to elected successors. Despite fraud, corruption and the exclusion of many (both native-born and immigrants) from suffrage, this was no small achievement and would continue until 1930, when the coup d'état that overthrew Hipólito Yrigoyen ushered in a new and no less corrupt system of political transition. At the same time, despite repeated efforts by Mitre to return to power, the presidency thereafter passed in turn to a series of men from the interior – Sarmiento, from San Juan, was succeeded by two presidents from Tucumán, Nicolás Avellaneda (1874–80) and Julio Roca (1880–86). Brief *porteño* rebellions – led by Mitre when he lost to Avellaneda in 1874, and by Buenos Aires governor Carlos Tejedor when he lost to Roca in 1880 – were rapidly defeated, undermining the grip of Buenos Aires on national power.

Avellaneda (1837–85), the youngest president ever elected in Argentina, defeated Mitre in the 1874 elections with Sarmiento's support and a coalition of provincial forces that joined the *Partido Autonomista* to become the *Partido Autonomista Nacional* (PAN), in effect Argentina's first national party and one that would remain significant well into the twentieth century. Avellaneda followed his predecessor's strategy of promoting immigration through the Immigration Law, which opened the prospect of employment and land for new arrivals. His government also introduced some protectionist legislation to bolster local production of flour, sugar and wine, while the easing of the economic crisis in Europe again opened markets for Argentina's increased production of agriculture-based products. The first wheat exports began in 1878 (a commodity that would remain a mainstay of the export economy for a century), and the development of freezing technology began to allow for the export of frozen mutton to Europe. After a decline in the 1850s, cattle breeding also saw a revival and, as in the case of sheep before, improvements in breeding and quality. From 1866, the Argentine Rural Society pressed to develop both better-quality cattle and more lucrative export markets, beginning to produce meat extract (from boiled beef and mutton) to ship to Europe. Although initially even the improved quality of livestock was insufficient to open up European markets (cattle exported on the hoof to Europe arrived in poor condition and were not readily saleable), in 1876 the first experimental shipment of chilled beef using a refrigerated cargo vessel proved successful, and the development of freezing technology made a boom in frozen beef exports possible from the early 1880s.

With pressures on land availability again coming to the fore, in 1878 Avellaneda's government adopted a law calling for the occupation of some 8 million hectares of land in the south, between the Negro and Neuquén rivers. The so-called Conquest of the Desert was financed through the sale of 4,000 public bonds that entitled the holders to 2,500 hectares of the land in question. The land, however, was not unoccupied, but populated by Indians of the Tehuelche, Araucanian and other tribes. As noted earlier, Indian attacks had already become a matter of great concern since the fall of Rosas, who had used a blend of coercion and tribute to ensure a degree of tranquillity, and expanded still further while troops were occupied elsewhere during the War of the Triple Alliance. These raids resulted in the loss of hundreds of thousands of cattle and horses, as well as the capture of many women and children. However, the Paraguayan war and the extension of greater technology made the Conquest of the Desert an unequal struggle: in 1879 General Julio Roca led 6,000 troops in five columns coming from Mendoza, San Luis, Córdoba and Buenos Aires, and armed with repeating rifles, into the Río Negro area, transmitting orders via the newly installed telegraph lines. The conquest was swift and one-sided, leading to the transfer of over 8 million hectares of land to fewer than 400 landholders (many of them Roca's officers, who either accumulated land titles or sold them to other members of the landed class). The remaining Indians were either sent to special reservations or apportioned out as servants or labourers, while their convincing defeat opened the way to settlement of the rest of Patagonia by the conquerors.

Roca (1843–1914), known as 'the fox', had already made a name for himself as an officer in the Paraguayan war, and cemented his national reputation with the Conquest of the Desert. In 1877 he was named war minister by Avellaneda, and was key in designing the military campaign in the south, shifting away from earlier defensive tactics in favour of an all-out attack. The motivation related not only to the threat from the Indians and the desire to increase the lands available for settlement (or sale by the state, at a pittance), but also to the perceived threat from Chile, which claimed parts of Patagonia and had proved successful at forming some alliances with tribes in the region – many of them originating from Chile. As a result of the successful campaign, much of what would become the territories of Neuquén and Río Negro came under state control and permanent garrisons were put in place, with border crossings to Chile closed down or placed under military control.

Almost before the desert campaign was over, Roca's name had been put forward as successor to Avellaneda as the candidate of the PAN, a move that had the support of much of the interior. Roca, a native of Tucumán, also had the backing of a powerful relative by marriage, Córdoba governor Miguel Juárez Celman; that provincial support, and his easy victory in the 1880 presidential election, helped to consolidate further the nascent nation. Indeed, the post-election rebellion by the *porteño* militia led by Buenos Aires governor Carlos Tejedor provided an opportunity for Roca to take a further major step in the process of national consolidation: after defeating the militia, Roca put Buenos Aires and its port under direct central government control, in effect 'federalizing' the capital and its customs revenues. As a result, the new city of La Plata was founded to become the new capital of the province of Buenos Aires, while the federal government not only took control of the port and customs, but also eliminated local militias and cemented the position of the national army. This would mark the start of a new phase, in which the rapidly consolidating republic would find itself on the brink of economic prosperity, growth and the prospect of becoming one of the world's most dynamic countries.

2 The 'Golden Age' 1880–1930

Julio Roca and the 'Generation of 80' presided over a period of national consolidation and (for the most part) prosperity that would last for the best part of 50 years. For 36 of those years, until 1916, the government was retained by the PAN, which was dominated by the landed elite and governed primarily in their interests. However, it remained, like other political movements before and since, a machine oiled by patronage and dedicated to retaining power, rather than a party with a real ideology or political programme. Described as the 'conservative' regime and liberal in economic policy, in practice the PAN was neither conservative nor liberal: its 'liberality' extended only to free trade policies rather than social and political inclusiveness, while at the same time it was not conservative because its policies were focused on creating a modern state dominated by the PAN, rather than conserving any pre-existing order.

At the same time, the PAN at the national level made use of alliances with provincial *caudillos* (although these increasingly represented local economic power rather than force of arms), doubtless aided by the fact that Roca and others were from the provinces themselves. This implied that, for much of the period at least, voter participation was limited and elections were only partially fair. However, this period of conservative and elitist government allowed for the expansion of state control, consolidation of institutions and predictable transitions from one president to another, the first time Argentina had experienced such a lengthy period of stability, although at times

Figure 2. Former Presidents Bartolomé Mitre and Julio A. Roca at the inauguration of the monument to Garibaldi (Courtesy of the archive, *Diario La Nación*)

it came to resemble stagnation as much as stability. Since 1930, democracy has advanced fitfully and government has periodically become more representative, but such long-term political stability has never been repeated.

Roca's government, and its support base, also succeeded in integrating Argentina with the global economy in line with what it saw as the most desirable model, that is, as an exporter of agricultural products and an importer of consumer and other finished goods, technology and capital. This model was criticized at the time by some urban sectors and has later been dismissed by revisionist historians as a misguided pandering to a small elite that left Argentina locked into a dependent role as a supplier of raw materials and purchaser of costlier manufactures. However, while reluctance to change a model that benefited the economic elite would indeed result in an increasingly disadvantageous position as global markets changed and overseas crises made themselves felt, it could be argued that it represented an intelligent strategy of capitalizing on Argentina's competitive advantages rather than seeking to produce locally what could be manufactured more efficiently elsewhere. Nevertheless, dependence on foreign capital and markets, and susceptibility to economic shocks elsewhere, would give rise to nationalistic and 'anti-imperialist' sentiments – directed in particular against Great Britain, still the main trading partner and source of capital, although in practice its share of trade was less dominant than is sometimes portrayed, accounting for around 20 per cent of Argentina's exports by 1887 (though its share of Argentine imports was roughly twice that figure). By 1914, 90 per cent of Argentine exports were farm products, and 85 per cent were shipped to Europe; Britain accounted for some 20 per cent of its exports and 33 per cent of its imports.

The landowning elites continued to show little interest in manufacturing, and indeed agriculture and industry were generally perceived as in competition for resources and political influence, rather than as complementary parts of an economic whole. It was not until the 1920s, after the First World War had undermined this model by reducing Europe's capacity to export the products Argentina needed, that manufacturing, in particular in the area of import substitution, began to be seen as a priority. For most of this period, small-scale industry and consumer-based businesses were largely in the hands of skilled immigrants; with the passage of time, they and their children swelled the growing middle class that would help to change Argentina's political structures. Moreover, increased prosperity and the need for labour boosted working-class immigration which would also create a new social class over time, with rising expectations and an increasing willingness to demand that those expectations be met. By the turn of the century, those demands would put pressure on a system that had become wealthier but not more democratic, and would see the elite forced to cede a share of political representation but without losing its control over the levers of political and economic power for some time to come.

Roca's government continued the expansion of the communications infrastructure, such as railways and telegraph lines – the railway network reached around 1,360 miles when he took office, and had burgeoned to 2,790 miles in 1885 and nearly 21,000 miles by 1914 – as well as the expansion of settlement in the south opened up by the Conquest of the Desert. That extension of the frontiers not only paved the way for greatly expanded agricultural production – in particular, sheep farming moved to the south as cattle and grains began to

dominate the Pampas area – but also gave Roca great patronage resources in the form of land titles for members of the military and
other allies. The general rise of agriculture boosted the resources available to the government and the attractiveness of landownership for
newer members of the political elite. In other words, the state would
become an increasingly attractive prize because the rise in its resources
spelled an rise in patronage and political powers. Foreign investment
in the 1880s expanded by some 800 million gold pesos, around half
of it in the railways.

The Roca government also had the good fortune to coincide with
the rise in technological advances, such as refrigerated shipping, that
favoured Argentina's exports, as well as a period of rising prosperity in Europe that increased consumer demand for food. Although
Argentina did not stand out as a cradle of technological innovation
during the period, the agricultural sector invested considerable money
and effort in importing improved breeding stock and cultivation techniques. The careful breeding of imported merino sheep led to a sharp
rise in raw wool exports towards the end of the century, coinciding
with improvements in technology at British mills. Grain and oilseed
exports increased exponentially, from a total of some 17,000 tons in
1880 to over 1 million tons a decade later; by 1910 Argentina was
second only to the USA in wheat exports. Greater demand in Europe,
and the extension of the railways, facilitated the rapid expansion of
grain cultivation, boosting both worker immigration (rural labour and
tenant farmers) and imports of agricultural machinery – and, significantly, barbed wire. The use of irrigation became widespread in the
Pampas, as well as in Mendoza, where the practice benefited the expanding wine sector, and some local industries, such as Mendoza's
wine and Tucumán's sugar production, flourished under a degree of
protectionism for those regional products. Even as sheep were increasingly driven south to Patagonia to make room for grain on the
Pampas by the 1880s, after 1900 cattle ranching again began to dominate the area, with rotation farming becoming increasingly common
and the quality of the cattle bred for the export of higher-grade meat
products rising. Culturally, too, developments mirrored Argentina's
ascendancy as a rising power. On 25 May 1908, the new Teatro Colón
opened with a performance of Verdi's *Aida*; regarded as second only
to La Scala in Milan, the opera house would continue to attract the
world's greatest artists – including Stravinsky, Toscanini, Pavlova,

Nijinsky, Nureyev, Callas, Pavarotti and Domingo – for most of the century.

Although Argentina's wealthy classes continued to evince little interest in industry, agro-industrial installations increasingly flourished along with export demand. With demand for salted beef long depressed (the commodity had been used to feed slaves in the early nineteenth century but was not popular with consumers able to choose what they ate), the *saladeros* that had sustained Rosas and his supporters in the earlier part of the century gave way to meat-packing plants (*frigoríficos*) that produced chilled and frozen beef and mutton for shipment to Europe. Similarly, milling capacity increased to allow flour as well as wheat to be produced. These developments increased the value of exports and reduced dependence on imported foodstuffs. Most smaller business enterprises came to be dominated by immigrants, who by the turn of the century far outnumbered native Argentines as owners of local industries.

The Roca government saw the beginnings of a rapid rise in both immigration and urbanization, as well as significant changes in the face of Argentina's cities. Nowhere was this more evident than in Buenos Aires, where, following the yellow fever outbreak of 1871, the wealthy increasingly abandoned the original centre of the city (in particular, the San Telmo area near Government House, known as the Casa Rosada) to move to more salubrious areas in the newer Barrio Norte, Recoleta and Palermo districts; the construction of a capital city increasingly known for its resemblance to Paris began at around this time, and British-financed trams, gas and electricity offered increasingly modern services to those that could afford them. As a result, the original city centre became dominated by tenement (*conventillo*) housing, with former family residences subdivided into small rooms to house the poor and, above all, poor immigrants. The population of Buenos Aires rose rapidly, from around 180,000 in 1869 to over 1.5 million at the outbreak of the First World War, with roughly one-third of the population being foreign-born. With wages high and the gold peso stable for much of the period, many immigrants were able to acquire houses and small businesses over time, as well as free public education for their children and the consequent opportunity for upward mobility. However, social mobility in general proved more difficult for the darker-skinned native poor in a snobbish society with European aspirations, and the relatively greater social advancement of many immigrants was a cause of resentment, as was the increasing desire of the rising urban classes to imitate elite tastes, at least in terms of culture, education and social mores.

From the 1880s in particular, Buenos Aires received thousands of immigrants, the majority from Spain and Italy. Others came from Ireland, Poland, Russia (notably Jewish refugees from the pogroms in Eastern Europe), while Arab immigration also rose in the early part of the twentieth century. A few came from England and Wales, many of whom went to the southern Patagonia region, either as railway workers or as sheep farmers. Railway employees were by and large a privileged group, benefiting from company housing and other advantages that made the British community a relatively elite enclave. Although rural wages were very high by European standards, landholdings were vast and concentrated in the hands of very few, leaving limited room for the immigrant who dreamed of owning his own farm. This, together with the somewhat inhospitable nature of much of the uninhabited countryside, caused the bulk of those immigrants to remain close to Buenos Aires, where work was available in the port, in slaughterhouses and tanneries, in small workshops, in service or as prostitutes. The immigrants who apparently adapted most readily to the inhospitable climes of the remoter provinces were Arab merchants, who settled in considerable numbers both in the Northwestern provinces and in the southern territory of Neuquén. Immigrants, or their children, who managed to rise to the middle classes, would become an important part of the consumer society in their desire to emulate elite fashions – not least due to the benefits to be gained from appearing European and prosperous, which opened doors to employment and lifestyle improvements not available to the darker-skinned migrants from the provinces.[1]

Nevertheless, most of the immigrants crowded into *conventillos* did not find entry into snobbish *porteño* society easy. Many dreamed of returning to Europe – many in fact did so, becoming known as *golondrinas* or swallows, as they migrated on a seasonal basis, depending on the money earned in Argentina and the seasons in which work was available. Others stayed in Argentina with the dream – still obtainable, albeit with difficulty, in a wealthy and advancing country – of moving up the social scale through work and sacrifice to reach the middle class, becoming shopkeepers or other small proprietors, and allowing their children to study for a better future in life. Many achieved this dream, becoming the cornerstone of the urban middle class. Still others maintained their position as members of the working class – in particular those who had worked in industry in Europe and had earlier trade union experience – and transferred their political and union affiliations to their new country. Most immigrants, whatever their occupation or position, had a community of compatriots which permitted them to maintain their roots and traditions and keep their nostalgia for the Old World, even as it also made them less likely to become fully integrated into Argentine culture. (The tango, the melancholic and passionate music of Buenos Aires, has its roots in that undefined and permanent nostalgia of the uprooted who made up most of Buenos Aires' less privileged classes.)[2]

Despite the squalid living conditions in which many found themselves, at least in their first years, immigrants were increasingly attracted to Argentina in the last two decades of the century by labour shortages and comparatively high urban wages, which rose substantially during the period despite chronic inflation in food prices. Far from being dominated by the Anglo-Saxon migrants Sarmiento and Alberdi had hoped for, the vast majority of those immigrants came from Italy and Spain, between them accounting for some three-quarters of new arrivals between the late 1850s and the start of the First World War. They would contribute strongly to Argentina's economy and, over time, its culture, although initially at least they did not form a favoured part of the national project envisaged by Roca and his colleagues. However, as they and their offspring increasingly joined the nascent middle classes, their demands for greater political inclusion and access to white-collar jobs began to represent a challenge to the elite political classes that had no intention of representing their interests. The native poor, if anything, faced even more squalid conditions than these migrants, and few prospects for advancement: by the early twentieth century, even as wealthy Argentines became famous in Europe for their elegance and extravagance, the introduction of compulsory military service led to the revelation that nearly half of the conscripts called up failed to meet physical requirements as a result of malnutrition and disease.[3]

Roca was succeeded by former Córdoba governor and senator Miguel Juárez Celman in 1886, who gained the PAN's support with backing from Roca, a relative by marriage, and following elections widely regarded as fraudulent. However, Juárez Celman was to prove an unpopular president, disregarding Roca and the PAN and imposing a virtual one-man government, known as the *unicato*. (In practice, the tendency towards presidential authoritarianism – the belief that the winning of elections represented a virtual carte blanche – was not limited to Juárez Celman and has remained characteristic of the strongly presidentialist system to date.) Moreover, his strong position on the separation of church and state, which led to the institutionalization of secular education and civil marriage – the latter thereafter obligatory before any religious wedding could take place – fell foul of the Catholic Church and many in the provinces who had earlier resisted what they regarded as *porteño* anti-clericalism. From this period, primary education became free, obligatory and lay, without Church oversight of state schools. It was Juárez Celman's misfortune that his tenure coincided with an economic crisis that undermined national optimism and belief in the PAN's dominance, caused in part by the rise in debt that had paid for modernization and imports of technology during Roca's tenure. At the same time, the economic crisis may have helped to stimulate the first stirrings of a middle class strengthened by immigration and education, unrepresented by the PAN but anxious to assume a more important place in the nation.

In addition to productive borrowing, to a large extent the economic crisis reflected a boom in land and stock market speculation and expanding issues of paper money that generated a rise in inflation. Provincial mortgage banks also boosted paper money issues, causing a sharp depreciation. Government efforts to force those banks to deposit the gold equivalent with the National Bank (in order to pay off national debt) led, in practice, to provincial borrowing and a worsening debt crisis. Moreover, guaranteed returns of 7 per cent offered to railway companies led to a proliferation of rail concessions, reaching a total of 30 in 1889, as well as a further burden on the state given that few of the railways were actually profitable. Government borrowing soared, generating an eightfold rise in foreign debt between 1880 and 1890. In late 1889, the failure of Baring Brothers to find subscribers for a loan to Argentina generated investor panic and a drop in revenues, while scandals surrounding corruption claims in connection with the loan damaged both Buenos Aires and London, and came close to bankrupting Barings. Combined with a financial crisis in Britain (which also hit indebted sheep farmers by cutting wool demand and prices), the crisis produced a rise in unemployment and a sharp fall in real wages for the first time in a decade. In 1890, the government suspended debt payments, in practice defaulting on foreign debt. The combination of speculation, inflation, capital flight and debt and banking crisis would become a recurring theme in Argentina, in particular a century later in 1989 and, most spectacularly, in 2001.

In July 1890, the government was shaken by the so-called *Revolución del Parque*, an uprising led by the newly emerging *Unión Cívica*, founded in 1889 and comprising a range of diverse and often mutually exclusive interests, including former members of the PAN, former followers of Bartolomé Mitre, Catholics and members of the emerging urban middle classes – many of them the children of immigrants who had grown relatively prosperous and who, having enjoyed the benefits of public education, now wanted greater opportunities within Argentine society. These included figures such as founder Leandro Alem, Bernardo de Irigoyen (once a functionary of the Rosas government), Socialist Party founder Juan B. Justo and Progressive Democrat Party founder Lisandro de la Torre, although the group had no concrete political platform other than opposition to corruption, fraud and the government of Juárez Celman. Though the revolution was defeated with relative ease, it pointed to both the existence of new political formations unwilling to accept the status quo and the sympathy of some members of the army, where many of the officers came from the same middle-class ranks, with the revolution. This, in turn, made clear that admiration for Roca and the availability of officer salaries and land grants in Patagonia was no longer sufficient to guarantee military support for an unpopular government; with relatively little resistance, Juárez Celman resigned and was replaced for the last two years of his term by Vice-President Carlos Pellegrini, formerly Roca's war minister. In 1891 Alem was elected as senator for the city of Buenos Aires.

In advance of the 1892 elections, the *Unión Cívica* proposed to back Mitre as its presidential candidate, with Irigoyen as his vice-president. However, in a bid to avert a challenge that looked likely to succeed, Roca (again in government, this time as interior minister) proposed a wider accord that would make Mitre the consensus candidate of both the government and the opposition, thus co-opting the former president and curtailing the threat posed by the *Unión Cívica*. Mitre's acceptance of the proposal, which would have allowed Roca to nominate a running mate to replace Irigoyen, fractured the *Unión Cívica*, with those opposed to the move rallying around Alem in the newly created *Unión Cívica Radical* (UCR), which would become the majority party after the First World War and the largest minority party for most of the decades following the Second World War. Although, perhaps predictably, Irigoyen lost the presidential election to Luis Sáenz Peña (who replaced Mitre as the 'official' candidate when the latter withdrew), the 1892 campaign helped to establish the UCR in much of the country as a party with electoral and political weight. This was illustrated by a series of uprisings in 1893 in Buenos Aires, Santa Fe, Tucumán and San Luis, organized by Alem and his nephew, Hipólito Yrigoyen. In the meantime, recession continued, with the government forced to renegotiate its foreign debt in 1893 after the wheat harvest failed and exports dropped. The central government took the opportunity to take over provincial debts in exchange for local control over some revenues, although whether this concentrated power in Buenos Aires, as David Rock argues, or merely concentrated weakness there, is debatable.[4] The cession of revenue powers to the centre was never fully reversed, and led eventually to the creation of a revenue-sharing system from the 1930s.

The UCR took its title from Alem's insistence on 'radical' opposition to the Roca–Mitre pact. Despite its undoubted middle-class roots, the UCR's discourse also focused on 'revolution' as a permanent objective, albeit with no clear revolutionary agenda beyond free and fair elections and a commitment to change. Alem himself, a former legislator who had migrated from the PAN to found the Republican party in the 1870s, was by nature an opposition figure rather than a politician, and one who found compromise unpalatable. Some of his followers, including his nephew, took issue with his overly personalist leadership. Increasingly disillusioned after the failure of the 1893 uprisings, and in particular with his political heir, Yrigoyen, whom he believed too susceptible to brokering deals with other political actors, Alem committed suicide in 1896. At the same time, the PAN itself was beginning to splinter; after finishing a second term as president in 1904, Roca (who was the only Argentine president to complete two terms until Carlos Menem in 1999) died in 1914 and the party itself was left with none of its original leadership, sustaining itself in power through fraud and questionable alliances.

Following Alem's death, Yrigoyen (1852–1933) assumed sole leadership of the UCR, and marked much of the movement with his own personality. Known as *el peludo*, the armadillo, Yrigoyen was a secretive and intransigent figure, who confided in few and was staunchly opposed to compromise. A former teacher of history, philosophy and civics, and sometime law student, Yrigoyen never married and was rarely seen in public, although his nocturnal habits gave rise to rumours of numerous romances; according to Felix Luna, 'his only passions were women and politics'.[5] He also came to be a substantial landowner and lived off the rents from those lands, donating his salary to charity. Briefly a legislator, Yrigoyen had backed the law federalizing the city of Buenos Aires, marking his first split with Alem. As a leader, he was given to communicating with only a few close colleagues and defined himself as involved in an 'evangelical task' and wanting his life 'to be seen by the public as a model, and indicating a path towards spiritual perfection'.[6]

A third revolutionary attempt, with significant military backing, was defeated in 1905 but nonetheless Yrigoyen briefly gained temporary control of a number of important cities such as Mendoza, Rosario and Córdoba. Despite this defeat, Yrigoyen adhered to the cult of 'intransigence', refusing any form of political alliance for the UCR and insisting on electoral abstention in the light of the impossibility of participating in fair elections. However, the degree of mysticism surrounding the UCR, self-defined as a 'sentiment' or a 'movement' rather than a party, its opposition to the status quo and the lack of a concrete political platform qualified it by definition to act as opposition rather than government. In these respects, as well as its personalist loyalties around the figure of Yrigoyen, the UCR shared many characteristics with the Peronist party that would arise in the 1940s – implying that Argentina's two main political parties since that time have been non-ideological, all-inclusive and consequently somewhat amorphous movements that sought to avoid excluding any part of their heterogeneous base, rather than parties with readily debatable policies. These amorphous qualities made both movements difficult to pin down, but also difficult to undermine: following the 1905 rebellion, former president Carlos Pellegrini warned that '[N]o one can destroy Radicalism: it is a temperament more than a political party, and to destroy it and annul it completely and forever, there is only one means, handing over the republic for it to govern'.[7]

In practice, by the beginning of the twentieth century, the success of PAN governments in promoting immigration, economic growth and education had begun to undermine the foundations of that government, based as it was on an elite minority rather than the popular vote. Indeed, the progressive elements of nineteenth-century governments had never been wedded to the kind of political and social progress that would involve universal suffrage and the need to compete seriously for political power. However, despite some repressive measures designed to reduce the threat of social and political unrest – such as the 1905 Law of Residence, which allowed for deportation of non-citizens accused of fomenting disturbances (aimed primarily at curbing the perceived threat from anarchists arrived from Europe) – growing pressures became increasingly irresistible. The assassination of Buenos Aires police chief Ramón Falcón by an anarchist in 1909 only increased fears, among both the middle and upper classes, of possible working-class violence.

In 1911, President Roque Sáenz Peña (1851–1914), the son of Luis, proposed what became known as the Sáenz Peña law, which provided for universal male suffrage for citizens aged over 18, a secret ballot and obligatory voting. The law, obviously, did not include women, those living in national territories that were not yet provinces or non-naturalized immigrants, who constituted a large proportion of the population – although they were counted as part of the population for the purposes of determining the number of legislators each district sent to the Lower House, and thus swelled the number of representatives without being able to vote for them. The Sáenz Peña law arose out of an accord with Yrigoyen, under which the latter agreed to abandon the course of permanent revolution and abstention in exchange for legislation guaranteeing free and fair elections. Hitherto, male citizens were allowed to vote, but were forced to do so publicly and vocally, which brought with it serious risks and reduced enthusiasm for what was then a voluntary process; typically, very small numbers of those eligible to vote did so. Moreover, the vote was by list, for all the candidates for all posts, which implied that the party most voted for received all of the posts up for election. Although Sáenz Peña himself had reservations, and many of his supporters in Congress feared its potential results, the president believed the measure would not seriously undermine the government, as the popular vote would favour the existing regime that had guaranteed prosperity and now electoral choice – or, alternatively, would allow the Radicals to destroy themselves, as Pellegrini had confidently predicted in 1905.

This concept was rapidly proved wrong. Only a month after the law was promulgated in February 1912, the UCR won elections in both Santa Fe and the Federal Capital (where the Socialists came second). In 1916, Yrigoyen became the first truly popularly elected president of Argentina, with about 45 per cent of the vote (some 370,000 votes, in comparison with 340,000 for the opposition), while the old conservative interests, rather than forming another national party in opposition, moved increasingly into other channels through which they exercised leverage. No longer able to win elections through the vote, the remains of the PAN and other traditional sectors focused on retaining the levers of economic power – now increasingly divorced from political power – and on influencing politics through business, the press and, by 1930, the armed forces. The conservatives also retained control of Congress and most governorships in 1916, although the UCR held the governments of Córdoba, Entre Ríos, Mendoza, Santiago del Estero and Tucumán. Within a short time, the Yrigoyen government would begin to use the constitutional facility of federal intervention to displace conservative governments in other provinces, and eventually even Radical governments viewed as competitors to the president (most notably in Mendoza and San Juan, where the Lencinas and Cantoni families built their own local support bases on more populist policies than those implemented by the national government, and represented a potential threat to Yrigoyen's own popularity).

At the same time, the Yrigoyen government did little to alter the prevailing economic model in Argentina, which benefited the continuity of elite power. The incorporation of the UCR and the Socialists into the political system served to reduce popular demands for greater representation, but the UCR, although prepared to back more progressive social and labour legislation, lacked the congressional support to put weight behind these measures or an economic programme designed to challenge the status quo. Indeed, it could be argued that the election of a popular government under Yrigoyen did more to give legitimacy to the prevailing model than to change it. Despite the scorn heaped on the new government by the old elite (like the Peronists 30 years later, the Radicals were caricatured as dirty, ill-dressed and vulgar), that old elite continued to dominate economic power even without being able to win the popular vote – a state of affairs that underscored Sáenz Peña's astuteness but also the limitations of a government with political support but reduced economic influence.

In many other respects also, the Yrigoyen government represented continuity more than change, despite the change in expectations among middle- and working-class sectors. Argentina's neutrality in the First World War was already well established when Yrigoyen took office, and no change in this policy was made – not least because it allowed Argentina to continue to sell meat, leather and grain to the British and to underpin continued economic growth.

There is no question of the genuine popularity of Yrigoyen and his election – indeed, at his inauguration, members of the crowd famously unhitched the horses from his carriage and pulled it themselves from Congress to the Casa Rosada. However, Yrigoyen's policies did not tend to favour the interests of the working classes, in part because his government lacked the support of the still-powerful conservative interests and thus suffered from an inherent weakness which prevented a substantial change in the power structure or in state policies. Primarily, however, the UCR represented middle-class interests linked basically to services or the public sector, who had little class identification and were readily attracted by measures such as University Reform, the expansion of public universities and the large increase in public-sector employment that favoured their chances of gaining government jobs. Like the traditional landowners, these were not especially sympathetic to labour or to industry in general, at a time when consumer goods for their use could be imported or produced on a small scale. At the same time, it could be argued that these middle-class interests rooted in public sector and services jobs were relatively remote from the most productive elements of the economy and offered little impetus for broadening the productive base or diversifying the economy.

By this time, too, the urban working classes were hardly a dominant segment of the population, although the War had curtailed European exports of manufactures to Argentina and had helped to boost the import substitution industries that would gain even greater ground in the 1930s. Argentina in the 1920s remained substantially rural, sparsely populated, with a scattering of provincial cities incorporating a middling sector of service, professional and light manufacturing workers. The whole was dominated by Buenos Aires, the capital and port which concentrated nearly all imports and exports, and was the point of entry and possibly final destination for most immigrants. The capital largely turned its back on the hinterland which provided its wealth, feeling itself spiritually closer to Europe than to the almost

Figure 3. Funeral of one of those killed during the 'Tragic Week', January 1919 (Wikipedia)

empty, barely modern interior of Argentina. Both the education system and, later, advertising would underscore the fact that the preferred image of the 'ideal' Argentina was European, not indigenous.[8] Buenos Aires, which had become the country's principal port and focal point from the late eighteenth century, and which became the federal capital in 1880, prided itself on being an elegant city, the Paris of South America. The *porteños* were strongly convinced of their own superiority over their provincial countrymen, hungry European immigrants and, of course, the rest of South America to which, apparently, Buenos Aires belonged only by geographical accident. The working classes were to be kept in the background.

The UCR government was, in point of fact, marked by two of the bloodiest and most famous acts of repression against labour: the so-called 'Tragic Week' in 1919 and 'Rebel Patagonia' in 1922. In January 1919, police repression of a metal workers' strike in support of improved working conditions at the Pedro Vasena factory blew up into a violent clash, causing the Argentine Regional Labour Federation (FORA) to declare a general strike which halted all work and transport activities in Buenos Aires for a week. Troops were sent in to quell both the strike and, in theory, the responding violence by groups of upper-class youths, known as the *Liga Patriótica*, who attacked Jewish-owned businesses and who were allegedly armed by the Navy. The activities of the *Liga Patriótica* marked the first such outbreak of xenophobia and anti-Semitism in Argentina, and the fact that the government remained largely passive in the face of these attacks pointed to its relative weakness vis-à-vis the urban elite. The appearance of the violent Right in Argentina was arguably encouraged by the Russian Revolution and the determination to avoid any similar event in Argentina (as well as, perhaps, the broader tendency to identify all Jews as 'rusos' due to the number of Jewish refugees from Russia, and therefore to identify them as possible subversives). Despite subsequent allegations by the government that the strike had been a communist conspiracy, the large number of deaths at the hands of the security forces (estimated at some 700, together with 4,000 wounded and 2,000 prisoners) tended to reinforce the image of violent repression of the working classes.

In 1921 and 1922, two military campaigns were launched in the southern Patagonia region aimed at the repression of rural workers, also linked to the FORA, who were protesting over their conditions. The first campaign in 1921 was peaceful, and Colonel Hector Varela, who had participated in the Tragic Week and was sent to Santa Cruz to survey the situation, was able to negotiate a deal under which the rebels would lay down their arms and the employers would comply with their demands on living conditions. However, a new rising followed after employers failed to honour the accord, and the 1922 campaign, also led by Varela, culminated in the order to execute the leaders of the strike. Martial law was also declared, and round-ups of suspected rebels took place throughout the region; in total, some 1,500 were killed.

While both the Tragic Week and Rebel Patagonia may have been somewhat overwritten in terms of their broader impact and what they illustrated about the Yrigoyen government's policies, there is little question that they had long-term implications for the Radicals' ability to claim to represent working-class aspirations. The government was by no means consistently anti-labour, although it favoured conciliation between workers and employers rather than more extreme measures. The government did, in fact, support worker action in some cases (such as in the 1917 railway strike), but in other cases it took repressive action (such as the meat packers' strike against Swift and Armour), an unclear and vacillating approach that left both workers and employers uncertain. To a substantial degree, the government appeared more willing to support Argentine strikers protesting against foreign-owned companies than to support strikes, particularly by immigrant workers, against Argentine state or privately owned companies. In practice, it would appear that the accession to power of the Radicals, together with the economic boom experienced during the First World War, increased the expectations and consequently the agitation of organized labour – especially after the post-war downturn led to a rise in unemployment.[9] This, in turn, increased concerns over possible labour agitation, in particular, following a spate of anarchist attacks, notably following the execution of the anarchists Sacco and Vanzetti in the USA in 1926. However, despite its good intentions, the Yrigoyen government represented more continuity than change, and indeed the need to reassure its middle-class constituency may have forced the administration towards a more intransigent posture as rising labour agitation generated fears in other sectors of society.

In 1922 Yrigoyen was succeeded by Marcelo T. de Alvear, also of the Radical party but of a far different stripe. Alvear (1868–1942), a member of an old political family and of the Buenos Aires landed elite, was nevertheless picked by Yrigoyen as his successor, and received some 458,000 votes, far above Yrigoyen's support six years earlier. However, by 1924 the party split into *personalistas*, who backed Yrigoyen as undisputed leader, and *antipersonalistas*, who argued that Yrigoyen had kept the party as a whole in his shadow. The *personalistas*, for their part, argued that the *antipersonalistas* were merely covert conservatives who wished to revert to the structure of the past. It was into the *antipersonalista* camp that Alvear, an aristocrat married to an opera singer with little support among much of the party base, fell, although as president he took an increasingly neutral position and avoided the reprisals against the *personalistas* demanded by much of his faction. However, *antipersonalista* sentiment was also strong in provinces such as Mendoza and San Juan, where the local ruling Lencinas and Cantoni families had suffered from federal intervention under the government of Yrigoyen, who saw them as potential rivals.

Following a sharp downturn after the war, when Britain virtually stopped importing meat and the livestock and meat-packing industries suffered a major regression, Alvear's government enjoyed a period of post-war recovery that arguably formed the basis of Argentina's most prosperous period, although that prosperity was as dependent as ever on agriculture. From 1923 onwards, nascent industries declined as the wartime need for import substitution disappeared and government policies did little to protect local manufacturing. Also, during this post-war period, Argentina's trading relationships began to shift, with Great Britain still absorbing most of its (agricultural) exports but the USA becoming the chief supplier of both capital and imports. An increasingly anti-US tone became evident from this time, in particular among economic nationalists and above all in relation to the oil sector. This was clearly illustrated by the cool government reception received by President Herbert Hoover during a visit in 1929. However, the railways experienced further expansion during this period, and although the area devoted to agriculture did not substantially increase, greater investment and specialization brought a rise in productivity and the expansion of related industries such as the *frigoríficos*.

Alvear sought to reduce corruption in government; despite Yrigoyen's emphasis on personal probity, the control of state patronage and the inclusion of thousands of Radical supporters on the public payroll had taken their toll on transparency. He cut thousands of public-sector jobs, generating resistance among Yrigoyen's supporters who had come to see those (economically unproductive) jobs as their territory. In practice, the split in the party left Alvear with minority support in Congress, reducing his prospects of innovation further, although his government succeeded in adopting some measures to control child labour, foment social security and boost exports of some key products. Alvear also named Enrique Mosconi as the first director of national oil company *Yacimientos Petrolíferos Fiscales* (YPF), first mooted by Yrigoyen in 1922 before leaving office, which became the first state oil company in Latin America. In 1924, YPF was given a virtual monopoly over the oil reserves in Patagonia, limiting the activities of foreign companies such as Shell and Standard Oil. The expansion of the domestic oil industry began to reduce dependency on imports, although the rapid rise in both car ownership and agricultural machinery outstripped local fuel production. Fiat and Ford both began manufacturing in the country during this period, as did the local SIAM, owned by the Di Tella family. However, in general terms, the economic boom and Alvear's more conservative bent probably tended to reduce political tensions with the elites, who regarded the president as less intransigent than his predecessor – although in fact Yrigoyen attempted nothing that would have threatened their economic interests, as noted earlier. At the same time, although over

Figure 4. President Hipólito Yrigoyen (second from right) and US President-elect Herbert Hoover (second from left) in Buenos Aires, 16 December 1928 (Courtesy of the archive, *Diario La Nación*)

500 strikes were called during Alvear's mandate, these did not spill over into violent confrontations such as those of Yrigoyen's term, and social tensions were relatively muted in the period.

In 1928, Yrigoyen became the second president after Roca to be elected to a second term, despite the split between his faction and that of Alvear and the fact that Alvear's record in office was largely positive. In concert with the conservatives and other parties such as the Independent Socialist Party, Alvear's *antipersonalistas* put forward Leopoldo Melo as their presidential candidate, only to see him defeated by Yrigoyen by nearly two votes to one in an election that became known as 'the plebiscite'. Yrigoyen's own vote more than doubled with respect to 1916, to over 840,000. However, far from a guarantee of success, this landslide victory may have contributed to the government's undoing. Yrigoyen himself appears to have believed that the 'plebiscite' implied strong public support for any policy course he adopted and that his government was thus virtually infallible, a common error that would be repeated by his successors, while the conservative opposition was alarmed by this vision of overwhelming public backing for a figure they still viewed as a danger to their hegemony.

In fact, policy-making would become distinctly sclerotic and confused during Yrigoyen's second term, and it would rapidly become clear that public support was not unconditional. By this time Yrigoyen himself was elderly and his lifelong habit of virtual seclusion, and of communicating in almost mystic terms through a few interlocutors, came to be seen as an oddity at a time when newspapers and radio were beginning to make communication more of a public good. Decision-making was slow and uncertain, giving rise to rumours that the president was ill or beginning to suffer from dementia, although it is more likely that Yrigoyen's political reflexes had simply failed to evolve sufficiently over the previous decades to adapt to a more modern and dynamic context. A key campaign promise – the full nationalization of the oil industry, a promise accompanied by anti-US rhetoric and a propaganda campaign against Standard Oil – foundered on congressional opposition and YPF's inability to meet domestic demand alone (the first but not the last time oil nationalism would run up against similar constraints, with politically unpopular results).

The broader political and economic context also became increasingly unfavourable to the government. In addition to the fear instilled in the conservative elites – still economically dominant but politically weak in terms of voter support – by the 1928 elections, the international environment was also changing, with dictatorships in Spain and Italy underscoring the possibility of replacing a chaotic civilian government with military-backed administrations. As early as late 1929, coup rumours began to surface in Buenos Aires, fanned by reports in newspapers controlled by those most interested in such an outcome.

The political climate also became more volatile as a result of the November 1929 killing of Carlos Washington Lencinas in Mendoza by an Yrigoyen supporter. Lencinas, like the rest of his family, was a local leader of an anti-Yrigoyen faction of the UCR. His father, José Néstor, was elected governor in 1916 and in 1919, but removed by federal intervention by Yrigoyen in 1918. Carlos Washington, who succeeded his father in 1921, also suffered intervention and was later blocked from assuming the Senate seat he had won. Although Yrigoyen almost certainly had nothing to do with his murder, events left open the opportunity to hint at possible presidential complicity. Yrigoyen's supporters also succeeded in impugning the election, in San Juan, of Federico Cantoni, leader of another anti-Yrigoyen Radical faction, the *Bloquistas*, and one of his allies to the Senate. A month later, an individual attacked Yrigoyen in the street as he left his home; the president's guards rapidly killed the perpetrator, whose motives were never clear, but thereafter Yrigoyen became even more inaccessible, going out only under heavy guard and isolated from the public.

In other respects, despite the looming Depression, the initial part of Yrigoyen's second term was not altogether rocky at the level of his middle-class support base. On the contrary, a relatively large and seemingly stable service and public-sector economy provided white-collar employment for a middle class with increasing aspirations to imitate the social and fashion trends of the elite. Although relatively few were able to visit the Europe their parents or grandparents had left, they were well aware that Argentina was seen in Europe as an equal if not an economic superior. Moreover, the dynamic theatre and cinema culture in Buenos Aires allowed for entertainments that were envied and exported elsewhere. Arguably the greatest exponent of the contemporary Argentine artistic scene, the tango singer Carlos Gardel enjoyed great success in Paris and throughout Latin America, as well as in European and Hollywood films. A virtual symbol of his age – born in France but an adoptive Argentine – Gardel was debonair, generous and successful; his huge success in Europe helped to make the previously lower-class tango socially acceptable in Argentina and broadened the genre's wider popularity. His death in a plane crash in 1935 was an occasion of great public mourning, and his funeral would be the largest seen in Buenos Aires until the death of Evita some 17 years later. (More than 70 years after his death, his trademark cigarettes are still regularly left in the hand of his statue at Chacarita cemetery, and the phrase 'he sings better every day' remains current.)

In the 1930 midterm elections, the UCR saw its support fall to around 600,000 votes, resulting in a virtual tie with the opposition; in the capital, the party lost to the Independent Socialist Party, further fuelling elite fears of atomized political power. The new Congress successfully blocked all government initiatives, adding to the atmosphere of stasis surrounding Yrigoyen. This political stalemate coincided with the full force of the Great Depression, which hit Argentina especially hard as export demand dried up, again highlighting how fragile its prosperity was and how dependent on outside events beyond its control. With falling export prices and demand and a sharp drop in foreign capital inflows, Argentine companies were forced to impose mass redundancies, measures that largely toothless labour legislation could do little to ameliorate. Public-sector workers also suffered as revenues fell and public spending rose, and by 1930 the government lacked funds to pay the bloated bureaucracy. Spending cuts had the effect of deepening the recession further, undermining wages and boosting unemployment. All of these events conspired to destroy the support base of Yrigoyen, increasingly perceived as chiefly responsible for the crisis.

Fifty years after General Roca won the presidency and consolidated the construction of a liberal and predictable state, in 1930 the armed forces would again take a direct role in politics, ostensibly to save the political system and the constitution from itself. They did so with the backing of a number of social sectors, not least a decadent conservative elite that could no longer win power through the ballot box. The coup d'état would mark the return of the armed forces to the centre of politics, where they would remain intermittently for a further 50 years, and a break with any vision of a consensual and pluralistic system in favour of a return to confrontation and zero-sum politics.

3   The Infamous 'Decade' 1930–43

On 6 September 1930 a military coup ended the presidency of Hipólito Yrigoyen, the Radical president whose accession to power in 1916 had given the middle classes of Argentina an important political role for the first time. The coup was the first military overthrow of an elected government since the 1853 constitution had helped to consolidate institutions, and the year 1930 was the first of what was to become known as 'the infamous decade' – in fact a 13-year period of military and fraudulently elected governments which began that year and which held power until 1943.

The coup had in fact been some time in coming, and if anything was delayed by disputes between rival factions within the army, as well as by an apparent desire to wait until the government's popularity had reached its nadir. This strategy was successful; despite Yrigoyen's massive popular support only a few years earlier, the small detachment of troops led by nationalist General José Félix Uriburu met no real resistance and not inconsiderable signs of support – indeed, Uriburu was welcomed by demonstrators while protestors attacked Yrigoyen's home. (One officer involved in the coup was an unknown captain named Juan Domingo Perón, who years later would express regret over what he considered an erroneous move that debilitated democracy.) Yrigoyen himself was taken under arrest to the island of Martín García and remained under house arrest until his death in Buenos Aires in July 1933, when the thousands that came out onto the streets for his funeral (having been conspicuous by their absence at the time of his overthrow) represented the largest popular turnout ever seen until that time.

Uriburu was proclaimed provisional president and took a number of measures to deal with the economic crisis, cutting government spending and padded payrolls while also seeking to implement public works projects in order to ameliorate rising unemployment and discontent. Some 20,000 public sector jobs were axed in Buenos Aires alone. However, his administration was short-lived; in 1931 he authorized elections in Buenos Aires province in the belief that the move would demonstrate his government's popularity. Instead, Radical candidates won a landslide, causing Uriburu to annul the elections and proscribe the UCR from political activity.

Shortly thereafter, in November 1931, the conservatives who opposed Uriburu engineered national elections, won by Uriburu's rival General Agustín P. Justo, who had links with the *antipersonalista* Radicals of Alvear. With the Radicals proscribed and the Socialists in disarray following the death of their founder, Juan B. Justo, in 1928 and subsequent splits in the party, General Justo enjoyed the support of the three parties that dominated Congress, the *antipersonalistas*, the Independent Socialists and the National Democratic Party (PDN). (As noted by Felipe Pigna, one was neither independent nor socialist, and the other was neither national nor democratic.[1]) This alliance became known as the *Concordancia*, which would become synonymous with electoral fraud and political opportunism, as well as an economic record that was at best mixed. With Justo and the *Concordancia*, the landed elites that had traditionally held power returned, albeit due only to ballot rigging and to the banning of the UCR, which saw its influence reduced to some local jurisdictions, such as Córdoba. Uriburu himself died shortly after handing over power to Justo at the beginning of 1932. From 1933 until his death in 1942, the UCR was led by Alvear, who split from the *Concordancia* and patched up divisions within the party, but who sought to convert it into an alliance between the middle classes and the elite that was virtually indistinguishable from the old conservatives.

In economic terms, the Justo government's most notorious legacy was arguably the 1933 Roca–Runciman Treaty, negotiated with Great Britain to avoid losing that important market to British colonies and former colonies, which in 1932 had signed the Ottawa Pact giving them trade preferences with Britain. Exports had fallen by 34 per cent in 1930 as a result of the Depression, and overall production fell by 14 per cent during the period 1929–32, leading to increased concerns over protecting the export outlets that remained.[2] In 1933, Vice-President Julio Roca (son of the former president) led a delegation to London that negotiated a treaty providing for Britain to guarantee that its beef imports from Argentina would not fall below 1932 levels. However, in exchange Britain received a number of trade and investment preferences, tariff reductions and guarantees that British loans would be repaid.

While the treaty guaranteed access to the valuable British export market, it has been argued that panic over the fallout from the Ottawa Pact led Argentina to adopt a short-sighted approach of focusing on its traditional partner, rather than taking the opportunity to broaden its export base and seek new markets at a time of global uncertainty. The treaty also provided for broader benefits for British interests, including exemption of British railways from pension funding requirements and the promise of protection of profit remittances in case of devaluation. In 1936 it was extended for a further three years, and Britain was allowed to impose excise taxes on Argentine meat imports. In addition, British pressures led to a supposed transport monopoly for the Anglo-Argentine Tramway Company in Buenos Aires, although in practice the government did little to enforce that monopoly and independent buses continued to expand to the detriment of the tramways.

Although arguably seen as a necessary move to ensure that a key market would not be lost, the treaty in practice committed Argentina to export raw materials and to import manufactures and capital from a dominant trading partner. This made it increasingly a target for nationalist critics, not least members of the *Fuerza de Orientación Radical de la Joven Argentina* (FORJA), a group of anti-Alvear, leftist Radical sympathizers led by important political figures such as Arturo Jauretche and Raúl Scalabrini Ortiz, who accused Justo of implementing policies that made Argentina an economic colony dependent on foreign capital, and of creating a Central Bank in 1934 primarily for the benefit of British interests. The FORJA's demands for popular sovereignty, economic emancipation and social justice would be taken up by Peronism in the next decade, and by dependency theorists thereafter. In more general terms, nationalist revisionism (often taking a far more authoritarian stance than the FORJA) was strengthened by anti-'colonial' sentiment fanned by the treaty, leading to a view of Argentine history that vindicated Rosas as a national hero (despite his favourable treatment of foreign interests) and argued that the country's ills were the work of Europeanizing currents and the creation of a neo-colonial state dependent on the export of raw materials and foreign capital.

As economic conditions deteriorated and labour and agricultural unrest grew Justo replaced his economic team, in 1933, and new economy minister Federico Pinedo announced a Plan of Economic Action to combat the effects of low commodity prices and the falling peso exchange rate. The plan established a currency exchange board, which issued permits for importers to acquire foreign exchange and thus gave the government considerable control over trade and allowed it to restrict imports, benefiting domestic industries. Pinedo also created an income tax to reduce dependence on export taxes, as well as establishing the new Central Bank to control money supply. Exchange controls also generated substantial profits for the government, which it used to purchase agricultural commodities at a base price set by the government, usually well above the international market price. This policy proved highly successful in ensuring solvency in the agricultural sector, which post 1934 was further benefited by the collapse of output in the USA and by drought in Canada and Australia, allowing the government to withdraw economic support for farmers. At the same time, however, the crisis encouraged farmers to adopt more efficient agricultural techniques that reduced demand for labour, swelling the already large number of unemployed who began to look for work in the cities. The government did, nevertheless, undertake programmes designed to improve infrastructure and reduce joblessness; for example, the road network doubled during the 1930s, financed in part through a fuel tax introduced in 1931.

In 1935, the first revenue-sharing (coparticipation) law was enacted to distribute revenues between the central government and the provinces, a system that has remained in place although the criteria for redistribution have been subject to frequent amendment and renegotiation. It would be broadly accurate to say that, since 1935, the provincial percentage of shared revenues has increased under civilian governments and diminished sharply in periods of military rule (the latter having no need to negotiate federal issues with Congress). However, in the 1930s the revenue-sharing policy concentrated distribution in the wealthiest and most economically advanced provinces. Under the 1935 laws determining collection and distribution of shared

revenues, the provinces received as a whole 30.6 per cent of the total, falling to only 19.6 per cent in 1946, with the bulk concentrated
among the wealthier provinces (a practice that would be reversed
later). This method of redistribution was not only inequitable, but
reduced accountability at the provincial level by removing tax collection for the most part to the national authorities, minimizing the
political need for local authorities to justify and limit spending.

Relative economic successes emboldened the Justo government to
take a more high-handed line politically, bolstering censorship and
engaging in corrupt practices. One of the most damning indictments
of the government came at the hands of Santa Fe Senator Lisandro
de la Torre, the Progressive Democrat who represented one of the
few voices of opposition in Congress. De la Torre was part of an investigating commission that examined claims by ranchers that meat
packers had formed pools in order to force producers to sell their cattle
at low prices, an allegation that the commission upheld. De la Torre
went further, investigating corruption in contracts between the government and foreign-owned meat-packing plants, and tax evasion by
the meat packers, and made repeated denunciations on the Senate
floor. In a confused incident in 1935, an attack that may have been
directed at De la Torre led to his colleague from Santa Fe, Senator Enzo
Bordabehere, being shot dead in the Senate chamber. Thereafter, the
antipersonalistas in Congress also became increasingly critical of the
government's political repression and economic policies. At the same
time, however, at least some members of the government took an important role on the international stage: Foreign Minister Carlos Saavedra Lamas was elected president of the League of Nations in 1936 and
also became the first Latin American to win the Nobel Peace Prize
that year for his efforts to mediate in the 1932–8 Chaco War between
Bolivia and Paraguay.

In a bid to undercut this shift against the government, in 1938 Justo
called elections, for which the *Concordancia* candidate was Roberto
Ortiz, an *antipersonalista* and former member of the Justo cabinet.
Elected fraudulently (in many districts the number of votes cast significantly outnumbered registered voters), Ortiz nevertheless came to
office promising reform. Ortiz himself sought to do away with ballot rigging, with the result that, in the 1940 midterm elections, the
UCR won a majority in the Lower House. He also carried out federal
interventions of Buenos Aires and Catamarca provinces against local

administrations accused of anti-democratic practices. However, the diabetic Ortiz's health deteriorated rapidly, leaving him blind within a year of taking office, and he was plagued by dissent within the *Concordancia* and renewed economic turmoil, as a series of bad harvests undermined the export sector. These were further complicated by a recovery in US agriculture, and by the outbreak of the Second World War, which affected shipping and reduced manufactured imports.

In 1940 Pinedo proposed a new economic reactivation plan (the Pinedo Plan), which reinforced financing to the agricultural sector and offered tax rebates on exports of manufactured products in order to stimulate industry and save jobs (as well as to limit the prospects of labour unrest). However, most of the funds envisaged were still to be channelled to the agricultural sector, and the revitalized UCR majority in the Lower House refused to debate the proposals. Calls by Pinedo to shift away from export agriculture in favour of import substitution industries met with limited support and were finally scuppered when Ortiz was permanently replaced by his vice-president, Ramón Castillo, in 1940.

Castillo, a highly conservative *caudillo* from Catamarca, was quick to reverse any hint at reform, in particular of economic policies that had been designed to benefit the agricultural oligarchy to which he responded. Castillo was also encouraged by the lack of real competition for power within the *Concordancia*, after the deaths of Justo, Alvear and Ortiz in the early 1940s. However, the unpopularity of his government was exacerbated by the state of the economy, itself affected by Argentina's neutrality during the war. Nazi victories in Europe deprived Argentina of much of its trade as a result, with Britain imposing a naval blockade, post 1940, that cut Argentine shipping by half. In particular, British blockades hit Argentine grain exports, as Britain continued to buy meat but accounted for relatively little grain demand. Adding to the dislocation this caused, Britain could not export products to Argentina during the war, which not only had implications for availability of the goods formerly imported, but also left the funds arising from Argentine exports to Britain frozen in London for the duration of the war. At the same time, US pressures to force Argentina to declare support for the Allies led to the loss of trade preferences and alternative export markets.

The policy of neutrality also led to frictions with the armed forces, factions of which were pro-Allied while other factions were pro-Axis;

Castillo himself, though representative of largely pro-Allied oligarchs (which alarmed some sectors of the military), saw little advantage to adopting a position and preferred to maintain neutrality. Perhaps more saliently, neutrality saw Argentina lose out on the military and lend-lease aid that the USA granted to its rival Brazil, raising fears that Argentina would lose its regional position economically, politically and militarily. This in turn boosted the position of the most nationalist elements of the armed forces, who called for increased domestic manufacturing of arms and other 'necessities', in particular after Washington imposed an arms embargo on Argentina. Public opinion, which had only limited influence over political decision-making, was not in general pro-Axis, but animosity towards British and US policies regarding Argentina also undermined any pro-Allied sentiment. These divisions, and Castillo's insistence on putting forward a member of the old *criollo* landed elite from the northwest, Robustiano Patrón Costas, as the official presidential candidate in 1943, would put in motion the June 1943 coup d'état that would add a new actor, the urban working classes – and their ostensible leader, Colonel Juan Domingo Perón – to the political mix.

The coalition of military and conservative interests that succeeded Yrigoyen was unsympathetic to both trade unionism and working-class aspirations. During this period, however, changes occurred in the nature and size of the manufacturing industry and the urban masses supporting it, which laid the basis for mass mobilization of the working classes in the 1940s. These changes were largely conditioned by external factors: the slowdown in immigration from Europe and the need to develop a new industrial base for the production of consumer goods, unobtainable from abroad during the Depression.

Import substitution during the 1930s was dominated primarily by small companies, along with a few large ones, and enjoyed little political support from the *Concordancia* governments anxious above all to boost primary exports and the 'comparative advantage' of Argentina as an agricultural powerhouse. The strongest growth occurred in the textile sector; locally produced textiles accounted for only 9 per cent of demand in 1930, but 82 per cent in 1943.[3] Import tariffs also played a role in boosting industry, with US companies in particular choosing to open local subsidiaries in order to avoid that charge on their Argentine sales. This process continued and expanded following the outbreak of the Second World War. These changes gave rise to a greater homogeneity among the working classes, while at the same time leading to ruptures within the middle classes and the oligarchy, between those who profited from import substitution and those who did not.[4]

Until 1929, Argentina had been almost exclusively dependent on foreign currency from exports of chilled beef and raw materials, such as leather, which paid for its imports of consumer goods that were destined for the relatively small part of the population who could have been described as consumers. Following the Wall Street crash, export markets dried up, producing a crisis in the agricultural sector and forcing many rural labourers to seek urban jobs, as well as temporarily reducing the power of large landowners. Even after the Depression had largely eased, in the late 1930s, Argentina saw a series of bad harvests which resulted in lower exports and a rising trade deficit. Both the large landowners and larger industries were dependent primarily on foreign capital, the lack of which undermined their position in the 1930s, while potentially strengthening small-scale business and labour, as they were more independent and with fewer financing needs. Import substitution industrialization aimed at replacing imported goods without necessarily seeking to create an industrial economy. This industrialization 'without industrial revolution' created a sharp rise in production of light industrial goods such as food and drink, textiles and metallurgical products (such as refrigerators and other primary appliances), as well as a rise in factory workers employed in industry, which was small-scale and dispersed.[5]

If *porteño* society was unenthusiastic about welcoming poor immigrants, it was even more unwelcoming in the face of internal migration from the provinces, which became large-scale from the 1920s and reached an even higher level in the 1930s as a result of the Depression's impact in the interior. By this time, internal migrants far outnumbered new European immigrants, and were conspicuous for being in general darker-skinned and less educated than their *porteño* compatriots. In short, they resembled everything which *porteños* preferred to think Argentines were not, being more Latin American than European in appearance and customs. Although many were from provincial cities, they were often used to a more patriarchal and traditional society, in which social relations were clearly defined and employers were also patrons to their employee-clients, offering them certain benefits such as extra pay, food, standing godfather to their children, in exchange for their votes. In Buenos Aires, the structure of society was radically different to that of 'the interior', where social relations were more rigid, but which offered a degree of containment not found in Buenos Aires.[6] By definition, they were not for the most part representatives of the provincial elites or relatively settled and respectable middle classes, but rather those in precarious employment.

Those migrants who came from provincial cities – the majority of the total – had some experience of industrial or manufacturing work, but also came from a culture which was more traditional and less fast-paced than Buenos Aires, and where social relations also offered a degree of personal contact and predictability which was absent in the big city.[7] The big city offered them few of its delights, with the elegant centre of Buenos Aires being tacitly off limits to the shabbily dressed inhabitants of the southern slums, in La Boca or Avellaneda, and offered instead factory or slaughterhouse work in poor conditions, or the fetid odour of the Riachuelo river which runs through the southern suburbs, receiving industrial waste from factories and slaughterhouses in the area. If anything, the aspiring descendants of immigrants who had some prospects of entering the middle classes through education and hard work were arguably more threatened by, and thus sensitive to, the influx of provincials than were the elites.

Labour organization was not a new phenomenon in Argentina at this time. The first trade union had been founded by the printworkers in 1857, and the first strike (also by the printworkers) was recorded in 1878. In 1887, the *Unión Industrial Argentina* (UIA), a union of owners and employers, was founded essentially with the purpose of opposing trade unionism and encouraging a hard government line towards labour. The UIA played a leading role against recognition of collective bargaining or the right to organize. During the later half of the nineteenth century, the majority of those in urban employment (more than 52 per cent in Buenos Aires) were foreign-born, and trade unions were dominated by immigrants, usually of socialist or anarchist orientation.[8] Perhaps ironically, the steady supply of immigrant labour in the last decades of the nineteenth century and the early part of the twentieth century meant that labour was plentiful and labourers were in a weak bargaining position, despite the organizing activities of some of those immigrants. This may, in part, explain the appeal which the Peronists' nationalist rhetoric held for labour in the 1940s: '[F]rom 1880 to 1930 uncontrolled foreign immigration was perceived by the labour movement as a source of weakness in its struggle.'[9]

In addition to the fact that the traditional working class in Argentina was primarily foreign-born and had formed specific political or union loyalties, it was characterized by the fact that workers had greater training in what was virtually artisan-scale production and greater stability in their jobs. From the 1930s, the majority of 'new' urban workers entering the manufacturing industry had little training or job security, becoming virtually part of the machinery they operated. At the same time, many had come either from rural jobs or from provincial cities, or were newly entering the labour force (e.g., urban women and the children of immigrants), and lacked a background in industrial discipline which characterized those who had laboured in a structured environment all their lives. They were also attracted by the possibilities of urban life and of improving their economic situation, rather than by factory work per se. Many in the 1930s were to see their expectations of an improved standard of living thwarted, as they found themselves forced to erect huts in the shanty towns of Buenos Aires, and became increasingly defined as 'poor' rather than as 'workers'. In any case, these workers had less self-definition than the traditional working class, being largely individualist in their often frustrated goal of upward mobility, and lacked a background of participation in trade union, political or other social organizations.[10]

The only relatively organized labour movement in the early years of the century which was not led by communists or anarchists from Spain or Italy was linked to the Catholic Church, which, following the 1891 Papal Encyclical *Rerum Novarum* on the issue of labour rights, made sporadic efforts to forge a confessional trade union tendency to counter anarchist or communist influences in the unions. The *Liga Democrática Cristiana* in the early 1920s made an attempt at confessional trade unionism which influenced early labour legislation.[11] The only official Church attempt to expand its role within organized labour in light of the increased urban working class, the *Juventud Obrera Católica* (JOC), founded in 1939, would become the only official Catholic body which initially gave unequivocal support to Perón, as it welcomed the emphasis he placed on Christian doctrine and the consequent lessening of trade union hostility to the Church, seen as favouring the interests of the elite and middle classes.[12]

Partly due to its unfavourable bargaining position, trade unionism had by 1930 made few gains for labour, and rising activism was met with rising repression. In 1907, a National Department of Labour

(DNT) had been established to collect statistics on workers' conditions, to arbitrate in labour disputes where this was agreed by both parties and to enforce rudimentary labour legislation which established Sunday as a rest day and regulated working conditions for women and children. In practice, however, the DNT was largely an ineffective body and the laws governing working conditions were routinely flouted with impunity. As a result of their weakness, trade unions did not attract members and unionization remained at a low level in most industries, further undermining the unions' effectiveness. At the same time, the internationalist vision of unions dominated by anarchists, syndicalists, socialists and communists failed to appeal to Argentine workers, while infighting among differing political orientations left the unions still more divided and ineffectual.[13]

By 1930, however, this scenario had begun to change. Firstly, the First World War, and then the Great Depression, had slowed immigration to a trickle. This meant that the majority of workers were now Argentine-born and labour supply was relatively static and thus in a comparatively strong bargaining position. Labour supply could only be increased by internal migration. Secondly, the fall in imports and consequent rise in import substitution manufacturing required an expanded labour force. Despite the lack of public policies to stimulate it, this import substitution process was actively encouraged by at least part of the oligarchy, who saw in it a new economic outlet which posed no real threat to the traditional agricultural economy, and by a sector of the middle class engaged in manufacturing. It was this sector of the middle class, engaged in the manufacture of light consumer goods, which would eventually support Perón's policy of subsidizing both production and consumption: whatever they lost in increased wages was compensated by the expansion of the consumer market. (It was in fact the professional and service sectors of the middle class which most strongly opposed both industrialization and Peronism, not least because the subsidy of production and consumption through increased wages and through protectionist policies increased their purchasing costs.)[14]

It has commonly been assumed that the bulk of internal migrants to Buenos Aires in the 1930s came from underdeveloped, rural areas and were therefore naive and uneducated enough to provide a constituency for Perón's brand of populism. In particular, it has been suggested that such rural workers were accustomed to submitting to the paternalistic authority of local landowners or *caudillos*, and that, once separated from this authority, they readily transferred that submission to Perón's leadership. However, as noted above, by 1943 the majority of these workers in fact came from relatively developed urban areas.[15] Indeed, it is perhaps worth noting that rural support for Perón appears to have been lower than in urban areas, at least initially, suggesting that rural workers were not particularly more susceptible to Peronism. For example, in the 1946 presidential elections, the vote for Perón averaged 55.2 per cent in cities over 50,000, while in rural areas of under 2,000 it averaged only 46 per cent.[16] This may be attributable to the fact that Perón's reforms had affected urban workers more than their rural counterparts – or it could be interpreted as reinforcing the view that rural workers were generally more submissive to their employers, who would presumably have wished them to vote against Perón. The exceptions to this rule were local *caudillos* in remote provinces who linked their careers to that of Perón as a means of increasing their own strength, and in exchange provided the support of their local clients.

What is most significant about the urban working classes in this period is their homogeneity rather than their distinctions. The greatest changes in their nature were their size and the fact that they were, in the main, native Argentines. In addition, despite the basically anti-labour governments of the 1930s, the rise in manufacturing and consequent demand for labour meant that by 1943 wages were already rising somewhat in real terms.

The policies of the governments of the 1930s, de facto or fraudulently elected, were repressive towards labour and towards labour organization. The 1930 coup d'état had marked a return to conservative government imposed by the traditional elites who had never sought the support of labour. Thus, despite its increasing size, the urban working class continued to be politically marginal. At the same time, the traditional labour leaders were divided and failed to represent the aspirations of the growing mass of workers: foreign-born leaders of the various tendencies were preoccupied throughout this period with events abroad, such as the Spanish Civil War and, later, by the Nazi–Soviet Pact. Their concerns were not shared by labour as a whole. (The communists resisted labour agitation in industries owned or monopolized by the 'democratic powers' – the USA and the United Kingdom – following the Nazi invasion of the Soviet Union.)

In addition to the repressive attitude of government to trade union-ism in the 1930s, the working classes were weakened further in the first half of the decade by a rise in unemployment resulting from the Depression, and by a rise in urban labour due to unemployment in the interior of the country. As a result, although urban employment increased in the period 1929–35, unemployment remained high and real wages fell during the period. From 1935, however, improving eco-nomic conditions led to increasing employment, which in turn led to better wages and somewhat greater bargaining power for the working classes, although real wages remained relatively static and the share of national income corresponding to the working classes, which had fallen in the first half of the 1930s, did not rise commensurately with the increase in industrial employment.[17]

By 1936, there were 356 trade unions in Argentina with a total of some 370,000 members, a figure which reached 473,000 members in 1940. However, trade union members accounted for only around 10 per cent of total salaried workers in 1940, and only around 30 per cent of industrial labour. Nearly all trade union members were concen-trated in the ports, transport or industrial sectors (including slaughter-houses), and nearly all were to be found in the cities of Buenos Aires and Rosario. Trade unions in this period were still largely leftist in ori-entation and concentrated among the more skilled sectors of labour. In 1935 the umbrella body *Confederación General del Trabajo* (General Confederation of Labour, CGT) was strengthened by a shake-up which resulted in the removal of most of its leaders, socialists and syndical-ists who were believed to have conspired with the government to the detriment of their members. Thereafter, the leadership of the CGT showed an increasing representation of communist trade unionists, especially strong in the textile and metallurgical sectors. (However, trade union membership would not rise significantly until after Perón came to power: in 1945 there were 969 trade unions with 529,000 members, while the number of union members rose to 1.5 million in 1947 and 3.0 million in 1951.)[18]

From the late 1930s, the number of strikes began to rise as labour's position became slightly stronger, and as their expectations of better wages also increased. In 1942, 113 strikes were held, of which 70 were wage-related and only 45 were successful in obtaining pay rises. The CGT divided at this time into two groups: the CGT-1, led by socialist José Domenech (of the railway workers *Unión Ferroviaria*), and the

CGT-2, led by municipal worker Francisco Pérez Leirós and dominated by socialist and communist leaders. The latter union was shut down by the military government in July 1943, one month after the coup d'état, and both the railway unions (*Unión Ferroviaria*, which represented the workers, and *La Fraternidad*, which represented the drivers) were also withdrawn from CGT-1. However, although the unions were initially weakened after the 1943 coup, real wages began to rise, increasing by 20 per cent for industrial labour by 1945.[19]

The Second World War brought with it the expansion of the import substitution process, as well as the increase in real wages and the numbers employed in industry. These classes continued to be marginalized from the sources of political power and either politically divided or apolitical. However, their expectations as well as their numbers (by this time the industrial working classes accounted for some 7 million out of a total population of close to 16 million) were increasing, and it was inevitable that labour must become a political actor, with or without the consent of the traditional sources of political power. What it required, and what it created, was a leader to bring this about: 'The Peronist movement drew strength from processes going on in Argentine society, and in turn it affected those processes.'[20]

Perhaps the primary significance of the 1943 coup d'état was that it occurred in the context of an increasing political vacuum. It was facilitated by the gradual discrediting of the traditional political groupings which occurred from 1930. The Radicals remained in disarray, while the traditional conservative party, which had historically represented the interests of the landed oligarchy and parts of the urban elite, had been virtually disbanded at the national level after the rise of the Radicals during the First World War, and continued to exist only through a few provincial parties such as the Democratic Party in Mendoza and the Autonomist Party in Corrientes. Although the conservative party remained strong in some municipalities, its lack of representation at the national level reduced its ability to distribute patronage and favours to the local level. The conservative and provincial parties would thus become increasingly isolated and reduced to a local expression, as true power to offer vote-getting favours was limited to the military coalition, the UCR and, later, the Peronists. (Both the Radicals and Peronists would adopt the conservative tradition of jobs for votes or jobs for the supporters of the local party boss or party affiliates.)

Even as the factions which made up the *Concordancia* were in decay by the early 1940s, the urban working classes were on the increase, both in numbers and in potential power, although to date they had failed to find sufficient bases for common action to overcome the general lack of political and union experience and organize their own movement. Nonetheless, by this time both the remains of the traditional working classes and the new members of urban labour were largely united in their desire to receive a greater share of the wealth they generated and to define a role in a society which in general saw them as poor and undesirable. (An exception were the immigrants and children of immigrants who were proud of their self-made status and of achieving some degree of upward mobility, usually in office rather than industrial jobs, independently of trade unions or government assistance, and who would later become violently anti-Peronist and critical of the *negritos* who depended on the Peronist government to give them the social benefits the immigrants had won for themselves.)

Thus, the 1943 coup represented the (temporary) eclipse of the traditional bases of power, replacing them with a new alliance of different, more radical military and civilian interests. The eclipse of traditional interests was neither permanent nor complete enough to permit a genuine political restructuring, but for the moment at least the existing levers of power were in new hands. At the same time, the nascent trade union movement was in disarray and had failed to produce a leader capable of fusing it into a genuine confederation. Arguably, unions from different sectors were seen as competing for a limited prize, rather than as forces which could unite to press their claims more effectively. Their leaders were thus seen as potential rivals, as well as considered unrepresentative by other unions, either higher or lower on the socio-economic ladder. As such, a leader to unite a range of sectors had to come from outside the movement, and had to be in a position to offer tangible benefits, rather than a proposal of class struggle or sector-based demands. This lack of a leader would soon be remedied, as the unionists were about to find that leader outside their ranks: they would mould that leader in the image they sought, even as that leader would also mould the trade union movement in his own image.

4 Peronism: The Original Protagonists

Official history indicates that Juan Domingo Perón was born in the town of Lobos, Buenos Aires province, on 8 October 1895. Like most other elements of the life of a man who was singularly economical with the truth on many occasions, even this simple fact is open to debate. Some sources indicate that Perón was in fact born a day or two earlier, in a small rural house outside Lobos, while other credible sources indicate that he was born nearby in Roque Pérez on 7 October 1893, and his birth was only registered two years later when his father decided to recognize his illegitimate son. According to this version, sustained by Perón himself later in life, the birth was registered in Lobos because it housed the Registry Office nearest to Roque Pérez. This minor dispute over Perón's origins is characteristic of the ambiguous nature of most supposed facts concerning his life, and suggests that that life began as it meant to go on.

Perón was the second son of Mario Tomas Perón and Juana Sosa Toledo; their older son, Mario Avelino, was born in 1891. Mario and Juana were not married at the time, and did not marry until 1901. Perón's paternal grandfather, Tomas Perón, had been a distinguished doctor and later a senator, and is said to have developed the first rabies vaccine in Argentina. When his father died in 1889, Mario abandoned his medical studies and left for the country, where he became a public employee in Lobos and formed a family with Juana Sosa. Juana was a young country girl of humble and apparently partly Indian origin, several rungs lower on the social ladder than Mario. The fact of having been an illegitimate son, of a mother not considered socially respectable, was later a bond between Perón and Evita, although Perón's resentments arising from this condition were less vehement than hers.

Outside the context of small-town Argentina, such resentments may seem unwarranted or hyper-sensitive, but this does not take account of the obsessions of that provincial society, especially those members struggling to be recognized as middle class and seeking characteristics which made them superior to others. Although it is estimated that some 30 per cent of all children born in Argentina in the early part of the twentieth century were illegitimate, this circumstance was one which separated genteel (albeit impoverished) society from the lower classes, who, for cultural and economic reasons, were often unwed. Another distinguishing characteristic was skin colour, as those of European origin hastened to distinguish themselves from the dark-skinned natives. The long-established *criollo* aristocracy, on the other hand, looked down on recent European immigrants, particularly of Spanish or Italian origin, whose skin tone and educational level were often difficult to differentiate from those of the despised *negritos*. The fact that Perón's parents were not married, and that indeed his middle-class father had taken up with a peasant girl with Indian features, were therefore issues which represented an overblown social stigma.

When Perón was five years old, Mario moved the family to the remote southern region of Patagonia, taking a job as administrator of the Chank Aike estancia in Santa Cruz province. The isolated childhood spent by Perón in Patagonia seems to have left a number of marks on his adult character and thinking: the miserable conditions in which rural workers lived became familiar to him, although in later years he would remember the peons as his companions and teachers, and he developed an independent and aloof personality (despite being outwardly ever-smiling and open, Perón maintained a certain distance in his relationships all his life, and very few people were close to him). He also developed an abiding admiration and affection for dogs, which he later described as his best friends in his Patagonian childhood and which he always held in higher esteem for their intelligence and loyalty than his human interlocutors. In 1904, the family moved slightly to the north, to Chubut province where the weather was less severe, although the limited accounts provided later by Perón of his parents indicate that both were austere and, in his mother's case in particular, iron-willed and prepared to withstand whatever came.[1]

Also in 1904, Perón and his brother Mario returned to Buenos Aires to study, although Mario shortly thereafter fell ill and returned permanently to Chubut. Thus Perón, at a very early age, found himself obliged to further develop his independent nature. His schoolmates later remembered him as dominating and bossy (words also later used to describe Evita by her own former schoolmates). While not an especially distinguished student, at 15 he began studying to enter medical school. He changed his mind and career abruptly when he was accepted by the military academy (*Colegio Militar*), following in the footsteps of several paternal uncles. The *Colegio Militar* was at the time under the direction of Prussian military officers and their disciples, and instilled an admiration for German military discipline and for authoritarian attitudes that remained with Perón and most of his colleagues for life – although the proclivity for authoritarian attitudes and the belief that government at both the family and national level must be authoritarian to be strong was, and remains, widespread in Argentine culture, and not confined to its armed forces.

In 1913 Perón graduated as a sub-lieutenant and joined the infantry, a less socially prestigious body than the cavalry. He was initially stationed in Paraná, Entre Ríos province, and transferred in 1920 to the Non-Commissioned Officers school at Campo de Mayo, near Buenos Aires, where for the first time he received glowing reports as an instructor. He was described by contemporaries as entirely devoted to his career and to the men under his command, teaching those from the most underprivileged backgrounds the basics of etiquette, hygiene and table manners in addition to their military training.[2]

In 1926, Perón was sent to the Superior War School, founded to train middle-ranking officers for higher command posts. He spent three years studying there before becoming a professor of military history in 1931, a post which developed both his vocation as a teacher and his intellectual pretensions. During the course of his tenure there, the then Captain Perón wrote three books on military history, as well as a history of Patagonian place names. Also during this period Perón took another step which formed part of the upwardly mobile career of any young military officer: in January 1929 he married a young lady of good family, Aurelia Tizón, known as 'Potota'. Aurelia, a music teacher by profession and the daughter of a middle-class Buenos Aires merchant with good connections in the Radical Party, was

14 years younger than Perón and deferred to her husband's greater experience. By the standards of the time she was doubtless considered to have made a good match, with a rising young army officer of good status and good looks, even if his earliest origins had been less than conventional.

At this stage, at least, Perón had shown himself to be extremely conventional in most respects, entering the military career as a traditional means of advancement (the military and the priesthood were among the principal career choices for upwardly mobile or academically minded young men of respectable but less than moneyed backgrounds). Aurelia was likewise of a conventional background, fond of music and painting, and the ten-year marriage was generally perceived as successful. A measure of the formality of the relationship, as well as a measure of Perón's frequent coldness with respect to other people, is that virtually his only public comment on Aurelia, made in a 1970 interview more than 30 years after her death, was: 'In '28 I married Aurelia Tizón. She was a very nice girl, a concert guitarist. She played very well. Unfortunately she died young.'[3]

The only unconventional aspect of the marriage was the lack of children. The question of Perón's infertility, which according to some sources was confirmed by a family doctor during this first marriage, was a thorny one for his followers in a *machista* society. It has been disputed by rumours that both Evita and his third wife, Isabelita, had been pregnant by him and had suffered miscarriages, and by Perón's own later statements that he had fathered a child by an Italian actress during his stay in Europe in the late 1930s. Subsequently, well after his death, a lady named Martha Holgado persistently claimed to be his illegitimate daughter (despite DNA tests indicating the contrary), even claiming to have maintained a close relationship with him during his term as president and to have been present at a number of historical events. However, other testimonies, as well as the fact that none of Perón's three marriages produced children, would tend to suggest that he was in fact infertile.[4]

THE BEGINNINGS OF A POLITICAL CAREER

In 1929, Perón graduated from the Superior War School, shortly before the start of the Great Depression. A year later, he would be caught up in the military plots to overthrow the ageing Yrigoyen. Perón was recruited to the ranks of the officers backing Uriburu, although a few days before the 6 September 1930 coup he withdrew from Uriburu's camp and joined that of Justo, whose supporters were more numerous and who favoured the formation of a joint military–civilian government. While the sudden shift from one side to another was an early sign of one of his more consistent traits, Captain Perón played a very minimal role in the coup, and one that he later regretted, noting the nefarious precedent it set in public life, the ending of the hopes of greater social progress and the strengthening of the most conservative sectors of the oligarchy.

Uriburu took rapid steps to rid himself of members of the pro-Justo faction, and Perón was sent to patrol the Argentine–Bolivian border for two months, before assuming his new post as professor of military history at the Superior War School. After Justo was elected president, Perón was promoted to the rank of major, and also served as aide-de-camp to the defence minister. However, at this stage of his career Perón was still far more devoted to his military and academic pursuits than to politics, honing his talents as a writer, teacher and communicator.

Early in 1936, Perón was named military attaché in the Argentine Embassy in Santiago, Chile, a delicate mission considering the less than cordial relations between the two countries, and one which demonstrated that he had reached certain prestige in the army. Perón and Aurelia remained in Chile until March 1938, during which time he was promoted to lieutenant colonel, although he was also accused of spying for Argentina and was rumoured to have been expelled by the Chilean government. In fact, Perón was later known to have formed a group of informers for the purpose of obtaining information on Chilean military plans, an activity which was not unusual for the holders of the post (being in fact its principal function). However, it was his successor, Major Eduardo Lonardi, who was eventually trapped by Chilean intelligence and deported, a cause for bad feelings between the two which may have influenced the fact that the same Lonardi was to lead the coup against Perón in 1955.[5]

In September 1938, Perón became a widower when Aurelia died of uterine cancer. At a loose end for several months, in February 1939 he was sent to Europe to receive training at a regiment in the Italian Alps, an assignment he would later inflate to suggest that he had been sent to analyse the military situation in Europe at the outbreak of the Second World War. In fact, in 1939 and 1940 he served at various Alpine outposts, not precisely at the heart of political and military strategy-making, although he is also said to have visited Germany and Vichy France during his stay. The use of mass organization and mass spectacle in both Italy and Germany doubtless made an impression on him as an example of how military discipline could be imposed on society for the good of society as a whole (sic), and of how the relationship between the masses and a leader could transform society.

However, this is not to suggest that Perón was a convinced fascist, as many anti-Peronists have automatically supposed. While Perón admired order and vertical power structures, and although he was unscrupulous enough (and superficial enough) to ignore many aspects of fascism in the name of convenience, he never favoured large-scale violence. Indeed, he was far from alone in the destructively naive belief that the corporate structure of the military, with vertical control and the subjugation of individual will to a common goal, could be transferred to civil society and would indeed benefit that society by making it more harmonious and efficient. At the same time, any sympathy for mass destruction would have been erased by his visit to Spain on his way back to Argentina in 1940, where he was appalled by the still-recent destruction caused by the Civil War and its ongoing effects, and the memory of which he would later cite as the reason for pulling back from violence which could have produced a civil war in Argentina in the 1950s.

Perón returned to Argentina in late 1940 and was almost immediately transferred to a mountain regiment in Mendoza province. A year later he was promoted to the rank of colonel and put in command of a mountain regiment, also helping young officers to prepare to enter the Superior War School. In 1942, Perón was assigned to inspect mountain troops, and placed under the orders of General Edelmiro Farrell, a complaisant superior officer whose relationship with Perón would help Farrell to the (de facto) presidency and Perón to the position of power behind the throne a short time later. Returning to Buenos Aires in March 1942, Perón quickly became involved in the political undercurrents of the army's younger officers (many of whom had been his pupils and with whom he had a good relationship). He was also involved at this time in another clandestine and dubious relationship: on his return from Mendoza, Perón brought with him a teenaged mistress, known as 'Piraña', who was kept in the background, and introduced as his daughter when it was necessary for her to appear.

The political undercurrents in the army were divided between those favouring the renewed candidacy of the pro-Allied Justo for the elections planned for 1943, a group of Axis sympathizers who wished to avoid the assumption of a pro-Allied government and a group favouring continued Argentine neutrality in the Second World War. Out of the third group was born the clandestine loggia *Grupo de Oficiales Unidos* (United Officers Group, GOU), of which Perón was a member and probable founder.[6] Despite his hitherto conventional military career, the experience in Europe would appear to have awakened Perón's taste for both politics and conspiracy. Within a short time, the GOU would play a role in the coup d'état of 4 June 1943, which would propel Perón to the post of secretary of labour, minister of war and eventually vice-president, posts from which his ability to lead would be extended far more widely. His leadership qualities were enhanced by his considerable charisma, good looks, energy and apparently permanent good humour.

THE SEARCH FOR THE 'REAL' PERÓN

Although the facts of Perón's biography to this point are relatively well-known, if not always clear-cut, it may be noted that this biographical sketch gives an idea of the public persona but does not conjure up a clear image of the private Perón or the personality behind the public image. There is a reason for this: the real personality of the private Perón seems elusive and largely undefinable even for those who knew him. Perón can be seen acting the role of teacher, studying military history and philosophy, acting as conspirator, disciplined officer, or as an audience displaying interest in what his interlocutor had to say and, in turn, saying what that interlocutor wanted to hear, smiling president or leader of masses. However, the person behind the public mask remains more nebulous. By all accounts somewhat cold, unspontaneous, distant and untrusting behind the mask of bonhomie assumed in public, he was also widely considered by those who knew him to be genuinely concerned for the poor conditions of his conscripts and, by extension, the social classes they represented.

These contradictions are not irreconcilable: the fact of being ambitious does not automatically rule out a genuine belief that those ambitions also involve the betterment of others, and the fact of being reserved does not rule out an interest (possibly a somewhat academic or impersonal one) in the sufferings of others. Both insecure and authoritarian, Perón could arguably be defined as similar to a rich uncle, happily distributing largesse to poor relations and enjoying their thanks, but on his own terms; a figure who would not cohabit as happily with peers as with inferiors or disciples. All his life, Perón was unquestionably happier in relationships in which his position was superior to that of the other party, a not uncommon characteristic which in his case had damaging consequences by leading him to surround himself with incompetents and sycophants within his government. At the same time, his more Machiavellian and megalomaniac characteristics co-existed with a basically simple and austere personality, and with a basically simple perception: just as in the barracks or on the *estancias*, problems should be resolved by the person in charge, who should have the capacity to do so.

THE SCANDALOUS ORIGINS OF EVITA[7]

The case of Evita is substantially different: her public and private personalities appear to have been largely the same, also including conflicting elements but evident to any observer. While Perón was working his way up through the ranks of the infantry, in what promised to be a successful but fairly typical military career, Evita was born in another small town in the province of Buenos Aires, smaller and more remote than Lobos, and in even less socially acceptable circumstances. Her mother, Juana Ibarguren, a pretty woman of Basque origin and poor family, was from the small village of Los Toldos, buried in the midst of the endless Pampas. At an early age, she went to work as a cook at the La Unión *estancia*, near Los Toldos, and soon became the official mistress of the *estanciero*, Juan Duarte. Duarte was from Chivilcoy, a larger town some 100 kilometres away, where his legitimate family stayed when he went to take charge of the administration of La Unión. Duarte and Juana were to have five children: Elisa, Blanca, Juan, Erminda and María Eva, who were informally acknowledged by Duarte to be his progeny but were not legally registered on their birth certificates with the surname Duarte. The youngest, María Eva, was born on 7 May 1919 on the estancia, where she lived the first few years of her life, until Duarte returned to Chivilcoy and Juana returned to Los Toldos with her five children.

Juana, invariably described as a hard-working woman of very resolute character, found a small adobe house on the outskirts of Los Toldos, literally on the wrong side of the tracks from where the town as such ended at the railway line. The house still stands (now surrounded by newer houses which have sprung up as the town grew outwards); it was bought by perennial Peronist politician Antonio Cafiero in the 1980s and converted into a rather understocked museum, featuring the sewing machine of Doña Juana. (As in the case of Perón, the house has been inaccurately described as the birthplace of Eva Duarte de Perón, although in this case there is no doubt that she was born elsewhere and came to Los Toldos as a small child.) Doña Juana was from all appearances an exceptional person who could well deserve her own biography, were the material available: as a young girl she had the courage to go to a remote *estancia* to work, on the grounds that the pay was better than working as a seamstress in Los Toldos.[8] Thereafter, she did not shrink from returning to Los Toldos and bringing up her children alone, working to support them and striving to give them more options in life than she had had herself.

The 1920s was a period in which a woman in her position had few employment options, and her most likely role in life would have been to set up family with a labourer and work in the house or in the fields with him. However, Doña Juana apparently did not yearn for this sort of life, and used her good looks to find, at least temporarily, more attractive partners. At the same time, she did not want her own daughters limited to the choice between being a labourer's woman, a mistress or a servant, and made remarkable efforts to ensure that their own good looks could be turned to the same advantage as their social betters, that is, finding a respectable husband who could give them a comfortable life. Working as a seamstress, she received the concession to make uniforms for the local school (allegedly through a subsequent lover who worked in the municipality) and eked out a sufficient living to feed and clothe her family.

That family, however, was even less socially acceptable in ultra-conservative Los Toldos than the Perón family might have been in

Lobos, and contemporaries were to recall years later that many families would not allow their children to play with the Duarte clan, calling
them offensive names and even throwing mud at them in the street.
That ultraconservatism and snobbishness was exacerbated by the fact
that Los Toldos was a very small, undistinguished and largely poor
village lost in the Pampas, where only a very few – the railway sta-
tionmaster, the teacher, the bakery owner, a few landowners and one
or two public employees in the post office and municipality – might
have had some claim to being socially a cut above the rest. Los Toldos
('the tents') was also, as its name implies, originally an Indian camp.
The fact that it still had a considerable Indian population (considered
the lowest of the low in proudly white, immigrant Argentina), and
that its inhabitants could be looked down on as poor, ignorant and
probably Indian as well, made those inhabitants all the more anxious to demonstrate their own respectability and to find means to
distinguish themselves from those who could be considered inferior.
Into that category fell unmarried mothers and illegitimate children.
Moreover, Doña Juana was far less circumspect than the norm: her
children used the surname Duarte (although they were registered on
their birth certificates and in school records as Ibarguren), and she
herself behaved as a hard-working, attractive and respectable matron
(albeit with occasional other 'protectors') rather than the abject figure
society might have accepted.

One of the more notable facts about Doña Juana is the fact that
she raised her children through her own efforts and without accepting
charity. Charity was certainly available at the time to people in her
position, through the Church and respectable ladies associated with
it, but only available at a high price: that of accepting humiliation.
In addition to accepting the position of miserable and undeserving
sinner, the price of a plate of food also included the humiliation of
having the children inspected for dirty fingernails and lice. This was
not an altogether wrong-headed or ill-intended act by ladies anxious
to impose their superior notions of hygiene on individuals whose own
sanitary concepts were often rudimentary, but the practice implied
the humiliating assumption that mothers did not know how to raise
their children, and that poor children could thus be assumed to be
filthy. Doña Juana disdained the aid, rejected the inspection and sent
her children to school scrubbed and immaculate in spotless white
uniform.

An indication of how little Doña Juana was prepared to accept social limits in this respect came in 1926, when Juan Duarte died in Chivilcoy. Doña Juana took her children to Chivilcoy for the funeral, insisting that they be allowed to say goodbye to their father. Such impropriety was considered completely shocking: Duarte's legal family had probably known (or at least imagined) that he had had another woman during the years they were apart, and probably accepted this as a normal fact of life – always provided that they were not confronted face to face with the fact, or with the other woman and her children. Their entry to the funeral was adamantly refused, and they were packed off with an earful of abuse. While accounts of the funeral differ, the total rejection they experienced at the hands of the representatives of petit bourgeois society remained with them all. (According to Raúl Suárez, a nephew of Juana Ibarguren who lived with them in Los Toldos as a child, Duarte's wife had been unaware of the relationship and, upon discovering the existence of Juana and five children, lost no time in travelling to the *estancia* with two police officers in tow, and in evicting her husband, his mistress and their offspring from the premises. Suárez also claims that the family refused to allow either Juana or any of the children to see Duarte's body when he died.)[9]

Suárez remembered Doña Juana and her daughters as being of very strong character, somewhat big-headed and with pretensions above their station, primarily due to the fact that all were fair-skinned and pretty. Suárez' reminiscences regarding his cousins go beyond even Peronist mythology in trying to make their history more respectable but give some insight into the mentality of Los Toldos, as even this relative of equally humble social origins felt the need to make the family appear less marginal than they really were. Los Toldos, which has expanded to a neat and attractive town of around 10,000 residents and shows the economic benefits of the rise in soya cultivation in the area in recent years, continues to show a strong conservative and basically anti-Peronist streak. Despite a statue in the main square, it shows little but distaste for the memory of its most famous daughter.

In 1930, when Evita was 11 and her older sister Elisa was established as a post office employee, Doña Juana arranged a transfer for Elisa (supposedly through another 'protector') and moved her family to Junín, a fairly large town some 50 kilometres from Los Toldos, and set about establishing them in a better social station. In Junín,

Doña Juana switched from sewing to cooking, offering meals to re-spectable single men at a time when restaurants in the interior of Argentina were largely unheard of. Given the number of single men working in Junín who needed meals and were unable to pay a servant, and given both Juana's experience as a cook and the presence of four pretty daughters, it can be assumed that this was a fairly good busi-ness. At the same time, while her daughters still faced the stigma of their illegitimacy, she was extremely strict regarding their comport-ment. In addition, while neither Los Toldos nor Junín offered many prospects for a woman alone, Junín at least offered a wider range of good marriage prospects, having both a military barracks and a sub-stantial administrative and professional sector, including the railway employees.

The policy of Doña Juana was highly successful with both Elisa and Blanca (by this time a schoolteacher), who eventually married an army major and a lawyer based in Junín. The mere fact that both Elisa and Blanca were employed could be considered remarkable at the time, and present-day residents of Junín describe the family as exceptionally progressive in this respect. That progressive tendency may have been due to necessity rather than design, but it is no less remarkable that two daughters of a family of such humble origin should have found employment and that that employment should have been not that of servants or laundry women, but more socially respectable posts. The fact that Blanca should have completed secondary school to become a teacher, when even most middle-class women did not do so, is an impressive feat that should not be taken lightly.

Evita, the youngest, however, was less receptive to her mother's plans for bourgeois respectability: from an early age, Evita, an avid moviegoer, dreamed of being an actress like her idol Norma Shearer, and was determined to go to Buenos Aires to launch herself in that less than socially respected profession. However, her later dedication to hard work, absolute determination and her firm belief in the possi-bilities of progress for the poor (who, to her frustration, often failed to share her vision of the progress they should desire) imply that Doña Juana's teachings nonetheless made a lasting mark on her youngest daughter.

Evita finished primary school at 14, where contemporaries recalled her as both sweet and shy, on the one hand, and – when convinced of something she wanted to achieve – persistent, persuasive and domineering (the latter characteristic frequently weighing in to win her point where persuasion failed). She was also recalled as a no more than average student, but with a passion for reciting and participating in school plays. When not declaiming before an audience, she was introverted, limited in her social circle by the continuing stigma surrounding her illegitimate birth, and very close to her mother and sisters, with a special soft spot for brother Juan, the only man of the house.[10]

THE HARD ROAD TO THE TOP

At 15 Evita left Junín for Buenos Aires, early in 1935. The circumstances of her leaving are the subject of various versions, the most common of which is that she was taken to Buenos Aires by Agustín Magaldi, a well-known tango singer who, depending on the version, either took a kindly interest in the young aspiring artist or was seduced by her and pushed into taking her with him to Buenos Aires. Other versions indicate that she went alone, or accompanied by her mother, or that her brother Juan, by this time working as a salesman, accompanied her to Buenos Aires. In any case, unlike the vast majority of young girls who dream of becoming actresses, she went.

With the exception of the fact that Evita went to Buenos Aires to become an actress, and did so, this story was and is not uncommon for people of poor family: the need to leave home at an early age in order to look for work, and often never to return, remains a common theme. One of the more popular television programmes in Argentina in the 1990s, *Gente que busca gente* (people seeking people), undertook investigations to try to locate long-lost relatives separated by hard circumstances: middle-aged women who were forced to leave home to seek work as servants as young teenagers and who lost all contact with their families; former maids seeking the now adult children they had been forced to give up as babies, when they became pregnant by their employer; the children of unwed parents who had never seen their father; or the mother who gave them up for adoption because she was unable to keep them alone. Poverty and deprivation usually play a role in these stories, and the extent to which these experiences are still common makes it easy to understand why Evita had a special rapport with the poor, and why her story struck a chord with so many, who had suffered the same privations and vicariously enjoyed the triumph which she, and so few others, finally achieved.

The role of Magaldi has always been disputed by many, who argue that there is no record that he played in Junín in 1934. Magaldi died, a young man, in 1938, before Evita became even moderately well-known and thus was unable to confirm or deny the story. This factor makes him a convenient protagonist: Magaldi, arguably second only to Carlos Gardel in popularity, was famous enough to make an impact in the story, while the concept of being picked up by a tango singer sounded sufficiently romantic for the soap opera public and sufficiently sordid for the anti-Peronist legend. Reasonably reliable contemporary witnesses assert that Magaldi and Evita knew each other in Buenos Aires, implying that contact was established either before or after she left Junín.

Magaldi, who had separated from his wife in the early 1930s, was above all known for his social sensibilities, generous nature and socialist leanings: his tangos speak frequently of exploitation and misery, the plight of the poor and forgotten prisoners, rather than romantic misadventures, and have a distinct ring of pre-Peronist propaganda. If indeed he did meet Evita in Junín in 1935, they might well have been genuinely attracted to one another, and Magaldi might well have been willing to help Evita to reach Buenos Aires, with or without a romantic attachment. In general terms, it was common practice at the time for visitors from Buenos Aires to take back young girls from the interior, to work as servants, to study, or for less above-board purposes, and the fact that he might have taken Evita to Buenos Aires would in itself have been nothing unusual.

If the version that Magaldi arranged an interview at a radio station is to be believed, it can only be assumed that his influence (which, like his career, was in fact limited by his political affinities) was insufficient to ensure that Evita got regular employment: the first several years she spent in Buenos Aires were lean ones, with walk-on stage or film parts and long periods of unemployment. However, even soon after arriving in Buenos Aires she did receive presentations which opened the doors to radio and stage auditions and a series of bit parts, which indicates that she was acquainted with someone in a position to open those doors. This period gave rise to the later version that she had been a prostitute, or at least something of a professional mistress, using the men who used her to further her career. Unfortunately, Evita was not the only young actress to learn that the casting couch was ubiquitous in Buenos Aires, or that her thespian talents were insufficient to ensure engagements without accepting that condition of employment – one which was also often forced on other working women, and one from which she would not have been exempt had she chosen an alternative employment.

This background, hardly the norm for first ladies of the land, was used to her detriment by critics who denigrated her for succumbing but did not question the system which imposed sexual oppression as a norm. While treated with total disregard by many in the system, during the difficult years of her early career she was also befriended by others, who recalled her as a sensitive and often sweet young woman and who made efforts to offer an occasional role or at least a meal when times were hard. Evita was later famous for having a long and detailed memory, for both friends and enemies, seeing both in black and white terms which were unable to admit defects in the former or virtues in the latter.

This attitude was also expanded to include whole groups of society: according to her way of thinking, the wealthy, the middle class and those with power over her had treated her with scorn and exploited her, and therefore would receive the same treatment. The poor and humble, who had not spurned her for her illegitimacy and had shown solidarity in times of need, were good and deserved her absolute commitment to ensuring that they received due retribution. At the same time, that identification gave her a clear idea, which she perhaps could not have explained but intuited perfectly, of what those people wanted and what they needed, or felt they needed, as opposed to what middle-class politicians thought they wanted or needed. Spontaneous and lacking in intellectual rigour, Evita did not philosophize about what was needed to bring about social justice, or contemplate the long-term cultural changes which would need to be patiently inculcated to do it: she saw injustice and went after it, to resolve immediate problems as immediately as possible, and to punish those she held responsible for that injustice. This attitude may not be optimal for a national leader, but it is understandable as the same unsophisticated reaction experienced by the common person in the face of cruelty: the difference is that the power which Evita would eventually have made the consequences of that reaction quite different from those of the ordinary person. A victim of many injustices, Evita could not bear to see injustice, and the methods she found to address it could be equally unjust, as well as being personal reactions to personal situations which did not change the fundamental sources of that injustice.

During the early years of Evita's less than flourishing acting career, she was said to have had an affair with Pedro Quartucci, a well-known actor. In the late 1990s Quartucci's daughter claimed to be the daughter of Evita, citing as evidence that blood tests showed she was not the daughter of Quartucci's wife.[11] This version was publicly supported by Quartucci's widow, who signed an affidavit in 1997 to the effect that Nilda Quartucci was in fact the daughter of the actor and María Eva Duarte. According to Nilda Quartucci's version, she had been born in 1940 in a clandestine clinic, and had been taken away by Quartucci to be raised in his legitimate family; on Quartucci's orders, Evita had been told that the baby had died (a not uncommon practice in cases of the kind).

This version remains unresolved – DNA tests showed that Nilda was not Pedro Quartucci's daughter – and does not at first sight appear probable. The authorities of the 'Liberating Revolution' which overthrew Perón in 1955 obsessively rooted out any fact, rumour or falsehood which could have served to blacken the reputation of Perón or Evita, and the possibility that they could have overlooked this bombshell seems remote. In particular, in 1955 many people who had known Evita in her early years in Buenos Aires were still alive, frequently anti-Peronist, and would surely have been aware of contemporary rumours. Nilda Quartucci claimed that Evita subsequently learned that her daughter had lived and was in fact the daughter of the Quartucci family, but by that time was first lady of Argentina and could say nothing about the issue. (One of the so-called 'proofs' cited of Evita's motherhood is a letter sent to her sisters by her confessor, Father Hernán Benítez, 33 years after her death, in which he refers to Evita's 'secret suffering', which was the true key to her greatness and which none but he and her sisters knew. According to the letter, that suffering, worse than the cancer that killed her, followed her to her grave and she frequently told him that she could not bear it and was disposed to take 'extreme measures'.[12])

From 1939, Evita began to enter what would be her metier as an actress: radio soap opera. Her brother Juan, working for the Radical Soap company, apparently got her into Radio Belgrano and into programmes sponsored by his employers. Beginning with secondary roles, she worked steadily in larger roles than she had received on stage or in the cinema, and by late 1943 she was signed to star in a series of biographical programmes about important women in history, playing Queen Elizabeth I, Sarah Bernhardt, the last Tsarina and others. Also, at around this time, she was presented to Colonel Anibal Imbert, the officer in charge of post and telegraph in the military government which had come to power in June that year (a position which included control over radio broadcasting). The introduction was apparently made by her friend Oscar Nicolini, Imbert's secretary and a supposed sometime lover of Doña Juana. The subsequent relationship unquestionably favoured her rising radio career, and may have furthered her entrance into Argentine history, as Imbert is sometimes supposed to have introduced her to Perón.

THE MEETING OF PERÓN AND EVITA

Given the fact that Perón and Evita were both public figures who flourished well within living memory, it should not in theory be difficult to pinpoint when, where and under what circumstances they met. However, as in most other aspects of their lives, there are a number of versions of their meeting and none is definitive. What is relatively certain is that they met in the context of the 15 January 1944 earthquake which devastated the western town of San Juan. Perón, in his capacity as secretary of labour, took charge of organizing relief efforts for the survivors: in his unreliable memoirs, he later recalled that he met Evita when she came to his office to offer her assistance in fundraising for the San Juan victims; other versions indicated that they met when she and a group of other actresses accompanied Perón in a street collection for that purpose.[13] (The version of cousin Raúl Suárez, again rather more puritanical than others, is that Evita went to San Juan, duly chaperoned by her sisters, to perform 'artistic numbers' to benefit the victims, and while in that city met Perón, also touring the site.[14]) The most common version is that they met at a fund-raising concert held at Luna Park stadium in Buenos Aires one week after the earthquake, and that Imbert may have introduced them. In any case, a short time later the two had moved into adjoining flats in Posadas street, in Buenos Aires' upmarket Barrio Norte area, and Perón had despatched his youthful mistress back to Mendoza (allegedly due to Evita's vigorous action in turfing her out of his flat).

There is no question that Evita's character was not the decorous and inconspicuous one demanded by society for a woman (including, in particular, the mistress of a prominent man, whose role should have been as self-effacing and invisible as possible). Whereas Perón was innately cautious, sometimes to the point of inaction, Evita invariably demonstrated determination, strength of character, impatience and impetuosity. At the same time, she was never shy about expressing her opinions forcefully, including on issues on which it was not considered acceptable for her to have an opinion, often in a rich and expressive vocabulary of a type which women of whatever social class were not expected to use. Evita was, like Perón, more comfortable in most cases in relationships in which her role was superior and where she could display kindness: with those who admired her, who came to ask her for favours, who needed her intervention, she was famous for showing patience, generosity, tact, respect and interest in seeking a solution for their problems. With those whom she suspected (doubtless with reason) of despising her, she could be brutally rude and abusive, as well as vengeful, counting on the fact that they had no choice but to accept that abuse, just as she had once had no alternative.

Whereas Perón had previously been discreet with respect to his private life, he became totally indiscreet in his relationship with Evita, living with her openly and allowing her free rein to intervene in his political affairs. At the same time, he turned his tutorial instincts to her, forming her in his own political thinking (and, consciously or not, having his own thinking partially reformed by his passionate and intuitive partner). Perón found a willing pupil in Evita, who absorbed his teaching, read the authors he recommended and, undoubtedly, rejoiced in being considered a person worthy of being a disciple and confidante.

While at this stage Perón certainly saw her as a protégée and an appreciative audience, rather than a future political tool, Evita's excellence as a pupil, combined with her own exceptional political instincts and charisma, would later make her an invaluable partner, both as a

tireless propaganda machine for her husband and as a vital link between the people and Perón, somewhat distant from personal contact
with everyday problems due to both his office and his nature. Perón
himself was to say years later, in one of his more truthful and perspicacious comments on his own career: 'One person had to take care
of the big things: the General. Another had to take care of the small
things: Eva. I took care of the Nation. Eva, of the personal problems of
its inhabitants. With her, with Eva, there was direct contact with the
people. For that reason, maybe, some remember her more.'[15] Evita's
impetuous nature also had its influence on Perón, who had shown a
lifelong characteristic of planning each step in his career with military
precision, seeing each goal as an objective to be taken, and who from
this time developed a strong talent for improvisation. Although this
relationship might be seen as strikingly progressive for its time, it also
betrays the underlying *machista* current that remains something of a
Peronist paradox: while Peronism has generated the most powerful
female figures in Argentine politics (including two presidents), all of
them have owed their position, to a greater or lesser extent, to the
convenience of their husbands.

While in 1944 and 1945 Evita concentrated primarily on her radio
and film career, she also took on a new radio programme, *Toward a
Better Future*, which offered propaganda for the military 'revolution' of
1943 and the policies of the military government. Her military links
were also said to have won her film roles, given military control not
only over content but over film supplies – indeed, her histrionic ability appears to have been limited in this metier, although it is worth
noting that, despite the interference of the de facto government,
Argentina continued to enjoy, from the 1920s, a thriving and highly
sophisticated film industry. She also took an increasingly high-handed
attitude with colleagues, reputedly leading to an acrid dispute with the
leading lady in one of her films, *La cabalgata del circo*. Libertad Lamarque, a famous and patrician actress, apparently came to words and
possibly blows with the rapidly rising second lead on the set of the
film, as a result of which Lamarque was obliged to transfer her career
and her address to Mexico when Evita became first lady. However,
Evita did not play an active role in politics at this stage and Perón's
machinations in power in this period cannot be attributed to her. Nevertheless, her visibility was irritating to the army, as was her disregard

for their codes of conduct and her habit of offering gratuitous opinions on political appointments and other matters far outside the normal remit of the mistress of a military officer. That irritation would form part of the impetus for the backfired efforts to remove Perón from power, which would culminate in the demonstrations of 17 October 1945 and his long-term installation at the centre of political life.

5   The Rise of Perón, 1943–5

On 4 June 1943, the government of President Ramón Castillo was overthrown by the second coup d'état of the century, the proximate cause of which was to avert the fraudulent election of his chosen successor, Robustiano Patrón Costas, a large landowner from Salta and former governor of that province. Unlike the overthrow of Yrigoyen, however, the '4 June revolution', as it was styled, was engineered primarily by a group of junior officers who had formed a secret society known as the GOU (initials variously said to stand for the *Grupo de Oficiales Unidos, Gobierno! Orden! Unidad!*, or *Grupo de Obra Unificación*).

The GOU's aims were not entirely clear and may not have been universally held among its members; however, it was at least heavily influenced by Juan Domingo Perón. It would appear that his own aim, at least, was the promotion of just such a 'revolution', albeit from a comfortable position in the second row, outside the immediate line of fire. According to Colonel Domingo Mercante, one of his closest collaborators (later governor of Buenos Aires and putative candidate to succeed Perón as president), Perón had created the nucleus of the GOU in December 1942, including Mercante and Perón's later opponent, Colonel Eduardo Avalos. However, its first general meeting open to other officers was held on 15 May 1943. At that meeting, 'at a given moment [Perón's] tongue ran away with him and he said: "we are going to make a revolution,"' to the apparent surprise of his listeners.[1]

Perón's ideological (as opposed to personal) influence over the GOU is somewhat hazy, as the group appears to have had little ideological coherence, not unlike Perón himself. However, GOU documents apparently authored by Perón consistently raise themes which were to become central to Peronism and to Perón's courtship of both the army and the working classes: nationalism, neutrality, the need for political and economic independence, industrialization, anti-communism and the need to redress the grievances of the poor against the rich: '[T]he great landowners enrich themselves at the cost of the peasant's sweat . . . ; the poor do not eat, nor can they feed themselves according to their needs. . . . The cities and the countryside are filled with lamentations which nobody hears.'[2]

Although the GOU seemingly agreed on the need to prevent Patrón Costas from becoming president, they agreed on little else. Even the reasons for objecting to Patrón Costas were not consistent. Some suggested he was unacceptable because he was pro-British and likely to abandon Argentina's policy of neutrality in the war. Others, including Perón, insisted that Patrón Costas was unacceptable because he belonged to the most reactionary element of the oligarchy, running his estates as a feudal fiefdom, and because the army was no longer prepared to tolerate either the political hegemony of the landed elite or the kind of electoral fraud which would be required for him to become president.[3] Beyond this, the GOU had no programme for government. Some of its members were reputedly democratically minded, others were thought to be seeking a military dictatorship, while still others sought a radical reshaping of Argentina's social and economic structure. Some of the officers were believed to be pro-Axis; others, pro-Allied. Many who participated in the June 1943 coup were unaware of the GOU's existence.

Following a short struggle for power among differing army factions, in which General Arturo Rawson was prevailed upon to take over the presidency from Castillo and shortly thereafter removed by the same military hands, General Pedro Ramírez emerged as president of the Republic, with General Edelmiro Farrell as his vice-president and war minister. Again, both were significant chiefly for their pliability: the sociable and womanizing Farrell was always willing to leave the decisions to his secretary at the War Ministry, Colonel Perón, and Ramírez was usually influenced by Farrell.

There were several bases for Perón's influence within the GOU and other sectors of the army. Simply by virtue of his experience (including periods abroad), he appeared to some erudite and politically sophisticated. More importantly, as secretary to the war minister and later as war minister himself, Perón consistently supported policies of interest to the armed forces, such as better pay and career prospects for junior officers, increased technology (such as the creation of an air force) and a programme of industrialization under the auspices of the armed forces. This was of particular significance owing to US wartime policy, offering Brazil increased military aid due to its entry into the war on the Allied side, and isolating Argentina because of its neutrality. Apart from sensitivities over this form of pressure, there was a real concern that as a result Brazil would become the dominant regional power.

Perón's policies, as discussed below, consistently sought to win the support of the army, especially the junior officer class (the navy, traditionally a more elite body, never supported him on the whole) and to marry their interests to those of the working classes. These two bodies thus became the two pillars of Perón's support, although the army's active role declined substantially even as that of the labour movement increased. 'The army and the workers, in patriotic conjunction, must form a splendid future for military industry.'[4] Their interests were not entirely harmonious, but for the moment the emphasis on nationalism, industrialization and opposition to the oligarchy, with which most sectors of the army (especially the infantry) had little in common, were adequate to make them seem so.

Another element of society which was taken to support the 1943 coup d'état was the Catholic Church, for a number of reasons. The Church had a long-standing link with the armed forces which went back to colonial times and contrasted with its generally poor relations with the Radical party and other liberal trends of thought which had gained impetus from the 1880s. Secularizing legislation such as lay education and civil marriage underscored the fact that the Catholic Church, although it represented the vast majority of Argentines in theory, was comparatively weak, with little economic independence or intellectual tradition, heavily dependent on governments increasingly dominated by supposedly anti-clerical (non-clerical would be a more correct term) interests such as the Radicals. At the same time, most immigrants to Argentina were from Italy and Spain, Catholic countries which were experiencing their own conflicts with the Church, and many of those working-class immigrants could be described as only nominally Catholic (when not anti-Catholic members of anarchist or other political movements).

In 1943 the Catholic Church in Argentina was, for evident reasons, influenced by prior events in Italy and Spain. Mussolini had recognized Catholicism as the state religion, made religious education compulsory and guaranteed the autonomy of the lay group *Acción Católica* (which also began functioning in Argentina in the 1930s); he also recognized the independence of the Holy See and the Pope as a foreign head of state, considered significant advances after a series of 'liberal' governments in Italy which had been more conspicuously anti-clerical than was the case in Argentina. In Spain, tensions between the Church and the Republican government were marked by strongly anti-clerical legislation and the burning of churches, and during the Civil War some 7,000 members of the clergy, including 13 bishops, were killed. In contrast, Franco explicitly recognized the central position of Catholicism in Spain (which under his government was officially Catholic rather than falangist). As the Church was inclined to view the fascist governments in both Italy and Spain in a positive light, at least initially, the 1943 coup in Argentina was easily translated by Catholic thinkers into a local version of Italian and Spanish nationalism, in which nationalist and Catholic were considered to be synonymous. Thus, rumours of Nazi influences and the fact that Perón had at least an element of fascist doctrine in his political thought were not per se anathema to the Catholic Church in Argentina. The Church also approved the opposition of the GOU to freemasonry and quasi-masonic entities such as the Rotarians, described in one GOU document as representing a threat to both the state and the army: 'The masonry is anti-Catholic, and thus is universally anti-Argentine by definition.'[5]

The influential Catholic magazine *Criterio*, directed by the Jesuit Msgr. Gustavo Franceschi, at least initially favoured the June 1943 revolution, described as a 'purifying wind through the social environment'. 'The providence of God wanted our armed institutions to come forward in time and save us.'[6] However, the magazine's (and perhaps the hierarchy's) later position vis-à-vis Peronism and the government of Perón would be much more ambivalent, and occasionally clearly hostile. Some strands of Catholic nationalism (a definition which might in itself be described as a contradiction in terms, given the explicitly universal, rather than national, nature of Catholicism) went further in supporting the military government, being openly pro-fascist and adding further right-wing elements to what would become Peronism.

In addition to the thinking of the Catholic intelligentsia, the military government also received support from other strands of historical revisionism stimulated by the decline of liberalism and the national and international crisis, including the FORJA, led by Arturo Jauretche and Raúl Scalabrini Ortiz. The FORJA, founded by dissident members of the Radical Party in the 1930s, also contributed its own slogan to the Peronist movement: popular sovereignty, economic emancipation and social justice. In the view of contemporary historical revisionism, if liberalism was discredited, then the vision of Argentine history imposed by its exponents such as Sarmiento, dominated by foreign influence, was also called into question. As revisionist tendencies rejected all positions held by political and economic liberalism, and as liberal thinking was believed to hold that the Hispanic, Catholic tradition in Argentina was the root of all evil, the logical inversion of this position was to vindicate Spanish and Catholic tradition, incidentally identifying both with *argentinidad* (Argentineness).[7] This nationalist tendency also rehabilitated the figure of the nineteenth-century *caudillo* Juan Manuel de Rosas as a nationalist hero, and with him, rehabilitated political authoritarianism and *caudillismo* as an acceptable Argentine phenomenon. Perón was later to be compared frequently with Rosas, including his relations with the Church, as both of them courted and later attacked the religious institution when it failed to offer uncompromising political support. While both viewed the Church as an institution favouring order and social control, the comparison reflects the ongoing dependency of the Church on those in power more than it demonstrates any real parallels between Rosas and Perón.

Another nationalist group forming an element of Peronism was the *Alianza Libertadora Nacional* (National Liberating Alliance, ALN), led by the pintoresque Guillermo Patricio Kelly (a perennial figure at the heart of various scandals until his death in July 2005). The ALN was an ultranationalist right-wing group which arguably found a form of containment in being absorbed into Peronism, which made it less dangerous than a completely loose cannon. (Indeed, Peronism has historically served the purpose on various occasions of absorbing extreme right-wing tendencies into a larger movement which served to soften the impact of those borderline groups by incorporating them into a less extreme structure. This tendency proved a double-edged sword in the 1970s, as those extremist groups which might otherwise have been marginalized would enjoy a rise which allowed them to use Argentina's largest party, then in government, to perpetrate organized violence.)

The ALN was not explicitly fascist, being more wedded to violence and extreme nationalism than to any pretence at ideology which might in theory have given it legitimacy. It contributed little in ideological or intellectual terms, although it would form the basis of the shock troops which took charge of violence when it was decided that this was called for. The ALN, like the FORJA and Perón himself, arguably committed the error of failing to recognize, in its nationalism, that Argentina was not in fact a world power but a weak and underdeveloped country with more potential than reality, an error which would lead to repeated bad judgements and undermine the positive achievements of the Peronist government.

Apart from the local currents which helped to form the identity of Peronism, Perón and his movement also received influences from other currents in contemporary Latin American political thought, informed by strong elements of nationalism, populism and authoritarianism combined with progressive ideas aimed at modernizing their societies. In Brazil, the *Estado Novo* of Getulio Vargas had been founded in the 1930s under an authoritarian leader with military connections, who enjoyed power for a decade and who used that power both to repress dissent and to industrialize the country. Vargas, although a less charismatic and less public figure than Perón, also sought to form state-manipulated trade unions which would help to underpin the rise in industry and modern labour relations, while at the same time ensuring that they did not clash with the state-led plan.

In Peru, also during the 1930s, Víctor Raúl Haya de la Torre had founded the *Alianza Popular Revolucionaria Americana* (APRA). Although Haya de la Torre certainly did not have military support – indeed, the military intervened to prevent his assuming the presidency – his platform was strikingly similar to what would become the platform of Perón. Haya de la Torre, together with Socialist leader José Carlos Mariátegui, was one of the creators of the concept of *indigenismo* in Peru, a largely indigenous country, which argued that the road to national consolidation lay in a return to indigenous traditions and principles. This contrasted with the position of liberal thinkers of the late nineteenth century who considered that the country could advance only through consolidation of a progressive oligarchy which would modernize and civilize its indigenous population. Haya de la Torre also had a platform of boosting import substitution industrialization, and represented a populist position which won the support of the working classes and sectors of the middle classes, that is, the same support base which would later support Perón.

Although the indigenous community in Argentina was small and largely ignored, unlike Peru, the concept of celebrating the national identity, in the form of the native-born working class, and disparaging the oligarchic concept which favoured all things European and despised its darker-skinned compatriots, was very similar in both countries. So was the incorporation of the urban working class as a support base, expanding it in turn through the increase in light industry. Also, like the APRA, the Peronist concept of *justicialismo* (social justice), which would eventually give that party its name, had the pretension at least of transcending national boundaries and becoming a regional movement. Perón, Vargas and Haya de la Torre were representative of a tendency common to much of Latin America, forced by the Depression to increase local industrial production and to come to terms with a new urban working class; all three also represented authoritarian and populist tendencies common to much of Latin American society.

THE NAZI TAINT

It is also necessary to mention the influence of fascism in the thought of both Perón and Peronism, although this should not be exaggerated in the manner of contemporary US diplomatic thought: this reasoning, which considered that Perón must be either communist or fascist, determined that, being anti-communist, he was ipso facto fascist. Perón, like all other products of the Superior War School of the time, had been trained by Prussian military officers and had a disproportionate admiration for German military prowess; as noted above, he had also been impressed by National Socialism in Germany and the role of the military in society under Nazism, and he was later to be horrified by the Nuremberg trials. At the same time, as also noted above, elements within Peronism – including the ALN and other nationalists and elements of right-wing Catholicism – were also highly sympathetic to fascism, some of them considering Argentina to be the Aryan nation of Latin America. The most fascist elements of Peronism would be, indeed, the notion of organized mass rallies and an 'organized community' (discussed below), in which the state would play a preponderant role in defining the supposed dynamics of society and would impose the requirement on members of the society that they play their assigned role – basically, that of supporting the party of Perón.

While authoritarian by culture, neither Perón nor Peronism was truly fascist. Perón combined a distaste for violence (at least while in power himself) with a total lack of orthodox ideological conviction which made him an unlikely candidate for wholehearted fascism (or any other doctrine). The fact that Perón provided refuge for Nazi war criminals and their Croatian collaborators (further discussed below) related largely to the desire to attract former Nazi professionals who might help to develop Argentina, the desire to please a largely pro-German officer corps and, apparently, petitions from the Vatican to grant a haven to Nazi and other refugees.[8] Allegations that Perón and Evita were Nazi spies or became rich selling passports to ex-Nazis are doubtful, although Argentine consular officials in Madrid and Lisbon appear to have done so.[9] Perón never gave any indication of being anti-Semitic or of justifying the Holocaust; rather, he was sufficiently naive to form a favourable image of the order in fascist society, and sufficiently cynical to turn a blind eye to its sinister nature. At the same time, given that Perón's labour policies were to be based on socialist legislation, and that Mussolini himself was originally a socialist, the crossed influences and parallels are not altogether irrelevant, as both fascism and Peronism aimed to make use of elements of socialism in order to avert a socialist rise to power.

The above is not intended as an apology for Perón's obvious authoritarian bent. It is intended to suggest that the picture of Perón and Peronism often painted abroad as a simple Latin American version of fascism is inaccurate and that the reality was both more complex and more simple. Neither Perón nor the majority of Argentines had (or sought to have, being distant from Europe and thus relatively unaffected by events there) a very true picture of what fascism really was, and therefore tended to reduce the phenomenon to its outward show. Some of that show could be considered impressive, especially for a relatively chaotic society such as Argentina's, and the belief that Mussolini had imposed order in a similarly chaotic society was even more stirring.

At the same time, both Perón and Argentine society in general were informed by an authoritarian culture which made the more obvious authoritarian elements of fascism easier to accept, if the greater violence which occurred underneath was ignored. Perón himself did indeed have acquaintances of unquestionable Nazi origin, and his movement incorporated elements of convinced fascists – many of whom would later become disenchanted by the fact that Perón was far less hard-line than they had believed. However, as the description of Peronist Doctrine below will show, Perón was a sort of ideological string-saver who pieced together the patchwork of Peronist 'ideology' by incorporating bits of any type of thinking, left, right or centre, which came to hand and which could serve a useful purpose.

PERÓN TO POWER – 'THE FIRST WORKER' AND THE TRADE UNIONS

An important component of Perón's policy was that of increased state involvement in the economy, intended to benefit the armed forces, industry and labour through redistribution of wealth and subsidized mechanization and consumption. The economic dislocation of the Second World War had made imperative

> intelligent state intervention in labour relations, to achieve the collaboration of all those who contribute with their muscle, their intelligence or their capital to the economic life of the nation.... To achieve this it is essential to guarantee welfare and just retribution to those who, as the large majority of the human masses of the Republic, may find themselves defenceless before the blind power of money or feel themselves tempted to assume violent attitudes.[10]

This last phrase also encapsulates another driving motivation behind Perón's desire for reform: the prudent goal of averting the violence which could arise if the less privileged did not receive a greater share of the cake.

In August 1943, shortly after he had taken over as secretary of the minister of war, Perón was called upon to face a strike by the meat packers' union, led by communist José Peter, who was jailed as a consequence of the strike. Instead of repressing the strike, Perón sat down to negotiate with union members, together with Domingo Mercante, and was able to convince the union to lift the strike in exchange for the liberation of Peter and a pay rise of five cents per hour. This experience apparently convinced Perón that a possible power base could be found here, giving rise to his desire to take charge of the National Labour Department (DNT).

In October 1943, Perón asked for and got the job of running the DNT, not least because few other officers were interested in taking on such a hitherto unimportant assignment. Another colonel, Carlos Gianni, had taken charge of the DNT in July 1943, and had acted with a policy similar to that of Perón's thereafter, opening the DNT to trade unionists and others in order to listen to different segments of public opinion, and cultivating a relatively high public profile, although Gianni has since been largely forgotten by history. Gianni resigned, apparently under pressure from the GOU, paving the way for Perón to add another important plank to his political platform. Thus, Perón already had in his hands the means to influence both his bases of support – the War Ministry (where he was still in charge of the secretariat) and the DNT. Perón indicated his intentions early on, announcing upon his arrival in the post that 'the DNT is a body which should have close ties with both labour and employer institutions, seeking in the best way possible the welfare of the working class and the tranquility of the factories'.[11] In other words, the interests of the working classes were of importance, but not at the cost of class conflict.

On 27 November 1943 the DNT was transformed into the Secretariat of Labour and Social Welfare, giving Perón his first cabinet post. More importantly, the Secretariat was rapidly converted from an ineffective body focused on collecting labour statistics into a government organ actively reshaping and enforcing labour legislation and industrial relations. Its achievements over the next two years were impressive: in addition to arbitrating in labour disputes and enforcing already existing labour legislation, the Secretariat produced legislation establishing labour courts; a national commission to supervise work by minors and schools offering training in professional, technical and factory skills; annual paid holidays, paid sick leave and minimum wages and the extension of pensions to all employees. Beyond the sphere of urban labour, the Secretariat also created the 1944 *Estatuto del Peón*, extending pension, sick pay and minimum wage rights to rural workers. In practice, the latter was less effectively enforced than the legislation affecting industrial labour, given the even more dependent relationship of rural workers with their bosses and the limited power of state regulatory bodies outside urban areas. However, it proved disproportionately irritating to the landowning class, changing the rules of traditional rural labour and at least theoretically modifying the dependence of the worker on the landowner.

Much of the legislation adopted during Perón's tenure at the DNT was not new, having been proposed or actually passed by the Socialist Party. However, Perón – who rarely invented anything but put to skilled use the creations of others – did implement those norms, making them his own and expanding the base of labour legislation in Argentina, also ensuring for the first time that that legislation was complied with.

Moreover, whereas past governments had discouraged or forbidden trade union organization, the Secretariat under Perón actively encouraged it, both in areas where no organization had previously been possible (such as among the sugar workers of Tucumán) and in industrial spheres where it had been largely unsuccessful. For the first time, union membership was found to be profitable (the unions often being granted more than they demanded by the obliging Secretariat), and posed no immediate dangers. Trade unionism rose substantially: between 1941 and 1945, the number of unions rose from 356 to 969, and from 500,000 members to over 2 million. Much of this increase came from newly unionized fields, but membership also increased in unions whose leadership had previously been in dispute or under socialist or communist control. During 1944 alone, 127 agreements were signed with employers' associations and 421 with trade unions, including gains such as paid holidays, job stability and pay increases included in collective contracts. All of this further encouraged new members to join trade unions, which were finally able to point to concrete gains.[12]

Another factor which encouraged a rise in trade unionism was the intransigent opposition of employers to Perón's activities, which made workers feel that their only option was to support Perón, as the only political figure likely to guarantee that their gains would be respected. Virulent and even irrational in their opposition to Perón, both business and political leaders, while not altogether mistaken in their misgivings, were so unbending as to make support for Perón obligatory for workers, creating part of the gulf which was to separate Peronists and anti-Peronists. The principal exception was the industrial sector, as the captains of industry were in favour of the military policy of promoting heavy industry and feared that industrial promotion could be eliminated by the government, undermining their activities.

One aspect of trade unionism under Perón soon became clear: those unions whose leaders were Peronists were favoured. As a result, out of self-interest if no other motivation, unions found it prudent to elect leaders of the right orientation. This process of 'Peronization' of the unions was furthered by the passage of Decree Law 23.852, which governed the organization of labour associations and granted exclusive recognition (*personería gremial*) to only one union in each field, thus allowing it to negotiate on behalf of its members. Unions whose leaders did not support Perón often found that a rival union in their field might be launched and granted *personería gremial*, thus depriving them of their right to engage in collective bargaining on behalf of their members. Perón made clear the importance he placed on labour organization and workers' rights, but also the role he envisaged for that sector: '[T]he well-organized trade union is one of the fundamental bases of the national organization of the modern state... in order to be efficient and useful, the union should defend itself against politicization.'[13]

Perón continued to follow the policy adopted in the case of Peter and the meat packers in August 1943: that of negotiating with unions rather than imprisoning their leaders. At the same time, he showed an astute ability to short-circuit strikes through division and conquest, wooing the unionists who were in disagreement or doubt over strike action, to the detriment of leaders pushing for more aggressive action. Unionists accustomed to meeting with repression by both military and civilian governments were seduced by a secretary of labour who invited them to the Secretariat to discuss their concerns and aims. They were further encouraged by the fact that the first unionists to accept the invitations could boast concrete results, including participation in the drafting of new labour norms later issued as decrees by the

Secretariat. That seduction was especially concentrated where unions were newly formed or contemplating new leadership, as the putative leaders were offered total support in exchange for their own loyalty. Those who were unwilling to offer that total support, such as Peter, were replaced in their leadership posts, in this case by Perón supporter (and later opponent) Cipriano Reyes.

What sectors of the urban working classes were most easily converted to Peronism? In general, those working in employment involving a high concentration of labour and a high level of mechanization, rather than in more privileged and more traditional sectors. In addition, a number of the most strongly Peronist unions worked in industries controlled by foreign interests, especially British interests (such as the railway workers, who were previously heavily unionized, and the meat packers, who were not). This may have influenced the injection of nationalism into Perón's rhetoric, which in turn attracted these unions to his position.

In addition, however, Perón made use of the factionalism plaguing the union movement to win new converts to his side. For example, he supported the efforts to Cipriano Reyes, an early key figure and early casualty of Peronism, to found a meat packers' union in opposition to that run by Peter, and used the split in the CGT between rival socialist and syndicalist forces to remove recognition from the more antagonistic faction. The CGT, an umbrella organization, accounted for some two-thirds of organized labour in 1943. Following the split in that year, CGT-2, as it was known, remained under socialist leadership, while CGT-1, the larger bloc, was seeking to form a Labour Party under its leader, José Domenech. CGT-2 was eventually suppressed, and many of its members joined the remaining CGT; its Labour Party eventually supported Perón in the 1946 elections.

Another case in point is that of the railway union, which Perón recognized as crucial given its size and power. (Mercante was of particular use in this case, as his father and brothers had been members of both the railway workers' union *Unión Ferroviaria* and the rail drivers' union *La Fraternidad*.) A telegram from the British Ambassador to the Foreign Office observed that the administrator of the (British-owned) railways was removed by Perón 'to win personal popularity from [the] powerful Railway Union in his own political interests'.[14] Perón himself is quoted as saying that 'the labour movement in the country is active and solid only in the railway organization. Whoever has control over this organization has control over everything'.[15] After the government took control of the union, Mercante was named to head the *Unión Ferroviaria* as a result of his family connections.

Perón recognized as early as 1943, even before the June 'revolution', 'the people are disillusioned with those who until now have been their leaders (socialists, trade unionists, labour leaders, etc.), and they are channelling themselves into other currents – independent, political, nationalist'.[16] It would appear that, having recognized this tendency (perhaps because he shared it), he came to power with the hope of directing these frustrated aspirations and sense of disillusionment into channels constructive for the country, the welfare of the working classes, and his own ambitions. However, according to some trade union leaders (such as railway worker Luis Monzalvo), it was the trade unionists who made the first approach to Perón when he arrived at the DNT, not the other way round. The fact that they found a sympathetic ear surprised and pleased them. Many of them, however, were not prepared to commit themselves to Perón or to link their fate with his. What finally forced them to forge this link was the attitude of their own rank and file and the attitude of the anti-Peronist factions in business and politics, which would soon appear to be gaining the upper hand.

In addition to the material benefits gained by labour under Perón, there were less tangible gains in prestige and self-respect. The new labour legislation, and the backing trade unions received from the state, raised their status and allowed them to bargain with employers on an equal footing. At the same time, Perón spoke of 'social justice', and of labour's gains as something to which they were entitled, not something to be magnanimously granted (although in fact his role as magnanimous granter was obvious, and doubtless one he enjoyed). His appeals to patriotism and loyalty found an echo in a working class not previously expected to display these qualities or to participate actively in the life of the nation. In repeated statements describing his programme as a local version of Roosevelt's New Deal, Perón stressed the priority to be given to public works and workers' housing. Perón gave the working classes 'social consciousness, social personality and social organization.... Peronism was born when the first Argentine worker...on meeting General Perón, felt he now had someone to protect him'.[17]

KEEPING THE CHURCH HAPPY

The de facto government also took a number of initiatives welcomed by the Catholic Church, such as the banning of local slang (*lunfardo*) in tango lyrics; however, the greatest triumph for Catholic activism was the imposition of compulsory religious education in state schools from 31 December 1943. The religious education decree was brought about by the Minister of Justice and Public Instruction, Gustavo Martínez Zuviría, a former *Acción Católica* activist.

Its own impetus having declined by the early 1940s, the Catholic Right attached itself briefly to Perón in the absence of an alternative, hoping that in Peronism the 'revaluation of Hispanic origins, explicit inspiration, accentuated in Peronism, in Christian principles, and even a certain support for the ecclesiastical institution, were expressions of the re-Latinamericanization of politics'.[18] It soon became obvious, however, that Perón was not Franco, and that he would 'not be the restorer of an Hispanic, Catholic and traditional culture'.[19] At the same time, the same sectors were distressed by the breaking of relations with the Axis in 1944, the eventual declaration of war on Germany and the signing of the Acts of Chapultepec, all of which they regarded as giving in to the imperialist power of the USA.

If *Acción Católica* and other Catholic groups ceased to play a major part in Perón's subsequent government, this did not mean that Catholic doctrine did not play a major role in the formation of Perón's social and political programme, borrowed as it was from a number of available sources. The body of Christian social doctrine had been left largely untouched by the Church in Argentina (elsewhere in Latin America, the Church tended to be identified with the policies of Christian Democratic parties). Inherently rather populist in its overtones, that doctrine lent itself to a populist political platform (and, more subtly, identified social justice as an effective mechanism of social control). At the same time, frequent references to Christian doctrine were calculated to appeal to the popular religious sentiment of the 'new' Argentine working classes, as opposed to the older labour leadership believed to consist of Marxists, anarcho-syndicalists and Spanish Republicans.

More importantly, perhaps, the presence of priests to bless political and labour meetings and the frequent references to recapturing the working classes for Christ were designed to elicit support from the clergy and the institutional Church for Perón and, eventually, for his presidential candidacy. Initially lacking a political party or even the solid support of the armed forces, Perón by 1945 sought an institutional base of support apart from that formed by the CGT to ensure his election in February 1946. The Church seemed well-suited to form a third base of institutional support, not least because, like Peronism, its reformist social doctrine was tied to a firmly anti-revolutionary stance favouring order and social control. On the other hand, however, the Church's links with (and dependence on) sectors that retained economic if not electoral power meant that it could not support policies which appeared to run counter to their interests.

Moreover, the Church as such was unable to form a political support base for Perón, just as Perón was unable to effectively recruit the working classes to Catholicism. The lack of real overlap between committed Catholics and committed Peronists reflected the – inaccurate – perception of both the Church and Peronism as class-based bodies. In reality both commanded (and lacked) the support of sectors throughout the social spectrum, and both had pretensions to a universal appeal. However, especially after the events of 17 October 1945, Peronism developed the image of a working-class movement, which alone would have prevented many middle- and upper-class Catholics from supporting Perón; the Church, in contrast, maintained an elitist image which aroused the distrust of many members of the working classes. Additionally, the Church at the time remained largely preoccupied with education and individual morality, rather than the more sweeping sociopolitical programme espoused by Peronism.

By 1945, Perón was vice-president, war minister and secretary of labour, and appeared to most observers to be the real power behind President Edelmiro Farrell (who had succeeded Ramírez in January 1944). Through judicious use of the radio as a means of mass communication and high-profile activities such as the organization of relief for the victims of the January 1944 San Juan earthquake, he had extended his influence far beyond the confines of organized labour. This increasing personal power was eyed askance by some sectors of the army (the navy had always opposed him), who distrusted his apparent ambition and wished to see government returned to civilian hands, or simply disliked the obvious rise in influence of the working classes. In addition, the armed forces were largely united in their disapproval of Eva Duarte, the radio actress who had become Perón's mistress and was believed to exercise disproportionate influence over him.

Business leaders had never accepted Perón's discourse to the effect that possible revolution could be defused only by concessions to labour which would maintain social tranquillity. Their opposition came to a head on 16 June 1945, with the launching of a manifesto demanding that the government change its social policy, a move rapidly countered by manifestos from trade unions. This conflict, with manifestos reproduced in street posters, would reach a climax on 19 September with the March for the Constitution and Liberty, which united anti-Peronists from all political and social spheres.

The unease on the part of the armed forces (echoing the stronger feeling of distaste and animosity by the oligarchy and many middle-class sectors) was strengthened by a demonstration in July 1945, in which a crowd 'spontaneously' appeared outside Perón's home, calling for his presidential candidacy. Although Perón disclaimed any such ambition, the prospect caused alarm in many military and civilian circles. Later that month, a number of senior military officers signed a communiqué demanding that anyone planning to stand for the presidency should immediately resign from any government post: if this was intended to flush Perón out, or to remove him from the exercise of his government functions, it failed. However, events were coming to a head between Peronist and anti-Peronist forces, a conflict which would soon make Perón and the working classes inseparable and the polarization of Argentine society a political factor for years to come.

6 The 'Revolution' of 17 October 1945

Because of his very high public profile and of what he already represented politically, Perón found himself the centre of dissatisfaction both within and outside the army by late 1945. In civilian circles this dissatisfaction crystallized in the 'March for the Constitution and Liberty' on 19 September 1945. Estimates of the turnout range from a police estimate of 65,000 to the organizers' estimate of 500,000,[1] despite a transport strike called to hinder the demonstration. The central demand of the March was the retirement of the army to its barracks and a return to civilian government. Although directed against the army as a whole, its particular target was clear: observers noted that, despite the generally orderly nature of the proceedings, 'such hostile cries as were uttered, were all directed against the person of the Vice President and Minister of War, Colonel Juan Domingo Perón'.[2] Earlier, in June, 319 commercial and industrial firms had issued a communiqué condemning the government's labour policies, which was endorsed by the UIA and the aristocratic Rural Society (*Sociedad Rural*).[3]

The March received widespread press coverage, typically describing it as 'essentially an occasion of the people . . . a remarkable demonstration of spontaneous and concerted action by people in the mass on a scale only possible under the uniting influence of some deep common experience or sentiment'.[4] What was not noted in the Argentine press, though it was noted elsewhere (such as *The Times* of London on 10 October 1945), was the fact that 'the people' on this occasion were almost exclusively of the middle and upper class. Despite the

UIA having called for the closure of factories and shops to enable the workers to attend, few did so. Had it been noted seriously at the time, this was an indication of the social division over Perón. The March was organized by many of the same sectors that had formed the 1930s *Concordancia* and would later come together in opposition to Perón in the 1946 elections: the UIA, conservatives, sectors of the UCR, professionals, students and the military hierarchy; an assortment described by meat packers' leader Cipriano Reyes as 'the whole association of fraud and corruption'.[5] This is not entirely accurate; however, the March's organizers did fail to consider that, far from representing the desires of 'the people', they represented only one segment of public opinion, which was in direct contradiction to another important, but on this occasion disregarded, sector of 'the people'.

With quarters within the army strongly in agreement with the March's desire for the fall of Perón and a return to constitutional rule, events moved rapidly after September. In early October matters came to a head over the appointment of Oscar Nicolini to the directorship of Posts and Telecommunications. Nicolini, a post office employee, was a friend of Evita's (and, according to some rumours, had maintained a sentimental relationship with her mother), and his appointment appeared to confirm her undesirable influence over Perón. Perón's one-time colleague General Eduardo Avalos led a rising against him from the Campo de Mayo barracks outside Buenos Aires and, after some confusion over Perón's situation, it was announced on 9 October that he had resigned all his posts. This move, however, did little to strengthen the hand of the sectors of the army opposed to Perón, given that neither Farrell nor the other officers had any idea of how to fill the power vacuum created by his resignation. Immediately following reports of Perón's resignation from government, rioting was reported in Buenos Aires. On 10 October, Perón demonstrated his still considerable power by making a farewell speech to the workers from the Secretariat of Labour and Welfare, which was broadcast nationally on radio. Although *The Times* commented on that date that Perón would address those workers 'for the last time, at least as far as can be foreseen', the speech was a very clear and indirectly incendiary political message:

> I have just signed a decree of extraordinary importance
> for the workers, which relates to salary increases and

> profit-sharing.... I have spoken with the President, and he
> has promised that the social work and the conquests at-
> tained will remain and will continue in course.... If one
> day it were necessary I would join your ranks to obtain
> what is just.... From now on I will be among you closer
> than ever.[6]

On 11 October, most of the cabinet resigned, elections were called for 7 April 1946, and moves to form a new cabinet began, while Perón began a supposed medical leave and he and Evita went to an isolated island in the Tigre delta, north of Buenos Aires. On 13 October, it was reported that Perón had been placed under arrest, and he was taken to Martín García, the island where Yrigoyen had been detained. On the 14th, at Perón's insistence, he was examined by an army doctor who stated that the island's climate had adversely affected his health, a ploy which two days later resulted in his transfer to the military hospital in Buenos Aires, closer to the field of battle.

While many trade union leaders still vacillated over whether to cast their lot with Perón, it rapidly became clear that labour's gains were in no way secure: after the 12 October holiday, when workers demanded payment for the holiday they were told to 'go and ask Perón for it': 'those days are now over'. At the same time, demands were made by opponents of the regime to turn the government over to the Supreme Court immediately. The same Court was at the time proposing to rule all decrees passed under the military government (obviously including all those relating to workers' rights) unconstitutional. The insistence on 'the government to the Court' by much of the elite made a confrontation inevitable.

By the early hours of 15 October, Cipriano Reyes was determined to call the workers into the street, if possible to march on to Buenos Aires and hold a demonstration at the military hospital. By the 16th, Reyes was urging his union members in the Berisso and Ensenada suburbs of La Plata to take this step, beginning with the aim of occupying the YPF oil refinery in Ensenada. That tactic was blocked by members of the navy. From there, Reyes and a group of slaughterhouse workers in Avellaneda decided to march on to Buenos Aires, word of which spread to other parts of the area. As a result, people began to move towards the city in small groups. Also on 16 October, the sugar workers of Tucumán began an indefinite strike, while 'groups of workers from

Figure 5. Crowds in the Plaza de Mayo, cooling their feet in the fountain, 17 October 1945 (Wikipedia)

Avellaneda paraded the city, . . . acclaiming Perón'.[7] After a long period of indecision, the CGT decided to call a general strike for 18 October to protest over the detention of Perón (whose whereabouts at this moment were unknown) and the threat to labour's gains. At this point, however, the CGT leadership was overtaken by the more direct action of its rank and file, and by those who still had not attained union membership.

THE ZOOLOGICAL DELUGE

Compared with the 19 September march, the events of 17 October received limited coverage in the largely anti-Peronist Buenos Aires press, which apparently failed to grasp the nature and significance of the day. (Ironically, referring to Perón's downfall, on 13 October the supreme bastion of anti-Peronism, the newspaper *La Prensa*, wrote that 'public opinion is winning'.) Although no account of the events of 17 October is entirely lucid, on the morning of that day a flood of workers from the industrial suburbs of Buenos Aires, and as far away as the slaughterhouses and shipyards of La Plata, began pouring into the city centre, chanting, 'We want Perón'. They were joined by metal workers, railway workers, women and children, halting all industrial activity and making superhuman efforts to reach the centre of Buenos Aires. Many even swam across the fetid Riachuelo River which separates the city from the southern suburbs. Although part of the impetus for this march doubtless came from Reyes' earlier efforts, and workers were aware of the idea of such a march, the original organizers were swept away by the level of popular fervour, especially when on the morning of the 17th the newspapers announced a new cabinet devoid of Perón supporters, and the possibility that government would be turned over to the anti-Peronist Supreme Court.

Many of those who participated had never previously penetrated the centre of elegant Buenos Aires, where the arriving hordes were regarded with astonishment, horror and fear by the *porteño* public. However, the urgency of the situation made them overcome fears, barriers, lack of transport and blocked bridges to make the pilgrimage to the Plaza de Mayo. 'From the early hours of the morning . . . groups of people began to form who had resolved . . . to go to Buenos Aires and demand the presence of Colonel Perón.'[8] One of the more striking elements of the events was that they took place in relative calm, without violence on the part of either the demonstrators or the police, many of whom also sympathized with Perón. The fact that neither the police nor the army intervened further encouraged the marchers, enthused by the apparent support of the security forces (for once) for the cause of the underclass.

The people continued to arrive in the Plaza de Mayo outside Government House, and remained there from mid-afternoon through most of the night. They scandalized the formal *porteños* by taking off their shoes and bathing their aching feet in the fountains, and refused to leave until Perón appeared. Avalos was forced to appear on the balcony of Government House to confirm that Perón had been released, although the crowd expressed scepticism and waited until Perón appeared on the balcony, where he was met by a storm of cheers and applause from a joyous crowd waving thousands of handkerchiefs. Although clearly taken by surprise and moved by the occasion, Perón had the presence of mind to delay his appearance until 10:30 that evening, when the crowd had reached its optimum size, refusing to take earlier desperate calls from Farrell asking him to appear. The crowd was variously estimated at between 100,000 and 1 million; between 300,000 and 500,000 is generally accepted. At 10:30,

Perón appeared on the balcony with Farrell, who presented him to the delighted crowd as 'the man who had won everyone's hearts'.

Perón's speech on that occasion to the *descamisados* or 'shirtless ones', as they were disparagingly described (referred to as the 'Peronist hordes' or a 'zoological deluge', in the words of Radical deputy Ernesto Sammartino[9]), was described by hostile observers as hollow and demagogic, although it was in fact remarkably effective and represented a permanent link between Perón and his following:

> I therefore put aside the sacred and honourable uniform given to me by the fatherland in order to put on civilian clothes and mix with that suffering, sweating mass which with its labour makes the greatness of the country.... I give my final embrace to this institution which is the prop of the fatherland: the army. And I give my first embrace to this immense mass which represents the synthesis of a sentiment which had died in the Republic: the real civility of the Argentine people.... I want now, as a simple citizen, mixing with this sweating mass, to press everyone against my heart as I could with my mother.[10]

Thereafter, Perón and the crowd maintained an extraordinary dialogue, with members of the crowd responding to his speech and asking where he had been, to which Perón evasively referred to the sacrifice he had willingly made for his shirtless ones. Perón ended the unique event with greetings for the workers in the interior of the country, and urged the crowd to sing the national anthem and to return home peacefully. He also urged them to take a well-deserved holiday the next day (when the CGT had already called a general strike), dubbed Saint Perón's day by the crowd. Effectively, 17 October passed into Peronist myth, justifiably, as the apogee of the mystical relationship between Perón and the workers, a unique relationship which produced a unique movement by those workers to rescue their leader when he needed them.

This is a highly condensed account of a mythic event whose emotive content remained unchanged for participants and observers decades later. That event involved elements unique in Argentine history, and largely unprecedented elsewhere: a spontaneous and peaceful uprising in defence of a leader, which above all was successful, despite the opposition of the traditional powers and the armed forces, and a spontaneous face-to-face dialogue and reciprocal expressions of affection with the rescued leader. It is difficult to convey the type of emotional reaction felt by the participants, not only due to the success of the event, but due to the exhilarating feeling of participating in a popular crusade, side by side with thousands of others focused on the same purpose, when those participants had previously been on the sidelines rather than playing a role in history.

The event not only involved a tremendous emotional charge, but represented one of the few occasions (at least until after Perón's overthrow in 1955) in which the masses took an initiative without orders from above. In this case, it is evident that 17 October was not planned by Perón, who was as surprised as anyone, but represented a genuine expression of at least an important sector of popular will. (Indeed, the evidence that the working classes were able to take such a step on their own initiative may have confirmed Perón's conviction that it was urgent to impose tight control from above to direct the trade unions and any further such expressions of popular will.) The day placed at centre stage the third permanent protagonist of the Peronist drama, together with Perón and Evita: the crowd.

THE SIGNIFICANCE OF 17 OCTOBER

The events of 17 October rescued Perón from political extinction. They also represented the final nail in the coffin of the Communist Party as a supposed bulwark of the proletariat, as the party itself committed the gross and fatal error of describing the 17 October demonstration as the work of armed bands led by the Nazi-backed Perón. The Socialist Party, in less violent terms, also interpreted the event as an outburst by an ignorant, indigent and weak-minded mob. These attitudes make it clear that both parties, which were supposedly the natural representatives of labour, were distanced from their putative constituency and unable to comprehend an attitude which was politically incorrect and therefore theoretically impossible.

But who organized 17 October 1945? To some extent it appears to have been a spontaneous outburst, in fact the last truly spontaneous workers' demonstration under Perón (later 'spontaneous' acts such as the annual repeats of the demonstration in the Plaza de Mayo on each 17 October, subsequently dubbed Loyalty Day, involved a significant degree of orchestration). This, however, perhaps underestimated the activities of union leaders such as Reyes, Luis Gay of the telephone workers and Luis Monzalvo of the railway workers: although the CGT leadership was unwilling to commit itself to Perón's future, these union leaders did a significant amount of agitating, if not literally organizing, in advance of the 17th. (Reyes later unequivocally claimed credit for the event, although his version omits the efforts of others.) According to Monzalvo, their purpose was 'to recover their leader at the cost of whatever sacrifice'.[11]

One of the more persistent myths surrounding 17 October was that the events were organized by Evita Duarte, who thereby rescued her future husband from political oblivion. This version has been perpetuated by both Peronist and anti-Peronist sources, for different reasons. For anti-Peronists, Evita's role demonstrated both Perón's weakness and dependency and her own malign influence over what was to come. According to this version, Evita snatched the cowardly Perón from the jaws of defeat and established her ascendancy over him and the *descamisados* for the purpose of exacting her revenge on respectable Argentines for her own obscure origins.

In Peronist folklore, Evita acted as the loyal comrade of Perón and the *descamisados* and spared no effort to mobilize 'her' workers on his behalf. This version is perpetuated in the memoirs of both Evita herself and Perón in his later years. For both of them, near the end of their lives, there may have been some sentimental reason for wishing this to be the case. However, within Peronist history (never notably addicted to accuracy) this version had its more practical uses: within a few years of Perón's election to the presidency, Evita had taken on much of the role he had earlier played with the trade union movement, while at the same time Gay and Reyes had both broken with Perón and become non-persons, cast into that outer darkness to which defeated political figures (later including Perón) were frequently consigned by the victors. Thus, it was convenient that their role should be forgotten and that Evita should be assigned a role she had not played.

Almost certainly Evita played no role in mobilizing the masses in October 1945. In her obituary in *La Nación* on 27 July 1952, that newspaper referred vaguely to her having 'moved actively in the shadows during the brief days of that separation and again been with him on the 17th.... What she did in the course of that decisive week as the one who stimulated the partisans will undoubtedly be recognized later by detailed chronicles'. It is noteworthy that no contemporary press report of the events of 17 October makes any reference to her name. Nor do the memoirs of those closely involved in the events, such as Reyes, Gay and Monzalvo.

In point of fact, as Felix Luna and Marysa Navarro have both argued, the Eva Duarte of 1945 was in no position to play the pivotal role later ascribed to her: at the time she was a radio actress and Perón's mistress, without contacts with union leaders and without, as yet, any standing in their eyes.[12] Moreover, in these early years, it is clear that she remained the pupil of Perón, not yet acting independently in the political arena, and it seems unlikely that Perón himself made any effort to stimulate the events of 17 October. On the contrary, a widely reprinted letter from Perón to Evita, written while he was imprisoned on the island of Martín García in the week before 17 October, makes it clear that he was not planning a political comeback at that time. In the letter, he promises that when he is released he will ask for his retirement from the army and they will get married and go to Patagonia to live quietly. This appears also to have been the main desire of Evita at the time; the political consequences of the 17th would change the future of both that couple and the nation as a whole.

In all probability, 'no one gave the call to come out. The people came out on their own. It was not Perón's wife (sic). It was not the CGT. It was the workers and the unions who themselves came into the street'.[13] If the CGT as a whole was unwilling to commit itself, the new unions and their members were already committed to Perón, both by loyalty and by necessity.

What was the significance of 17 October 1945? To begin with, it was the first great political success of a previously marginalized class. Cipriano Reyes would describe it as the first step towards transforming Argentina's political, economic and social structures, although this is not wholly accurate: precisely the failure to *transform* the political, economic and social structures of the country, as opposed to shifting the balance of power within them, was to prove a major weakness of Peronism. However, it would be fair to say that 17 October represented in some respects the Argentine people's finest hour. Unlike other occasions, such as the overthrow of Yrigoyen, when people turned their backs on a leading figure and subsequently mourned his fate when it was too late, on that date a popular movement took action to defend a leading figure and the ideals that he – at least ostensibly – represented. At the same time, those people were justifiably proud of their action in rescuing their leader from disgrace. This created a bond between the people and their leader which was arguably never completely broken, even 50 years later and after the death of most of the protagonists.

Another significant element of the demonstration is that it marked a shift in the balance of forces involved in the evolution of Peronism: in particular, it marked the rise of labour's importance and the decline of the army. The army remained divided over the question of Perón's fate at this time: some elements had engineered his overthrow, some had even been prepared to participate in a plot to assassinate him,[14] while a reservoir of support remained in other quarters, especially among the lower ranks. However, the army as a body remained paralysed on 17 October when faced with a united mass mobilization of Peronist support. Even the most anti-Peronist officers refused to take action to suppress the demonstrators. Thus, the initiative was seized by the working classes, which thereafter overshadowed the armed forces as a Peronist power base.

It also marked a new and deeper rift in public opinion, particularly defined by its attitude towards Perón and Peronism. While the March for the Constitution and Liberty was considered an expression of middle- and upper-class public opinion, 17 October represented an even more fervent expression of opinion from a large and previously ignored sector of the public: the working class. (It should be noted that not all sectors of the working class were represented: some members of that class, in particular the children of recent European immigrants, considered themselves more civilized and more upwardly mobile than those who put their feet in the fountains in the Plaza de Mayo.) This was recognized in some quarters: an editorial in the *Buenos Aires Herald* on 18 October 1945 called for 'an immediate and serious attempt at national understanding and reconciliation', noting that 'the rival demonstrations of recent days and the passions these have provoked reveal the threat of social cleavage'. However, in general such calls for understanding went unheeded, as the success of the *descamisados* on 17 October provoked incomprehension and fear among members of the 'other' Argentina, who failed to perceive that the masses were not acting in an aberrant manner, but were rather motivated by logical self-interest as well as genuine affection: if Perón had granted them benefits and those benefits were threatened by his disappearance from the scene, it was only sensible that the masses should mobilize on his behalf.

Equally, the events tended to distort the picture of Peronist strength, equating it exclusively with the lower classes. In fact, Perón had sympathizers among middle-class nationalists and industrialists: the latter in particular, also out of self-interest, supported his policies, given his emphasis on industrialization and on increasing consumption through raising wages. As early as 1944, Perón had spelled out the importance of such a policy, noting that:

> when it is no longer possible (post-war) to export...the only solution will be to increase home consumption.... (This) can only be accomplished by raising salaries and wages so that each wage earner may consume much more,...making it possible for each industrial concern, manufacturer or trader to produce as much as he is doing today, without being obliged to close down his works and dismiss his workmen.[15]

'It thus becomes obvious', concluded the *Review of the River Plate* on 19 October 1945, 'that the country is in virtually the same position as it was a fortnight ago'. On the contrary, an appraisal of the events in the context of both the issues leading up to them and their aftermath demonstrates that 17 October 1945 changed the nature of Argentine politics more than was generally understood or accepted at the time. The structure of economic power had not fundamentally been altered, but a new force had been introduced into the political structure, which was thereafter central (if not dominant) in Argentine politics, and which invariably affected the balance of political power.

Despite a weakening of the forces excluding it from political power, coupled with an improvement in its living standards and an increasing social homogeneity, the Argentine working class had grown and matured but had remained marginalized, factional and isolated from the mechanisms of political power. Specifically, it had failed to produce a leader from within its own ranks capable of forming and driving it in a particular direction; without such a leader it had little ability to emerge as a coherent force in its own right. In this context, therefore, 'the proletariat sought in Perón the political leadership it could not itself provide'.[16]

Perón had a gift for saying what his audience wanted to hear and following rather than leading the desires of that audience. This allowed him to fill the vacuum between the working class and the country's rulers, a vacuum the working class had not filled with one of its own. At the same time, whereas other movements such as socialism, communism or syndicalism were imports which clashed with aspects of the expanding Argentine working-class culture, Peronism was a reflection of rather than an imposition on that culture, comprehensible because it represented that cultural reality. That it mixed a range of concepts taken from nationalism, European fascism, socialism and falangism with Argentine paternalism, authoritarianism and sentiment was a benefit rather than a detriment – Argentina itself was a not entirely coherent mix of European, Latin and local customs and ideas and could well be represented by just such a mix as Peronism.

At least in part, of course, it may be that Perón demonstrated a shrewdness and political judgement much greater than that of his colleagues. On the basis of his later career, it may be observed that Perón was also adept at sensing and going along with the tide of public opinion. However, he personally had a genuine affinity for the problems of the working classes, an affinity which led him to adopt their cause for political ends (both theirs and his own), while his innate conservative tendency made him anxious to institute reforms which would prevent what his political instinct told him could lead to revolution, or at least serious social conflict. In addition, Perón's travels in Europe during the late 1930s had seemingly given him ideas as to the incorporation of the working classes into society under the auspices of state control. This seems to have informed his notions of social welfare and cooperation as the responsibilities of a corporative model of government.

Finally, Perón's military background moulded his cast of thinking, as it applied both to problems of discipline and structure and to Argentina's modernization. In particular, many progressive infantry officers favoured modernization and industrialization, as a means of increasing the state's efficiency, independence and prestige, as well as for diminishing the reactionary power of traditional forces in society. (Certainly the army was the state apparatus most susceptible to industrialization, and the infantry was a logical constituency for such a policy.) To achieve these aims required a modern and organized workforce under the guidance of a leader (or 'conductor'); Perón repeatedly stressed the uselessness and potential danger of a disorganized 'inorganic mass'.

The coming together of both circumstances – the tensions and changes in Argentine society and the position of the labour movement – and the right person to channel such circumstances into a dynamic new force is, of course, crucial in explaining the relationship between Perón and the working classes. However, this relationship between the main protagonists was cemented and to some extent defined by the position of the antagonists, that is, the traditional sectors of society. These sectors came together to oppose Perón and Peronism for the most reactionary of reasons: to maintain the status quo. According to Luna,

> in attacking Perón they really sought to prevent the transformation of the country which was already taking place and which Perón himself could neither greatly promote nor stop, ... an unstoppable evolution which at that moment was accelerated by the particular conditions inside and outside the country.[17]

This is perhaps slightly overstated, but it is true that in seeking to prevent the course of change the anti-Peronist factions demonstrated clearly to the working classes that they must support Perón, their only defender, by identifying him, just as the working classes had done, as their leader. 'Though Perón's schemes may in practice come to nothing, the fact remains that it is the first time any Argentine government has seriously interested itself in the conditions of the working classes at all.'[18]

Thus, one outcome of 17 October was to brand Peronism forever as a working-class movement, although this is only partially true, and to link the *descamisados* permanently to Perón as their only source of recognition. Other political forces made it clear that they would oppose Perón and Peronism at all costs and, as part of this attitude, would seek to keep labour in its marginal position. As Ernesto Sabato, one of the few anti-Peronists honest and clear-eyed enough to consider the reality of the situation, put it:

> There was a justified desire for justice and for recognition, faced with a cold and egocentric society, which had

always forgotten (the poor).... This is fundamentally what
Perón saw and mobilized. The rest is only detail.... It is also
what our political parties continue not to see and, what is
worse, do not want to see.... If it is true that Perón awoke
in the people their latent hatred, it is also true that the
anti-Peronists did everything possible to justify and increase
it.[19]

THE TRIUMPHAL RISE TO POWER

Following 17 October, the presidential elections were brought forward
to 24 February 1946, and a comparatively quiet phase ensued before
the campaign began. In the meantime, on 22 October, Perón and Evita
were married quietly in a civil service, and later in a religious service in
the Franciscan church in La Plata on 10 December. In late October Gay
and Reyes founded the *Partido Laborista*, not least as a potential future
alternative to Peronism, and in November the party offered Perón
its nomination for the presidency. Perón was also nominated by the
FORJA-influenced dissident branch of the UCR, its *Junta Renovadora*,
and he stood as the candidate of both.

At this point the extent of Perón's middle-class leaning was also
apparent. While the *Partido Laborista* put forward Luis Gay as its vice-
presidential candidate, the UCR put forward the unimpeachably bourgeois Dr. Hortensio Quijano; at Perón's insistence, Gay withdrew in
Quijano's favour. This led to the suggestion in some quarters that 'the
"sans culotte" section of labour has lost some influence'.[20] This was
more than compensated, however, by Decree 33.302 in December
1945, providing for new workers' benefits including indexed wages
and the so-called *aguinaldo* (literally a year-end bonus of an additional
month's wages – 'the thirteenth month'). The refusal by employers
to pay this year-end bonus led to strikes and lockouts, and further
polarized opinion. At the same time the armed forces, which remained divided and almost immobilized over the question of Perón's
candidacy, were also being won over by Perón with increased spending on military equipment, training and expansion.

The assortment of forces opposing Perón's candidacy, including
the mainstream Radicals, conservatives, communists, socialists and a
host of others, coalesced into the *Unión Democrática*, which selected
Dr. José Tamborini as its presidential candidate and which took as its

slogan 'Against Nazism, For Democracy'. As a slogan it was difficult to disagree with, but its obvious implications were hardly conciliatory. In practice, the *Unión Democrática* confined its platform to opposing anything which Perón proposed, to such an extent as to drive many voters towards the Peronist camp simply for fear that a win by Tamborini would see the reversal of all the gains won by the working class, and possibly a sustained persecution of the Peronists. The way in which the *Unión Democrática* was seen by the working classes may be gauged by the comment of Cipriano Reyes: it included 'those who during the past 14 years had continued denying citizens' rights, persecuting and imprisoning workers' leaders, closing down trade unions, . . . stealing the elections, denigrating the dignity of the people'.[21]

In the same way that the UCR government's attitude during the Tragic Week had undermined its position with the working classes, so the support of socialists and communists for the anti-Peronist coalition would further distance them from their supposed natural constituency, since their position appeared to be militating against the rights of the workers they had, in theory, been backing. Moreover, the socialists in particular tended to be drawn from the ranks of middle-class intellectuals, a group which as a whole was not favourable to Perón and his seemingly authoritarian bent. Nor was the Perón government to be especially tolerant of much of the intellectual class – the slogan 'alpargatas yes, books no' (alpargatas are a type of canvas and rope shoe worn by the poor) was a popular one among his supporters, while the great Argentine writer Jorge Luis Borges (by no stretch of the imagination a socialist) was famously removed from his post at the national library and made an inspector of poultry by the administration. This was arguably less the case in the cinema and music industries, where a number of famous artists – notably Hugo del Carril, who recorded the first and most famous version of the Peronist March – were strong supporters, although others who were not would eventually find it prudent to continue their careers elsewhere.

Perón also received a boost from the Catholic Church, which issued a pastoral letter in November 1945 forbidding its members to vote for any candidate who advocated secular education, divorce or the separation of Church and State (all of which Perón opposed at this time). In an extraordinarily foolhardy move, the *Unión Democrática* thereafter announced that it advocated all of these steps. Thus, Catholics were

also faced with the choice of voting for Perón or disobeying a direc-
tive from the Church hierarchy, although it is questionable whether in
fact this had a significant influence on voter decisions. In any case, although the Church repeated its standard admonitions in this famous
pastoral letter, there is no question that it did not adopt Perón as its
favoured candidate, not least because there appeared to be at least a
reasonable possibility that the *Unión Democrática* might win the elections, and any open preference for Perón by the Church would have
strained its relations with the new government with which it would
be forced to co-exist.

BRADEN OR PERÓN

The *Unión Democrática* also suffered from its apparent alliance with
'imperialist' interests, in particular with the US Embassy. The ambassador from April (when Argentina and the USA restored diplomatic
relations, after their breakdown over Argentina's equivocal position
during the Second World War) until September 1945, Spruille Braden,
was an outspoken and tireless opponent of Perón, and had formed
many ties with like-minded Argentine elites. Braden even participated
prominently in a series of June 1945 pronouncements by the Rural Society and other anti-government sectors, giving the impression that
the US ambassador was the leader of the anti-Peronist movement. Effectively, just as Perón became the leader of movements which had
failed to generate a leader from their own ranks, Braden became the
leader of an opposition movement which included the full spectrum
of political parties and other sectors, which had few interests in common except their opposition to Perón, and which was thus equally
unable to generate its own leader. In character, Braden had little
of the diplomat, being aggressive, forthright, a stereotypical 'Yankee imperialist' who had already made his presence felt in Colombia
and Cuba, adopting an interventionist and political role not entirely
appropriate to his diplomatic status. At the same time, he was violently
anti-communist, anti-fascist and, possibly due to his upbringing in
Chile, more than slightly anti-Argentine. Above all, he was anti-Perón,
and as early as July 1945 had expressed the view, in a cable to the US
State Department, that US security could only be guaranteed by the
downfall of the military regime and of Perón in particular. Personal

relations between Perón and Braden were largely choleric in nature, with each carrying out a public campaign against the other ranging from accusations to outright insults.

On leaving Buenos Aires, Braden made a speech at a farewell lunch in which he promised to continue his battle against the Argentine government, a speech which received a standing ovation from the well-heeled audience. Upon returning to Washington, Braden kept up his anti-Peronist crusade, and was responsible for the launch of the so-called 'Blue Book' (the real title of which was 'Consultation among the American Republics with Respect to the Argentine Situation'), a US government report purporting to demonstrate wartime links between Perón and other members of the military government with the Third Reich. (In his memoirs *Diplomats and Demagogues*, Braden himself accuses Perón alternately of both Nazism and communism, and even accuses him of having paid communist agents in the State Department in his employ – at one point, he appears to suggest that Alger Hiss may have been one of them.) The Blue Book accused Perón of having 'established a "corporate" labour organization subservient to the government', while making clear that relations between the USA and 'the military regime or any Argentine government controlled by the same elements' should not be expected to improve.[22]

The Blue Book was embraced by the *Unión Democrática* and widely reported and reproduced in the press. However, it appeared to be – and indeed was – a blatant interference in the national presidential elections scheduled a few days after its release. It provided Perón with an opportunity to launch a highly inflammatory reply (called 'the Blue and White Book', the colours of the Argentine flag) denouncing imperialism and interventionism, and allowing him to dismiss his political opposition with his best political slogan – 'Braden or Perón', again suggesting that his real opponent for the control of Argentina was the former US ambassador, rather than Tamborini.

Perhaps due as much to the errors of the opposition in further deepening political and social rifts as to his own actions, Perón won the 24 February 1946 elections with about 52 per cent of the votes cast. During the first term of his presidency, legislation favouring the labour movement and rises in real wages continued. However, there was a qualitative change in the freedom of movement of the unions at this time (not, as was suggested by his opponents, prior to 17 October 1945). The *Partido Laborista* was dissolved when it became apparent that its support was not unconditional; those who refused to accept its disappearance, including Gay and Reyes, either disappeared from the political scene or found themselves in prison (having 'deviated from the correct path', in the subsequent words of Evita). Gay was replaced as leader of the CGT by the wholly subservient José Espejo (supposedly the elevator operator in Evita's apartment building), and the CGT as a whole became more 'verticalized', with virtually no independent union activity tolerated and all unions led by approved Peronist cadres.

This period after the elections also witnessed the rise of Evita as a power with the trade unions: once Perón was president and effectively unable to exercise the same personal contact and authority over trade union activities, Evita moved into his old office in the Ministry of Labour and exercised it in his stead. The necessity for this would appear to be simple: as his wife, acting at least initially under his instructions, Evita's role was complementary rather than threatening to Perón's position vis-à-vis organized labour, whereas an independent individual (such as Mercante) might have come to replace or at least challenge Perón in the loyalties of the workers. Similarly, it is not difficult to guess at the reasoning behind the increased controls placed on the union movement. Having become a numerous, powerful and organized movement, due largely to the influence of Perón, the labour movement now possessed the potential to become a political threat as as well as a support. Therefore, as it became more mobilized and more effective, it also became potentially dangerous and required careful control to ensure that that the threat would not become a reality.

7 Peronism in Power 1946–52: The First Presidency

Perón, summarily promoted to the rank of general a few days before, was sworn in as Argentina's president for the first time on 4 June 1946. The date represented the apogee of the aspirations of many, who saw it as the vindication of the demands of Argentina's underclass. For many others, it was 'a date which will live in infamy', the rise of a fascist rabble-rouser rousing an uncultured rabble, which threatened to mark the end of the country they knew. Both views were to prove exaggerated, as the rise of Peronism marked neither the end of oligarchic exploitation and the death of the elite nor the birth of a revolutionary new Argentina.

Neither Perón nor his putative party had any long-term experience of grass-roots politics or of opposition. In 1946, Perón was a talented novice politician who had entered power before entering politics, and who had no experience of the negotiations and flexibility which must invariably form part of the political process. Similarly, his party was born when its leader became president, and was not to have the experience of being in opposition until after his overthrow. This is somewhat ironic: by the nature of its platform, which represented it as the underdog opposing the oligarchy and the established political system, Peronism was in some respects by nature an opposition party, and one which was only sporadically effective at ruling.

Despite the fact that large and powerful sectors of society were opposed to Perón, and indeed legislators of opposition parties refused to attend his inauguration, he assumed government in apparently favourable conditions. Having won clean elections by a reasonable margin, he was assured of at least significant short-term support, and he controlled both houses of Congress. He governed a country which had come out of the Second World War in unusually solid financial condition, a benefit of its neutrality. His inaugural speech promised social justice and reconciliation for all, promising, as many have done since, to seek to be president of all Argentines, both supporters and opponents. At the same time, the difficulties faced by his government included the very nature of his own support base, which incorporated a wide range of unruly interests which did not always coincide or were altogether contradictory, as well as Argentina's isolated post-war diplomatic position (useful for nationalist rhetoric but less convenient in practice), and the need to comply with at least some of the wide range of promises made for social justice and a new Argentina.

On the personal level, both Perón and Evita stirred animosity among the upper and substantial sectors of the middle classes. While some sectors of the middle classes adhered to Peronism by conviction or because its policies favoured its members in the public sector, manufacturing and service sectors, other elements of the middle class were more firmly anti-Peronist even than the oligarchy so hated by Evita. Although the elite rejected Perón and Peronism, they retained a certain conviction that their loss of power would not be permanent. They could give themselves the luxury of doing business with the government where convenient, while comfortably contemptuous of Perón and his actress wife. However, the anti-Peronist bourgeoisie was far less certain of its position or of its future return to favour. Moreover, many had struggled to *hacer la Argentina* through their own efforts and had achieved, over one or two generations, a tolerable economic position, home ownership, a job or business. They were, with some logic, outraged that Perón's *descamisados* were given homes, jobs and other benefits which they had been forced to fight for.

This is a factor which is central to both Peronism and anti-Peronism: the fact that party loyalty and party membership were sufficient to gain jobs and other favours previously reserved for other sectors. With the foundation of the Peronist Party, this crystallized into possession of a party card. Those working in public dependencies often found themselves obliged to join the party in order to keep their jobs, while voluntary party members found new doors opening to them which they had never imagined. This was not new:

traditionally, friends of a local conservative or Radical politician had been given jobs due more to their connections than other virtues. However, the anti-Peronists argued, in the past, 'jobs for the boys' had required that the boys in question have at least minimum qualifications for the job. In the case of the Peronists, they said, the only qualification needed was the party card. This was a key element of anti-Peronist hatred. Conversely, it was a strong basis for loyalty to Peronism by those who suddenly found that a party card meant they belonged, and not only to the party. No heavy political commitment or reflection was required, which meant that it was not even necessary to take responsibility for the direction taken by the party or the government, but merely to support it. (Osvaldo Soriano, in his acid novel *No habrá más penas ni olvido*, translated as *A Funny Little Dirty War*, accurately summed up this position in the words of one of his characters: 'I've always been a Peronist. I never got mixed up in politics.')

This also raises another question central to Peronism: responsibility, and lack thereof. Argentines were used to, and not strictly opposed to, *caudillos*, patron–client relations and authoritarian government; as a whole, they were not anxious to assume major civic responsibility. Perón fitted in nicely, taking charge from above and taking responsibility out of the hands of those below, who could either feel satisfied that their interests were represented or place the blame for what went wrong on Perón instead of contemplating possible shared responsibilities elsewhere.

THE ELIMINATION OF OPPOSITION

Despite sweeping victory in the 1946 elections, Perón was soon to demonstrate a negative characteristic which marked his entire career: that of requiring absolute support and no opposition whatsoever. The first move was to dissolve, on 23 May 1946, all the parties which had supported his campaign, including the *Partido Laborista* of Cipriano Reyes and Luis Gay, and to create a single official party, first called the Sole Party of the Revolution and, shortly thereafter, the Peronist Party. (This would officially be titled the *Justicialista* Party, known as the PJ, which is the title which remains today.)

Reyes resisted the move, becoming for a time the only *Partido Laborista* representative in the Lower House. Gay resigned as president of the party and became secretary general of the CGT. Reyes, a man of strong convictions but hardly an apostle of peace, with a long history of participation in violent actions in defence of his trade union positions, made it clear that he was wedded to his goal of trade union rights, but not to Peronism, automatically turning him into a foe. On 17 October 1946, while an official rally commemorating the demonstration of a year earlier was held in the Plaza de Mayo, Reyes held his own rally in front of Congress, at which he denounced the officialist rally, saying that the events of 17 October 1945 had been designed to defend the people and not any political party or leader. The move demonstrated courage but also, as in the case of Perón, a lack of political finesse which led to outright confrontation rather than constructive opposition. In July 1947, Reyes suffered a machine gun attack, which he miraculously survived with minor wounds. In early 1948, when his two-year mandate as a legislator expired, he left the Chamber and the *Partido Laborista* disappeared forever. Not long thereafter, in September 1948, it was announced that a plot to assassinate Perón and Evita had been discovered, of which the instigators were Reyes and a nationalist economist named Walter Beveraggi Allende. There is no evidence that such a plot ever existed, but it provided the excuse to eliminate a political opponent with a high profile if limited power. Reyes and Beveraggi were arrested, and Reyes was severely tortured, remaining in jail until the fall of Perón in 1955.[1]

Despite being apparently more pliable than Reyes, Gay and the CGT were to fare little better under the increasing institutionalization of Peronism. The unions had little to complain about in material terms, given the significant improvement in the position of their members and the number of trade unionists who rose to political posts or important jobs in nationalized companies, and in fact there is very little to suggest that they were not largely and sincerely loyal to Peronism at this time. However, Perón's mindset required that all elements of society be corporate, coordinated and vertically controlled (a mistaken military concept of perfection which has little chance of success in civil society), and distrusted an even theoretically independent trade union movement. The 1945 law of professional associations, which allowed the government to recognize only one union in each sector, had already established a significant level of control over organized labour, withdrawing legal recognition from non-Peronist trade unions. However, the CGT under Gay was willing to accept loyalty but not government control, contending that the government had more important things to attend to and that unions should attend to their own problems.

As in the case of Reyes, a pretext was found to accuse Gay of treason and remove him from play, in this case, the visit of a delegation of the American Federation of Labor (AFL) in January 1947. The delegation included one Serafino Romualdi, a refugee from Mussolini's Italy who took it upon himself to prove that the CGT was no more than a puppet organization controlled by a fascist regime. Perón took advantage of the vociferous criticisms and blatant interference of Romualdi (who announced that he was 'investigating' Argentine trade unionism) to accuse Gay of having reached an agreement with him to sell out the CGT to US interests. On 29 January, Gay resigned, although he had the good fortune not to end up in jail. He was replaced briefly by the obscure graphics worker Aurelio Hernandez, and subsequently by the even more obscure José Espejo. Thus, the CGT was to become one more appendage of the government apparatus, and would later be used to defend government actions before the workers, instead of defending the position of the workers before the government.

The five-member Supreme Court was, likewise, seen as a source of implacable opposition to the Perón government: indeed, three of its members had been on the Court for many years and held views considerably at odds with those of the government. In order to eliminate opposition to the measures taken by the government, those three members were impugned on the outstandingly cynical grounds that they had acted illegally by recognizing the de facto governments which took power in 1930 and 1943 (the latter of which had brought Perón to power) and by failing to resign when those illicit governments took office. A second contradictory accusation argued that they had then unlawfully impeded the actions of the second de facto government by taking decisions which blocked its measures. Despite the grossly obvious absurdity of the charges, in April 1947 all three justices in question were removed from their posts by Congress, allowing the government to pack the Court according to its own designs.

Opposition within Congress was limited, and not distinguished by its stellar actions. The attitude of the Radicals in Congress was to be as obstructive as possible, rather than representing a constructive opposition (similar to the experience they had faced at the hands of the conservatives under Yrigoyen's presidency), although in the light of their numbers their ability to be either obstructive or constructive was limited. The Radical legislators were led by Ricardo Balbín, known as 'El Chino', who would become an eternally unsuccessful presidential candidate between 1951 and 1973 and who adopted a 'no surrender' position of constant provocation and insults which offered a convenient pretext, if not justification, for frequent sanctions. Balbín was later to face imprisonment and exile in Uruguay.

The unnecessarily bitter conflict which was entered into enthusiastically by both sides also cemented a relationship which went beyond mere political opposition to an attitude of enmity for Peronists and anti-Peronists. Each side saw the other as threatening to annihilate their members, achievements, and everything they stood for. The anti-Peronists tended to base their strategy on opposition to all things Peronist, without making substantive alternative proposals. The Radicals, in any case, were traditionally inclined to get bogged down in style rather than substance, obsessively favouring the appearance of democratic process (if not necessarily real democracy) and the appearance of legality (if not necessarily legality itself). They were legalistic and pedantic in their internal debates to the point of being largely inoperative, both within and outside government. The Peronists, who on the contrary were too little concerned with even the appearance of democratic practice and legality, were far more dynamic in deciding and putting policies into practice, something which made them easier to criticize, but less sclerotic in the exercise of power.

THE FIRST FIVE-YEAR PLAN

On taking office, Perón announced a cabinet which constituted a mixed bag of competents and incompetents, who were to oversee the hive of activity which was to follow. The competents included the secretary of technical affairs of the presidency, José Figuerola (the Spanish lawyer who had been at the head of the National Labour Department when Perón arrived in 1943), and Foreign Minister Juan Atilio Bramuglia, who was to distinguish himself as chair of the UN Security Council during the Berlin blockade. The moderately competent members included former socialist Angel Borlenghi as interior minister, and the relatively incompetent included the 'super-minister' of economy, Miguel Miranda. The latter was a successful industrialist appointed by Perón in the apparent belief that his Midas touch would extend to the national economy as well.

Although Miranda was the government's economic guru, it was Figuerola who was charged with preparing the government's Five-Year Plan, 1947–51, announced on 21 October 1946. The plan, which focused on national production and investment, boiled down into 27 draft laws relating to the state's planned role in politics, education, health, justice, culture and foreign relations over that period, an ambitious role aimed at filling large gaps in areas such as education and health and at changing the dependent position of Argentina in the world market to make it an independent economic power.

This policy was decried as corporatist by its opponents and celebrated as a watershed by its supporters, although in point of fact parts of the plan foundered on the inexperience of many of those carrying it out, and on the fact that Argentina remained a dependent player in the world market and did not control many of the external factors which affected the possibilities of the Five-Year Plan's success. Moreover, it focused heavily on industry, to the detriment of agriculture, while efforts to utilize agriculture to sustain other economic developments reduced incentives to boost production, needed for both export and increased domestic consumption. The creation of the Institute for the Promotion of Trade (IAPI) gave the state a monopoly over both purchases and exports of grains and meat, a mechanism to redistribute income away from a landed oligarchy regarded as anti-Peronist, which nonetheless undermined output in what was still the country's most competitive sector.

Many of Perón's ambitious projects looked ready to be completed. During the first three years of his government, real wages went up by some 27 per cent in the case of skilled workers, and 37 per cent for unskilled labour, and the number of salaried workers increased to reach 55 per cent of the workforce, while GDP expanded by close to 30 per cent. In addition, the working week was reduced: the six-day working week had been slightly reduced in the 1930s, by the adoption of 'the English Saturday', which implied only a half day of work, but from 1949 it was decreed that the public sector would not work on Saturday at all, a move followed by banks and most companies. This in addition to an ever-lengthening list of national, religious and Peronist holidays, as well as the annual day off enjoyed by the members of each sector's trade union. More money and more leisure time meant more possibilities to enjoy entertainments, or shopping for previously inaccessible consumer goods now more widely available. (One of them, the radio, was not only the most widely available form of entertainment, but also the most wide-reaching vehicle for propaganda.) Other diversions were also to become available, such as more sports facilities for the poor and seaside holidays for underprivileged children at state-owned hostels.

At the same time, this was a government which did not forget that popular participation had been fundamental in putting it in power. The government continued to foment that mass participation, in order to remind its followers of their role. Every 17 October, Loyalty Day, a mass demonstration was held in the Plaza de Mayo to commemorate that first event. Thereafter, 18 October was also declared a holiday (popularly known as San Perón). Other days which provided an opportunity for similar mass encounters between the workers and their leader, Argentina's First Worker, included 1 May, national holidays and other one-off occasions such as the announcement of a nationalization, or of the discovery of a plot to assassinate Perón. There is no question that many entered enthusiastically into these mass rallies throughout the duration of the government. However, they undoubtedly lost their initial spontaneous nature, becoming increasingly organized and controlled by the government, in part to ensure both attendance and order. Their increasingly official nature stemmed in part from the unfortunate Peronist practice of seeking to control every element of society to ensure harmony and avoid possible chaos, as well as the need to maintain the visible image of popular support for the government. It is difficult to maintain spontaneity and improvisation in the long term, even with good intentions, without becoming increasingly mechanical and regimented. Under such control, spontaneity of course ceased to be spontaneous. While Peronism continued to command the sincere support of many Argentines for the duration of Perón's presidency (and of a large percentage for many years thereafter), its consolidation reduced its spontaneity and innovation, which had been among its most positive qualities.

Although industrial policy under Perón went little beyond continuing the model of import substitution and the production of consumer goods for avid new consumers with money in their pockets, this was sufficient at the time to generate a rise in production and in new jobs. The fact that industrial policy was limited to this model would have longer-term consequences, given that the lack of locally produced ma-chinery maintained the dependence on imports. Most had to come from war-ravaged Europe, because the USA considered many machin-ery products to be strategic at this time and denied export licences. At the same time, the limited industrial model meant that Argentina continued, as ever, to be dependent on its exports of agricultural products, whose value was less than that of the industrial machinery and other finished goods imported from abroad. The assumption that Europe was hungry and would need to buy Argentine beef and grain at Argentine prices proved to be a mistake, given that Europe lacked funds to pay for the food it needed, and the financing from the Marshall Plan was used primarily to acquire the same products from the USA. In one of his more strident debacles, Miguel Miranda in-sisted that Argentina would not sell grain on the world market except on its own terms, with the result that the country was landed with two unsold harvests which remained in storage and generated losses for the productive sector. Even given these shortcomings, however, in the initial stages of the Five-Year Plan, Argentina's reserves were sufficient to keep the economy buoyant, and the effects of this less than optimistic panorama were not widely noted.

In addition to the fact that new jobs made the period after 1946 a time of plenty for many, the Perón government expanded educa-tion facilities to an extent which ensured that more people would be trained as skilled workers, and thus readily employable, in the future. Increased real wages and lower unemployment also boosted education numbers: with fewer pressing unmet needs, more children could stay in school, while the government (and later the Eva Perón Foundation) invested heavily in the installation of new schools to make education more freely available. In 1949, the government would found the Na-tional Technology University (UNT), a tertiary institution aimed at providing higher technical training for skilled workers, which pro-vided free higher education for those who previously would have had virtually no possibility of attending university.

In addition to greater access to education, the government in-vested heavily in public health care, increasing training facilities for nurses and other health care workers and installing medical centres and modern, well-supplied hospitals throughout the country, avail-able free of charge. This was a true breakthrough in a country where the majority had had little access to health care. The downside (it was characteristic of the Peronist government to create a downside even in its most laudable achievements) was that, as in other public-sector services, all doctors and nurses working in public hospitals were obliged to join the Peronist Party or face dismissal, a move which served no useful purpose and only generated discord and a further source of anti-Peronist propaganda. In 1947, Bernardo Houssay became the first Argentine to win the Nobel Prize for medicine – hardly an achievement attributable to the Perón government, but indicative of the level of excellence in scientific and medical research. (Luis Federico Leloir and César Milstein would respectively win the 1970 Nobel in chemistry and the 1984 Nobel in medicine.)

At the same time, at the local level, the Peronist machine was also active, ensuring not only that everyone could participate and that local needs were identified and addressed, but also that the governing party could pinpoint its supporters and the extent of their loyalty. Throughout the country, local party delegations (*unidades básicas*) sprang up, charged with affiliating new members, addressing the small-scale problems of the local community and offering a range of useful services such as contacts, information, classes and training courses, low-cost hairdressing and manicure facilities, and a forum for local participation in the wider movement. These were to become even more widespread with the launching of the Women's Peronist Party.

Favourable international factors also boosted morale during the early years of the Perón government. The defeat of Braden at the hands of Perón and his withdrawal by the US government, as well as the nationalization of the British-owned railways, made Argentines feel that their country was assuming its rightful place as a nation of importance, as did Argentine donations of grain and other foodstuffs to hungry Europe (principally Spain) after the War. However, Perón's calculation that international factors would remain favourable – and indeed, that new conflict with the Soviet Union would boost demand for Argentine agricultural products – proved to be ill-founded, encouraging the squandering of resources that would not prove easy to replace.

THE ENTREPRENEURIAL STATE

Another facet of Argentina's international relations during the period, which boosted morale for some and caused others to despair, was the programme of nationalization between 1946 and 1949, beginning with the purchase of the United River Plate Telephone Company from ITT in September 1946. Claiming that the need to nationalize public services could not be allowed to violate the rights of their multinational owners, and incidentally showing off the financial resources the country then enjoyed, Perón was to pay 95 million dollars for the telephone company, at the same time granting a ten-year exclusive contract to ITT to provide equipment and materials for a network already in serious need of investments and modernization.

The most famous nationalization involved the purchase of British-owned railways, also in serious need of major infrastructure investments. Moreover, from 1 January 1947, the railways lost the franchise which allowed them to carry out imports tax-free, one of their principal advantages. Thus, the sale of the railways implied a much greater advantage for their British owners than for Argentina, apart from the symbolic value of the takeover. After protracted negotiations, on 13 February 1947 the Argentine government paid 150 million pounds for the railways, to be paid for by Argentine beef exports to the United Kingdom. Despite the initial proposal to use Argentine funds blocked in London, arising from British debts for wartime beef purchases from Argentina, in August 1947 the British government took the unilateral decision that those funds could not be converted or used for purchases outside the United Kingdom, making them unavailable to pay for the rundown and unprofitable railways. The railways were formally handed over on 1 March 1948, to national celebration, although the triumph was more symbolic than economic.

Another nationalization which caused sharp criticism was the acquisition of the Dodero shipping lines, owned by Alberto Dodero, a close friend and frequent financial backer of Perón, said to have paid for Evita's Rainbow Tour of Europe in 1947 out of his own pocket. Dodero and his brothers had acquired the line in 1942, but the shipping company was in the red by 1946, a situation which was not resolved even by being awarded an exclusive government contract to transport 30,000 refugees from Europe at a rate of 600 pesos each. In 1949, Dodero decided to sell the line, which was bought by the government on the grounds that it provided an essential public service, despite fierce opposition by the miniscule Radical bloc in the Senate on the grounds that the company was bankrupt and that its nationalization was designed only to favour its owners.

Dodero was also one of the shareholders and a member of the board of directors of the electricity company CADE, the only public utility not losing money at the time and, curiously, the only energy company not to be nationalized. As early as 1944 the military government had planned to take over CADE, and in May of that year Perón was alleged to have received a bribe to halt the nationalization, although there is no proof of that transaction. In any case, the relationship with Dodero is illustrative of a situation which frequently placed the government in a bad light. Dodero was alleged to have given Perón large sums of money on several occasions, and to have given Evita a property in Montevideo, in addition to financing the delegation which accompanied her to Europe in 1947. He was also one of the first to discover that gifts of jewellery to the first lady were a good means of remaining on good terms with the government, a strategy in which he was imitated by many others. In effect, the Perón government frequently appeared to go to great pains to give its critics as much ammunition as possible.

The Peronist practice of spending large sums on the nationalization of foreign-owned companies did not relate only to propaganda or poor administration, but also rested on the belief that the Second World War would be followed by a major devaluation in the USA and Europe. This belief implied that it would be more beneficial in the long term to spend the currency reserves which might tomorrow be worthless, acquiring capital assets which could increase in value. As a result of that policy, currency reserves fell from 1,697 million dollars in 1945 to 721 million in 1948, a situation which would impact on the economy when exports began falling in 1949. The concept that public services should be in state hands was a widespread trend in the post-war era: throughout Europe and much of Latin America, governments were nationalizing services and creating new state companies – many of which, as in the case of Argentina, would be privatized in the 1980s and 1990s. This is not to say that Perón or his counterparts elsewhere were mistaken in their belief in nationalization in the 1940s (or, necessarily, that their successors were mistaken in privatizing 40 years later). This was the era of the welfare state, public health services and a state structure aimed at serving the needs of the working class and the newly expanding middle class, after the war broke down the traditional classist society and the previously neglected people below the top rungs of the social ladder had to be taken care of. In addition, despite its long-standing pretensions to be a major world power,

Argentina had long experience of being a virtual economic colony, principally of Britain, and the aim of eliminating that dependence was a driving force in the nationalization of foreign-owned companies which were of essential interest to the country's functioning.

SIGNS OF DISSENT IN THE JUST SOCIETY

Some insight into the contradictory reactions generated by Perón and Peronism throughout Argentine society may be gained from the wide range of reactions within the Catholic Church. Members of the right-wing clergy who had supported falangism in the 1930s were notably hostile, including Msgr. Gustavo Franceschi. At the same time, other members of the clergy supported Peronism, either for its social content or for its anti-communism. Arguably the most influential of the clergy allied to Perón was the Jesuit Hernán Benítez, a friend of Perón's who became confessor to Eva Perón, spiritual adviser to the Eva Perón Foundation and Rector of the University of Buenos Aires. In his enthusiasm for underscoring that religious content and his influence over Eva Perón, it is not unrealistic to assume that he may have encouraged Perón to go further than he ever intended in competing with the Church on its own territory.[2]

The legislation adopted by the Perón government in its early years continued to favour Church interests, at least at first sight, although it also increased the Church's dependency on the state. In 1946 legislation was brought requiring the registration of non-Catholic religious institutions and placing them under the control of the newly created *Dirección General de Cultos*. In addition, Protestant missionary activity among indigenous communities was prohibited and missionaries not connected to a recognized religious institution were prevented from working altogether. In March 1947, a decree was ratified making religious education compulsory in primary and secondary schools, and two months later the *Dirección General de Enseñanza Religiosa*, under the control of two priests, was established to oversee religious education, appoint teachers and approve religious texts.

The 1949 constitution did not alter the status of Catholicism as the state religion or the favoured position of the Church as an institution. However, the text stressed the social function of private property (i.e., raised the possibility of expropriation if the common good so dictated, a position regarded as quasi-communist), expanding the faculties of the state over private property, as noted below. Most importantly, it provided for the re-election of the president. This issue was important to Catholic opinion especially because Domingo Mercante, considered Perón's likely successor until that time, incorporated into his provincial government members of *Acción Católica*, who were notable for their Catholic rather than Peronist militancy and who subsequently distanced themselves from Peronism.[3]

Even more central to the issues raised by the constitution was the increased role it gave to the state – specifically, the Peronist state – in educational and family issues previously regarded as the province of the Church. The new constitution provided that the state would 'orient official education and control private education', in order to 'create in young people virtues... in line with Christian paradigms'.[4] While the widening of access to education was one of the highly positive features of the period, overeager government propagandists found it necessary to utilize that educational system as another means of political indoctrination, a move which generated rejection and probably did little to increase admiration of the government among its supporters. By the early 1950s, small children learned 'Perón and Evita', 'Evita loves me' as the first words they read, and by the time of Evita's death her ghost-written autobiography *The Reason for My Life* was required reading in all schools.

PERONIST DOCTRINE

It was not until the late 1940s that serious attempts were made to define the doctrine of the Peronist Party, variously referred to as Peronism or *Justicialismo* (social justice). The motivation for seeking, somewhat after the fact, to define this Peronist ideology would seem to be the fact that it did not exist in reality. Perón, in part a product of the religious, political and cultural realignments of the 1930s, had assumed office with the support of divergent social and political sectors and without a clear political platform or even a party. However, as Peronism came to have a clearer notion of its importance as a permanent rather than transient political force, and as it now governed a

Figure 6. President Juan Domingo Perón and Eva Perón, November 1949
(Courtesy of the archive, *Diario La Nación*)

country still hoping to play a major role in the post-war international
order, its lack of substantive content likewise became inconvenient
and had to be addressed.

However, the fact that Peronism still needed to maintain the
adherence of as many sectors as possible meant that its definition
must avoid excluding any potential support base. *Justicialismo* was
thus defined in 1951 as 'a doctrine whose object is the happiness
of man within the society of mankind through the harmonising of
material, spiritual, individual and collective forces, appraised from
the Christian standpoint'.[5] The previous year, one of the 'Twenty
Truths of *Justicialismo*' handed down to the faithful on 17 October
1950 informed that '*Justicialismo* is a new philosophy of life, simple,
practical, popular, profoundly Christian and profoundly human'.[6] If
these definitions were rather pretentious, they were vague enough not
to exclude almost anyone (their ideals were, on the whole, difficult
to disagree with).

The incessant comparisons between Christianity and Catholicism
on the one hand and Peronism on the other, in which the former
tended to appear inferior, became even more aggressive in the writings
of Eva Perón, who routinely compared Perón with Christ (whom the

Figure 7. Eva Peron receiving a delegation of maritime workers from Mar del Plata (27 August 1951)

rich also scorned and the poor followed). 'Perón is the face of God in the darkness.... Here the case of Bethlehem, 2000 years ago, was repeated; the first to believe were the humble.'[7]

If all of this pseudo-religious doctrine might have been considered offensive by the Church and by many members of society, however, the concepts put forward by Perón in *La comunidad organizada* were potentially even more threatening. Appearing in 1949, the Organized Community was essentially a blueprint for the Peronist state (as well as representing the rather naive concept that civil society could be ordered in the same way as the armed forces), in which all its elements strive towards a common goal, the 'overcoming of class struggle by social collaboration and the dignifying of man. Society will have to be a harmony in which there is no dissonance'.[8]

Apart from the fact that the underlying thesis behind the Organized Community was that all individuals and institutions must follow the line marked out by the Peronist state, in itself an alarmingly absolutist idea for all but those already converted, it also suggested that modern society had been deprived of the traditional moral absolutes needed to sustain it, and that substitutes must be found; implicitly, these absolutes would be provided by the state rather than religion. In fact, in such a scenario, the state appeared to almost supplant the Church altogether as a community of souls, representing the highest common good.

Most importantly, to arrive at 'an ideal of better humanity, the sum of individualities tending to continuous improvement'[9] would visibly require massive state intervention in precisely those areas of society considered the property of the Church: education and the family. The greatest practical difficulty in the increasing importance given to the Peronist Doctrine was the extent to which the governing party became identified with the state. (It is worth noting that the highly personalist and centralized presidential system in Argentina has often led to a closer than desirable identification between the ruling party and the state, although Perón was the first to try to turn that identification into a doctrine extending to the whole of society.)

THE THIRD POSITION

The international face of Peronist Doctrine was defined as the 'third position' in global politics, a forerunner of what would shortly become the non-aligned policy in the Third World, although the third position was defined as something beyond a mere decision to avoid close ties with either side of the Cold War. According to Perón, '[O]ur Third Position is not a central position. It is an ideological position which is in the centre, on the right or on the left, according to specific circumstances'.[10] While thus arguably too nebulous to be a position at all, in the post-war era it created tensions with both the USA and the Vatican, as it was not specifically pro-Western and anti-communist. Like the Peronist Doctrine itself, it represented an effort to be all things to all people. Although the doctrine was surprisingly successful in that respect, containing positions attractive to all tastes which could allow for virtually any inference the interlocutor wished to make, as foreign policy it tended to have the reverse effect, with governments on all sides of the political spectrum suspecting Argentina of being hostile or downright subversive, as a result of being too far to the left or the right. In point of fact, the third position was rarely a defining factor (how could so indefinite a notion have defined anything?) in Argentine foreign policy during the period, which involved rhetorical anti-imperialism in theory but pragmatic efforts to maintain good relations in practice, in particular with the USA and Britain.

The 'third position' made its debut when Argentina restored diplomatic relations with the Soviet Union the day after Perón assumed office in 1946. The move was followed by assurances to Washington that the new government was above all committed to regional defence and therefore on the side of the USA in the case of a hypothetical conflict between the two powers. Indeed, although Perón did not deprive himself of the opportunity to blast US imperialism rhetorically as often as possible, the Peronist government in fact took no position basically negative for the USA. At the same time, he lost no opportunity to remind the increasingly anti-communist USA that his government represented a bulwark against revolution and communism. Despite his early clashes with Braden, Perón maintained good relations with subsequent US ambassadors, and was frequently at pains to reassure them that his government would take no actions detrimental to the interests of the US government or its private companies. The Argentine government did not endear itself to other countries in the region (to the extent they noticed) with the grandiloquent suggestion that they should follow Argentina's foreign policy lead by adopting the third position, although this was far from the first or the last time that Argentina felt itself qualified to take a leading role in the region which its neighbours saw no reason to accept.

THE 1949 CONSTITUTION

After imposing so many changes (some of them more cosmetic than profound) in Argentine politics and society, it was not surprising that the Peronist Party should have turned its attention to a reform of the 1853 constitution. The first proposal of constitutional reform came in early 1947, although it was not until he opened the annual session of Congress in 1948 that Perón came out in favour of the reform. By this time, the reform was facilitated by the fact that the midterm legislative elections had increased the Peronist majority in Congress. On

5 December 1948, constituent elections were held, and were amply won by the ruling party with 110 members. The UCR, whose access to the media had been severely restricted during the campaign, accounted for only 48 members.

While the need for a constitutional reform was bandied about in previous debates, there was little concrete discussion of why it was needed, or of what was to be reformed. This gave members of the constituent assembly virtual carte blanche to modify what they wanted, and made it impossible for voters to know what they were authorizing those members to reform. In point of fact, although it was not stipulated in any prior debate, the fundamental element of the constitution to be reformed was Article 77, which prohibited immediate re-election of the president, in theory, forcing Perón to step down in 1952. (Prior to the reform, Buenos Aires governor Domingo Mercante had been widely tipped to succeed Perón as the party candidate in 1952, and the reform which allowed Perón to stand again marked a distancing in the relations between the two and the beginning of the end of Mercante's political career.) Thus, the draft reform presented by Secretary of Technical Affairs José Figuerola modified Article 77 to read 'The president and vice-president of the Nation will remain in their posts for six years and may be re-elected', in lieu of the original wording which indicated that they 'may not be re-elected except after an interval of one electoral period'. Despite this change, Perón announced to the constituents that he did not anticipate standing for re-election.[11]

The constituent assembly was inaugurated on 24 January 1949, presided by Mercante himself and including among the Peronist members the constitutionalist Arturo Sampay, mainly responsible for drafting the reformed constitution, after the text prepared by Figuerola failed to please either Perón or his followers. Mercante, who had distinguished himself as an able governor who worked well with the opposition and was considered far less authoritarian than many of his fellow party members, was also to distinguish himself as an able and comparatively non-sectarian assembly leader. After acrid debates which made it clear that the fundamental issue of the reform was the re-election of Perón, the Radical members of the assembly withdrew in early March, although the Peronist majority was sufficient to allow a quorum which rapidly approved the reform on 16 March.

In addition to the re-election question, the reformed 1949 constitution contained various modifications to the 1853 document, including the elimination of the electoral college and direct election of the president, and the insertion in the preamble of language recalling the Peronist slogan of social justice, economic freedom and political sovereignty, as well as the creation of the instrument of a 'state of prevention and alarm', similar to the state of siege (and never used while the 1949 constitution was in force). The new constitution also contained clauses relating to the rights of the worker (not including the right to strike), of the elderly and of the family, and specifically denied recognition (i.e., legality) to organizations considered opposed to the liberties or political system established by the constitution. This implicitly allowed for the suppression of opposition parties although none was outlawed during Perón's term. It also authorized provincial legislatures to carry out similar reforms of provincial constitutions, with the evident intent of 'Peronizing' those texts as well.

EVA PERÓN

When her husband assumed office, Eva Perón had recently turned 27 and had minimal political experience, although her theatre and radio days gave her at least a modicum of experience in public speaking. She had played little part in the presidential campaign, accompanying her husband on speaking tours but remaining decorously and decoratively in the background. On the only occasion when she attempted to address a political meeting, filling in for an otherwise engaged Perón, her nerves only allowed her to stammer out a few sentences, and the disappointed crowd which had expected her more illustrious husband had little patience with her inexperience and booed her off the platform. Rather astonishingly, only some six months later the gauche radio actress had become an accomplished speaker who not only received delegations and official visitors, but also gave speeches and headed political meetings alone. In these early months her activities were limited primarily to the formal role of first lady, and to informal political functions such as receiving trade union delegations or other groups on Perón's behalf. After Perón took office, she moved into an office in the Central Post Office building (where her mother's old friend Oscar Nicolini still held sway), although a short time later she moved into her husband's old office in the Secretariat of Labour. There, she gradually began assuming the social role she would later play, receiving petitions from representatives of the poor and acting as 'a bridge of love', as she put it, between the *descamisados* and the increasingly occupied Perón. Even at this early stage her role represented an integral part of the image of a caring and accessible government, and would eventually lead to the slogan, 'Perón fulfills, Evita dignifies'.

From 1947, however, Evita began to assume a more formal and more prominent role in affairs of state. In early 1947 Spanish dictator Francisco Franco invited Evita to make an official visit to Spain, and the 'Rainbow Tour', as the visit was called, seized the opportunity to include visits to other countries, including Italy, Portugal, France and Switzerland.

A nervous Evita left Buenos Aires on 6 June 1947 with a delegation including her brother Juan Duarte (by this time Perón's secretary), confessor Hernán Benítez and Liliane Lagomarsino de Guardo, the wife of Dr Ricardo Guardo, head of the Peronist bloc in the Lower House, and one of the few scions of the Argentine aristocracy to adhere to Peronism. Her sharp instincts and Liliane Guardo's counsel appear to have prevented any serious breaches of etiquette: despite a few gaffes, Evita carried off the Rainbow Tour with remarkable poise, attracting large crowds in Franco's Spain and leaving a generally favourable impression elsewhere. Although in Italy she was the subject of an anti-fascist demonstration outside the Argentine Embassy, and in Switzerland her car was pelted with tomatoes on one occasion, the European press was largely positive, commenting on her beauty and comportment, if far more discreet than the paeans of praise for her triumphal visit in the official Argentine press. In France in particular her youth and beauty were applauded, her few press conferences produced no glaring errors to pounce on, and her stay in Paris gave her her first contact with the haute couture designers in fashion, an experience which would be reflected in a less gaudy and more elegantly tailored wardrobe in the future.

Two principal disappointments stood out in Evita's European tour. One was the failure to receive an official invitation from the United Kingdom, including a reception by the Royal Family, a crowning achievement which Argentine diplomacy had been angling to arrange. The UK government confined itself to indicating that the Royal Family would be at their summer home in Balmoral and unable to receive her; the prospect of tea with the prime minister did not appease the offended Evita, and the visit to England was called off.

The other disappointment was Evita's audience with Pope Pius XII on 27 June, where by all accounts she received a friendly reception but did not receive the papal decoration she was allegedly hoping for as a reward for her social work. At her 27-minute audience with the Pope, 'Sra. de Perón was accorded the most elaborate Vatican reception extended to a visiting dignitary since the war' and also received His Holiness' thanks 'for the aid Argentina has given the war-stricken nations of Europe, and for Argentina's collaboration in the relief work of the Pontifical Commission'. However, 'the Pope, although occasionally permitting photographs of himself with distinguished visitors, did not do so on this occasion'.[12]

In point of fact, the Vatican was engaged at this time in the delicate diplomatic mission of finding countries willing to accept European refugees in the post-war period, including in some cases those whose wartime activities might make them susceptible to accusations of war crimes, and the fact that Argentina became a source of financial assistance and potential exile for some of those refugees made the Holy See willing to give a cordial reception to Perón's envoy and to Eva Perón. This was certainly the gloss placed on Evita's visit by one Vatican official, who stated:

> that he did not believe any subjects of political importance had been touched on seriously at the Papal audience.... He gave the impression that good care had been taken to make this part of the visit successful from the Argentine point of view. In view of Vatican interest in Argentine assistance as a supplier of relief to Europe and a receiver of displaced persons, it is not surprising that the Vatican should have received in such good part the Argentine effort to dramatize and intensify its good relations with the Vatican.[13]

Among the displaced persons who the Vatican was seeking to place in the period were former Nazis and war criminals, although it may have been unaware of the full extent that it served people who had played a significant role in the Holocaust and other major war crimes. Be that as it may, a not inconsiderable number of those criminals found their way to Argentina, including Adolf Eichmann and others such as Erich Priebke, who were later extradited. This was to give rise to the allegation that Perón and Evita were pro-Nazi, or that they had enriched themselves by selling passports to former Nazis. It is fairly certain that Evita's visit to the Vatican resulted in the acceptance of a long list of refugees which included war criminals such as the Croat Anke Pavelic.[14]

While it is implausible to see this as a sign of true Nazi convictions, this is not to suggest either that Perón would have been overly perturbed: unscrupulous and devoid of ideology, he would probably have had few strong feelings either way. At the same time, if Argentina became a preferred haven for Nazis, this was due not only to its open door, but to its large German-trained military community and the presence of a sincerely pro-Nazi current which made it a welcoming refuge. (Some insight into the Catholic Church's own attitude with respect to Nazi and Croatian Uztachi refugees may be gained from the fact that, when Eichmann was kidnapped from his Buenos Aires refuge in 1960 by Israeli agents, Argentine Cardinal Primate Antonio Caggiano protested that Eichmann had sought refuge in Argentina and deserved Christian pardon.[15])

VOTES FOR WOMEN

In September 1947, the law giving Argentine women the right to vote was promulgated, after being adopted by Congress without undue disagreement. Some 20 similar bills had been presented in the preceding 20 years, without generating strong support.[16] However, the timing of the initiative in 1947 was more propitious, in both regional and national terms. Women were granted the vote in most Latin American countries between 1946 and 1952, and it was natural that this should also be the case in Argentina. However, in that particular case, the issue was also an obvious one for both Evita and Perón to take up. Evita was certainly not a feminist, and may have felt that activism on behalf of the rights of the poor and oppressed as a group was more vital than on behalf of women alone, though they were among the most poor and oppressed of all. However, in February 1947 she had made a radio speech calling for women's suffrage and periodically returned to this issue. For Perón, the question of women's suffrage offered obvious advantages, since it presented the chance to double the voting population at a stroke, with a reasonable possibility that a large number of those new voters would favour the party which had given them the vote.

The granting of the vote for women opened the possibility for new political organization, with the creation of the Women's Peronist Party, as an entity separate from the regular men's party. The Women's Party was formed in 1949, with Evita as its leader, and its initial activists were a group of women largely inexperienced in politics. This made it even more dependent on the government apparatus than its masculine counterpart, and at the same time more easily moulded in the government image. The Women's Peronist Party formed a series of local delegations in electoral districts throughout the country, with paid delegates commanding the local level and the wives of provincial governors usually being named as head of the provincial party. While Evita, not Perón, was its formal head, the party was arguably something of an anomaly among her functions, not least because she was not a woman at her happiest in the company of other women, but also because she basically disapproved of political activity by women, who in her view were meant to take care of their families and vote for Perón.

THE EVA PERÓN FOUNDATION

The function which unquestionably did become Evita's principal passion came into formal being in mid-1948. In July of that year, the Eva Perón Foundation received legal recognition and became the formal face of its founder's social welfare activities. The Foundation was of course in direct competition with the more traditional forms of charity practised by the *Sociedad de Beneficencia*, an elite body organized under Church auspices, which had been intervened in by the government in July 1946 when it refused to accept the new first lady as its president. The Foundation was by no means an anti-religious body: Hernán Benítez was appointed its spiritual adviser, and ensured it had a staff of priests and nuns to cater to the spiritual needs of its clients. However, it did explicitly reject the Church's concept of 'charity' in favour of 'social justice'. Moreover, it was able to dispense assistance far more lavishly than the Church (though its methods were in practice often virtually indistinguishable from the 'charity' it rejected),

Figure 8. Perón and Evita, 17 October 1951 (Wikipedia, National Archive)

and it used its largesse to inculcate Peronism where the Church had used its charitable institutions to inculcate religion.

The Foundation, launched with a modest contribution of 10,000 pesos from Evita herself, came to receive funding unheard of for an ostensibly private foundation. It received public funds, private donations (some of them less than voluntary, such as the requirement that trade union members should contribute one day's wages per year, or the donations in cash and kind made by companies threatened with official inspection, fines and possible closure if they failed to 'donate') and semi-public funds such as inheritance taxes and fines collected by the government, a percentage of the taxes imposed on the lottery and gambling operations, and properties which came into state hands due to lack of legal heirs. No official budget or records of income were ever published, leading to widespread allegations of corruption and whispers that much of the money ended up in a numbered Swiss bank account held by the first couple. However, despite the lack of tidy accounting practices, in general it would appear that the funds were administered honestly, if somewhat haphazardly. That much of the fortune that entered the Foundation may have been squandered is another issue, but there is little doubt that the vast majority of the funds went to the works for which they were intended.[17]

Evita herself attended to petitioners every day, often well into the night. The petitions she heard, and the solutions offered, were wide-ranging and extended from requests for a football or a bicycle, a sewing machine, a mattress, to medicines, a house, a job, false teeth, a community centre. At the same time, the Foundation undertook much larger-scale works, constructing schools, housing complexes, hospitals, the Children's City near La Plata (a scale replica of a town for children, still open to visitors), orphanages, shelters for the elderly, nursing schools, hostels for working women and single mothers. All of these facilities offered a level of comfort and elegance fit for the oligarchy, and far beyond the spartan conditions which the wealthy ladies of the *Sociedad de Beneficiencia* had thought suitable for working women and orphans. In addition, the Foundation undertook larger-scale but lower-cost activities such as delivering a bottle of cider and fruit cake to virtually every family in the country at New Year's (decorated with a photo and greeting from the first couple).

The amount spent on giving luxury to the poor was decried by many, with Evita's detractors delighting in stories such as the version that slum dwellers given new homes by the Foundation had torn up the parquet floors to use as firewood. However, what the Foundation unquestionably failed to do (as traditional charitable institutions had also failed to do) was to change the social conditions which generated poverty, ignorance, unprotected working women, abandoned children and the need for a paternalistic body such as the Foundation. In fact, as in the case of the charities it despised, this was not the real aim of the Foundation, as its founder had a boundless and sincere desire to aid the poor, but no strategy aimed at reducing poverty rather than sporadically alleviating it.

Another important aspect of the Foundation, both for and against, was that it changed the requirements for the receipt of charity. Whereas Evita had no qualms about meddling in people's lives, she sought not to humiliate: thus, to receive assistance, it was no longer necessary to be inspected for clean nails and head lice. However, while petitioners could be dirty and still considered respectable, there was a new requirement: they were supposed to be loyal to Perón.

Although the Foundation spent huge sums on projects which did not leave a lasting effect (not least, it must be said, because many of its hospitals, schools and other institutions were closed down when Perón was overthrown in 1955), it also contributed to the services available to the poor through the establishment of well-equipped hospitals and schools, the training of nurses and teachers, and also through small-scale practical aid. The daughter of a working woman who had supported her five children with her sewing machine, Evita knew the practical requirements of those who needed a means to feed and clothe themselves, and frequently gave her petitioners the tools they needed for that purpose. Such a large-scale operation, and the personal intervention of the first lady, was arguably not necessary to distribute sewing machines, but the personal touch was doubtless necessary for both Evita and her devotees, demonstrating her personal concern for each one and maintaining the personal nature of a government which claimed to represent and work for the people. Populist and socially compassionate, like the image of the government itself, the Foundation served to bring the mass ethic of Peronism down to the individual level, carrying the emotion of belonging to a mass movement to its most personal expression.

The wide acceptance of such an interventionist state, however paternalistic, and the need for a first couple who acted as the wise and loving parents of a nation may be difficult to understand from outside. However, it must be borne in mind that the rather reactionary Catholic culture in Argentina had long since inculcated the notion that the receipt of charity and care from one's superiors was right and proper, representing both noblesse oblige and the right of the poor to receive alms. Although the Peronist message was that the government practised social justice and not charity, which was frowned upon, in practice the message was likewise that the people should be the passive and grateful recipients of what the mighty chose to bestow. From that point of view, this was the first government to honour its obligation to bestow, and was therefore considered a paragon by many. At the same time, the notion of a protector (*caudillo*) was in general commonly accepted, and the fact that that patron should have reached the highest office in the land without forgetting his clients below was also considered cause for celebration. (At the same time, the continuation of the social relation in which the patron bestowed and the client received was a two-edged sword for the government: Perón himself would become frustrated at the lack of initiative of a people to whom, according to his view, he had given the tools to become more independent.)

Similarly, personalism was and is always a predominant character-istic of Argentine government, and thus in this case was not consid-ered especially worthy of comment, except by those who specifically objected to the person of Perón or Evita. On the contrary, the high level of personalism inherent in Peronism had much to do with its enduring appeal: although social justice was an attractive idea, it is generally easier for people to adhere to a person than to a system, or to feel loyalty to a specific leader rather than to more abstract ideals.

THE 1951 ELECTIONS

By 1951, although the economic situation was deteriorating and the voice of protest could sometimes be heard even within the trade unions, via a series of strikes, Perón had effectively no real opposi-tion in Argentina, with political parties stifled and a still high level of support for the regime. In July of that year, a law was passed bringing forward the new general elections from early 1952 to 11 November 1951, a short period giving the opposition little chance to prepare a campaign. Another twist to the presidential elections also emerged in August, when it was announced that the CGT had called an open fo-rum for 22 August to promote the candidacy of Evita as vice-president. This would undoubtedly have been the culmination of her meteoric political trajectory, and a fitting symbol of the new role women were to play in the elections. (Perón himself was to remark, with excep-tional prescience, that he had won the first elections with the men and would win the second elections with the women, and the third with the children.) It is not at all clear that Perón himself was in agreement with this proposal, and it is certain that it was completely unacceptable to the armed forces. However, in reality the question was academic: by August 1951, Evita was gravely, and increasingly visibly ill, probably another motive for the early presidential elections. There was no possibility that she could have been vice-president, even if all other factors had been in favour.

The first signs of the uterine cancer which would kill Evita had supposedly been noted in January 1950, when she had an emergency appendectomy. Whether or not she was aware of the nature of her illness in 1950 and 1951 is not clear, although by August 1951 Perón certainly knew. This, and the equally implacable opposition of the armed forces to her candidacy, makes it virtually certain that he never harboured any illusion that she could become vice-president, although he did depend on her presence in the electoral campaign.

A general strike was declared for 22 August, and free transport laid on to bring in workers from all over the country for the public forum which was to take place in front of the Ministry of Public Works, with the aim of confirming Evita's candidacy. The demonstration, which far surpassed government expectations, was estimated to have gathered 2 million people. When the ceremonies began, Perón and CGT leader José Espejo were alone on the platform, until the insistence of the multitude brought Evita to the stand. Arguably, this was one of the few times in her life when she did not know how to proceed, apparently pressured by Perón to reject the vice-presidential nomination but faced with a multitude calling for her immediate acceptance. Her speech, one of the peak moments in Peronist mythology, was one of the most impassioned moments of an always passionate speaker, although initially she evaded giving any reply to the central question of her candidacy. Espejo announced that the forum would be suspended until the following day, but the crowd refused to move until Evita had responded, leading to an extraordinary dialogue (only comparable to that between Perón and the crowd on 17 October), in which she begged to be allowed four days to consider her position and the crowd demanded immediate acceptance. Meanwhile, Perón ordered them to disperse, to no effect, and it became increasingly clear that the situation was out of control. After seeking to evade the question, saying 'I am not giving up my place in the struggle, but only giving up the honours', she was understood to have said 'I will do what the people want' and the crowd finally dispersed, content in the belief that she had accepted.[18]

As a result, on 27 August, the Peronist Party announced that it had designated Perón and Evita as its presidential and vice-presidential candidates, making it necessary to resolve the question urgently and finally. On 31 August, Evita broadcast a short, tragic and emotionally charged radio message, communicating her 'irrevocable and definitive' decision to not stand, stating firmly that this was a personal decision responding to her sole ambition to go down in history as the

Figure 9. Funeral of Evita (Wikipedia, *Caras y Caretas*)

woman at the side of Perón, who dedicated her life to the people.[19]
Thereafter 31 August became known as 'renunciation day', while rumours multiplied over the real reason for her decision, including illness, threats by the armed forces and, most probably, the fact that
Perón had nothing to gain by imposing his wife's candidacy. The
aged and ailing Hortensio Quijano was prevailed upon to stand again
as vice-president (although he would die before the inauguration in
1952), and the presidential formula was thus concluded.

The short campaign was marked primarily by two major incidents.
One was a coup attempt on 28 September, led by General Benjamín
Menéndez, which attracted minimal support within the armed forces
and was quickly quashed, although it provided substantial fodder for
electoral propaganda. The other was the collapse of Evita, who had
been confined to bed four days previously. After the coup attempt, the
first public acknowledgement of her illness was made by the government press office, although it was described as anaemia rather than
cancer, and needing a long period of treatment and rest. Despite her
illness, the day after the uprising she summoned members of the
CGT to her bedside and gave them money from the Foundation to
buy weapons in order to form armed workers' militias to defend the
government.

On 17 October 1951, Evita made her first public appearance since the 22 August forum, receiving from her husband the Grand Peronist Medal on the balcony of the Casa Rosada. Visibly ill and profoundly moved, her speech that day was again one of the peak moments in her extraordinary relationship with her public. In addition to a passionate call for those assembled to shout 'My life for Perón' in unison for a full minute, responded to by the crowd with equal passion, the speech was clearly a farewell, as both she and her listeners knew, and tears were shed abundantly on both sides. It was also arguably the only moment in which Perón was unable to conceal his emotion in public. As though she were already dead, the government declared that 18 October would be Santa Evita Day.

The Radicals had chosen Ricardo Balbín as their presidential candidate, seconded by Arturo Frondizi, and presented a platform showing few differences from that of the ruling party. The Radicals were severely hampered in their campaign by the fact that radio stations refused to sell them air time and only the newspaper *La Nación* covered their campaign to a limited extent. The police broke up various political rallies and the Socialist candidate, Alfredo Palacios, was jailed after the coup attempt. The government would again later claim that the elections had been clean, which they arguably were in the technical sense, although the fact that the opposition was not allowed to campaign makes the claim slightly risible. The efforts by the government to block the opposition campaign were undemocratic and clumsy, and also seem to have been unnecessary, given continuing high levels of support for Perón and the fact that the public illness of Evita was far more dramatic a vote-getter than anything the Radicals could have offered even had they been absolutely free to conduct an all-out media onslaught. (The exaggerated need of the Peronists to have absolute, rather than majority, support, frequently led them to go a step too far, with negative consequences. Enormous popular support, genuine devotion to Evita and a loyal voter base made it entirely unnecessary for the propagandists to impose Perón and Evita, the Twenty Truths of Justicialismo and the Peronist Doctrine on old and young alike, and the absolute insistence on total 'Peronization' would only become an effective propaganda tool for the opposition, without either increasing genuine support or generating new support among the government's detractors.)

On 6 November, five days before the elections, Evita had emergency surgery, apparently without her being informed of her condition. On the 11th, a ballot box was brought to her sick bed to allow her to vote for the first time, a move requiring a special law to be adopted by Congress to allow for an exception to electoral laws.

The results of the elections were unsurprising, with 4.7 million votes for Perón and 2.4 million votes for Balbín, while the Senate was 100 per cent controlled by the Peronists and the Radicals achieved only 12 seats in the Lower House. There were now virtually no visible impediments to Perón's government, except an overall exhaustion of the model and its leaders which would make it increasingly difficult for that government to maintain itself in operation. It could be said that many of Perón's greatest achievements had occurred before he became president, while Evita, Peronism's most sincere and impassioned (if also its most violent) exponent during his government, was fading away.

8 The Death of Evita and the Fall of Perón

The last months of Perón's administration and his second inauguration were marked above all by the painful and public last illness of
Evita. In October 1951, Evita's ghost-written autobiography, *La razón
de mi vida*, had been published and was shortly to become required
reading for all school children. The book represented a blend of Evita's
genuine feelings, always expressed in somewhat melodramatic style
(the description in the book of her first meeting with Perón as 'her
wonderful day' rings true), and the out-of-control propaganda machine which was no longer content to make Perón and Evita appear
great political leaders, but was virtually turning them into religious
icons. The book became a bestseller, not only due to political exigencies, but also due to Evita's illness; the resistance it generated is
illustrated by the fact that its publisher, Peuser, was the target of a
bomb on 3 November 1951, even as Evita herself was hospitalized for
cancer surgery.

The period between the November 1951 elections and Perón's second inauguration on 4 June 1952 was marked by another coup attempt
on 2 February 1952, the death of Vice-President Quijano in April and
a rising economic crisis spurred by a post-1948 decline in GDP, the
high cost of imports as a result of the Korean War, a drought which
hit agricultural production at home and the effects of rising domestic food consumption on prices and exports. None of these events
attracted nearly as much attention as the health of Evita, not even
the drastic austerity programme announced by the government on

18 February, including cuts in public spending and a two-year freeze on prices and wages. Beef and white bread consumption were also curtailed, in a country where these formed the staple of even poorer people's diets. However, public spending cuts proved recessionary and untenable for a government for which public-sector employment was a key source of support; as a result, high inflation and the printing of money (and the use of supposedly untouchable resources such as pension funds) became key to financing the public deficit, not for the last time. In this respect, the illness of Evita was a blessing for the government, as it distracted public opinion and possible protests from these alarming developments, which indicated that the fiesta of Peronism was over. Her appearance on the balcony of the Casa Rosada on 1 May, when she received the Grand Peronist Medal, reconfirmed the suspicion that little time was left for the most beloved and detested figure in Argentina.

On her 33rd birthday, 7 May 1952, Evita was named 'Spiritual Leader of the Nation' by Congress though, in theory, the Church had jurisdiction over spiritual matters. Thereafter, her only public appearance occurred on 4 June, when she insisted on participating in Perón's second inauguration, aided by heavy doses of pain killers. Although Perón was widely accused of having cruelly exploited her by obliging her to participate in the ceremonies, there is no doubt that she would have refused to be left out, in particular since she herself was also aware at this stage that she had no more time to make public appearances. After the inauguration, she was never to leave her bedroom in the presidential residence again, dedicating her lucid moments to helping to design her future monument, which she wanted to resemble Napoleon's tomb, and which was never constructed.

A week before her death, Evita entered into a coma and Dr. Pedro Ara, a Spanish embalmer, was summarily brought to the residence with the intention of embalming her body to be placed on display in the future tomb. The crisis passed, however, and the wait for death continued. On the last Sunday before her death, 20 July, Father Hernán Benítez preached before a mass gathering in central Buenos Aires, aiming to prepare the public for the inevitable; the radios in the presidential residence were cut so that Evita could not hear the broadcast of the sermon. Her state, and the state of the nation, was so desperate that even many who were not government supporters came to pay their respects or to offer prayers. During her last week, scores of people gathered permanently before the residence to pray, offering a wide range of religious objects and pledges for the purpose of finding a miracle cure. The miracle did not occur, and on 26 July, Father Benitez gave last rites to the again comatose Evita, and Dr. Ara was again summoned to begin preliminary embalming proceedings. That night, it was officially announced that the Spiritual Leader of the Nation had entered immortality at 20:25.

The 'necrological bacchanale' unleashed by her death brought forth further verbal excesses, naming her Martyr of Labour, the Joan of Arc of America, the Standard-Bearer of the Suffering and so on. Moves were made to seek her canonization. Her embalmed body was placed on public display for some days at the CGT's headquarters, while the public queued for long hours in the persistent rain to pay its respects to 'the Guiding Star of the People'. The city was deluged with floral offerings, and an estimated 65,000 people per day filed past the coffin until the wake was abruptly called off on 8 August, due to Dr. Ara's fears that the body could be damaged if the embalming process were not completed. The final funeral service was held at Congress the following day, with some 2 million people gathered in the plaza outside, before the body was returned to the CGT building for Ara to continue his embalming work. As in other cases in which the government was unwilling to trust its genuine support base entirely, the funeral became an excuse for obligatory mourning and public employees and students were in some cases obliged to participate in the rites, again giving the opposition the chance to claim that the mourning was a question of obeying orders rather than genuine emotion. However, there is no doubt that genuine grief ran high among millions of Argentines who mourned the loss of an idol, a protector and a friend.

The funeral, and the outpouring of public grief which surrounded it, was arguably more similar to the death of Princess Diana nearly a half century later than to any other event in living memory. Like the death of Diana, the death of Evita involved a beloved figure who had been so much in the public eye, and had been taken to heart by so many millions, that it seemed to many to be the death of a close friend or relative. At the same time, she was a person so famous and so fabled that she appeared to be untouchable, making her death more incredible. Also, like the death of Diana, the death of Evita was a poignant and emotive event which moved even many who had not expected to feel a sentimental reaction. With the exception of her (numerous) avowed enemies, many who had never been admirers of Evita suddenly felt themselves jolted by the high level of real public emotion, on the death of someone who had represented part of their lives for some years. Admirers of both Evita and Diana would doubtless dislike the comparison, feeling that one was unworthy of comparison with the other, but by the time of their deaths both had reached quasi-sainthood in the eyes of many admirers, which their youth, beauty and glamour enhanced, as well as their early death.

REPRESSION, AUSTERITY AND DECLINE

Following Evita's death, Juan Duarte (who during his sister's lifetime had used her protection and his position as the president's secretary to receive bribes and to become involved in a number of questionable business dealings to support his playboy lifestyle) became the subject of allegations of corruption, relating to the shortage of meat and spec-ulation with beef stocks, and was investigated by a team of military officers. Duarte was one of a number of close collaborators of the presi-dent alleged to be using their positions for corrupt purposes, and Perón announced in a violent radio speech at the beginning of April 1953 that investigations would be carried out and all those found guilty of corruption severely punished. On 6 April 1953, Duarte resigned as the president's secretary, and three days later his dead body was found with an apparent suicide note. Again, rumour and speculation were rampant, with many (including his mother and sisters) not believing the death to be a suicide. Others claimed that he was seriously ill with syphilis, causing him to kill himself, while after the 1955 coup it was alleged that the calibre of the bullet in his head did not match that of the gun found in his hand.

The possibility that Perón might have ordered his death seems highly unlikely, given his tendency to silence or send into exile those who proved embarrassing, rather than to kill them. However, the pos-sibility that others might have thought Duarte's death beneficial for the government is not entirely unrealistic (though given the probable genuineness of the suicide note and the lack of signs of struggle or vi-olence about the body, any outside intervention probably would have taken the form of pressure to commit suicide, rather than a third party actually pulling the trigger). In fact, the truth about Juan Duarte's death was never entirely resolved and remains obscure, although the disappearance of another person whose presence was inconvenient for the government was ominous and appeared as a sign of things to come.[1] More fortunate, but still a victim of political death, was Domingo Mercante, once considered Perón's probable successor, who was expelled from the Peronist Party at the end of April 1953 on the grounds of disloyalty and lack of ethics. Other former Evita allies such as Lower House leader Héctor Cámpora and CGT Secretary General José Espejo also disappeared from public life during this period.

Another element of Peronism which disappeared during this period was the personal contact with its followers supplied by Evita. Although Perón initially announced that he would take her place at the Eva Perón Foundation on some afternoons, personally receiving visitors and hearing their petitions, this unrealistic idea was, unsurprisingly, short-lived. This role had been created by Evita and was now part of the package of government. As Perón could not fill this role (and probably did not relish the thought of doing so anyway), there was no one who could replace Evita in that unique function, and the relationship between the government and the people became more distant. Although, for his supporters, Perón and his movement continued to be the subject of affection and gratitude, the personal element which had formed a unique component of that relationship was weakened.

A further example of the violence and rising repression which marked the decadence of the Perón government occurred on 15 April 1953, when two bombs exploded, killing five people, near the packed Plaza de Mayo where Perón was making a speech about his anti-inflation plan. The speech rapidly degenerated into a violent call for violent response to the explosions, after which right-wing groups present in the Plaza de Mayo attacked and burned the Socialist headquarters and their newspaper, *La Vanguardia*, as well as the local headquarters of the Radicals and the National Democratic Party and the aristocratic Jockey Club. Neither police nor firemen answered calls for help from the institutions under siege. Following the attacks, which did not produce deaths, prominent members of the targeted opposition parties were imprisoned, being released only in August when the government was seeking to improve relations with the USA. The authoritarianism of which the opposition had frequently complained was becoming dangerously more real.

The year 1953 also marked Perón's first major forays into international relations, in part due to the worsening economic situation which made new foreign capital necessary. In the case of Latin America, Perón made his first foreign visit, to Chile, which was reciprocated by Chilean President Carlos Ibáñez mid-year, while he also made considerable efforts to court the USA. The Chilean visit formed part of the Peronist international strategy of regional integration, with Perón interested in forming an economic bloc with Chile and Brazil in particular, similar to the eventual Mercosur. In this respect, he was unusually far-sighted, as the notion of regional economic integration was not yet widely imagined. However, his irrepressible desire to push Peronist Argentina as the principal power and political reference point for that united Southern Cone was a stumbling block to any real progress, as was resistance by President Getulio Vargas in Brazil and generally poor Argentine–Brazilian relations. During 1953 and 1954, however, treaties were signed with Chile, Ecuador, Bolivia, Nicaragua and Paraguay to reduce trade barriers and take steps towards forming an economic union.

In the case of the USA, whose ambassador Albert Nufer had a cordial relationship with Perón, the government took all possible steps to welcome Milton Eisenhower in April. A month earlier, Perón had announced a draft law to favour foreign investments, facilitating the repatriation of capital and profits by investors, and after Eisenhower's visit, he agreed to lift restrictions on US publications circulating in Argentina. If the moves served to attract more US businessmen to Argentina, they failed to create a warm relationship with Washington, and provided a new front on which the president, formerly nationalistic and anti-imperialist in his rhetoric, could be attacked by his enemies – who were increasing in number. The only important contract reached under the new foreign investments law, an agreement with Standard Oil to exploit oil areas in Santa Cruz and sell oil production to state oil company YPF, was not signed until April 1955, and offered further ammunition for the political opposition who accused Perón of selling the country's oil reserves. (In reality, Perón was a Latin American leader who, like many of his colleagues, saw genuine attempts to foster independent economic development founder on the rock of US dominance in the region. This forced them to accommodate their positions in order to improve relations with the USA, even as those relations undermined their position at home by leaving them open to charges that they were Yankee lackeys, or 'sepoys', one of Perón's own favourite terms of abuse.)[2]

The second Five-Year Plan, announced by the government in December 1952 for the period 1953–7, also provided grist for the opposition's mill, as it maintained the previous year's anti-inflation measures including wage and price controls. Although real wages had fallen between 1949 and 1952, they were still nearly 50 per cent above 1943 levels, implying that the Five-Year Plan was not an unbearable burden for the working classes, despite the fact that their purchasing power was reduced. The problem was not that the working classes received a smaller portion of resources, but rather that these resources themselves were shrinking, and if they could not be made to grow in the longer term, there would be no solid basis to maintain the gains of the average working-class Argentine. The Plan also placed far greater emphasis on agriculture, as well as support and incentives for major companies able to carry out important investments, rather than the earlier emphasis on supporting the workforce, and increased the focus on the role of private enterprise in economic development.

As controversial as the plan was, by the time of Perón's overthrow the economic measures taken had succeeded in improving the economic picture, reducing inflation and the trade deficit and boosting real wages, despite a drought which put paid to the plan to increase agricultural production. At the same time, the announcement in 1954 that the government would receive a 60 million dollar loan from the US Eximbank to buy equipment for the installation of steel mills implied that the economy was recovering. Due to the economic improvements apparent at the time of the 1955 coup, many Peronists (and even the less convinced) clung to the belief that their leader's economic policies would have been able to bring the country out of crisis, increasing support for his eventual return. His overthrow made it impossible to say with precision whether the recovery would have endured or not.

THE CHURCH–STATE CONFLICT

The precise reasons for the rapid decline in relations between Perón's government and the Catholic Church – later widely seen as the main source of his downfall – are difficult to determine, and the decline appears to have been accelerated by a number of relatively minor issues rather than by any one major crisis. Perón was the first to make expressly combative gestures, at least in public, which made him appear the aggressor. Some of the impetus may have come from elsewhere, from Cabinet ministers or others seeking influence. Pablo Marsal, for instance, indicated that the proposed canonization of Eva Perón – one of the many initiatives which offended Catholic opinion – was instigated not by Perón but by minions seeking favour.[3] The final responsibility for any bad judgement exercised, however, lay with Perón as head of an increasingly verticalist administration.

From the perspective of the Catholic hierarchy, there were already reasons for disquiet, again stemming from the ever-increasing emphasis on the Organized Community. These included the threat to private property implicit in the 1949 constitution, and provisions of the second Five-Year Plan. These called for greater state involvement with the family unit and defined the basic objective of education as 'to realize the moral, intellectual and physical formation of the people on the basis of the principles of the *national Peronist doctrine*' (emphasis added).[4] Even the much-vaunted third position between capitalism and communism provoked disquiet in a Church increasingly affected by Cold War politics. However, as late as 1954 Cardinal Caggiano could say:

> it is an undeniable fact that the name of God frequently pronounced by the highest authority of government and by the Chief of the Revolution, has exercised a visible influence.... Today no one is disconcerted when God is spoken of, ... the people and the local and trade union authorities imitate the good example of the First Magistrate of the Nation and name God.[5]

Indeed, Perón continued to name God at frequent intervals well into his second term of office, consecrating the country to the Virgin in December 1953. This made his sudden public antagonism appear all the more startling and inexplicable. The verbal attacks on 'certain priests' – Perón himself never criticized the Church per se – were probably motivated by a sincere belief that the Church had failed to collaborate with Perón's reforms (or had even opposed some of his projects) and by a desire to bring the Church under greater state authority. It is not likely that they were intended to provoke the conflict which occurred, but rather to shock the Church into compliance; the method chosen – an attempt to co-opt some elements and accuse others – was the same as that earlier employed to coerce opposition within political parties and the trade union movement. However, the effect on the Church was to cause it to close ranks and to adopt the role of martyr, while the seemingly unprovoked attack created a certain sympathy for the Church among even the tepid Catholic majority.

The Church question was secondary to other problems which the government faced in its second term. The increasing institutionalization of what had been a fairly fluid political movement, especially with respect to its trade union base, and the economic reverses suffered by Argentina in global terms had led to a decline in the government's dynamism in the social and political context. The lack of new economic initiatives, and the economic decline which curtailed government subsidy of production as well as consumption, led to a drop in support from the industrial bourgeoisie and others (including sections of the working classes) hit by economic austerity, many of whom were already less wedded to (and less favoured by) Peronism than organized labour. Increasing repression of political dissent was used to keep disgruntled sectors in line. Some nationalist sectors, too, were alarmed at Perón's overtures to the USA, necessary in the economic context, which contrasted with his characteristic anti-imperialist rhetoric. In this context, the Church represented a possible structure within which dissent could coalesce, which the opposition parties, in disarray, did not.

Perón may have been aware that the Church was not inherently a very strong institution in Argentina, and thus assumed that it would not be hotly defended. (He even told the US ambassador in June 1955 that he expected the conflict to increase his own popularity.[6]) However, its devotees were drawn largely from the traditional middle classes, 'now on the outside of politics looking in',[7] and from the elites, whose loyalties did not lie with Peronism. As was the case in the 1930s, when sectors of the middle classes had also been politically marginalized, the Church thus became a facade for political activity. In addition, increasing restrictions on religious liberty (one of the few civil liberties thus far unimpaired) resulted in increased Church attendance and greater possibilities for political organization.

CAUSES OF CONFLICT

Perón, according to his own later accounts, attributed the split with
the Church to its political use of religious education and to the
foundation of a Christian Democratic Party (PDC) in July 1954. On
the face of it, the foundation of another opposition party could have
little impact on his own power base, and might have fractured the political opposition still further, especially as electoral coalitions were at
the time prohibited. In addition, the Church remained insistent that
the new party was not 'a Catholic party, . . . but a party with Christian
inspiration, and the Church has nothing to do with this.... It is not
convenient to tie the Church to the vehicle of a party, nor to link a
party to the vehicle of the Church'.[8]

Certainly the Catholic hierarchy had not encouraged the founding
of a Christian Democratic Party in the past, and the party itself claimed
not to oppose Perón, although the fact that it sought to reclaim the
Christian doctrine adopted by Peronism, and that it appeared to provide a possible rallying point for political opposition, was a matter of
concern. Indeed, its manifesto was in some points hard to distinguish
from that of Peronism, not least in its desire for involvement at all
levels of society:

> It would be an illusion and an injustice to try to disregard
> the conquests reached by the working people.... For Chris-
> tian Democracy, the end of society is the common good
> of all.... Thus, all intermediate organizations... should
> be promoted: professional and labour associations, fam-
> ily associations, schools, cultural entities and political
> parties.[9]

The PDC numbered among its political proposals greater industrial development outside Buenos Aires and greater social advantages for rural and non-industrial labour, thereby giving rise to the
fear that it might attract more working-class support than would
existing opposition parties. In addition, the PDC might arguably
have occupied the favourable position which Peronism had occupied in 1946, that is, a new political movement not yet discredited
by past actions or past alliances. The fact that the PDC appeared
to have adopted positions which were previously the province of

Peronism was not the only reason that it appeared to offer competition. Perón's long-term lip service to Catholic social content had led the Vatican to believe, in the past, that Peronism might in the longer term develop into a Christian Democratic party. However, regardless of its inclusion of Catholic social doctrine, Peronism was (and remains) a platform for its leader and not for Catholic activism.

An editorial in the Peronist newspaper *Democracia* on 4 October (apparently written by Perón) attacked the PDC as 'a political manoeuvre', though it claimed that 'some believe that the Church is behind these agents provocateurs'. The article warned that the foundation of a PDC 'would unleash a struggle now non-existent in the religious field, and it would proceed by giant steps toward incidents difficult to foresee in their results between the State and the Church'.[10]

A further point of contention between Perón and the Church (and others) was the foundation of the Peronist Union of Secondary Students (UES). The UES was designed to provide organized activities for adolescent students and to counter anti-Peronist sentiment in secondary schools. Incidentally, it was also in competition with Catholic youth groups, and thus seen as a further challenge to the moral territory of the Church. The UES was widely criticized by the Church and strongly opposed by middle-class parents, who objected to the indoctrination of their children and were concerned both by the morality of this state intervention in the family and by rumours of immoral activities within the UES (fundamentally, that its real function was to make nubile young women available to Perón and members of his government). The rumours, unfounded or otherwise, were doubtless fuelled by increasing press censorship, which added to their speculativeness. Even the verifiable relations between Perón and the girls of the UES, who met at the presidential residence, were considered at best highly undignified for a head of state approaching 60 years of age, and who apparently enjoyed riding scooters with the teenagers as an antidote to the increasingly burdensome routine of exercising presidential power for so many years. (Although other members of the UES have contended that no impropriety took place, one student, 14-year-old Nelly Rivas, would become Perón's mistress, remaining with him until he left Argentina for exile.)

While the controversy over the UES and the foundation of the PDC were seen as provocative, and likely to drain Church support away from Peronism, it is difficult not to assume that the desire to place the Church more solidly within the Organized Community already existed and that the decision had already been taken to attain that end. For example, in mid-1953 new legislation had been adopted introducing increased controls over religious activities in frontier zones and mission areas. While this was ostensibly designed to curb Protestant missionaries, it was also intended 'to curb the exclusive powers and privileges of the Catholic Church in its frontier missions'; an official of the US Embassy noted that 'my own impression ... is that the Decree is aimed primarily at obtaining greater control by the Perón regime over the activities of the Catholic Church in Argentina'.[11] Thus, while the foundation of the PDC and the tensions over the UES provided an excuse for anti-Church rhetoric:

> the character of this government is such that it could not forever live happily alongside another power as influential in temporal affairs as the Catholic Church has been, even though, for a time, this situation was probably beneficial for Peronism. The campaign against the Church was launched at a time and in a manner chosen by the Peronists, when they were not facing other serious domestic or international political pressures.[12]

The 'character of the government' had in fact become increasingly absolute, and in truth could not perhaps continue to tolerate an institution which might challenge its quasi-spiritual authority as well as its political power. Finally, however, it must be noted that Peronism had consistently manifested the need to identify sources of opposition against which flagging support could be rallied and to identify itself – not without reason – as a target of the forces of reaction. In the absence of a coherent political opposition, the Church could be cast in that role, as the institutional representative of anti-Peronist factions. Moreover, because its staunchest adherents were not in general those of Peronism, an attack on the Church appeared unlikely to alienate most sectors still loyal to the government.

The economic decline which curtailed the government's spending on social justice programmes and necessitated its approaches to the USA may to some extent have hastened the campaign against the Church. Given his lack of firm economic power (which remained on the whole in the hands of the famous oligarchy and foreign interests), Perón may have felt weak enough to fear pressure even from the Church, or may have viewed the Church–State conflict as a way of diverting attention from the economy. Equally, intelligence reports may have suggested that clerical opposition was greater than it was: as early as 1952 intelligence reports spoke of clerical provocation of protests; the driver assigned to the Bishop of La Plata was a member of the police intelligence service, and it is reasonable to suppose that other members of the hierarchy were under similar surveillance.[13] Visibly, the conflict was orchestrated by Perón himself. However, it is possible that it may have been exacerbated by the actions of Peronist groups who identified the Church as the representative of the middle and upper classes and who therefore joined in the attacks with enthusiasm.

In late 1954, Perón began a series of attacks against 'certain priests' who were meddling in politics. Complaints of 'clerical infiltration' were alleged to have come from organizations such as the CGT and UES, with Perón casting himself in the role of mediator. In November 1954 he insisted that 'the Church has nothing to do with this affair.... Some have believed that this is a question of the Church.... There is no such thing. This is a political question.... What is the clergy? It is an organization like any other, where there are good, bad and very bad men'.[14] Perón then went on to name a series of priests considered anti-Peronist (most of whom were briefly arrested), and also accused the bishops of Córdoba and Santa Fe of political opposition. 'I've never had any conflict with Christ. Precisely what I am trying to do is defend the doctrine of Christ, which... priests like these have tried to destroy and have been unable to.'[15] He went on to suggest that organizations which acted against the government and popular organizations such as the CGT should have their legal recognition revoked and be charged with illegal association; the legal recognition of the *Acción Católica* was revoked shortly thereafter.

Although Perón declared that the problem was thereupon resolved, it resurfaced at a rally a few days later. The Peronist faithful carried banners demanding legalized divorce and prostitution, and separation of Church and State – hardly demands likely to be raised spontaneously. They listened to speeches again giving Perón a rather Divine nature and indeed suggesting that God was Peronist, rather than Perón being Christian ('if there was a single man who could preach Perón's doctrine before Perón, that man was God, precisely'). The opposition, it was said, 'had decided to conceal themselves under the guise of men of Christ', in order to oppose 'this shining living gospel which is the doctrine of Perón'.[16]

It is notable that not only was the conflict cast in terms of the recalcitrance of 'certain priests', rather than the Church as a whole, but that those priests were described as enemies of 'the people' (and indeed of God) rather than of the government or Perón himself. This line was continued well into 1955: in a May Day speech calling for separation of Church and State, CGT Secretary General Eduardo Vuletich said, '[T]he workers are against the priests not for religious reasons,... but for political and economic reasons'.[17] Perón himself on 13 June referred to the 'clerical oligarchy' as the only sector of that favourite enemy of the people which had not given up the struggle against Peronism.

These verbal assaults were accompanied by a series of new laws undermining the Church's temporal power and its moral concerns. These included the granting of equal legal rights to illegitimate children (September 1954), the closure of the General Direction of Religious Education, the prohibition of public religious demonstrations, the legalization of divorce and prostitution (December 1954), the abolition of religious education in state schools and the General Inspectorate of Religious Education, the derogation of tax exemptions granted to religious institutions and the calling of a referendum on the separation of Church and State (May 1955). Most of these laws could have been justified on their merits, as part of the Peronist programme of social reform – indeed, the legalization of divorce and the recognition of the rights of illegitimate children could be seen as major advances in terms of individual rights – although religious processions were banned due to their potential political overtones and the suppression of religious education was justified on the grounds that the classes were used to promote the PDC and spread anti-government propaganda.

The official response of the hierarchy came in a series of agitated pastoral letters and letters directed to Perón and the education minister. The tone of these letters, however, was more querulous than combative; if anything, their moderation and repeated insistence that Catholics as such should refrain from politics were taken as a sign of submission. However, *Acción Católica* and other lay Catholics were inclined to take a more combative role. With media censorship increasing, the pulpit came to be used as a medium for anti-government propaganda; a number of priests were detained for contempt or disrespect for the government (*desacato*) during the first six months of 1955. Another time-honoured form of propaganda, the pamphlet, was widely used to ridicule the government, to deplore anti-religious legislation and to call on Catholics (and the armed forces) to take action against Perón. Some of 'the Catholics' went further, forming armed commandos ostensibly for self-defence.

In particular, the religious procession became a vehicle for political dissent, and one which attracted many non-Catholics. This was in part because they sympathized with the Church's new position as a victim of repression, although many observers were still ready to point out that the Church had shown little solidarity with other victims of repression and had remained publicly uncritical of the government until it suffered repression itself. However, the Church attracted support once it had been forced into opposition primarily because it represented the only institutional entity within which dissent could be nurtured, and because religious processions initially remained legal while anti-government political demonstrations did not.

THE BEGINNING OF THE END

The first such procession to compete with the government to 'win the street' took place on the Feast of the Immaculate Conception on 8 December 1954. While official statistics are not reliable, photographs indicate that attendance far surpassed that at a rival government-sponsored rally (held in honour of the boxer Pascualito Pérez, returning from an overseas victory). The event which sparked the climax of the Church–State conflict, however, was the Corpus Christi procession on 11 June 1955 (when the protagonist of the government's counter-demonstration was again the unfortunate Pérez). The crowd which attended Mass in the cathedral filled the cathedral and much of the Plaza de Mayo. The sermon was preached by the auxiliary bishop of Buenos Aires, Msgr. Tato.

Following the Mass, the participants marched to Congress, where some sort of assault on the national flag is reported to have occurred. According to the official press, 'the Catholics' burned the flag flying in front of the Congress building. Several Catholic pamphlets accused Interior Minister Angel Borlenghi of having burned the flag. Other sources indicated that the Argentine flag had been torn when demonstrators attempted to replace it with the Papal standard. Another observer noted that no flag appeared to have been burned, though an Argentine flag was torn. However, he recorded, 'whoever is responsible for the flag incident had planned it in advance since both the Papal and Argentine flags involved... were carried to the Plaza Congreso.... No Argentine flags were originally flying'.[18] Clashes apparently occurred between *Acción Católica* and members of the ALN.

Two days later, Msgr. Tato and Msgr. Novoa, the Deacon Canon of Buenos Aires, were relieved of their duties by a decree signed by Perón and his full cabinet. (The last Catholic activist in the government, Commerce Minister Antonio Cafiero, had resigned two months previously over the Church–State issue.) This was later justified by Perón on the grounds that Tato was leading the Catholic opposition and had in fact led the procession to Congress for the purpose of burning it in retribution for the anti-clerical legislation it had recently adopted.[19] The immediate Vatican response was a decree of excommunication encompassing all those who had violated the rights of the Church, including the use of violence and the expulsions, and those who had induced the use of violence. The Vatican still stopped short of naming Perón explicitly in the excommunication order, though its meaning was implicit. The decree was suppressed in Argentina, although it was reproduced as a pamphlet. It was, however, seemingly interpreted as having sparked off the unsuccessful revolt by the Armed Forces on 16 June 1955, carried out under the slogan '*Cristo Vence*'.

The 16 June revolt was to be the bloodiest coup attempt in Argentine history until that time, leaving some 355 dead and 600 wounded, according to official figures. It was planned that an air force squadron would fly over the cathedral, located in the Plaza de Mayo, in honour of Liberator José de San Martín, whose tomb is located there. In the morning, intelligence reports indicated that the naval school ESMA (which became a notorious torture centre in the 1970s) had mutinied and that similar events were occurring at the air force base in Ezeiza. Loyal army troops took up positions to defend the Casa Rosada and Perón left the building and moved to the Ministry of War. Shortly after midday, air force planes supposedly ready to participate in the homage to San Martín began bombing the Plaza de Mayo and Casa

Rosada, with a notable and wanton disregard for the lives of the people gathered in the plaza to watch the expected flyover. Their aim was above all to kill Perón, and they had few scruples about the method chosen, which put hundreds of other lives at risk under the bombs. After the bombing started, members of the navy attacked the Casa Rosada and the Ministry of War, where Perón was concealed in the basement.

The CGT, echoing the events of October 1945, called unionists to come to the Plaza de Mayo to defend the government. On hearing this, Perón countermanded that call, ordering the CGT to ensure that no one was to go to the plaza, now a battlefield, but this second order was too late to prevent groups of workers from heading for the plaza to become cannon fodder. After several hours of carnage, in which the air force and navy rebels managed to massacre hundreds of civilians without coming close to either killing Perón or overthrowing the government, army tanks entered the plaza and ensured that the rebellion was quelled. The air force pilots and a number of civilians involved left for Uruguay, and one of the admirals involved committed suicide. Perón announced at 18:00 that the rebellion had been suppressed and called for calm, but that call was to go unheeded.

It may be that the conflict between Perón and the Church appeared to offer propitious circumstances for the 16 June revolt. There is, however, no evidence that the Church hierarchy was apprised of or acquiesced in the rebellion, and the PDC refused any involvement.[20] Some participants indicated that the revolt had been planned some months in advance, while others indicated that 'it was inspired partly from fear that Perón's policy was leading to communism in Argentina and partly because of the rapidly increasing campaign against the Church'.[21] However, on the night of 16 June, a number of priests were detained and 12 churches burned in Buenos Aires, while the cathedral was sacked and one elderly priest died as a result of a blow to the head. Like the incident of the flag, responsibility for the burnings was disputed. Borlenghi, a former socialist, was again accused by some for authorizing the acts, while Perón himself variously blamed 'communists' and 'the people'.

Eyewitnesses were in no doubt that the burnings were officially sanctioned, as the perpetrators moved freely through a city under state of siege. (Perón himself was initially to accuse the communists, a palpably unrealistic idea given the restrictions imposed on them and the difficulty they would have had in disregarding the state of siege with impunity.) After the fall of Perón, the burnings were openly attributed to the ALN acting under the direction of Perón, who was even accused of having planned the incident in advance.[22] In any case, if Perón had once been looked upon as a Franco-type figure by some Catholic nationalists and officers, the burning of churches was more reminiscent of the Spanish Republicans, for whom neither the armed forces nor the Catholics had any affinity. Despite frequent accusations against Borlenghi and the left within Peronism, and eyewitness claims that members of the ALN clashed both with Borlenghi's supporters and Catholic activists, make it not unreasonable to believe that increasing conflict with the Church may have been stimulated by the ALN as a tactic to discredit the left.

The burnings of the churches represented both the apogee and the end of the Church–State conflict: the issue disappeared overnight from the speeches of both Perón and the opposition. It has been suggested that this represented the influence of the army, which held the balance of power following the coup attempt. Certainly the army was influenced by a Catholic formation and thus viewed the conflict with disquiet. Moreover, from the perspective of some officers the conflict was evidence of leftist influence in the government, and in addition, '[I]t was endangering internal order and damaging Argentina's prestige abroad'.[23] However, the efforts by Perón to make peace with the Church also stemmed from the fact that the events of 16 June left him in an untenable position, one in which he would be forced to either smash opposition or accept the fact that his hours in power were numbered.

In order to avoid provoking further conflict, Perón sought to make peace with the Catholic Church and with opposition parties. Ministers such as Borlenghi, who had been criticized for supposedly fomenting crisis, resigned and, on 5 July, Perón made a speech proposing a truce with opposition parties, whose innocence in the 16 June coup attempt he proclaimed (although radio time was still denied to them). Ten days later, he announced that the Peronist revolution was over, and that the country must now live in peace and in line with constitutional rights and responsibilities, in order to avoid further infringements of civil liberties (which he justified in the past on the grounds that they were inevitable in times of revolution, as a result of which revolution must be temporary in nature).

Figure 10. Crowds celebrating the victory of the coup d'etat in Argentina's
'Revolución Libertadora' (Liberating Revolution) that overthrew Juan Perón
(Wikipedia)

The announcements, rather than pacifying the opposition, gave
the impression that Perón was weak and thus an easier target. In any
case, the truce was brief: on 31 August, it was announced that Perón
was to resign, providing an excuse for another mass meeting in the
Plaza de Mayo in order to 'dissuade' him and to demonstrate the level
of popular support he still enjoyed. His speech on that occasion was
the most violent of his career; apparently improvising in the heat of
the moment, he lost control and called for violence against violence,
saying that 'when one of ours falls, five of theirs will fall'. Although
this call was not immediately answered by those gathered in the plaza,
it represented the beginning of the end, and the beginning of a war
with no quarter, with fear and hatred running high on both sides.

According to some sources, the army was responsible for maintaining Perón in power as a figurehead after the June 1955 coup attempt, on the condition that steps be taken to 'de-Peronize' the government. The army is also said to have demanded the replacement of
the CGT secretary general and of the interior and education ministers

(all of whom resigned within a few weeks of the rebellion), and a 'call for a plebiscite to resolve the State–Church problem without official propaganda, political or religious, of any kind'.[24] Certainly the campaign against the Church was dropped overnight, and no further reference was made to it.

THE COUP D'ÉTAT

The overthrow of Perón in September 1955 was even less attributable to the Church than the June revolt. Eventually, it was the army, supported by various civilian groups, which was to bring down the government. The initiative was to come from troops stationed in Córdoba, where the uprising was led by retired general Eduardo Lonardi. A general on active service, Pedro Aramburu, had reportedly pulled back from the rebellion on the grounds that it had no guarantee of success, although once the uprising started he assumed command of the rebel forces in the west of the country. Army unease was increased by reports that the CGT had proposed to create armed worker militias, a proposal flatly rejected by Perón but which nonetheless appeared as a further threat to be averted.

On Friday, 16 September, troops from the artillery school attacked the infantry school in Córdoba, provoking its surrender a few hours later. Similar uprisings took place in the western provinces of Mendoza and San Juan, while the navy took control of the southern ports of Puerto Madryn and Puerto Belgrano and warships began to move on Buenos Aires. Although government radios continued to announce that the rebellion was under control, by the weekend sporting events had been cancelled and queues formed at markets as citizens sought to provision themselves for the pending crisis. It was announced that Admiral Isaac Rojas, the senior and most rabidly anti-Peronist naval officer involved, had taken command of the fleet, and by Monday, 19 September, the final assault was expected. Some 10,000 loyal troops were sent to Córdoba to defeat the 4,000 rebel troops, and the army advanced on the ports held by the navy.

On 19 September it was announced suddenly that Perón had resigned, urging the army to find a peaceful resolution to the conflict. The resignation, which was ambiguous enough to leave open to interpretation whether it was really a resignation or not, was apparently brought on by reports that the navy planned to destroy the 400 million dollar oil refinery in La Plata, and according to Perón's later statements was intended as a bargaining chip to be used in negotiations with the rebels, rather than as a real resignation. However, on 20 September, the military chiefs of staff agreed with Rojas that Perón and the rest of his government should resign, and that Lonardi should assume the presidency on 22 September. Lonardi, who proposed the slogan 'neither victors nor vanquished', was proclaimed provisional president that night. Perón, meanwhile, without resisting, packed his bags and requested asylum at the Paraguayan Embassy. The Embassy transferred him to the warship *Paraguay*, anchored off Buenos Aires, beginning Perón's 16-year exile. The 'Liberating Revolution' had succeeded.

It may seem improbable that a figure who had enjoyed such wide powers as Juan Domingo Perón should have abandoned the presidency and the country virtually without resistance. In this respect, it could be said that Perón was true to his belief in national unity and order, and wished to avoid the disorder which would surely have arisen from any attempt to put down the rebellion. In any case, his chances of success were questionable, given the increasing weakness of his government and the fact that another rebellion would probably have followed had the September 1955 uprising been crushed.

Perón himself was later to blame the generals and the trade unions who failed to support him, saying that his disillusionment caused him to resign. There may be a grain of truth in this: although Perón spent a decade ensuring that the trade unions were inhibited from independent action or initiative, paradoxically, that lack of initiative appeared to provoke his annoyance on more than one occasion. Basically, it appears likely that he wished to avoid massive bloodshed, and indeed that after nine years in the presidency he was exhausted, bored and disillusioned. In any case, in packing his bags and leaving Argentina without any serious attempt at negotiation, Perón appears to have shown a marked disregard for the future of his supporters – left to the vengeance of those who had reluctantly suffered nine years of Peronist rule – and for the gains made by the working classes with the apparent end of the so-called Peronist revolution.

Apart from the festival of revenge which was to follow, the departure of Perón was sincerely celebrated by many, who saw the (improbable) possibility of a return to democracy – if 'return' is the correct word in a country which had little experience of real democratic practice – and a better future. It was equally sincerely mourned by millions of others. The socialist writer Ernesto Sabato noted that, while he and others were celebrating the fall of Perón in the city of Salta, two servants of the house were weeping in the kitchen, representative of millions of other workers and poor people who had no other protector and who were genuinely devastated both by the fate of their leader and by fears for the future. As noted by Sabato, 'in the Peronist movement there were not just base passions and purely material appetites: there was a genuine spiritual fervour, a para-religious faith in a leader who talked to them as human beings and not as pariahs'.[25]

It could be argued that political malaise, evidenced by a deteriorated economy and an increasingly repressive government, might have been sufficient to produce the natural end of the Peronist cycle, had that cycle been allowed to run its course until the end of the presidential mandate in 1958. This might have allowed the election of a new president (even a new party) who could have governed without necessarily seeking to destroy everything done by the government of Perón. This too might have averted the disastrous return of an aged leader, years later, expected to complete the unfinished cycle. However, the cutting short of the cycle by the 1955 coup left open the belief that, given time, Perón could have resolved the ills of the country, or indeed that he could act as its saviour in the future.

Even had Perón remained in office until 1958 and retired under normal conditions, it is doubtful whether he would have been relegated to the history books and a quiet retirement, given the passions surrounding his movement and the figures of Perón and Evita. In addition to the pragmatic and idealistic reasons for those passions, there was an element of the irrational, inexplicable and unquenchable, similar to the passion the true football fan feels for his club, regardless of whether it is winning or losing. The mirror image of that passion was the hatred of many anti-Peronists, which also combined the pragmatic and idealistic with the irrational, inexplicable and unquenchable. Those two conflicting passions, coupled with the sense that the history of Peronism had been cut short and remained unfinished, would generate tragedy for more than a quarter of a century.

9 Peronism Proscribed

Lonardi and his slogan of 'neither victors nor vanquished' would enjoy only a very short reign: after assuming the provisional presidency
on 22 September, Lonardi was soon considered too moderate by those
aiming to smash Peronism and demonstrate precisely who were the
victors and who the vanquished. Suffering from cancer, he was soon
made to resign in favour of the much harder-line Aramburu, who was
sworn in on 13 November 1955. Although Lonardi had intervened
the provincial governments and dissolved Congress, he proposed to
leave the CGT intact, a move his supporters were not prepared to
accept. Vice-President Admiral Isaac Rojas, a notoriously *revanchiste*
anti-Peronist, would remain as vice-president after the internal coup
which allowed Aramburu to succeed Lonardi.

For the new de facto regime, the overthrow of the government,
prison for its ministers and dissolution of its party were insufficient:
the so-called Liberating Revolution sought to destroy all traces of
Perón and Peronism in the country, to the point of gross waste through
the destruction of important public works. The CGT, which attempted
a general strike on the overthrow of Lonardi, was intervened by the
government, and its leaders who remained in the country were arrested, together with legislators and public functionaries of the former government. The works of the Eva Perón Foundation were closed
down or dismantled, plazas, parks, buildings, monuments or anything
else bearing the name or image of Perón or Eva Perón were remod-
elled and renamed, and their names were literally stricken from school

textbooks. Even the presidential residence, one of the oldest stately homes in Buenos Aires, was torn down. These efforts ran from the absurd (picking out the embroidered name of the Foundation from the linens used at its hospitals or hostels) to the criminal, such as the destruction of hospitals and the halting of work on others which were close to completion.

On 9 March 1956, it was decreed that the very existence of Perón and Peronism was a crime. Newspapers were obliged to refer to Perón as 'the fugitive tyrant', rather than mentioning his name, and reference to Perón, Evita, Peronism or its symbols or discourse was made illegal. The use of the Peronist flag or the party march (*Los muchachos peronistas*, The Peronist Boys) became a crime, as did the use of any type of image of the former president and his wife. Perón himself was tried in absentia for a long series of crimes including having attacked the Catholic religion and burned the flag, as well as rape, and he was stripped of his rank of general on the grounds of having betrayed the honour of the armed forces. A series of books purportedly offering lurid revelations of the regime's crimes were published, combining truth with the wildest possible rumours, which were cited as though they were gospel.[1]

Evita, metaphorically speaking in her grave more than three years before the Liberating Revolution, was to become one of its first and most bizarre victims. At the time of the coup, the embalmer Dr. Pedro Ara was still putting the finishing touches to his master work, which had been residing in a laboratory set up in the CGT headquarters since August 1952 and was planned for permanent display. In December 1955, troops led by Lt. Col. Carlos Moori Koenig of army intelligence entered the building and took charge of Evita's mortal remains (allegedly subjecting them to necrophilic abuse and mutilation). Thereafter, the body of Evita was to become a heavy burden for the de facto government, which did not know what to do with such a powerful symbol of what it was seeking to destroy. Despite its fear that the body would become a rallying point to unite the Peronists, the government was unwilling to destroy it, given that Aramburu was a strict Catholic who could not countenance the burning of a body. For some six months the body was repeatedly moved, always in an unmarked box, and always flowers and candles mysteriously appeared. Paranoia surrounding the corpse, fed by the inexplicable appearance of the flowers and candles, caused one officer with custody over the body to shoot his wife dead in the middle of the night, believing the shadow he saw to be that of a Peronist bent on recovering Evita's mortal remains. The army also refused to hand the body over to Evita's mother, who, with her other daughters, would be arrested and forced to go into exile in Chile. After a spate of rumours as to its fate, the body was despatched to Europe to be buried under the name of Maria Maggi de Magistris in a cemetery in Milan. The body would remain there until 1971, and Evita would thus become one of Argentina's first disappeared (like many other mothers afterward, Evita's mother would die in 1971 without ever learning where her daughter's body was).

Among the Peronists imprisoned by the Aramburu government were a number of loyalist military officers, some of whom were kept under house arrest from early 1956. Among the officers transferred from detention on a naval vessel to house arrest were Generals Juan José Valle and Raúl Tanco. They were shortly to begin planning a counter-coup, with the intention of calling elections and halting the destruction of works of public interest. The uprising led by Valle was not strictly speaking pro-Peronist, although some Peronists supported the movement, but it was interpreted as the first Peronist rebellion against the dictatorship.

The uprising, planned for the night of 9 June 1956, was a fiasco, and all the rebels were quickly captured. What set the Valle rebellion apart from previous uprisings was the fact that the government decided to execute the rebels, rather than simply imprisoning them. The first groups of rebels detained were taken out and shot summarily wherever they happened to be, still on the night of 9 June, while in the Greater Buenos Aires district of José León Suárez a group of imprisoned workers who had not been implicated in the events were also taken to a garbage dump and shot dead. Tanco sought asylum in the Haitian embassy, from which he was removed by force by the army; on the following day the government ordered his return to the embassy, given the international reaction to such a blatant violation of sovereignty and asylum rights.

Valle surrendered himself on 12 June, in an effort to prevent further killings. He was taken to the prison which formerly stood in the Palermo neighbourhood of Buenos Aires and executed by a firing squad on the same night. A total of at least 27 people were executed after the backfired 9 June rebellion, the first time that either civil or military rebellion against the Argentine government had resulted in the firing squad for those involved, as opposed to prison or the widely respected practice of allowing dissidents to leave for exile. It was to be the first in a long and increasingly savage series of acts of bloody repression over the following 25 years, and further deepened the rancour between Peronists and anti-Peronists. It would also initiate the rise of a new generation of combative leaders from within the Peronist movement who, in the absence of Perón, were to be more independent and more willing to fight force with force than any of the movement's figures in the past. Although most anti-government actions were sporadic and small-scale, the clandestine movement would keep Peronism (and anti-Peronism) alive and sustain pressure for its eventual return to power.

In the meantime, Perón had begun a long odyssey through various Latin American exiles, which would eventually end in Spain in 1960. On 3 October, he left for the Paraguay of General Alfredo Stroessner, but departed on 1 November, principally due to pressure applied to Stroessner from Buenos Aires and the fear that he could be the subject of an assassination attempt. Although his destination was ostensibly Nicaragua, the DC-3 in which he was travelling made a stop in Panama, where, after spending the night and making a brief visit to President Ricardo Arias, he announced his desire to remain. He was to stay in Panama for a nine-month period, until President Aramburu's visit to that country for a meeting of Latin American heads of state made his departure diplomatically prudent. It was during this period of Perón's exile that another personality would appear who was to have an important role in the history of Peronism: María Estela Martínez, who would become Perón's third wife and eventually, through an incongruous chain of circumstances, president of Argentina – the first woman president of that or any other republic.

María Estela Martínez was born in La Rioja in February 1931. She was the daughter of a bank employee and a housewife in the provincial capital, who already had five other children. Like Evita, she never studied beyond primary school. When she was still a small child, her family moved to Buenos Aires, where her father died when she was seven and where, in the style of a young middle-class girl of the time, she studied French and piano. She later studied ballet with the intention of becoming a classical dancer. As a young girl, she would

leave her family (with whom she had virtually no further contact) and
would go to live with a spiritist, José Cresto, and his wife Isabel, who
trained her in esoteric practices and the occult, interests which would
affect her strongly. By her early 20s she had found work with a dance
troupe led by one Joe Herald, alternately described as a group of folk
dancers or a cabaret act. Known by the stage name Isabel, in honour
of Cresto's wife, she also failed to stand out in this environment: moderately attractive but without any particular beauty, physical presence
or remarkable physique, she filled a space on the stage and eked out a
living.[2]

Isabel met Perón at Christmas 1955 in Panama, and within a short
time was living in his home. As with so many aspects of Perón's life,
there are many discrepancies over that meeting and how she came
to move almost immediately into the *caudillo*'s household. Some versions suggest that she was presented to him by the former Argentine
ambassador in Panama and that she offered herself as a secretary.
Others claim that she was a spy, introduced by either the Argentine
government or the CIA (and that, indeed, Perón was aware of this),
and that the intimacy of their living arrangements led her gradually
to shift her loyalties to Perón. Yet others, which do not necessarily
contradict the previous version, indicate that she arrived at his door
shortly after their first meeting, saying that she had left Herald's troupe
after being asked to entertain customers, and asking for refuge.[3]

Perón had played by the rules in choosing his first wife when he
was an up-and-coming young officer, and had flouted them outra-
geously in choosing his second, secure in the knowledge that at the
time his power was untouchable. Now in exile and drummed out of
the army, he had no reason whatsoever to try to be respectable in the
eyes of military society, and every reason to choose what appeared to
be a comfortable alternative – and one which could even serve to further annoy his former comrades in arms. However, even while their
living arrangements may have been considered dubious, Isabel was in
many respects more similar to 'Potota' than to Evita. Despite the un-
kind and unfair representation of her as a cabaret dancer of ill repute,
she was in fact a conventionally brought-up, middle-class girl who,
notwithstanding this unconventional relationship, possessed the sort
of education appropriate for a discreet and respectable military wife.
Much contemporary comment remarks on Perón's mistress in exile –
often with some surprise – as a *señorita* and a cultured young lady able

to dance, speak French and play the piano, in line with the conventions of her time.

At the same time, Isabel shared with Evita the more unusual quality of determination in pursuing unconventional ambitions, leaving home at an early age to become a dancer, and subsequently leaving her country alone to do so. This in itself was highly unusual for a young lady of conventional background, and may provide a glimpse of the determination which led her subsequently to pursue the presidency. (Paradoxically, given these rather progressive beginnings, Isabel would appear anachronistic later in her career. Despite being the first woman president of a republic, at a time when Argentine women were rapidly advancing in academic and professional life, Isabel remained a product of an earlier age, with little formal education and an emphasis on social deportment. This image, even in the first woman president, was increasingly outdated at a time when many young women were far more highly educated, and more qualified for public office, than she.)

Isabel would become vice-president of Argentina in 1973, president on Perón's death in 1974, and her reign would see the rise of death squad activities, violence by both the Left and Right and the initial stages of the clandestine detention centres where so many Argentines would disappear. Despite this high profile, she has been an amorphous but controversial figure, with many considering her to be an evildoer deliberately intent on destruction, and others considering her a hapless and somewhat innocent victim of evil forces, chiefly on the unflattering grounds that she was too unintelligent and too incompetent to be evil. Certainly she appears to have lacked full consciousness of the horrendous events which occurred during her regime, or her degree of responsibility in them. When she was questioned by Spanish judge Baltázar Garzón more than 20 years later in connection with his investigations into human rights violations in Argentina, she seemed so little aware of events that he later remarked publicly (sarcastically or not) that she appeared to be autistic. In late 1955, however, she was an unremarkable 24-year-old who passed from a seedy dance troupe to a somewhat seedy exile with the former president, and gave no hint that her future might give rise to such a debate.

In August 1956, Perón and Isabel would leave Panama for Venezuela, then under the dictatorship of General Marcos Pérez Jiménez. There they would continue the frugal lifestyle they had maintained in Panama, apparently at odds with the fortune Perón had supposedly stolen and smuggled out of Argentina. In addition to giving his new protégée her first lessons in politics, Perón was to spend much of his period of exile writing repetitive books filled with self-justification and little factual history, as well as giving frequent interviews to the foreign press. Following the overthrow of Pérez Jiménez, Perón would move to the Dominican Republic in January 1958, where he would lecture local strong man Rafael Trujillo on his failure to adopt suitable social programmes. However, following the Cuban Revolution, when fallen dictator Fulgencio Batista also sought refuge in the Dominican Republic, the political climate became too rarefied for Perón's liking, particularly as the Venezuelan government began to increase the pressure on Trujillo.

Interestingly, revolutionary Cuba was mooted as a possible refuge for Perón, reportedly due to the good offices of the Argentine Cuban Revolutionary hero Ernesto 'Che' Guevara. Although the son of an anti-Peronist middle-class family from Rosario, Guevara, who left Argentina after completing his medical training and had no political trajectory there, had apparently become convinced that Perón represented the closest Argentine approximation to 'national socialism'. At least, he had been persuaded by the leftist Peronist Youth leader John William Cooke that no revolutionary project was feasible in Argentina without Perón. On his recommendation, Fidel Castro extended an invitation to Perón to relocate to Cuba. However, in January 1960, Perón, Isabel and his poodles left for Spain, where they were received coldly by General Francisco Franco but allowed to remain in relative security until 1973. In November 1961, under pressure from the ultraconservative Catholic government, Perón married Isabel after a six-year relationship.

PERONISM: PROSCRIPTION AND MILITANCY

In Argentina, meanwhile, Peronism was proscribed, suppressed and officially non-existent, yet paradoxically it was regaining its strength and combativeness after becoming increasingly sclerotic in the last years of Perón's government. The removal of its leader led to a rise in grass-roots activism and the emergence of new leaders, just as its inception had been a largely fluid and participatory movement. In particular, the curtailing of political activity meant that these figures in general came from the rank-and-file. The years of repression allowed Peronism to assume the mantle of opposition which had always suited it, but which in fact it had never really exercised. It also allowed its leaders to assume responsibility for the movement, in the absence of the father figure who had been its only real decision-maker. This process created a greater maturity and independence among other political activists, which would affect the movement in future.

Also, with the trade union bureaucrats installed by Perón in recent years now imprisoned and the CGT intervened, a new generation of more independent and more militant union leaders would spring up. These would eventually cause headaches both for the military government and for Perón, given the willingness of those leaders to consider the possibility of a 'Peronism without Perón', a concept with little appeal for the *caudillo* himself. This would lead to a series of successful strikes against the regime's economic policies (generally pro-agrarian, elitist and anti-labour), which would result in the loss of millions of workdays and cause the government to try to re-float the CGT as a more moderate interlocutor. This resulted in a split within the CGT, among those willing to reach agreement with the government and the Peronist-run unions, which would withdraw from the CGT and form a separate body, the 62 Organizations.[4]

Economically, too, the government faced continuing, though by no means new, problems that further undermined stability. Throughout the later half of the 1950s and 1960s the economy continued to suffer boom–bust cycles, arguably worsened by the lack of tax or other incentives to improve agricultural competitiveness, and frequent periods of high inflation. Repeated stabilization plans between the 1950s and 1980s had no long-term impact on inflation. While instability represented a deterrent to foreign investment, frequent devaluations, designed to boost exports and curb imports, in practice fostered further inflation, unemployment and declining output. Public spending cuts designed to offset the resulting lower revenues also contributed to repeated recessions. First Lonardi and then Aramburu subscribed to a range of measures to deregulate the economy, including devaluation, spending cuts and a reduction of state intervention, all of which added to economic dislocation without improving competitiveness.

When it became clear in early 1957 that the Aramburu government would be forced to call elections in the relatively near future, a split was formalized in the UCR between the followers of Ricardo Balbín, an unconditional anti-Peronist and supporter of the Aramburu government, and the followers of Arturo Frondizi, more critical of the military government and dedicated to the policies originally followed by Hipólito Yrigoyen. Frondizi's bloc would become the UCRI (Intransigent Radicals), while Balbín's bloc was known as the UCRP (the People's Radicals); both were selected by their respective factions as presidential candidates for the elections held in 1958. It was clear that these elections would scarcely be free and fair, given that the Peronists were strictly proscribed and the electoral majority was thus not represented by any candidate. Seeing the possible advantages of this situation, Frondizi increased his criticism of the de facto government and wooed the working classes, even as Balbín was firmly in favour of the anti-labour economic policies of the military regime.

Frondizi's efforts to reach an accord with Perón's followers were further encouraged by the 28 July 1957 constituent elections for an assembly to reform the constitution yet again. From Venezuela, Perón ordered his followers to cast blank votes, and the blank vote won, with nearly 2,120,000 votes in comparison with 2,117,000 votes for the UCRP and 1,821,000 votes for the UCRI. Once presidential elections were announced for 23 February 1958, Frondizi and his principal political operator, Rogelio Frigerio, began forming close relations with Peronist figures. Although Perón wished to avoid a return to constitutional government which would leave him more marginalized from politics than a repressive de facto regime, he reached a secret agreement to order his followers to vote for Frondizi, in exchange for Frondizi's agreement to adopt Peronism's past economic policies, reform the constitution and to call new elections thereafter. Frondizi was later to deny having signed such an agreement, the content of which he would in any case have been unable to implement in the light of military and other opposition to any return of Peronism.

The announcement that Perón had ordered his supporters to vote against the ruling government stimulated strong criticism of Frondizi's evident agreement with Perón, but did not damage his electoral result: with the support of Peronism, Frondizi received 45 per cent of the votes to Balbín's 29 per cent, while the UCRI won all provincial governorships, all Senate seats and an absolute majority in the Chamber of Deputies. A further 690,000 blank votes were cast, demonstrating that Peronism was still more than a force to be reckoned with.

The main political figure to emerge within the Peronist movement during the period was the leftist John William Cooke, a former legislator who became Perón's authorized representative, while the main trade union leader to appear on the scene was metalworker Augusto Timoteo Vandor. Cooke, imprisoned by the Aramburu regime in the southern prison of Rio Gallegos, escaped to Chile in 1957 with other Peronist prisoners including the businessman Jorge Antonio, ex-CGT leader José Espejo and former Lower House leader Héctor Cámpora. Despite his intelligence and resourcefulness, Cooke's leadership of the proscribed party and its assorted and contentious exile communities dotted throughout Latin America was made virtually impossible by Perón's tendency to communicate, from exile, with a wide range of other figures.

Cooke was further hindered by the fact that his own leftist, non-labour background made him suspect for many traditional Peronists. Cooke would leave Chile for Venezuela in 1958 and share part of Perón's exile in that country and the Dominican Republic, before returning to Argentina under the amnesty announced by Frondizi – then returning to prison when a state of siege was declared in November of that year. From his prison cell, Cooke maintained a long correspondence with Perón, who urged him to lead a campaign of civil disobedience and violence against the Frondizi government in order to force an extension of the amnesty, arguing that Frondizi had not kept his pre-electoral promises. When this failed to achieve the desired effect, Cooke became increasingly marginalized within the party, moving to revolutionary Cuba in 1960 where he died, aged only 48, in 1968. However, he was to have a posthumous ideological influence in the Peronist guerrilla movements of the late 1960s as well as, crucially, defining Perón as a figure of national liberation. At the same time, Perón would make public his pre-election pact with the UCRI, effectively undermining any possibility Frondizi had of maintaining real power and provoking widespread calls for his resignation.

Even as Cooke was losing his power within the fractured movement, Vandor (known as *El Lobo*, the Wolf) was rising rapidly in the trade union sector, becoming known for both his capability as a union leader and for his realist's ability to adjust to the political exigencies of the moment. After having been imprisoned, following the 1955 coup, Vandor had risen to become the leader of the metalworkers' union UOM and a strong voice within the 62 Organizations, which represented Peronist resistance at the trade union level. The unions also put increasing pressure on Frondizi's government, which implemented long-term economic policy goals that offered few short-term benefits. At the same time, the IMF imposed a policy of devaluation and salary cuts in order to try to stabilize an economy which, after a sharp increase in foreign investment in Frondizi's early years, was again floundering. This left the government even more vulnerable to union opposition, despite having ordered a 60 per cent salary increase shortly after taking office in May 1958. Frondizi was further buffeted by the reaction to his announcement that the government had signed oil exploitation contracts with foreign oil companies, despite his famed and virulent opposition to similar moves by Perón five years earlier. These considerations made it impossible for Frondizi to achieve the trade union support he hoped for, despite his 'developmentalist' approach to encouraging heavy industry through state activism, although he lifted the intervention of the CGT and returned it to union control in 1961. The decision to crack down on strike actions marked the end of any rapprochement with the unions.

THE RETURN TO MILITARY INTERVENTION

Caught between the rock of intransigent military and political anti-Peronism and the hard place of the militant trade unions, Frondizi enjoyed little chance of survival. Even that slim chance was further reduced by Guevara's decision to receive Che Guevara on his sole visit to his homeland, and to abstain from the vote to expel Cuba from the Organization of American States in 1961. This came precisely at a time when US-led anti-Cuban fervour ran high and the Argentine military (enthusiastic about the National Security Doctrine propagated by the CIA, which espoused an enhanced role in internal security matters for the armed forces) saw his non-aligned policy as representing a pro-communist stance. Although Argentina broke diplomatic relations with Cuba in February 1962, tensions were only partially reduced. At the same time, measures to appease the trade unions, such as price freezes and sharp wage increases, foundered on the state's parlous fiscal position; an attempt at stabilization through foreign loans, coupled with devaluation, produced hyperinflation and a new recession.

The reduction in tension was not sufficient to allow Frondizi to survive the next blow to his presidency. Gubernatorial and legislative elections were held in March 1962, and Frondizi took the dangerous decision of allowing the Peronists to present candidates, in the hope of re-capturing part of his lost support from that quarter. Although the Peronist party remained proscribed, Peronist candidates were allowed to stand for related parties, in the hope that this would allow for their gradual reincorporation into the electoral process and avert possible future violence. The principal party to present candidates, the Popular Union, included a number of trade unionists, among them textile worker Andrés Framini, a candidate for governor of Buenos Aires province, backed by Vandor. At the rally called to announce Framini's candidacy, it was also announced that Perón would be his candidate for vice-governor, a move probably designed to ensure that the Popular Union was proscribed, rather than to lend Perón's explicit support to Framini. Framini's eventual victory in any case strengthened the position of Vandor, whose support had been crucial, rather than the position of Frondizi, Perón or Framini himself.

Perón's putative candidacy was formally rejected, but the Popular Union was allowed to compete in the elections. The result was worse than Frondizi had expected, with the Peronist candidates receiving 32 per cent of all votes and winning nine governorships and 41 seats in the Lower House, eliminating the UCRI's majority. In an effort to forestall the looming coup d'état, Frondizi announced the intervention of five provinces where Peronist candidates had been elected, a move which lost him popular support and failed to improve his position with the armed forces or the UCRP. On 29 March 1962, Frondizi was placed under arrest on Martín García island, where both Yrigoyen and Perón had been before him. However, for the time being, internal struggles between the so-called legalist and hard-line military factions prevented the imposition of a military government, and Senate President José María Guido assumed the presidency. Guido, widely known as 'poor Guido' during his provisional presidency, had the support of the so-called 'Azules' faction within the army, led by General Juan Carlos Onganía, which favoured a military withdrawal from politics and which prevailed in internal struggles with the 'Colorados' faction, who were violently anti-communist, anti-Peronist and in favour of military dictatorship. However, the splits came to a head after Guido named a constitutionalist officer as secretary of war. Violent skirmishes between the Azules and Colorados at several military bases only served to reinforce the evident helplessness of the civilian government, while Guido's attempts to reduce frictions by compromising over cabinet appointments lost him the support of the Azules.

In the mid-1963 presidential elections, the Popular Union was not permitted to present a presidential candidate, although it was allowed to participate in elections for other offices. The Popular Union was to form a coalition with a range of smaller parties, to be called the National Popular Front, including the Popular Conservative Party, whose leader, Vicente Solano Lima, was chosen by Perón as the coalition's presidential candidate. Frondizi's UCRI chose former Buenos Aires governor Oscar Alende as its candidate, while Balbín's UCRP chose the little-known Córdoba doctor Arturo Illia, to become known as 'the turtle' for his physical appearance and slowness of action. Illia was elected president, with the minimal vote of around 25.0 per cent, while blank votes reached nearly 19.0 per cent, Alende received 16.4 per cent and General Pedro Aramburu, who had formed a new party, received just under 14.0 per cent.

The elderly Illia, who was 73 when he took office in October 1963, was honest, unambitious and undramatic, all of which counted for little in face of the fact that he had a minority in Congress, minimal support among the armed forces or the working classes, and little economic policy. He faced strong opposition from the CGT, led by textile worker José Alonso, which pressed for economic measures to benefit the working classes and began a series of strikes and occupations from the first half of 1964. In addition, discontent was rising in the industrial and agricultural sectors over his lack of dynamic economic policies. The balancing act between the demands of Peronism, to the effect that all limitations on their political activities be lifted, and those of the armed forces and business interests, would have been practically impossible even in more favourable circumstances, and Illia had virtually no real support base to shore him up against the waves of opposition battering him from all sides.

In this unfavourable context for the Argentine government, 'Operation Return' was carried out. An attempt to bring Perón back to Argentina finally came to fruition at the beginning of December 1964. Vandor, whose own power in the movement was increasing rapidly due to his shrewdness and his insistence on maintaining a relatively low profile, played a leading role. (His very power and shrewdness were eventually to be his downfall, as they allowed him to represent a serious competitor for Perón in the possible scenario of 'Peronism without Perón'.) Vandor was in this respect caught in a difficult situation: on the one hand, Perón's return would reduce his own power, while on the other hand, his need to maintain control of the 62 Organizations in the face of a challenge from Framini and others made it necessary for him to lead the year-long efforts to plan Operation Return.

On 2 December 1964, Perón boarded an Iberia flight in Madrid, using a passport issued under a false identity, with long-time Peronist activist Delia Parodi, using a passport which identified her as his wife. They travelled with Vandor, Framini, Jorge Antonio and others, expecting to arrive in Buenos Aires after a stop in Rio de Janeiro. However, on arrival in Rio, the aircraft was surrounded by Brazilian troops, and a member of the Foreign Ministry advised the group that, acting on a request from the Argentine authorities, the Brazilian government would prevent them from travelling on to Buenos Aires. The first attempted return had been a failure, and one which led many, both supporters and detractors, to suppose that Perón's time had passed and that he would be fated to spend the remainder of his life in Madrid. It also encouraged Vandor to persist in his efforts to create a Peronist trade union movement without Perón.

Illia allowed the Peronists to stand in the March 1965 legislative elections; their triumph, by some 3.4 million votes to 2.6 million for the Radicals, disconcerted the armed forces and made Illia's eventual overthrow a virtual certainty. Thereafter, Vandor and his followers would attempt to increase the trade union movement's weight in the Peronist movement. This effort generated opposition both from the politicians blindly loyal to Perón and from the left-wing segments of the party who advocated revolution rather than an attempt to return to the bourgeois political system. Although Perón was obviously unable to travel to Argentina to influence the outcome of internal disputes, he used his unskilled third wife. Isabel was sent as a 'messenger of peace' who would be used by the orthodox Peronists to undermine the position of Vandor and his followers prior to the 1966 elections, in which Vandor had planned to back his own candidates as a further sign of independence. Although Isabel showed no nascent talent for political leadership, and Peronists of all sides paid her lip service,

rather than serious attention, her presence polarized the existing factions within the movement.

Further efforts by Vandor's faction, at a meeting on 21 October
1965, to create a new neo-Peronist political party through internal
elections would represent a serious rupture between Vandor, Perón
and his messenger of peace. Within the trade union movement, a further rupture also occurred, with Vandor remaining as secretary general
of the 62 Organizations and José Alonso becoming leader of a rival
body called the 62 Organizations Standing with Perón, as a result of
which Alonso was ejected from the CGT. Efforts to prevent Vandor's
candidate from winning the governorship in Mendoza included send-
ing Isabel to the province to campaign for his rival, whose victory left
Vandor's political power significantly reduced. Shortly thereafter, in
a new attack from which Vandor escaped unscathed, his close collab-
orator Rosendo García was shot dead at a pizzeria in Avellaneda in
circumstances which were never clarified (although Vandor himself
was accused of responsibility by several versions).

LÓPEZ REGA AND ONGANÍA: THE WARLOCK
AND THE ARGENTINE REVOLUTION

In addition to undermining the 'Peronism without Perón' faction, the
visit of Isabel had two important consequences. The first was her meeting with a former police corporal, José López Rega, who had at one
time served as part of President Perón's police guard, and who apparently prevailed on one of his former military aides, Bernardo Alberte,
to present him to Isabel. The second (at least partially a consequence of
Isabel's activities) was the 28 June 1966 military coup which overthrew
Illia, led by the former 'legalist' General Juan Carlos Onganía. Onganía's previous support for the Illia government made him vulnerable
to attacks from colleagues furious over Illia's tolerance for the Peronist
circus led by Isabel and Vandor, which also undermined the Azules'
approach of seeking a rapprochement with some of the more pliable
trade unionists. Again, Illia had no power base to which he could
turn in the face of military hostility. Moreover, there was a total lack
of support from all other factions of political and economic power,
alarmed as they were by the economic crisis and rampant inflation.

Indeed, members of Congress – notably Peronists elected in 1965 – did everything possible to block Illia's legislative agenda, increasing political paralysis.

López Rega, like Isabel, showed little sign at first sight of being a person who would leave an important mark on his country. An undistinguished record as a police corporal and a frustrated desire to become an opera singer did not mark him out as exceptional. However, his attraction for Isabel stemmed in particular from his strong interest in spiritism, translated into various unintelligible works on the subject. While most others, including Perón, apparently did not take this seriously, Isabel did. When she returned to Madrid in July 1966, she was accompanied by López Rega (also known as Daniel, and later to be known as the Warlock), who would become Perón's valet. Thereafter, his obsession with the occult would become truly sinister, and his influence over those around him would grow, allowing him to play a major role in the greatest tragedy in Argentine history.

In the case of Onganía, it shortly became clear that he was planning a lengthy stay in the presidency, rather than a transition period until new elections could be called. The 'Act of the Argentine Revolution' announced the end of civilian rule, and the military government ceased to be referred to as 'provisional'. This was not universally seen as negative in a country wracked by political instability. The coup, which was widely expected, followed a demand by Illia for the resignation of an army general. Onganía, who had resigned as chief of staff in late 1965, took steps to unite the army while hinting at a more accommodating form of military rule. He initially received the wide range of support that Illia had lacked, including that of Vandor, most of the trade union movement and the Peronist leadership, as well as other political and economic sectors. Vandor attended Onganía's inauguration, and hoped to be able to influence the military government in light of his failure to influence electoral processes.

Onganía, however, proved not to be open to outside influences, being authoritarian, ultra-Catholic, violently opposed to 'subversives' of whatever political tint and determined to stamp out immorality, in part through the prohibition of miniskirts. He also promptly closed Congress, banned political parties and intervened in the national universities, which for the first time experienced systematic repression of students seen as potential Marxists. His economic plan, to be called the Argentine Revolution, was aimed at controlling prices and wages in order to reduce inflation, and at stimulating industry through devaluations and import promotion aimed at bringing in foreign investment. This was to be accompanied by strict measures to ensure 'social peace' and avoid derailment of the economic plan.

Onganía's more active economic policies, carried out by the energetic Economy Minister Adalbert Krieger Vasena, included unpopular but not necessarily erroneous attempts to modernize the economy. These were not always conceived with due thought to their immediate consequences: for example, in attempting to shore up the bankrupt sugar industry in Tucumán province, in the period 1966–1968 11 of the province's sugar mills were closed and production was concentrated in the hands of the largest remaining mills. The government sought to promote alternative industries such as textiles, citrus and sugar-related products such as alcohol, through the use of subsidies and tax exemptions to investors locating industry in the province. However, these industries take time to develop, and are not in any case as labour-intensive as sugar production, thus unemployment in Argentina's most densely populated province increased.

In these policies, it rapidly became clear that Onganía was not open to influence from Vandor or the CGT, and he had no qualms about using draconian measures to squash union protests. A port strike in Buenos Aires led to military intervention and imprisonment of the leaders. Vandor continued to attempt to negotiate with the government, which undermined his position vis-à-vis more militant sectors, including the unions that followed Raimundo Ongaro in forming the rival organization CGTA (CGT of the Argentines), devoted to opposing the regime and supporting Perón's leadership. Repression by the regime, in particular within the universities, also generated a more militant response, and caused some of the more radical elements to move from the city and province of Buenos Aires to provinces such as Córdoba and Tucumán, where at this stage repression was less acute.

Perón himself, from Madrid, encouraged the more extreme sectors of Peronism, and also received and played off representatives of most of the political spectrum against each other, in a bid to retain a grip on the levers of power. Those visitors reportedly included, in late 1966, a disguised Che Guevara, who made a clandestine visit to Madrid to seek (unsuccessfully) Perón's support for Guevara's failed Bolivia campaign.[5] The former president sent a message to the Peronist Youth in 1967 calling for a 'revolution within Peronism' and showing less distaste for violence – as an exile living at a safe distance – than he had when in office. In a political context in which repression of dissent was fiercer than ever, the call was soon answered. Efforts to form a guerrilla movement in the rural north had begun in the early 1960s, while the right-wing Tacuara movement also formed in the period would eventually provide the leaders of the new Peronist guerrillas, including Mario Firmenich, Rodolfo Galimberti and Joe Baxter. The guerrillas were purportedly leftist in orientation, although many came from the falangist Tacuara, influenced by the pro-fascist priest Julio Meinvielle.

Guerrilla violence would increase following the *Cordobazo*, an outbreak of civil unrest in the city of Córdoba in May 1969. The immediate cause was police repression of protests over an increase in prices at the university cafeteria in Resistencia, Chaco province. Further protests followed in the cities of Rosario and Córdoba, causing troops to occupy both cities. The uprising in Córdoba included a strong trade union element, much of it communist or socialist rather than Peronist in origin. Unlike most of Argentina, Córdoba had a long history of class-based trade unionism, as well as Peronist unions, generally linked to the automotive and other metal-working industries which were strong there.

Córdoba also had a strong tradition of student militancy, having generated the protests which led to the 1918 university reform. Students at its university, the oldest in the country, were unusually politicized, even for the period, and represented a range of positions from the far Left to far Right. (Córdoba, in addition to its classist tradition and also significant Peronist union base, had traditionally supported the UCR, as well as anti-Peronist putsches such as those led by Menéndez, Lonardi and Aramburu.) In the case of the *Cordobazo*, student and trade union militancy came together (despite the traditional distrust between the two sectors), to produce the largest civil uprising against the military government and the security forces until that time. In Córdoba, at least 14 people died during the ensuing conflict. The CGT and CGTA both declared a general strike, and on 2 June, a series of supermarkets linked to the Rockefeller family were bombed, marking an upsurge in violence which would continue to climb for a decade. Although Economy Minister Krieger Vasena was dismissed following the protests, the *Cordobazo* marked the beginning of the end of Onganía's government.

The first important victim of the spiral of violence was Vandor, shot five times at point-blank range at the UOM headquarters in Córdoba on 30 June 1969. As a result, a state of siege was declared, although those responsible were never identified. Vandor's death was later claimed by one of the 'special formations' formed by young revolutionary Peronists, calling themselves the 'Descamisado Command', who described him as a traitor to the working classes. Violence from both the Left and Right would thereafter continue unabated. A number of attacks on military and police posts and thefts of weapons were carried out in 1970 in particular.

On 29 May of that year (the anniversary of the Cordobazo), the former leader of the Liberating Revolution, General Pedro Aramburu, was kidnapped from his home by two men in military uniform, who proved to be members of the Montoneros, a Peronist guerrilla movement inaugurating its publicly known activities with the kidnapping. Aramburu was subjected to 'revolutionary justice' on a number of charges including the destruction of working-class gains, the theft of Evita's body, the execution of Juan José Valle and the sell-out of national assets to international interests. On 31 May, it was announced that Aramburu had been sentenced to death, and he was 'executed' by his captors, reportedly showing great calm and bravery in the face of the event. Shortly thereafter, other Peronist guerrilla movements such as the Fuerzas Armadas Peronistas (FAP) and Fuerzas Armadas Revolucionarias (FAR), as well as the Trotskyist Ejército Revolucionario del Pueblo (ERP) began to appear.

Its inability to avert Aramburu's kidnapping and murder was the death knell for Onganía's battered government, whose support had rapidly shrivelled among nearly all social sectors after initial hopes that he would bring a measure of stability. An internal coup replaced Onganía with the anonymous and unknown General Roberto Levingston on 8 June 1970. Levingston himself was to enjoy a brief presidency, marked by the remarkable coming together of the political parties (banned since Onganía's assumption) to issue a joint demand for a return to civilian government. Levingston was replaced by General Alejandro Lanusse in March 1971.

THE CATHOLIC CHURCH AND
THE PERONIST OPPOSITION

Following the fall of Lonardi in November 1955, the Church had found it prudent to move slightly away from its recent anti-Peronist stance. Given the assumption that some 90 per cent of Argentines were at least nominally Catholic and perhaps half considered themselves Peronists, there obviously existed considerable overlap between the two groups, and a long-term conflict of loyalties was in the interests of neither. The principal impetus for Catholic overtures to the working classes came, as had the impetus for opposition to Perón, from the clergy and laity rather than the hierarchy. The 1950s had not yet witnessed the commitment to the poor on the part of some priests which later led to an active clerical presence in factories or in *villas miserias* (shanty towns). However, the institutional Church presence in working-class areas was strengthened after 1957, with the majority of new dioceses concentrated in the industrial suburbs of Greater Buenos Aires. Following the example of French priests and the encouragement of Pope John XXIII, a small minority of 'worker priests' became active in the late 1950s and began to espouse Peronism actively. While initially seen as a means of neutralizing labour activism, the priests' own rising militancy alarmed the hierarchy; many were defrocked, and others were exiled by the government, apparently with the acquiescence of the Church.

The Second Vatican Council, inaugurated in October 1962, emphasized the responsibility of the Church to take an active approach to social problems, especially of the poor and oppressed, and also resulted in the explicit recognition of the autonomy of temporal authority. The documents which emerged from Vatican II, as well as the conclusions of the Medellín conference, made the Catholic social doctrine, which had hitherto been cited by *Justicialismo*, central to the Church's mission. The reforms involved a major shift of emphasis from the Argentine Church's traditional concerns (mainly sacramental, moral and educational) towards an active role in social issues. In several cases, priests came into conflict with their bishops over the implementation of the Conciliar reforms, and a number were dismissed.

The end of the Second Vatican Council took place only a few months before the June 1966 coup d'état of General Onganía, which was unintentionally responsible for encouraging the greater social action sought by the Vatican. The 'Argentine Revolution' of Onganía aimed at economic growth through support for industry, requiring a climate of political stability attained through the exclusion or repression of all sectors of potential opposition. These included many middle-class professional and intellectual sectors, the working classes and the poor. As was the case in similar circumstances in the 1930s and 1950s, many of those excluded from political participation found a common cause with elements of the Church, particularly the Third World Priests Movement.[6]

At the same time, the political expression adopted by much of this coalition was Peronism, of late a largely working-class movement, which by now had been in political opposition for over ten years. Its consequent position as a 'movement of national resistance' (entirely consonant with its traditional self-image as a 'movement of political and social opposition'[7]) attracted middle sectors newly suffering political repression themselves. The proscription of political parties was to lead to a new convergence between intellectual and middle-class sectors and the working classes, including middle-class Catholic activists.

The Argentine Third World Priests Movement, which came into existence in 1967, never included more than 3 per cent of the Argentine clergy, although they attracted the support of at least four bishops, including La Rioja bishop Enrique Angelelli, assassinated by the dictatorship in 1976. Drawn primarily from the priests who worked in the *villas miserias*, the movement tended to accept Peronism at its own valuation, although they tended to be concerned with the situation of the very marginal – only rhetorically of central interest to Perón's government – rather than the organized working classes which were the main beneficiaries of Peronism. However, they found in Peronism the definition of liberation theology and social action applicable in the Argentine context – in part because in the 1960s Peronism was re-evaluated as a uniquely Argentine phenomenon and therefore valid in the national context.

The parallels between Peronism and Catholic social protest were strengthened by Perón's statements in exile, especially his 1968 book *La hora de los pueblos* (*The Hour of the Peoples*). This emphasized the 'third position' as the precursor of the concept of the Third World, and claimed that the Peronist government had formed a transition to national socialism without reactionary or communist influences.

In the years after the Cuban Revolution, *La hora de los pueblos* called for Latin American unity against exploitation ('the continental integration of Latin America is indispensable: the year 2000 will find us united or dominated') and announced popular revolution and the death knell of imperialism: '[E]volution will lead us imperceptibly toward revolution and there will be no force able to stop it.... The reign of the bourgeoisie in the world has ended. The government of the peoples begins.'[8]

The position of *La hora de los pueblos* was far more revolutionary than any stance adopted by Perón during his nine years of government, representing an attempt to widen his support base in the new political context. The more radical posture reflected therein was attractive not only to the Third World Priests, but to a range of idealistic Argentine youth who lacked a national figurehead for currents of revolution and social commitment, and who were to adopt Perón and Peronism as their national expression.

Neither Perón nor the Third World Priests unequivocally rejected the use of violence in the late 1960s and early 1970s; indeed, Perón's political position in this period was further obscured by his unwillingness to exclude any potential source of support. Although most priests rejected the use of violence personally, they accepted its use as a legitimate defence against greater institutional violence. Those who defended the use of violence most often cited Eva Perón as their example (as did the Montoneros, for whom '*si Evita viviera, sería montonera*' – if Evita were alive, she would be a Montonero – was a favourite slogan). Citing her dictum that 'Peronism will be revolutionary or it will be nothing', and her overriding concern for the poor, the Third World Priests called Eva Perón 'the prototype of a certain revolutionary militant.... [H]er voice is the most clearly classist which has been raised in the country'.[9] This represented a shift away from her popular, quasi-religious image of a saint of Peronism (which was taken up by the Peronist Right in the early 1970s) to that of a more revolutionary figure; these years also saw the restoration of her central role in Peronism, which had been downplayed in the years following her death.

At their fourth 'National Encounter', in July 1971, the Argentine Third World Priests identified the path to national socialism as specifically Peronist. The 'Document of Carlos Paz', issued by the 160 priests present, stated that 'the Peronist movement, revolutionary, with its massive force,... will necessarily lead to the revolution which will make possible an original and Latin American socialism'.[10] This position represents a quantum leap from the original aspirations articulated by Perón in the 1940s – and indeed begs the question whether he had any interest in creating socialism even if the possibility had existed.

LANUSSE AND THE GAN: COURTSHIP OF PERONISM

President Lanusse was an astute military officer who, like many military officers since 1945, harboured dreams of becoming a new Perón. He faced, however, increasing violence from the revolutionary Left, primarily the Montoneros. Their influence over the Peronist Youth would reach important levels, to the tragic extent that the later military dictatorship would erroneously conclude that members of the Peronist Youth were ipso facto guerrillas, marking them out for elimination.[11] Another highly publicized action by the Montoneros was the 27 August 1970 murder of trade union leader José Alonso, described as a traitor to the working class and to Peronism. At the same time, right-wing violence also became increasingly common, as did torture of detainees; the killing of 16 guerrillas seeking to escape from Trelew prison in 1972 produced a new wave of riots.

Despite the difficulties surrounding the process, Lanusse had the intention of returning Argentina to civilian rule, a process which necessarily required negotiations with Perón. His interior minister, the Radical Arturo Mor Roig, announced the lifting of the proscription of political parties, and Lanusse began to send out signals that he was willing to begin talks with Perón, a non-person for Argentine governments over the past 16 years.

However, Lanusse mistakenly based his policy of talks on the belief that Perón himself would no longer wish to be a presidential candidate, a position which would have facilitated a return to constitutional rule. His emissary, Colonel Francisco Cornicelli, visited Perón in Madrid in April 1971 for the not particularly fruitful start of a long period of negotiations. These invariably foundered on the issue of violence, which Lanusse wanted Perón to curb and which Perón argued would disappear of itself when conditions in Argentina changed. During this period, Perón received not only Lanusse's emissaries, but also a wide range of acolytes from both Left and Right, looking for a blessing, or at least a wink and a nod, from the aging *caudillo* who could still make or break a political future. As had always been his wont, Perón gave the impression to all of being in agreement with their views, however extreme or however opposed to those of the previous visitor, and gave the impression that any and all acts of violence might enjoy his blessing if the circumstances were right.

The Perón who sat in Madrid awaiting his chance to return in 1971 was a man of nearly 76 years (or 78, if versions that he was born in 1893 are accurate), with serious health problems and an increasing dependence on Isabel and his sinister valet. José López Rega also became his nurse and later secretary. The two, Isabel and López Rega, took steps to ensure that his contacts with others were limited and controlled by themselves. Even long-term collaborators, such as Perón's faithful financial backer Jorge Antonio, were blacklisted and prohibited access to the residence in Puerta de Hierro. The bizarre nature of their doings is illustrated by the results of one of Lanusse's principal goodwill gestures towards Perón. In September, the body of Evita was disinterred from the Milan cemetery where it rested under the name of María Maggi, and returned to Perón in Madrid. Although its subsequent burial in Madrid might have seemed appropriate thereafter, at the insistence of Isabel and López Rega, Evita was installed in the attic of their home, making a most peculiar ménage à trois (or à quatre, taking López Rega into account).

In order to progress with his plans to allow for open elections, Lanusse announced his Great National Agreement (known as the GAN), which imposed a number of limitations on any future government but which sought to mark out an agreement that could allow for relative political stability in future. The GAN included the armed forces as participants and guarantors of the accord, in itself sufficient to disturb civilian politicians, although this alone was less disturbing than the suspicion that the GAN's real purpose was to open the way for Lanusse himself to announce his candidacy. In October 1971, Lanusse announced presidential elections for 11 March 1973, with the new government to take office on 25 May, and in December Isabel and López Rega began a three-month visit to Argentina to prepare the Peronists for the internal elections which would be held to choose a candidate during 1972.

Meanwhile, negotiations between Perón and Frondizi led to an electoral alliance between the Peronists and the party of Frondizi (now called the MID). This was to be called the Civic National Liberation Front or, more colourfully, the FRECILINA for its initials in Spanish, which made it sound more like an antibiotic than a political party. Perón also sought a 'social pact' with the trade union movement, including an agreement on temporary wage and price controls. The pact was negotiated between José Rucci, the right-wing leader of the CGT, and José Ber Gelbard, a former leader of the Peronist General Economic Confederation (CGE). However, ongoing negotiations between Lanusse and Perón were complicated by the continuing rise in violence (which now included widespread reports of torture by the police and military, and of attacks on left-wing Peronists by right-wing groups in addition to guerrilla violence, focusing increasingly on the kidnapping and murder of prominent business or military figures), and by Perón's refusal to condemn that violence.

With rumours of a coup against Lanusse increasing, in July 1972 it was announced that all candidates for the 1973 presidential elections must be resident in Argentina by 25 August 1972. This was a bold stroke designed to ensure that Perón would be unable to stand, even if Lanusse realized that his own candidacy was impossible. Perón promptly broke off negotiations and his representative, one-time Lower House leader Héctor Cámpora, tried to drive a wedge between Lanusse and the military by suggesting that Lanusse had not acted in accordance with the wishes of his colleagues. This provoked Lanusse into a virtual challenge, saying that Perón would not return before 25 August because he lacked the courage. Perón did not rise to the bait, waiting for a month before announcing, via Cámpora, that he would return to Argentina before the end of 1972, even if not before the deadline required to present his candidacy.

Other events in Argentina further weakened Lanusse's negotiating position. On 15 August, a guerrilla commando attacked the maximum security prison in the southern city of Rawson, liberating 25 members of the Montoneros, ERP and FAR guerrilla movements, six of whom successfully escaped and requested political asylum in Salvador Allende's Chile. A few weeks later, 16 of the guerrillas who had been recaptured were massacred at a prison in Trelew and three others were gravely wounded; the fact that they were under heavy naval guard made the official version that they had tried to escape implausible, and one of the survivors later testified that they had been lined up and shot down. Public opinion, which would shortly become exhausted by acts of brutality, was horrified by the killings, and any hope of national accord appeared further away than ever.

Given that it had been announced that Perón would return to Argentina before the end of 1972, it was imperative that he do so. On 7 November, it was announced that he would arrive on 17 November, at the age of 77 and 17 years after having last set foot in his homeland. The move was apparently designed to put more pressure on Lanusse by demonstrating the support still commanded by the elderly elder statesman, including the support of the so-called 'special formations' of the violent Left, as well as the violent Right. Perón arrived at Ezeiza international airport on the 17th, where he was met by a range of political figures, although troops halted efforts by his youthful supporters to hold a welcoming rally. Until the following day, he was held a virtual prisoner at the airport hotel, being allowed to leave for a rented house in the Buenos Aires suburb of Vicente López only on the 18th. Once there, crowds began to form to see Perón wave periodically from the window, but, unlike other occasions, the atmosphere was largely one of happiness at his return, with little sign of the violence to come. However, it became widely rumoured that Perón was virtually under the control of Isabel and López Rega and access to him was extremely limited, while his decisions were shaped to a large extent by the imposition of their will.

However, Perón remained sufficiently lucid to hold a series of meetings with other political leaders, including Ricardo Balbín, with whom he famously made peace after decades of enmity. However, Balbín, also a presidential candidate, was not disposed to support a move to have the residence limit lifted in order to allow Perón to stand. It was subsequently announced that the candidate of the FREJULI, the electoral alliance of the Peronists, MID and other minor parties, would be perennial loyalist Héctor Cámpora, seconded by Vicente Solano Lima, the 1963 presidential candidate of the Peronist-backed National Popular Front coalition. Cámpora was designated directly by Perón, who had been symbolically chosen by the FREJULI as its candidate and who delegated that honour to the obedient dentist who had remained loyal since the 1940s. The nomination of Cámpora was also blamed on Isabel and López Rega, on the grounds that they considered him easily controllable and therefore a guarantee of their own hold over the movement. However, it is likely that Perón himself chose Cámpora as his proxy, a safe candidate who commanded no party loyalties himself and could be trusted to step down when the time came.

With the nomination of Cámpora assured, Perón left Argentina on 14 December after less than a month in residence. At the end of the year, he made a series of inflammatory declarations calling the military 'gangsters' and condoning bombs and vigilante justice – statements that made the Lanusse government prohibit him from entering the country before the elections. The elections were no more tranquil without his presence. Guerrilla actions included the killing of a high-ranking naval officer and the theft of a truck-load of arms from a military base in Córdoba. Intranquillity ran so high that Lanusse apparently considered suspending the elections, although the armed forces held firm in the intention of returning civilians to government. Lanusse's anti-FREJULI attitude, moreover, made the public feel that the military government was again returning to its anti-Peronist stance, an attitude which favoured the candidacy of Cámpora. Lanusse's final statement, virtually calling on citizens not to vote for the FREJULI, was the icing on the cake: even without Perón's presence, on 11 March, the FREJULI enjoyed a sweeping victory, with nearly 50.0 per cent of the vote for Cámpora in contrast with 21.3 per cent for Balbin. The FREJULI also won all but one of the provincial governorships and an outright majority in both houses of Congress. After 18 years of proscription, the Peronists were set to return to power, and the stage was set for the last act of an increasingly tragic drama.

Although Peronism had always touted itself as the representative of the marginal and the oppressed, from its inception it had enjoyed the upper hand: Peronism was born when its leader was already effectively in power. After 1955, however, Peronism could speak from much greater experience of marginalization and oppression, having suffered torture, imprisonment and proscription for its main figures and, in the case of its grass-roots supporters, the indignity of being completely unrepresented and forbidden even to remember its political loyalties.

In light of this, and in light of the failure of any other political alternative to take up their aspirations, the possibility of a return to power, and a return to the ideal of social justice, was heady stuff. This alone could be said to justify the election of Cámpora, given the absence of any other alternative which could bring Peronist goals back to the forefront and Perón closer to power. The year 1973 was the first time in two decades that the large number of Argentines who supported Peronism, or at least wanted the option to vote for it, had been accorded the dignity of having their wishes respected. That what it stood for was even less clear than in 1946 was secondary: it represented, again, opposition to all the forces which had proscribed Peronism and undermined both the economic and social gains of the working classes (gains in terms of both salary and dignity). It also represented the failure of any other political figure or movement to capture the imagination as Peronism had done.

10 Descent into Chaos

CÁMPORA TO THE PRESIDENCY, PERÓN TO POWER

On 25 May 1973, 64-year-old Héctor Cámpora was sworn in as president. The years of proscription and ongoing crisis made many cling to the hope that the restoration of Peronism, even in the person of this weak representative, could bring some calm and a semblance of hope for the future to Argentina. Cámpora, known as 'Uncle' to the Peronist Youth and other sectors of the movement (for whom the father figure is obvious), was by no means a malign figure, but a decent man with a wealth of good intentions on assuming the presidency. However, Cámpora had carved out a long but undistinguished political career solely on the basis of his absolute loyalty towards Perón and Evita. This was, of course, the key to his political longevity, but his lack of any other political capacity meant that his long career (he entered Congress in 1946 as deputy for San Andrés de Giles and became leader of the Lower House in 1948, largely due to his good relationship with Evita) had scarcely attained the level of mediocrity.[1]

However, the Cámpora government was not immune to malign influences. López Rega was named Minister of Social Welfare, and would use his post to develop the apparatus of a right-wing death squad, the Argentine Anti-Communist Alliance (Triple A), to begin the work of physical extermination of so-called left-wing sectors or other enemies which would later be carried on by the official security forces. The president of the Chamber of Deputies, third in the line of succession after the vice-president and president of the Senate, was López Rega's son-in-law, Raúl Lastiri.

Now, with good intentions and the hopes of a weary nation pinned to his success, the luckless Cámpora was president of a country virtually ungovernable even for someone of infinitely greater capacity. After years of weak and short-lived civilian governments interspersed among unsuccessful and increasingly resisted military governments, Argentina's economy was in tatters, social polarization had reached an unprecedented scale and violence from both Left and Right was spiralling out of control. Worse, Cámpora had no political base and no power of his own, having been chosen by Perón precisely because of his total lack of independence, and no one in Argentina was ignorant of this fact. Indeed, the campaign slogan 'Cámpora to government, Perón to power' left little to the imagination in that respect.

On the very day of his inauguration, Cámpora signed an amnesty allowing for the release of a number of political prisoners and convicted terrorists held at Devoto prison in Buenos Aires, a well-intended but politically perilous move which went beyond the script prepared for him by Perón. The release of members of the ERP and Montoneros not only went against the wishes of the Peronist Right, who formed an important part of the forces dominating Cámpora's government, but made the police and military feel that the government was their enemy, given its celerity in releasing prisoners convicted of killing members of those forces. The principal effect of this move was to harden the determination of the security forces to ensure that terrorists and their accomplices would not be released in future: if putting them in prison meant that they could be free within a short time, in the future they would not face charge or trial, and would never officially make it to prison. The fact that members of the Peronist Left were represented in the Cámpora government gave a false but even greater image that their power was growing, making the backlash even stronger.

Cámpora showed little sign of calming the situation in Argentina during his first weeks in power, although in early June the CGT and Peronist business chamber CGE signed a 'social pact' aimed at backing the government's economic policy by freezing wages and prices in an attempt to reduce inflation. Left- and right-wing violence continued unabated, as both sides sought to 'win the street' and demonstrate that they had greater power, while the government was unwilling to send the police to repress violence (or even to maintain a modicum of order) by groups considered to represent 'the people'. Cámpora did, however, invite representatives of guerrilla groups including the Montoneros to a meeting at the Casa Rosada, further infuriating the security forces and provoking the Peronist right-wing to action, in the belief that they would soon lose power if they did not strike hard and fast.

THE EZEIZA MASSACRE

The backlash would be felt on 20 June 1973. On that day, Perón was finally to return to Argentina, an event which had its mythic element but which in fact would force Argentina to view Perón close up as an aged politician, rather than a rather diffuse legend far away in Madrid. Some 3 million people (10 per cent of the total national population) made the pilgrimage to Ezeiza airport, making it the largest mass gathering ever held in the country. Cámpora, still closer to the role of servant than commander-in-chief, had flown to Madrid to accompany Perón and Isabel on their final return to Argentina. However, the occasion, rather than a celebration, became a massacre whose extent was never accurately reported, and one which spelled out clearly the extent and dangerous nature of the split within the movement. The Peronist Left attempted to dominate the event, taking up strategic positions surrounding the platform where Perón was to address the crowd, in order to press home the call for socialist revolution. However, the Right, which included right-wing Peronist shock troops, members of the security forces and trade union mafiosos, was determined to seize the moment to squash the Left. Shooting started near the platform, causing panic as the crowds tried to flee; many were trampled even as others were caught in the crossfire. Warned of the carnage, Perón's plane was diverted to the military airport at Morón, and even the survivors were deprived of the opportunity to see the *caudillo*, for many, the first opportunity to see first-hand the leader with his people.

It has never been entirely clear what started the massacre at Ezeiza. At around midday, with the entire area seething with anxious participants, a column of the Peronist Youth from La Plata apparently circled round to one side of the platform in an effort to get close. Rightist forces, which included not only official guards and security

forces but also the Triple A, trade union hit men and other uniden-
tified participants armed with heavy weapons and dark glasses, responded by dropping to the ground and opening fire. Members of
the Left tried to occupy the platform, and were massacred by members of the Right who took the platform and continued to fire on the
crowd. Given the huge number in attendance, an orderly withdrawal
under fire was impossible, and escape was cut off by the panic-stricken
crowds who first ran forward towards the platform, where the shooting was taking place, and then back in an effort to flee the area.
Pandemonium reached its peak by mid-afternoon, although the crisis continued into the night. Rooms at the airport hotel were turned
into improvised torture centres. Final police reports were to claim that
the violence had been started by the Left, although initially the police stated that the shooting had begun from the platform, occupied
only by security agents and trade union gunmen, according to photos
and eyewitnesses. The police also stated that 25 people were dead,
although later reliable sources estimated the casualties at 13 dead and
365 wounded.

Despite his considerable displeasure over the events at Ezeiza, Perón
lost no time in advancing his political activities on arrival, probably
in the knowledge that in any case he had little time to lose. His first
speech, however, which concentrated on moderation, gave little encouragement to the Left and the youth who thought he was on their
side, as he denounced violence and efforts to introduce new and unacceptable ideas into Peronist doctrine. Shortly after his arrival, he
paid a visit to UCR leader Ricardo Balbín to agree to a consensus for
the future. A few days later, Perón suffered a heart attack; although he
recovered well, the signs were that his health, shortly before his 78th
(or 80th) birthday, would not bear up indefinitely.

PERÓN-PERÓN

On 13 July 1973, Cámpora announced his resignation after 49 days
in office. It is uncertain whether it was Perón himself or Isabel and
López Rega who pushed for his immediate withdrawal. However, the
most credible version appears to be that Perón's heart attack made it
clear that, if he was to return to the presidency, it would have to be
as soon as possible. This was of course of interest to Perón himself,

but arguably of even more interest to Isabel and López Rega, whose ambition for power at this stage was probably greater than Perón's own, and whose grip on that power was far more tenuous. If Perón were to die suddenly as an elder statesman without elected office, their power would dissipate immediately.

Whatever the reason, Cámpora's loyalty did not vacillate, and he and Vice-President Vicente Solano Lima obediently resigned, allowing Lastiri to assume as provisional president. New elections were called for 23 September and, although initial rumours and new meetings with Balbín led to speculation that the ageing Radical would be Perón's vice-presidential candidate, politicians of various Peronist factions (including Cámpora himself) were the subject of frenzied lobbying to occupy that post. However, at a party congress on 4 August, Isabel was proposed as vice-presidential candidate (the nomination of Perón himself as presidential candidate was never in doubt). Thus, where Evita had been thwarted in her desire to reach the vice-presidency, 22 years later the formula Perón–Perón was finally announced.

In many respects, Perón was to blame for actions and decisions which had a strong effect on the nation as a whole, and for the choice of such an inept individual to succeed him in presiding over the worst crisis in Argentina's history to date. However, the country had no obligation to act as his hostage for a generation, and the fact that it chose to do so was primarily the responsibility of the nation and its citizens, not of a single individual well beyond retirement age and long out of touch with the daily realities of his country. This, again, reflects distaste for accepting personal responsibility which has been a factor in the willingness to accept a series of strongmen at both the national and local level. This has the disadvantage of putting the strongman's adherents at the mercy of whatever erratic or erroneous actions he may take, but has the advantage of reducing the need for personal choice or the obligation to accept responsibility for the events which ensue. This was translated to a national level to such an extent that Perón was permitted to take disastrous decisions, when he was not realistically in a condition to make them wisely, and was then cast as scapegoat for the failings of a nation that followed those decisions without insisting on an alternative.

Ironically, this was arguably the moment in which Perón reached the apogee of his universal appeal in Argentina, a universality he had claimed but never achieved in the past. Peronism had never been a

left-wing movement by any means, and its strong working-class constituency included a large degree of conservatism which favoured material gains and security over revolution. By this time, however, it had
its own large left-wing, composed primarily of those who did not remember its days of glory and had some confusion as to what Peronism
really was in substance. By 1973, Perón also attracted the support of
a large number of those who sympathized with traditional left-wing
parties, who now saw him as the closest thing to a representative of
the Argentine working class, and the only leader possibly capable of
bringing about real social change – and, incidentally, of halting the
right-wing violence plaguing the country. At the same time, in 1973
Perón also attracted elements of the traditional Right, historically im-
placably anti-Peronist, as the only possible guarantor of social peace
and a firm government.

This extremely wide range of consensus (a consensus based largely
on despair and the lack of other apparent options) seemed on the one
hand to favour the success of the government – as did a brief period of
economic boom, bolstered by high global commodity prices. On the
other hand, however, a coalition extending from far Left to far Right
would impose conflicting demands which no government could possibly satisfy, implying that Perón would inevitably be forced to opt for
one side or another once elections were out of the way. Although the
Left naively believed otherwise, there was little question as to which
side it would be. Perón might laud the unruly and even revolutionary
youth from his exile, when their activities helped to destabilize the
country and promote his return, but Perón as president had no need
for, and no wish to tolerate, guerrilla groups whose violent activities
could not fail to destabilize his own government. The announcement
that Isabel, at least indirectly associated with the far Right and the
death squads of López Rega, would be vice-president made it clear to
the relatively astute viewer that the die had been cast in favour of
the Right. The excuse for putting forward Isabelita as vice-presidential
candidate was the impossibility of choosing anyone else, given the
conflicts between different factions of Peronism and the fact that a
choice of a member of the Left, Right or any other grouping would
have provoked serious rifts within the movement.

Both within and outside the party, there was a widespread view that
Isabel was not competent to assume leadership of a country in crisis,
and a widespread awareness (however suppressed) that Perón's failing

health would almost certainly lead to his vice-president being forced to assume that leadership at some point. As such, society as a whole, and the political class in particular, must carry some responsibility for the course of events. The unwillingness to do so has led to a collective tendency to draw a veil over Isabel's presidency, to treat her largely as a figure of derision, and to gloss over this period of recent history, one which does not reflect creditably on most people of any political leaning. However, although stubbornly clinging to power rather than resign and call early elections, Isabel was not solely responsible for the disastrous course of events, nor for the blind (and often misguided) pursuit of self-interest which led the armed forces, the trade unions, the business sector, the insurgents and others to do everything possible to weaken her position further and make it untenable. The desire to deny history and to use someone who, despite their position, had only limited influence over the situation, as a scapegoat has done nothing to help Argentina come to terms with a part of its history that remains to be addressed.

The Perón–Perón candidacy was formally accepted by the former president on 18 August, little more than a month before the 23 September elections. On 31 August, the CGT organized a mass demonstration in his support, in which the Peronist Youth also insisted on taking part, although on this occasion both sides were careful to avoid a repeat of Ezeiza. The event, involving some 1 million marchers, passed off peacefully, despite the drain on Perón's limited physical strength implied by spending eight hours on the balcony of the CGT reviewing the scene. Shortly thereafter, Perón met with guerrilla leaders Mario Firmenich (Montoneros) and Roberto Quieto (FAR), in an effort to reduce the impact of his obvious lurch to the Right since his return, and during the campaign López Rega was conspicuous by his absence. Perón obviously needed the Left for the elections, although he was unwilling to give ground to their demands (the example of the coup against Salvador Allende in Chile came as a bombshell in the middle of the campaign). However, while he continued to exercise his experience and adeptness in managing both extremes of his movement, Perón was no longer a young man able to play one faction off against another without getting caught in the middle. At the same time, he was no longer an idealized leader in far-off exile, giving his blessing 'urbi et orbi', like the Pope, as he himself put it,[2] when the moment was right and acting as arbitrator among different factions. He was a politician involved in an electoral campaign who could no longer remain above party politics and faction fighting and was forced to participate in the down-to-earth political struggles which intensified daily.

After the short political campaign, the Perón–Perón formula won the 23 September elections with over 60 per cent of the vote. Ricardo Balbín was again the UCR candidate, after having been rumoured to be Perón's likely running mate (a candidacy Balbín was seemingly enthusiastic over although his party was not). The notion that Perón's triumphal return would end the bloodshed and chaos which had rocked Argentina for so long was quickly crushed when, on 25 September, CGT leader José Rucci was assassinated, probably by the Montoneros (although the journalist Martin Andersen argues that Rucci was killed by a group linked to López Rega and the Montoneros claimed to have carried out the crime in order to strengthen their image[3]). However, the inauguration on 12 October was peaceful, with the hostile factions occupying the Plaza de Mayo maintaining order and avoiding conflict. The occasion marked Perón's first appearance on the balcony of the Casa Rosada since his ill-conceived 'five for one' speech 19 years earlier, and also the first time in as many years that he had used military uniform, as his rank and privileges had been restored shortly before. After a short and unremarkable inaugural speech, given the historic nature of the occasion, Perón turned his attention to imposing order on the youth movements and guerrilla groups which he had encouraged in exile but which now represented a threat to the stability of his government. The armed elements initially accepted a halt to violence, and turned instead to indoctrination of workers or slum dwellers, and the Montoneros entered strongly into the leadership of the Peronist Youth, with the eventual consequence that all of its members were later to be considered subversives.[4]

Before Perón's inauguration had taken place, the Peronist Superior Council had issued a document ordering all supposedly Peronist groups to repudiate and fight against Marxism, using all means necessary to combat Marxist subversion. Shortly thereafter, and following the murder of Rucci, the number of attacks on members of the Peronist Left escalated sharply, with the suspicion that López Rega and the Triple A were responsible. While the government as such was not

Figure 11. President Juan Domingo Perón and Vice-President María Estela Martínez de Perón receive Bolivian President Hugo Banzer (Courtesy of the archive, *Diario La Nación*)

explicitly implicated in the wave of terror, it was apparent that it made little effort to halt it or to discover those responsible. One of the sharpest responses of the Left came not from the Peronist groups but from the ERP, which on 19 January 1974, attacked a tank brigade in the city of Azul, Buenos Aires province. The event led Perón to accuse the provincial government of tolerating subversion, forcing the left-leaning provincial governor Oscar Bidegain to resign in favour of his rightist vice-governor Victorio Calabró, a former activist of the metal-workers' union which had produced Vandor and Rucci. Shortly thereafter, the ruling party presented a draconian anti-subversion law in Congress which implied ominous consequences for even non-violent dissent. The legislators of the Peronist Youth were to resign over the law, after being publicly castigated by Perón, and the Right increased its hold in Congress. The other left-wing Peronist governor, Ricardo Obregón Cano of Córdoba, was overthrown by a putsch led by his provincial police, and he and Vice-Governor Atilio López were forced to resign after the federal government announced the intervention of the province thereafter.

The influence of López Rega continued to increase, to the point where Perón was virtually never seen in public without him. Despite Perón's poor health (he suffered a serious crisis in late November 1973 and nearly died), his doctors' orders that he should rest were counter-manded by López Rega, who ensured that he walked long distances for exercise and maintained a punishing schedule which would have tired a younger and fitter man. At the same time, López Rega was ap-parently convinced that he was able to resuscitate Perón in the event of his death, even claiming to have done so in Spain on one occasion. López Rega continued to act as private secretary and nurse to Perón, in addition to retaining his post as social welfare minister, and he continued to live with the first couple.

During 1974, right-wing attacks on left-wing activists continued, and Perón himself increased the decibels against the Left. In a 7 February speech, he attacked the left-wing 'infiltrators' in the Peronist movement as 'useful idiots' or fellow travellers attempting to subvert Peronism. (This was not altogether untrue: the Left had not accepted the fact that Peronism, for all its revolutionary rhetoric, was not a leftist ideology, if it was an ideology at all, and their attempts to turn it into one could be described as a type of subversion. Some members of the Left were perfectly aware that Peronism was not socialist in its basis, but attempted to use it to influence the solidly Peronist working classes, also a kind of subversion.) On 1 May, he went further, at the May Day rally in the Plaza de Mayo, his second appearance there following his inauguration. The Peronist Youth attempted to 'win the street' through organizing a massive presence, painting signs on the spot after they were prohibited from carrying banners and signs to the Plaza. Montonero slogans were chanted, and a Montonero flag was burned, probably by trade union sectors. On the arrival of Perón and Isabel, things went from bad to worse, with the Youth shouting 'there is only one Evita', and also shouting slogans celebrating the deaths of Vandor and Rucci, even as Perón praised the memory of trade union leaders murdered by subversives. The chants of 'what's happening, general, why is the people's government full of gorillas (right-wing thugs)' provoked an irate response from Perón, who called the 50,000 members of the Peronist Youth in the Plaza 'beardless' and 'stupid', among other epithets. The Youth turned their back on their leader and filed out of the Plaza, leaving it half empty; thereafter, trade unionists and right-wing sympathizers in the Plaza attacked the unprepared members of the Left as they withdrew from the scene, throwing sticks and stones and producing a pitched battle which led to dozens of injuries.

The 1 May catastrophe would be Perón's virtual swan song. Although a few days later the Peronist Youth announced that they remained loyal to Perón, on 13 May he accused them of trying to produce a civil war, and urged others to find means of self-defence against such an outcome. These words were interpreted as encouragement for the death squads already in operation. In addition to the thorny question of subversion, these last days were marked by rising trade union demands for salary increases (despite the social pact which had agreed a wage and price freeze), an issue which again produced accusations of disloyalty and psychological warfare. On 12 June, Perón made his perennial threat to resign, producing a general strike and a rally by the CGT in the Plaza de Mayo. The rally marked his last appearance in the historic plaza.

By 19 June, Perón was bedridden. At 10:30 on 1 July 1974, his heart had stopped, despite cardiac massage and mouth-to-mouth resuscitation, and despite repeated efforts by López Rega to force his soul to remain with his body. At 13:15 he was officially pronounced dead. The man who had dominated Argentina for 30 years was suddenly gone, with no apparent successor to guide the fate of the country, leaving that country in the hands of Isabel and López Rega.

Although news of the death did not come as a surprise, it caused profound grief and consternation, as the one man many had hoped might end the calvary of violence and instability in Argentina disappeared. A measure of the general sorrow was the moving speech by Balbín at the funeral, the high point of his own career, in which he ended saying 'this old adversary says farewell to a friend'. His grip on power and personal charisma had captured the public imagination to such an extent that, even in spite – or because – of official efforts to eliminate his existence for over a decade, for two generations he was the centre of public life in Argentina. As such, his disappearance left a void that left the nation stunned and unable to look for alternative figures. In any case, possible successors had had no chance to develop in the shadow of a leader who had come to represent the incarnation of Argentina, both good and bad.

Indeed, Perón in many respects was *the* incarnation of Argentina and the Argentines: intelligent, charming, naive, cynical, quick, improvisational, energetic, sentimental, contradictory, irresponsible,

Figure 12. A soldier cries at Juan Perón's funeral, 1974 (Wikipedia)

individualist, egocentric, authoritarian, superficial, arrogant, and a *chanta* (an Argentine word describing a condition so familiar to Argentines that it has no real translation in either English or standard Spanish, charlatan being not too far off the mark). Although the style and persona of the *chanta* differs from province to province, he is a universal figure in Argentina. Though decent Argentines may pretend contempt for the *chanta*, there is a cultural tendency to harbour at least a sneaking admiration for the successful one. Perón was arguably the greatest and most successful *chanta* of them all.

So Argentine is Peronism, in fact, that even anti-Peronists were Peronist in their thinking, casting themselves as the opposition to that inherently opposition movement and accepting the general concept that Perón was the centre around which all political life and political power revolved, and the basic symbol of Argentina (of everything good, in the case of Peronists, and everything bad, in the case of anti-Peronists). The anti-Peronists also did more than the Peronists themselves to ensure Perón's continuity at the centre of national political life, by demanding revenge after 1955, and by seeking to destroy all

Figure 13. President María Estela Martínez de Perón (Isabelita), addressing the crowds on 1 May 1975 (to the left, Social Welfare Minister José López Rega) (courtesy of the archive, *Diario La Nación*)

of the gains achieved by the working classes in the preceding decade. Lonardi's original slogan of 'neither victors nor vanquished', if taken seriously, could have led to respect for working-class gains, the normal resumption of political life and the eventual realization that Perón himself was not necessary to ensure that the bad old days would not return. However, the anti-Peronists, in their Peronist insistence on permeating all levels of society and dictating from above in order to make anti-Peronist doctrine as universal as Peronist doctrine had attempted to be, made Perón himself fundamental.

ISABEL IN THE PRESIDENCY

Isabelita assumed the presidency on Perón's death, burdened by the political and economic crisis facing the country and by her own inadequacy, and found herself forced to depend increasingly on López Rega. During her speeches, he stood behind her whispering her words as she spoke, a peculiarity he explained on the grounds that he acted as a medium to transmit Perón's message for her to speak. However, while shrewd in acquiring power, López Rega had little more idea of how to exercise it than Isabel, allegedly dedicating much of his energy to expanding the activities of the Triple A and, purportedly, embezzling government funds.

Violence, which had been kept at bay until after Perón's funeral, was soon on the upswing again. The Montoneros assassinated former interior minister Arturo Mor Roig, while a series of murders of left-wing politicians, including former Córdoba vice-governor Atilio López and President Arturo Frondizi's brother Silvio, were attributed to the Triple A. A total of 29 killings were blamed on the Triple A in May 1975 alone. The Montoneros would go underground in September after the government closed down their publication *La Causa Peronista* (the last issue of which included a report by Mario Firmenich and Norma Arrostito of the details of Aramburu's kidnapping and murder). Shortly thereafter, they carried off two high-profile raids, kidnapping the Born brothers of the Bunge & Born grains holding and receiving a multi-million dollar ransom, and stealing Aramburu's body from the Recoleta cemetery and announcing that it would not be returned until Evita's remains were brought back to Argentina.

The Montoneros' effort to appear a larger and more dangerous group than they really were was to prove useful to the armed forces later, when the supposedly massive guerrilla presence provided an excuse for massive counter-insurgency operations which targeted thousands of people with no guerrilla links whatsoever. At the same time, the ERP was conducting a very visible rural guerrilla campaign in Tucumán, which also included a series of high-profile attacks, such as the taking of a police station in the capital and the murder of an army major, Roberto Viola, and his small daughter, making it appear that breaking point was near.

ANNIHILATION OF SUBVERSION

The first concrete step towards officializing the war against subversion and related carnage was taken in Tucumán. On 10 February 1975, Isabel signed Decree 261, ordering the security forces to 'annihilate subversion' in that province. The communiqué announcing the military intervention of Tucumán indicated that:

> subversion attacks . . . the entire Argentine people. Thus, the fight against subversion requires the participation of the whole community. The National Executive Power . . . has decided the intervention of the army in the fight against nationless subversion. Once again, the armed forces are united and identified with the people in the defence of our own way of life.[5]

Some days later, on a visit to Tucumán to inaugurate public works, López Rega told journalists that he would like to be 'the first to take up a gun to eradicate subversion. . . . If this operation which Social Welfare is carrying out can be a means of collaborating with the cleansing of those who are part of the subversion, I will be very happy'.[6]

Operation Independence, under the command of General Edgardo Acdel Vilas mobilized 5,000 members of the infantry, federal police and gendarmes to combat a purported 600 guerrillas of the ERP operating in the province. (In fact, according to army intelligence, the operating force of the ERP was estimated at between 120 and 160.) Thereafter, press reports referred to armed clashes but did not identify guerrillas captured or killed, although losses suffered by the security forces were extensively reported. The national CONADEP commission charged with investigating disappearances after the return to democracy in 1983 was to note that Tucumán was the first testing laboratory for the irregular methods later used to combat subversion in the rest of the country, relying heavily on the use of clandestine detention centres, torture and forced disappearance. *La Escuelita* in Famaillá was to become the first clandestine prison in Argentina, and some 565 people would disappear in Tucumán, including 107 under Vilas' tenure, through the end of 1975.[7] Vilas himself, in his unpublished memoirs, attributed the necessity for this methodology to the fact that:

> if detention procedures had been carried out by my men wearing army uniforms, then there would have been no choice but to hand (the detainee) over to the courts, so that he could be released a few hours later; but

if the operation was carried out by officers in civilian clothes...the situation changed....(In 1975) 1,507 people accused of maintaining close relations with the enemy passed through the detention centre in Famaillá...; the most dangerous and important never reached the courts.[8]

Economic policy aimed at reducing inflation included severe austerity measures under new Economy Minister Celestino Rodrigo, including a sharp devaluation and the freezing of wage increases, which provoked a huge protest march by the unions on 27 June 1975, the first such march against a Peronist government. Isabel was forced to give in to pressure and approved collective contracts with large salary increases, boosting inflation further. She was also forced to give in to pressure on López Rega, the principal focus of hatred against the government. On 20 July, he was named 'extraordinary ambassador' in lieu of his cabinet post, and promptly disappeared from sight for a decade, until he was caught and extradited from the USA in 1986. Shortly thereafter, Isabel took leave for health reasons from mid-September, leaving Senate President Italo Luder as provisional president. While many Peronists and others saw this as a possible chance to replace the hapless president, Isabel was tenacious in clinging to her at least symbolic power, and by 17 October she was back in office. During September, the state of siege imposed in Tucumán was extended to the rest of the country, and the armed forces likewise charged with 'annihilating subversion' throughout Argentina.

Peronists from all sides of the spectrum sought to persuade Isabel to step down and call early elections, given that there was no doubt that the country would not endure the present situation until 1977, when presidential elections were anticipated. Others, such as navy chief Admiral Emilio Massera, also tried to persuade her to call elections and suggested that she stand as his vice-presidential candidate. However, Isabel was determined to remain in office, refusing to take seriously the widespread rumours that a coup d'état was again imminent.

One of the few tactics which occurred to Isabel and López Rega in the midst of the chaos that reigned in Argentina had been to return Evita's body to Argentina (at which time, as promised, the Montoneros returned the body of Aramburu). The body was again put on display, next to the closed coffin of Perón, but after an initial flurry of interest

Figure 14. General Jorge Videla, Admiral Emilio Massera and Brigadier Orlando Agosti, the junta that seized power on 24 March 1976 (courtesy of the archive, *Diario La Nación*)

it did little to distract Argentines from the more pressing problems of daily life. Evita and Perón would remain in the chapel at the presidential residence in Olivos until another military government was faced with the quandary of how to dispose of them.

THE COUP D'ÉTAT AND INDUSTRIAL BLOODSHED

In the early hours of 24 March 1976, when Isabel's government had tottered on for 20 months, she left the Casa Rosada in a helicopter bound for Olivos. Her naval attaché informed her that, due to technical difficulties, the helicopter would be forced to land in the city airport, where it touched down in the military zone. Isabel, alone, was escorted to another military aircraft and placed under arrest, marking the fifth military coup against a civilian government since 1930. Isabel was placed under relatively comfortable house arrest in the southern lake district, although she later claimed to have been tormented frequently with threats that she would be executed. She was held on charges of embezzlement, first in Neuquén and later at a military base

in the city of Azul and at Perón's residence in San Vicente, before finally being released in 1981 without trial. She immediately returned
to Spain, where she has maintained a low profile. Although Isabel had
the misfortune to be imprisoned by the military government, events
would show that she had been lucky in comparison with many of her
countrymen.

Cámpora would also become one of the victims of the dictatorship,
although he managed to escape the fate of the disappeared or a return
to prison. Cámpora sought asylum in the Mexican Embassy, having
served as ambassador to that country after resigning as president. The
refusal of the military government to allow him safe conduct to the
airport, however, meant that he was forced to remain in the embassy
for nearly four years until, suffering from an advanced cancer, he
was allowed to leave for Mexico in October 1979. He died there in
December 1980.

The 'National Reorganization Process' (*Proceso de Reorganización Nacional*, PRN) instituted under the new military government marked a
watershed in the history of Argentine military governments, in terms
of both the violence which ensued and the effort to make a lasting
change in society. According to the Act of the PRN, issued on 24 March
1976, the armed forces' intention was to:

> restore the essential values which serve as the base for the
> integral direction of the state, . . . eradicate subversion and
> promote economic development in national life based on
> the balance and responsible participation of the various sec-
> tors, in order to ensure the subsequent installation of a re-
> publican, representative and federal democracy, adequate
> for the reality and exigencies of solution and progress of
> the Argentine people.[9]

With the intention of making a permanent change in the country's culture and economic structure, the regime was characterized
by repression and a penetration in the national life without precedent. Congress was closed and replaced by the Legislative Advisory
Commission, made up of three members of each branch of the armed
forces; all provincial governors were replaced by military officers or,
later, military appointees; the federal and provincial justice systems

were suspended, together with the Supreme Court; and the national universities were also intervened.

The upsurge in disappearances and killings was immediate after the coup, and would reach a total number of disappearances estimated at up to 30,000 (the National Commission on the Disappearance of Persons, CONADEP, established in 1983 documented 8,961 cases).[10] While these would affect all elements of society, the Peronists represented the largest number of victims, with those suspected of guerrilla links including the Peronist Youth, trade unionists, and anyone who happened to be acquainted with people in those categories. Most Peronist governors, political and trade union leaders were imprisoned. Unlike the post-1955 period, however, the rank and file had little chance to increase their independence by throwing up new leaders to fight against the repression, given the all-out nature of that repression and the fact that their ranks were physically decimated. Many of the leaders of the guerrilla groups, as well as hundreds of others suspected of political activity, would also flee the country, further reducing the body of activists able to maintain some cohesion in a movement which had already lost its principal figure and had suffered the breakdown into faction fighting which predated the coup.

The strong idealistic tendency always present in Peronism, and the suffering of its members at the hands of two vengeful military dictatorships, made it understandable that there would be a strong Peronist presence in the human rights movement which sprang up in Argentina from the late 1970s. However, there was also a stronger element of collaboration with the military government by some sectors of Peronism than would later be willingly admitted. This, not surprisingly, included close links between rightist elements of Peronism – some trade union leaders, political survivors and former members of the Triple A – and the murderous practices of the dictatorship. However, it also included possible links between the supposedly leftist Montoneros and members of the armed forces, most notably Admiral Emilio Massera, member of the first junta and director of the ESMA clandestine detention centre. The Montonero leadership was widely accused of having betrayed the Trotskyist ERP to the armed forces. They would also be accused, with justification or not, of cutting a deal with Massera to ensure relative calm during the 1978 World Cup, which was held in Buenos Aires and won for the first time by Argentina, a major public relations triumph for the dictatorship.

The unprecedented human rights crisis, which drew widespread condemnation from international organizations such as the United Nations and Organization of American States, as well as the administration of US president Jimmy Carter, would arguably draw Argentina into alliances with apparently strange bedfellows such as Cuba and the Soviet Union. Both countries acted in concert with Argentina at the United Nations (UN) to ward off investigation of their respective human rights records; indeed, the UN's political difficulties in coming to grips with the Argentine case led to the establishment of its working group on disappearances, the first of its so-called 'theme mechanisms' to investigate specific human rights violations internationally.[11] At the same time, Carter's boycott of the Soviet Union following the invasion of Afghanistan opened a business opportunity for Argentina to substitute US grain exports to that country. While the ties between the anti-subversive PRN government and two communist states might appear odd on the surface, it is worth noting that, unlike Chile, the PRN did not overthrow a Marxist government, nor were the principal targets of the 'dirty war' communist, but rather Peronist.

Nor was the PRN's economic record more stellar. Under Economy Minister José Martínez de Hoz (known as the Wizard of Hoz), efforts to reduce inflation and the trade deficit again centred on moves to cut wages and consumption; the CGT was outlawed and workers' leaders faced the same treatment as suspected subversives. Despite low unemployment, the share of wages in national income was the lowest for 40 years, and the shift of resources to agriculture and banking hit the urban middle and working classes exceptionally hard, producing an increase in structural poverty rates that has yet to be reversed. By 1980, capital flight and collapsing banks led to a sharp rise in foreign debt from 8 billion dollars in 1975 to some 40 billion dollars – 42 per cent of the GDP – in 1981. Much private foreign debt was also taken over by the state in the early 1980s, at the initiative of the then Central Bank president Domingo Cavallo, further boosting the public debt burden, although a key factor was military enthusiasm for foreign borrowing to strengthen growth, often through grandiose public works that were never completed.

Eccentric foreign policy-making, as well as the deteriorating economic situation and rising popular pressures, would also be responsible for the risk of war with Chile over the Beagle Channel dispute in the late 1970s (a project of Massera's), as well as the disastrous decision to invade the Falklands/Malvinas islands in April 1982. Although the sovereignty question is one that stirs strong nationalist sentiment across a range of public opinion, the expectation on the part of the then junta leader General Leopoldo Galtieri that the government of US president Ronald Reagan would support Argentina over the United Kingdom, and his ally Margaret Thatcher, is bizarre and inexplicable (as is the calculation that the United Kingdom would back down in the face of force). The catastrophic and ill-prepared military campaign, which saw untrained conscripts without supplies pitted against professional British troops, led to a rapid defeat and the inevitable conclusion that Argentina's professional military officers were corrupt and incompetent even in their purported professional sphere. Mass demonstrations in support of the invasion rapidly turned to anti-government protests, as rumours of Galtieri's alcoholism and abuses by military officers against their own soldiers compounded shame over the initial enthusiastic popular reaction and over the ignominious result.

The military government would eventually withdraw in late 1983, pushed out of office primarily as a result of its complete failure to improve the economy and its disastrous performance in the 1982 Falklands/Malvinas War. Their withdrawal was not, however, especially attributable to a popular struggle for freedom and democracy, concepts which were still somewhat nebulous in a country whose history of military and personalist governments and authoritarian culture meant that it had never developed a base of 'democratic habits'.[12] Prior to allowing elections, in October 1983, the junta decreed a self-amnesty, which public opinion widely rejected. However, the Peronists were widely perceived as having been prepared to negotiate the issue, despite being the most numerous victims of repression, with well-known party leaders such as Catamarca Senator Vicente Saadi arguing for the need for national pacification.

This was yet another obstacle for the Peronists to face in their first presidential elections since the death of Perón. The Radicals had also lost their long-time leader, Balbín having died in 1981, but had greater good fortune in the choice of a presidential candidate: Raúl Alfonsín, a relatively young man, had led an internal anti-Balbín *Renovación y Cambio* current within the UCR for a number of years, for which he stood as presidential candidate in 1973. He was also charismatic and a good orator, giving him an aspect closer to that of a Peronist than a Radical candidate. The Peronist candidate eventually chosen was

Italo Luder, who, together with vice-presidential candidate Deolindo Bittel, was closely associated with the 'old' party. Luder himself, a decent man with long political experience, was devoid of charisma and unable to find a new message to stir voter passions, certainly not sufficiently to offset a perception of the party as overly linked to the violence which had exhausted the country. That perception increased when its candidate for governor of Buenos Aires, Herminio Iglesias, set fire to a coffin, supposedly that of the UCR, at the party's closing rally, provoking a shudder in a society which had seen far too much violence and division. Alfonsín, benefited by his personal charisma and the Peronists' disarray, won the elections with 50.5 per cent of the vote, losing only in a few strongly Peronist provinces such as Tucumán, La Rioja and Chaco. To many, it appeared that the Peronists' long hold on power might have ended, with the death of Perón marking also the death of his party. However, this opinion did not consider the historical adaptability of the Peronist movement, now without historic national leaders but disposed to face a new metamorphosis, nor its traditional strength in provinces which would now represent the backbone of its recovery.

11 Provincial Perspectives

Even a thumbnail sketch of each of the 23 provinces (plus the city of Buenos Aires, the Federal Capital) would occupy a separate book. To illustrate these broader areas more specifically, therefore, particular attention will be paid to four divergent case studies: the more traditional, northwestern provinces of Tucumán and Catamarca, the western province of Mendoza and the Patagonian province of Neuquén, incorporated fully into the republic only in 1955. These provinces come from different political, historical and economic traditions, and fall outside the Buenos Aires and Pampas area on which much attention is concentrated. They also illustrate each of the four categories into which the government and international organizations group Argentina's provinces: *advanced* (Buenos Aires, Córdoba, Mendoza, Santa Fe and the Federal Capital), having both high-density population and high per capita gross provincial product; *intermediate* (Entre Ríos, Salta, San Juan, San Luis and Tucumán), with a middling population and intermediate per capita product; *underdeveloped* (Catamarca, Chaco, Corrientes, Formosa, Jujuy, La Rioja, Misiones and Santiago del Estero), characterized as provinces with low per capita product and high poverty levels, concentrated in the northwest and northeast; and *low density* (Chubut, La Pampa, Neuquén, Río Negro and Santa Cruz), Patagonian provinces with small populations but high per capita product.[1]

Although the traditions and contemporary circumstances of each province are to some extent unique, these four are at least partially characteristic of the categories they represent, and offer differing patterns of political and economic development:

- Although the poorest of the five advanced provinces, Mendoza is the furthest from the Littoral area and, like other wealthy provinces, received significant European immigration from the late nineteenth century in particular. It also offers an example of family-dominated politics at the provincial level, the motivations behind the practice of federal intervention and a largely efficient provincial administration.
- Tucumán has been representative of the political and economic problems facing a number of interior provinces since the 1860s, and since the mid-1970s has been especially hard hit by repression, economic crisis and unemployment. After becoming an important agricultural centre in the colonial period, Tucumán became largely dependent on domestic demand for a single product – sugar – after falling under the economic dominance of Buenos Aires in the latter half of the nineteenth century.
- A marginal part of the Viceroyalty of Peru in the colonial period, in the twentieth century Catamarca represented almost a caricature of the underdeveloped province, noted primarily for *caudillos*, contraband and corruption. Dominated by the Saadi family and its hold over the patronage system for some 50 years, the province gave the Saadis a springboard to national influence but saw its own position diminish as scandal and political manoeuvring marginalized the family from the early 1990s.
- Incorporated as a province only in 1955, Neuquén has experienced rapid growth since the 1970s, primarily as a producer of oil and gas. With the exception of periods of military rule, it has been governed since 1962 by the neo-Peronist *Movimiento Popular Neuquino* (MPN), dominated for most of that time by the Sapag family. Despite the province's wealth and reputation for efficient administration, poverty levels have often been comparable to Argentina's poorest provinces.

To a greater or lesser extent, all of these provinces illustrate the fact that Argentina's federal relationships have become (for both the provinces and the central government) yet another mechanism of party politics and clientelism, in which both provincial and national governments use each other to retain power, but rarely for the purpose of good government or to the benefit of the population or the economy as a whole. The relationship illustrates not only the weakness of the provincial states and their dependence on the national state, but also the inherent weakness of the national government and its need for provincial support – often gained through economic favours which prejudice the remaining provinces or through outright coercion. The ability of provincial administrations to exercise leverage over the national government depends in many cases on the ability of local *caudillos* to mobilize or control votes, which in turn flourishes in a context of limited economic alternatives to political patronage, and on the over-representation of small provinces in the Lower House of Congress and the Electoral College.

MENDOZA

With an agro-industrial economy falling outside the traditional model of the Littoral provinces (based on large-scale landholdings and production of beef and grain), Mendoza has been disproportionately dependent on the fluctuating internal market for its principal products. It has also been known for social mobility, efficient administration, democratic practices and popular participation; although this reputation is not wholly deserved, its record is better than that of the country overall or of the majority of provinces individually.

With an arid climate making agriculture difficult, and a small settled indigenous population isolated from trade routes linking Peru and Bolivia with Buenos Aires, Mendoza in the colonial period was a military outpost heavily dependent on Chile. Incorporated into the Viceroyalty of the Río de la Plata in 1776, the Mendozan economy was badly affected by the free trade with Spain introduced in 1778, as its products – chiefly fruit, olives, grapes and wine – could not compete with imported goods; thereafter Mendoza depended still more heavily on commerce with (and between) Chile and Tucumán, as products from Tucumán and Paraguay passed through Mendoza on their way to Chile.

Mendoza and the Cuyo region increased in importance from 1813 with the creation of the intendancy of Cuyo, governed from 1814 by General José de San Martín. Under San Martín, local industry was organized and expanded to produce goods needed for the war of independence, including arms, gunpowder, lead, sulphur and blankets.

Within the Argentine Republic, Mendoza's elites followed the pattern of other traditional forces dominant in the country. Between 1854 and 1916, all of Mendoza's members of the Electoral College voted for all the winning presidential candidates, and enjoyed in particular close relations with Julio Roca, the principal force in Argentine politics for over 30 of those years. Provincial political elites continued to exercise a stranglehold on political powers: in 1866, 21 of the 25 members of the provincial legislature were related to the governor, while between 1880 and 1943 members of 35 families occupied nearly half of all political posts.

Mendoza became the first Argentine province to produce oil, with the establishment in 1885 of the *Compañía Mendocina Exploradora del Petróleo*. Production was minimal because the price of oil was inflated by high transport costs imposed by the British-owned railways, due to the fact that petroleum represented potential competition with British-produced coal imports. However, this early involvement of private capital and the provincial oligarchy in oil production represented a conflict of interest between the province and the national state as oil production became more concentrated in state hands, especially after the founding of state oil company *Yacimientos Petrolíferos Fiscales* (YPF) in 1922. After the 1930 coup d'état, the *Mendocina* yielded its oil rights to YPF, in exchange for royalty payments which would become a key factor in relations between the province and the nation by the 1980s, when Mendoza produced a quarter of Argentina's total oil output.

Although as undemocratic as their counterparts elsewhere, the governing elites in Mendoza in the late nineteenth century pursued an unusually active policy of fostering economic development, which also promoted immigration and social mobility. Such a policy was arguably necessary in a province where agricultural production required technological innovation, especially in terms of irrigation. Moreover, due to its proximity to the wealthiest and most populous part of Chile, Mendoza enjoyed greater commercial opportunities, although its economy was geared largely to the national market rather than to exports. The emphasis on wine production was increased with the arrival of the railway in 1885, in the same way that sugar production increased in Tucumán to take advantage of the expanded domestic market it created. However, whereas the sugar industry created a class of large landholders and industrialists, on the one hand, and a class of peasant proprietors and waged labour, on the other, the expansion of wine production in Mendoza tended to create a middling sector of medium-scale landholders and vintners who joined the provincial middle and upper class.

The provincial government, by virtue of controlling access to water, controlled access to the livelihood of the bulk of the population. The General Water Law was passed in 1884, with a water department created the following year. Foreign technicians were contracted to study irrigation methods and new methods of vine cultivation and wine production. Improvements in irrigation systems were financed by the sale of public lands, many of which were sold to the same immigrants contracted to improve agricultural output; private landholders likewise sold parcels of land to finance their own improvements. At the same time, the provincial government encouraged mass immigration to provide a labour force for economic expansion, paying an agent in Buenos Aires one peso per head for each immigrant who came to Mendoza. Between 1880 and 1905 an average of 2,000 immigrants arrived annually, rising to an average of 6,000 between 1906 and 1914, and lands dedicated to vines increased from 1,500 hectares in 1873 to 53,000 in 1911.

The availability of technology to extract water supplies changed the face both of Mendozan agriculture and of its landholding patterns. Prior to the widespread use of irrigation, much of the province was usable only for pastoral farming, the sparse pasture requiring vast tracts of land. However, as irrigation became more widespread, the cultivation of vines, which did not require large units of production, became viable; moreover, control of above-ground water supplies ceased to be a significant source of political power. In addition, many of these smaller tracts were bought by immigrants who had come to Mendoza originally as labourers or technicians. Whereas in the mid-nineteenth century almost all lands were in the hands of the *criollo* aristocracy, a century later 93 per cent of all cultivated lands were owned by families of recent immigrant origin.[2]

The promotion of economic expansion and immigration created a settled and industrious population in Mendoza and a prosperous provincial economy, although Mendozan wine was forced to compete with imports from France and Spain. However, over time it also undermined the political and economic dominance of the traditional elite, whose political power had been largely based on their economic power and control of water supplies. While the local representatives of the liberal elite continued to govern until 1917, they did so against rising opposition by 'new' middling sectors, both urban and rural, who eventually supported the UCR. Though their economic dominance was already a thing of the past, restricted political participation permitted them to retain government until the 1916 elections that brought Hipólito Yrigoyen to the presidency and Radical lawyer José Néstor Lencinas to the governorship of Mendoza.

Lencinas, a wealthy lawyer known for his defence of the rights of the poor, was arguably a *caudillo* of the same nature as those who had gone before. Between 1916 and 1930, Lencinas and his three sons Carlos Washington, Rafael Néstor and José Hipólito captured two governorships, two Senate seats and three Lower House seats. However, with universal suffrage attained in 1912, Lencinas was a populist rather than an elitist *caudillo*, and necessarily more responsive to the popular mood than those governors who had been hand-picked by the ruling families. Under him, legislation was introduced regulating pensions, working hours and minimum wages (advances not achieved nationally until the Perón era some 25 years later).

Lencinismo was arguably a local populist current incorporated for convenience into the UCR (like the *bloquismo* of Federico and Aldo Cantoni in San Juan), and both the Lencinas and Cantonis suffered from poor relations with Yrigoyen. Mendoza was intervened by decree by Yrigoyen in 1918, on the grounds that Lencinas was not operating within the boundaries permitted by the constitution. In the 1919 elections held to 'normalize' the province, Lencinas was re-elected, dying in office in 1921. His son Carlos Washington was elected governor on his death, but the province was again intervened from 1924 to 1926, this time by a Congress which in the majority supported Yrigoyen, and against the wishes of anti-Yrigoyenist President Marcelo T. de Alvear. In 1926 Lencinas' candidate, Alejandro Orfila, was elected governor, but the province was again intervened under Yrigoyen's second presidency in 1928; it was still under federal intervention at the time of the September 1930 coup d'état that overthrew Yrigoyen. Carlos Washington Lencinas was twice elected senator, but his credentials were rejected on both occasions by the pro-Yrigoyen Congress. He was assassinated in 1929, purportedly on the orders of Yrigoyen (a suspicion that was a factor in his own overthrow a year later).

The aftermath of the coup brought the old conservative elite back to power in Mendoza, in the form of the *Partido Democrático Nacional* (renamed the *Partido Demócrata*, PD, in 1946), which was elected repeatedly during the 1930s on the basis of widespread allegations of fraud. The PD shared with the conservative provincial governments of the late nineteenth and early twentieth centuries a reputation for efficiency, an element of personalism and a progressive outlook with respect to the province's social and economic infrastructure. However, while ostensibly a 'federalist' party representing provincial interests, the PD in the 1930s was notable for its support of the centralizing initiatives of the national government. In the 1934 debate on tax reform (which gave the Nation the right to collect and redistribute taxes), a member of the PD stated that 'the provinces renounce constitutional rights to place themselves at the service of a higher concept'.[3]

Perón won the 1946 presidential elections in Mendoza with some 52 per cent of the vote, a more modest level than that recorded in provinces such as Tucumán. However, following Perón's 1955 overthrow and the proscription of his party, the neo-Peronist party *Tres Banderas* was founded in Mendoza, although it never succeeded in winning an election, with the PD winning most provincial elections until 1973. In that year, the left-wing Peronist Alberto Martínez Baca was elected governor, although he faced impeachment the following year following accusations of financial irregularities connected with *Bodegas y Viñedos Giol*, the winery founded in 1896 and acquired by the provincial government in 1954. The impeachment was aborted by federal intervention of the province. Nevertheless, Mendoza, already socially conservative, was not one of the provinces most central to the 'war on subversion' from 1976 and was not radically changed by the experience. However, there are testimonies of six clandestine detention centres and some 150 disappearances in the province. Economically, the province remained dependent on national funds for over half its financial resources during the dictatorship, and GDP per capita declined over the period.

In 1983 the UCR won both the presidential and gubernatorial elections in Mendoza, a break with recent political trends in the province; with the exception of the period 1958–61, no Radical had governed Mendoza since 1928, with the UCR typically the third force behind the Peronists and PD. Moreover, the popular former PD governor Francisco Gabrielli was beaten into third place, while traditional *caudillos* returned to office in Tucumán, Catamarca and Neuquén. However, the economic crisis of the mid-1980s, exacerbated by the fall in wine prices, led to a new fall in provincial GDP, and in 1987 Peronist José Octavio Bordón captured the governorship. Bordón, who would later come second to incumbent president Carlos Menem in the 1995 presidential elections, gained a reputation for efficiency and honesty, although in practice he did relatively little during his four-year term and benefited from the coming to fruition of projects launched under his predecessor and from Mendoza's history as a well-ordered and prosperous province. That very reputation appears to have done little for its influence at the national level, where more problematic provinces have often carried more weight if only by virtue of their ability to cause trouble.

TUCUMAN

While the northwest remains the most traditional, *criollo* region of Argentina, Tucumán is in some ways the least traditional province in the region. Historically a commercial centre, from the late nineteenth century Tucumán experienced significant industrial development based largely on the production of sugar, and also significant immigration attracted by commercial and industrial opportunities; in some limited respects the provincial capital of San Miguel de Tucumán is thus closer to Buenos Aires or Rosario than to the rest of the northwest. Following a period of significant political and economic influence in the nineteenth century, Tucumán declined both politically and economically, especially since 1930. In many ways an atypical province, Tucumán is sometimes said to represent the future of the entire country, in the sense that it has at times experienced phenomena which later became generalized throughout Argentina. This was most obviously true in the case of the counterinsurgency methods introduced in Tucumán in 1975 (involving the use of torture, disappearance, extrajudicial killing and the setting up of a network of clandestine detention centres to eliminate real and perceived political opposition, violent or non-violent), which from 1976 became the norm throughout the country.

An important agricultural, commercial and manufacturing centre serving the mining centres of Alto Perú during the colonial era, Tucumán – situated on the route between Potosí and Buenos Aires – became wealthy in the eighteenth century through the production of wooden products including carts, trade and contraband, relying on the available pool of slaves and indigenous labour. Known as 'the cradle of independence' (a number of important battles were fought by General Manuel Belgrano's Army of the North in the province, in particular the Battle of Tucumán on 24 September 1812, and Argentina's independence was declared by the Congress of Tucumán on 9 July 1816), Tucumán's economic links with Buenos Aires and other provinces of the interior gained in importance post independence, with its international trade declining until the latter half of the nineteenth century.

The production of sugar (depending then as now on a dense population which guaranteed a supply of cheap labour) began in 1821 at the initiative of Bishop Colombres, and expanded moderately at a small-scale level over the next 50 years. It did not, however, achieve a level of industrial development until the opening of the railway linking Tucumán with Buenos Aires in 1876, an event which altered its development and partially underlay the subsequent divergence between Tucumán and other traditional provinces such as Catamarca.

The development of the sugar industry, which grew rapidly post 1870, marked the subsequent development of Tucumán in at least three significant respects. To begin with, it created an industrial base around the sugar mills more extensive than any other outside the Littoral region. This industrial power remained concentrated in the hands of a traditional commercial and landed elite which, while it retained significant political power until at least 1946 and economic power until the present, was extensive enough to prevent the concentration of power among a handful of families, unlike Catamarca, Salta or La Rioja. The diffusion of power also reflected the fact that agriculture in Tucumán did not depend on irrigation, and power therefore did not depend on the control of water supplies.

At the same time, a significant proportion of sugar cane production remained in the hands of independent small-scale producers who sold their product to the large mills. This created a substantial class of producers who were simultaneously peasant proprietors and labourers, and independent only in nominal terms, since they had no option but to sell to the large mills on the latter's terms. This differed sharply from Salta and Jujuy, where nearly all cane was grown on plantations owned by the mills themselves. Moreover, the growth and labour intensiveness of the sugar industry created labour shortages redressed by migrant workers from the north or Bolivia, often in conditions of near-slavery.

This relatively diffuse ownership was due in part to the lack of capital available to concentrate both plantations and mills in the hands of a small elite, which was also partially responsible for the third phenomenon distinguishing Tucumán: the arrival of significant numbers of European immigrants and foreign capital in the late nineteenth century. Although attracted in part by the availability of land in the northwest, European and later Middle Eastern immigrants were principally involved in commercial or industrial activity. Drawn especially by the shortage of skilled local labour in the sugar industry, by 1895 some 10,000 Spanish, Italian and French immigrants had settled in Tucumán, contributing to the broadening of a professional middle class and a 'Europeanization' of cultural outlook, especially in the capital. By 1914, nearly 10 per cent of Tucumán's population was European-born, as opposed to some 8 per cent in Salta, less than 4 per cent in Santiago del Estero and around 2 per cent each in Jujuy, Catamarca and La Rioja.[4] In 1914 the National University of Tucumán opened, further widening the province's cultural life.

The rise in Tucumán's economic importance coincided with a period of political influence at the national level. Three of Argentina's most prominent statesmen, Juan B. Alberdi, Julio Roca and Nicolás Avellaneda, were from Tucumán; Avellaneda and Roca in their presidencies pursued policies which benefited Tucumán's political and economic elites. The railway was extended to Tucumán during Avellaneda's presidency, in 1876, while Roca allegedly sent members of the Mapuche and other tribes captured in the 'Desert Campaign' in Patagonia to work as semi-slave labour in Tucumán's sugar industry. From the 1880s the sugar industry enjoyed the protection of high import tariffs on foreign-produced sugar. (Wine was the only other regional product to enjoy such protection.) As a result, sugar prices in Argentina have typically been two to three times higher than the international norm, but the practice created a wealthy elite dependent on the central government and willing to use its influence in the province to support it. It also created an industry with no need to be efficient. However, perhaps because no family or group had achieved hegemony in the province, provincial politics were noted for their factionalism. Between 1887 and 1906 the province was intervened by the federal government three times (although never by Avellaneda or Roca), to stabilize combustible situations caused by infighting among members of the local oligarchy.

From the 1920s, however, with the sugar industry declining despite legal measures to fix the internal price (due to the limited internal market, increasing competition from Salta and Jujuy and, from 1929, the decline in agricultural exports), Tucumán played a diminishing role in national affairs. The sugar mills depended increasingly on government subsidies or loans to finance the annual harvest and milling of sugar; that financial support continued to be granted year after year in the face of threatened closures and mass unemployment in a province already characterized by poverty and the greatest population density outside Greater Buenos Aires. Those subsidies likewise contributed to the province's financial insolvency, given the large number of unsecured debts that sugar mills accrued with the provincial bank. Perhaps most importantly, central government subsidies kept the province dependent on the central state and on a sole product, while contributing to the inefficiency of its production.

The population density and the high percentage involved in small-scale production or industrial employment undoubtedly explains the high level of support for Perón in the province from the 1940s. While Peronism from its origins tended to adapt to local conditions, its principal expression in the 1940s was based on urban industrial labour and small- or medium-scale proprietors; as such, its main bastions of support were the few urban centres with a significant industrial and commercial presence. In the case of Tucumán in particular, unionization began on a large scale from June 1944, with the creation of the sugar unions FOTIA, FEIA and UCIT, as well as other unions which affiliated to the CGT. However, the railway unions *La Fraternidad* and the *Unión Ferroviaria* already had a significant presence in Tucumán: the railways had long represented a major source of employment, due to the importance of the railways generally and the presence of large workshops for the maintenance of rolling stock in Tafí Viejo. The FOTIA, railway workers and others participated in demonstrations in support of Perón in Tucumán on 17 October 1945; in 1946, Perón received the highest percentage of the vote anywhere in the country in Tucumán, and between 1946 and 1991 the Peronists won every presidential and gubernatorial election in the province in which the party was not proscribed.

Following the 1966 coup d'état, the government of General Juan Carlos Onganía launched 'Operation Tucumán', seeking to redress the economic crisis in the province through the closure of 11 sugar mills, the concentration of production among the largest, and the promotion of alternative industries. These moves reflected growing concern over possible unrest in a province where population was dense, unions politicized and poverty and unemployment, always endemic, on the rise. A wave of strikes hit Tucumán in 1966, 20 of them in the sugar industry alone; repressive action ensured that by 1967 the number was dramatically reduced. The industrial promotion scheme had some success in creating or expanding production in areas such as textiles and sugar-related products such as paper and alcohol (and other agricultural sectors such as citrus or soya production also witnessed significant growth). However, that growth could not absorb the workforce made redundant by the closure of sugar mills, and some 200,000 left the province between 1966 and 1970 – indeed, Tucumán was the only province to register a decline in population between the 1960 and 1970 censuses.

Tucumán was also influenced during the Onganía regime by an influx of academics, students, artists, political activists and other intellectuals from Buenos Aires and Rosario, which suffered considerably greater political persecution. Culturally, the province enjoyed an expansion of artistic activity, as well as an infusion of intellectual stimulus (and political militancy) in the university, even as the economic situation deteriorated. This arguably also brought a radicalizing influence whose vision of Tucumán did not entirely square with the reality facing its working class and rural population.

The economic displacement and political mobilization in Tucumán in the 1960s and early 1970s also contributed to the activities of both urban and rural armed opposition groups. (An earlier guerrilla experiment in Tucumán, the pro-Perón *Uturuncos*, had been active in the late 1950s and represented the first attempt at rural insurgency in Argentina in the twentieth century.) By far the most important of the groups operating in Tucumán, the Trotskyist *Ejército Revolucionario del Pueblo* (ERP) was dominated by middle-class professionals, most of whom had their early political formation in the Radical party. The ERP perceived in Tucumán the same set of conditions that had facilitated the Cuban Revolution: economic dependency (Tucumán being seen as an 'internal colony' of Buenos Aires), a heavy concentration of population, dependency on a depressed sugar economy which in turn exploited the high level of poverty and unemployment in the province, a history of political militancy and a mountainous region suitable for guerrilla warfare. In addition, the ERP drew parallels with Vietnam, where the Viet Cong had established liberated zones with local support and had thereafter been able to generate international support for its struggle.

This perception was palpably a gross miscalculation of the support base available, and indeed such an insurrection could scarcely be successful if confined to a small province in the centre of the country. Following years of decline, rising poverty and unemployment, and brutal repression of protests, Tucumán's poorer classes – traditionally conservative at best – did not offer a strong support base for any such adventure. Moreover, political militancy, to the extent it existed, was overwhelmingly Peronist and hence offered scant support to a Trotskyist insurgent group operating in the early 1970s under an elected Peronist government. In this respect, however, the ERP was no different from other groups of Marxist orientation in Argentina which had historically been blind to the level of working-class loyalty to Peronism, apparently because it was politically incorrect from a Marxist perspective.

On 10 February 1975 the government of President María Estela Martínez de Perón ordered the security forces to 'annihilate subversion' in Tucumán, and *Operativo Independencia*, under the command of General Edgardo Acdel Vilas, mobilized 5,000 troops to combat the ERP in the province. The irregular methods used, which would later spread to the rest of the country, included the use of clandestine detention centres, torture and forced disappearance. Although the ERP was purportedly eradicated by the end of 1975, a new wave of political disappearances in the province followed the 24 March 1976 coup d'état. However, the military government led in the province by General Antonio Domingo Bussi – later accused of personal involvement in human rights violations – also undertook a number of highly publicized public works that enhanced his prestige.

At the time of the return to democracy in 1983, Tucumán represented a bleak panorama: unemployment and underemployment reached 16.6 per cent, rising to 26.1 per cent in 1987 and 29.2 per cent in 1991, while infant mortality reached 41.5 per thousand by 1984 and those below the poverty line accounted for 42.4 per cent of the provincial population, well above the national averages. Despite an ever-more discredited political system, significant elements of all social sectors became increasingly dependent on the state, while a degree of nostalgia for the more free-spending military government saw a rise in support for Bussi as a civilian figure. The bankruptcy of the political system was illustrated by provincial elections in the 1990s: following a federal intervention that removed the incompetent José Domato from office, in 1991 the governorship was won by a former popular singer, Ramón 'Palito' Ortega, backed by the then President Carlos Menem and federal intervener Julio César Aráoz as an alternative to Bussi; Bussi himself was elected in 1995.

CATAMARCA

One of the last outposts of the Inca Empire and later of the Viceroyalty of Peru, Catamarca – a name of Quechua origin, meaning fortress on the hillside – has historically been on the margins of every political and geographical entity to which it has belonged. Prior to independence Catamarca was largely a producer of cotton, economically geared to trade with Chile and other provinces of the northwest, and declined in importance as Argentina's economy became increasingly orientated towards Buenos Aires in the later half of the nineteenth century. Catamarca continued to enjoy a trade surplus until the 1870s, chiefly due to its copper, gold and silver mining industry in the north of the province (the Bajo la Alumbrera mine near Santa María, opened in the mid-1990s, has been the province's leading industry for a decade). However, its marginalization within the country was cemented by the expansion of the railway, which favoured Tucumán to the detriment of the rest of the northwest. The railway reached the capital of Catamarca, in the south of the province, only in 1889 – and terminated there, isolated from the zones of greatest mining and agricultural production. The end of the century thus saw an irreversible decline in Catamarca's production, which in demographic terms signified mass migration to the provincial capital or to the sugar plantations of Tucumán.

In religious terms, the strong (for Argentina) Catholicism of the province was very evident. Owing to a large and fairly settled indigenous population it had attracted, since colonial times, missionaries and a strong institutional Church presence uncommon in most of Argentina. The wooden statute of the Virgin of the Valley, the patron of Catamarca, now housed in its cathedral, was discovered being worshipped by Indians in a grotto in 1620 (the origins of the statue are mysterious and supposedly miraculous). The 1854 provincial constitution, drafted by an assembly presided over by four priests, made no reference to the recognition of freedom of religion, unlike the national constitution, and members of religious orders, uniquely in Argentina, were not excluded from voting. The cult surrounding the Virgin of the Valley had, even in colonial times, spread beyond Catamarca, attracting (and continuing to attract) pilgrims whose food, lodging and other contributions sustained much of the provincial economy.

Due to its economic stagnation, Catamarca attracted minimal European immigration. By 1914 only 2.3 per cent of its population was foreign-born (as compared to nearly 10 per cent in Tucumán); the immigrant community included 674 Spaniards, 568 Italians and 469 Arabs.[5] As a result, Catamarca remained, with Salta, one of the last solid bastions of traditional *criollo* society. The conservative elite retained power from independence until 1943, in an economy based on public patronage, subsistence farming and artisanal production. Prominent among the few families who retained control of the province was the Cubas family; José Cubas, governor several times in the 1830s and 1840s, led the province's resistance to Buenos Aires *caudillo* Juan Manuel de Rosas and was executed in 1841. One of his descendants, Alicia Cubas, married Vicente Saadi a century later and became the matriarch of another ruling family which was to control Catamarca for nearly 50 years. The continuity of power in the nineteenth century did not, however, indicate political stability: the province was intervened by the federal government seven times between 1880 and 1918. (Catamarca has been intervened more times than any other province. Governor Agustín Madueño, who left office in 1928, was the last governor to complete his mandate until

Ramón Saadi handed power to his elected successor – his father – in 1987.)

Catamarca perhaps reached its apogee of national importance under the presidency of *catamarqueño* Ramón Castillo, who was elected vice-president in the fraudulent elections of 1938 and replaced President Roberto Ortiz in 1940. Castillo was deposed by the 'Revolution of 4 June 1943' when he sought to impose the candidacy of another member of the *criollo* elite, the *salteño* Robustiano Patrón Costas, as his successor. The coup d'état, which laid the foundation for the rise of Perón, arguably represented the final blow to that elite's political dominance, already in decline following the introduction of the Sáenz Peña law in 1912 and the election of Yrigoyen in 1916. Thereafter, the entrenched aristocracy of the northwest (more socially than economically powerful) played an ever diminishing national role, while more modern urban sectors (chiefly of recent European origin) rose in importance.

As a chiefly urban movement, based especially on industrial trade unions and sectors of the professional middle classes, the Peronism of the 1940s had no obvious support base in Catamarca. However, it was adopted as an alternative to the old conservative party (which at the time represented the losing side) by elements of that now-debilitated elite and by a new political class in the northwest which, without seeking to alter the basic power structure prevalent in the region, sought greater insertion for its own members within that structure. Those elements arguably represented a transition from the old oligarchy to a new, populist oligarchy in underdeveloped provinces, but not a clear break with the politics of the past.

This new sector included, in particular, members of the professional middle class, a small group in Catamarca but one which by this time was expanding, especially due to the incorporation of the children of Arab and other immigrants. A small group at best, it had no possibility of dominating provincial politics alone. However, the old elite was likewise weak. The Catamarca oligarchy was made up largely of the old *criollo* aristocracy, which enjoyed social prestige but limited economic resources of its own. This was and is a constant factor: the local elite, while wealthy in relative terms, was based in a province with little economic output and thus had little economic power at the national level. Until the 1940s they had been able to exercise power chiefly through their ties to other, more economically influential elites, and through the control of state payrolls and patronage gained through their access to provincial government. However, as the oligarchy's political weight diminished nationally after 1943, the Catamarca elite lost its useful political connections. With no other source of political power, some members of these conservative elites joined the Peronist bandwagon, together with members of the small but rising middle class. Neither had the strength necessary to control the province alone, but a good relationship with the national government ensured access to economic resources and therefore political power; economic assistance, on the other hand, was channelled by the national government precisely because its influence was weak in remote parts of the country and could only be exercised through local collaborators.

The new coalition of forces represented by Peronism offered an entree to political power which the old elites would not (and arguably could not) provide to ambitious outsiders. That new political class was represented by rising provincial *caudillos* such as Carlos Juárez in Santiago del Estero, Fernando Riera in Tucumán and Catamarca lawyer Vicente Saadi, who in 1947 became a Peronist senator at the age of 33. (By the 1980s, all three of these now aged *caudillos* were still in power.) According to most versions, Saadi acceded to the Senate through a rather original piece of fraud, allegedly telephoning the governor and, claiming to be Perón, ordering that the provincial legislature elect Saadi as Catamarca's new senator.

The son of Lebanese immigrants, and married to the daughter of the prominent but impoverished Cubas family, Saadi had already passed through the Radical and conservative parties before attaching himself to the Peronists in the mid-1940s. In consolidating his and his family's domination of the province over a period of 45 years, Saadi did not fundamentally alter the tradition of nepotism and *caudillismo* in Catamarca politics, but rather represented a transition from one oligarchy to another, from a traditional oligarchy to a populist one. His power remained based on clientelism, local power brokers (many of them sharing his surname) and the lack of political or labour organization in the province. Within a year of joining the Senate, Saadi had become president of the majority bloc in the Senate and president of its Foreign Trade Commission, as well as president of the party in Catamarca. The latter two posts in particular are alleged to have provided the basis for the personal fortune he eventually accumulated; as noted above, the province itself offered only limited economic resources to be exploited or misappropriated.

Catamarca was intervened by the federal government at Saadi's instigation in 1947, on the grounds of a political conflict between the governor and vice-governor, and again in 1948. On the latter occasion Saadi was appointed governor, possibly with a view to removing him from national influence given his often tense relations with Perón and Eva Perón. The province was intervened again in 1949 and Saadi expelled from the party, due to the 'nepotism that rules in the government of Catamarca. There is a climate of persecution and denial of fundamental rights'.[6] Saadi was subsequently arrested on the grounds of *desacato* (slander) on the basis of anti-government articles published in his newspaper *La Verdad*, and of theft of public property. He was imprisoned until 1952. Resurfacing in 1955 as a political ally of General Eduardo Lonardi after the overthrow of Perón, Saadi subsequently allied himself to Radical President Arturo Frondizi, under whose government he returned to the Senate, besides maintaining ties to Perón in exile, insofar as their interests coincided.

Re-elected to the Senate in 1973, Saadi pursued a sinuous political trajectory in the 1970s and early 1980s, maintaining relations with both the post-1976 military government and representatives of the Montonero guerrilla movement. On the return of electoral democracy in 1983, Saadi again became senator for Catamarca, president of the Senate and first vice-president of the Peronist party, a position effectively guaranteeing control of the party. As a skilled negotiator more dedicated to his role as power broker than to any presidential ambition, Saadi represented a powerful figure to be courted rather than a competitor for the highest office. Also in 1983, son Ramón Saadi became governor, a post to which Vicente succeeded in 1987 while his son replaced him in the Senate. On Vicente's death in 1988, Ramón returned to the governorship and his sister Alicia succeeded him in the Senate. The hold on provincial politics remained a springboard for numerous relatives to gain influential posts in both the national and provincial administrations.

The funds necessary to sustain the Saadis' hold on the province, as noted earlier, flowed from their national connections. By 1992, the provincial administration accounted for 46 per cent of employment in the province, with a larger number of employees per capita than any province except the more sparsely populated provinces of La Rioja (home of President Carlos Menem) and Santa Cruz (home of President Néstor Kirchner). It also contrived to pay its employees on time during the 1980s financial crisis, unlike provinces such as Tucumán, while the Saadi electoral machine was also noted for using resources to distribute gifts to voters prior to elections. (In particular, they were alleged to have given one shoe to each voter in a given district, with the promise that the other shoe would be handed over if they won the district.) National influence also boosted Catamarca's share of federal shared revenues, to more than twice the per capita amount received by Tucumán, not least to gain Saadi's support for the initiatives of the increasingly beleaguered Alfonsín government in the 1980s. At the same time, Saadi's influence in the fractured party was crucial in gaining the presidential nomination for his 'political heir', Carlos Menem, in 1988; Vicente Saadi died the day after Menem won the party primary.

Unlike adjoining Tucumán, Catamarca was little affected by the political upheaval and repression of the 1976–83 military regime. A traditionally Catholic province lacking political militancy, Catamarca offered no real or perceived subversive target to attack. Educational levels remained on average poor, and the provincial university, opened in 1973, had a poor academic reputation and a conservative hierarchy, while the long history of patronage and dependency on the state had essentially stifled independent political or social initiatives. In short, the passive provincial society already conformed to the approximate model which the dictatorship sought to impose throughout the country. The province suffered only one serious clash between the military and guerrilla forces, although it became a haven for political activists from provinces where repression was more severe. For the same reason, arguably the return to democracy in 1983 was less of a watershed than in other parts of the country; from 1983 to 1991 the provincial government remained in Saadi hands.

However, in April 1991 the Menem government intervened in the province against Menem's former ally. While the causes are somewhat ambiguous, the proximate cause was the discovery of the body of María Soledad Morales, a 16-year-old student, on 10 September 1990. Although the precise circumstances of her death were never clarified, she seemingly died following a party given by the son of a Saadi associate, at which members of the family were allegedly present; her death, whether accidental or deliberate, appeared to involve cocaine and sexual abuse. The case attracted extreme national and provincial attention and was taken up by members of the Catholic Church and others as symptomatic of the decadence of the provincial administration. A series of weekly 'marches of silence' kept the case in the public eye, and the apparent impunity of those responsible for the death provoked a wave of indignation; public opinion was particularly horrified when Catamarca federal deputy Angel Luque told the press that had his son been responsible, her body would never have been found (a comment that saw him expelled from Congress and the party).[7] However, while the intervention served to end the Saadis' dominance, it did little to modify political structures (a niece of Vicente Saadi was elected governor in 2011).

NEUQUÉN

Unlike the provinces of the northwest or Cuyo, Neuquén has little history of belonging to the Argentine Republic or to any of the colonial administrative entities that preceded it. Settled by Argentines only in the last two decades of the nineteenth century, Neuquén voted in presidential elections for the first time in 1951 and became a province only in 1955, having been a national territory since 1884. In that respect, Neuquén and the rest of Patagonia fall outside the traditional federalist argument that the provinces pre-date the nation; from 1884 to 1955 Neuquén and the other territories were 'simple administrative or geographical divisions, subsequent to the national constitution'.[8] Whereas the nation was ostensibly created by the provinces, the territories were created by the nation and as such had no autonomy. Indeed, they were created precisely in the period when the national state was consolidated and beginning to dominate even the existing provinces, and their initial 100 years of social, political and economic development did not occur as semi-independent states or recognizable cultural entities – a fact which influenced the development of social structures more than usually dependent on the state. Until 1955, Neuquén's officials were all named directly by the national government and it had no power to fix or collect taxes, also in the hands of the nation.

However, despite its lack of traditional social structures and its 'new' and fluid society, from 1960 Neuquén consolidated a system of political *caudillismo*, in the hands of the Sapag family, as entrenched as that in any northern province. Arguably, the Sapags' position was for a long time stronger, being based on control of Neuquéns's considerable economic resources and their ability to distribute greater largesse to their political clients, as well as a certain consequent independence from the federal government as a source of funds. Having laid the foundations of their political and economic power before 1955, the Sapags predated the province, even as the provinces predated the nation. The instrument of their power has been the provincial political party, the neo-Peronist MPN, founded by them in 1961, when the Peronist party was proscribed, and consistently in power since then.

There are many seeming paradoxes in the rise and continuing success of the Sapags and the MPN (at least until 1991 the two were largely synonymous). The fact that a system of government based on patronage, clientelism and economic dependence can so easily be constructed in a province which is patently not a feudal or rigidly structured society is curious, as is the fact that the Sapags insistently claimed to represent 'true Peronism' in the province. However, at the national level the MPN's independence from both major parties has allowed it to exercise leverage in Congress, at least when the governing party has lacked a safe majority. Moreover, the exclusive focus on Neuquén meant that the Sapags and the MPN played little national role and consequently have not disturbed the central powers or provoked close national scrutiny of the political situation in the province. (Whereas a poor province like Catamarca can only serve as an access route to other sources of power, which forced the Saadis to look outside the province, Neuquén as a major oil producer offers more than adequate economic resources, many of them state-controlled.) Likewise, the construction of a patron–client system in a 'new' society full of economic migrants without pre-existing local loyalties is readily viable, especially where no pre-existing political force dominated. The Sapags, immigrants from Lebanon, arguably came to power in Neuquén at a moment similar to that at the national level when Perón first became president, and their use and abuse of power was reminiscent of the early years of Peronism.

Neuquén and other Patagonian provinces came within the effective control of the Argentine Republic as a result of the 'Conquest of the Desert' (1879–85) led by Julio Argentino Roca, first as its commanding general and later as president. The so-called 'desert' was at the time populated by Chileans and by indigenous groups dominated by the

Araucanian Indians, and the chief objectives of its conquest were to expand the area dedicated to livestock production in an era of increasing
foreign trade and to secure the frontier with Chile (finally established
in 1881); the latter was facilitated by Chile's concurrent involvement
in the War of the Pacific. However, the reasoning behind the Argentine settlement of the south also contained an element of Sarmiento's
'civilization versus barbarism': the existing tribes were assumed to be
nomadic, primitive and thus inferior (indeed, the insistence on referring to the region as 'desert' suggests that it was considered effectively
uninhabited by human beings).

The desert campaign was financed by public subscription and by
the sale of some 400 titles to parcels of land of 2,500 hectares each
(at the time still inhabited by local tribes); a further 6,000 land titles to parcels of varying sizes were distributed to participants in the
campaign. From 1876, under the 'colonization law', parcels of 40,000
hectares were distributed to concessionaires for the purpose of being
subdivided to attract settlers to the area but, by 1928, 92 per cent of
those lands remained in the hands of the concessionaires and the experiment was abandoned. The lands in Neuquén were mainly of limited value for agricultural purposes, the only areas suitable for pasture
being the areas around the northeast and the confluence of the rivers
Limay and Neuquén. Sheep were increasingly moved to the area from
the more fertile Pampas, although markets were not readily accessible
before the railway reached the area in 1902. As such, the territory attracted few settlers, reaching a population of only around 14,500 by
1895 (much of it of Chilean origin, with only 70 immigrants from
Spain and Italy recorded at that time). However, the railways later
brought Europeans into influential social and economic positions; indeed, the railways and public employment were from the first key
sources of economic activity. From the early twentieth century merchants of Syrian and Lebanese origin became increasingly important:
the centre of early twentieth century merchant activity was Zapala,
the territory's second city and birthplace of the younger members
of the Lebanese Sapag family.

Oil was discovered in Plaza Huincul in 1918, at which time only
eight towns (most of them ex-military installations) existed in the
territory. As much oil-related activity was state-operated – first under
the auspices of the *Dirección de Explotación de Petroleo*, created in 1910,
and later state oil company YPF – the discovery marked another stage

in the state's incursion into Neuquén's development. Although the creation of YPF in particular raised tensions between oil-producing provinces and the nation, the small amount produced by Neuquén in the 1920s and 1930s and its status as a national territory with no autonomy to defend made these considerations less important than elsewhere. The local elite, to the extent it existed, was dependent on, rather than in competition with, the national state; following provincialization in 1955 the elite (still mainly state employees and bureaucrats) continued to rely on, rather than dominate, the provincial state.

Oil exploitation in Plaza Huincul created a new economic centre in Neuquén and gave rise to the town of Cutral Có, primarily populated by YPF employees in the 1930s, which attracted merchants originally based in Zapala, including Elías and Felipe Sapag. In the absence of elective political bodies the Sapags rapidly came to dominate local commissions, and both joined the *Partido Laborista* and later the Peronist party from 1946. In the 1951 municipal elections, Felipe was elected councillor, pursuing a programme of public works and occasionally intervening with the national government to demand benefits for the residents of Cutral Có, most of them state employees.

The granting of the presidential vote to the national territories in 1951 was of course designed, like the concession of votes to women in 1947, to ensure a greater majority for Perón in his second presidential election. The strategy proved successful in the territories, where the vote for Perón was higher than the national average; in Neuquén he received nearly 80 per cent of the votes cast. (Although Neuquén and other territories had small populations and therefore meant few votes in absolute terms, the president was elected by the Electoral College, where provinces and territories with small populations were disproportionately represented.) Neuquén was in any case a natural support base for Perón, dominated by public-sector employment and urban-based industrial labour. However, this electoral manoeuvre also created the beginnings of the MPN's support base, which would later usurp the position of the Peronists in the province.

Neuquén and the other remaining national territories (with the exception of Tierra del Fuego) became provinces of the Argentine Republic on 15 June 1955. As the Patagonian territories represented the most important sources of oil production, their provincialization was arguably delayed until that late date in order to maintain greater central control over their natural resources – although the timing also reflected the need to generate support for the sagging Perón government (overthrown three months later). Neuquén thus came into existence as a province with a strong Peronist identification, at the precise moment the Peronists were proscribed by the military government. In 1961 the provincial chapter of the Peronist Party founded the MPN, which won the gubernatorial elections the following year with Felipe Sapag as its candidate. After those elections were annulled, Sapag and the MPN again won the 1963 contest, remaining in office until the 1966 coup d'état, although its leading members remained on good terms with the military government; Felipe Sapag was appointed federal intervener of the province in 1970. Although other neo-Peronist parties would fade away after Perón's return in 1973, the MPN has remained the province's key power base.

As after the 1966 coup, the Sapags maintained good relations with the junta that overthrew President Isabel Perón in 1976, despite the fact that two of Felipe's sons were killed by counterinsurgency forces. The designation of high-ranking army officers at the head of the military government, as opposed to civilians or lower-ranking officers (as was at times the case in Catamarca and Mendoza), points to the considerable importance placed on the control of Neuquén, given its hydrocarbons reserves and the fact that much of its territory remained the property of the armed forces. Although no terrorist attack was ever reported in the province, a clandestine detention centre was established in the city of Neuquén and 32 disappearances and numerous acts of torture were reported there in 1976 and 1977. While a small number in comparison with provinces such as Córdoba or Tucumán, the cases generated a strong local human rights movement, under the auspices of Bishop Jaime de Nevares.

In terms of economic development, the period of military government saw a sharp rise in gross provincial product and in royalty payments from the national treasury, although strong dependence on national funds in the form of royalties, shared revenues and other contributions reinforced the loss of autonomy implied by the dictatorship. Defence spending was also unusually high, due to the province's hydrocarbons resources and to rising tensions with neighbouring Chile.

With the return to democracy, President Raúl Alfonsín won the 1983 elections in the province, and his Radical party gained more congressional votes than the MPN, although Felipe Sapag returned to the governorship and the party got nearly 30 per cent of the presidential vote. However, the MPN lost the 1985 legislative elections to the Radicals amid slowing growth and charges of corruption and other crimes involving members of the Sapags' inner circle. The Sapags' own influence in the party began to decline thereafter, although the MPN continued to hold the governorship, with both Pedro Salvatori and Jorge Sobisch taking the party's nomination in the late 1980s and early 1990s. However, the MPN has retained a low-profile but significant leverage at the national level owing to its ability to supply 'independent' congressional votes to support government projects – in particular where government support in Congress has been a minority or a slim majority. This has tended to guarantee receipt of federal revenues on a disproportionately large scale given the province's small population, which, in turn, has strengthened the MPN's hold in the province. This is reinforced by widespread dependence on the provincial government, creating a striking concentration of power in a province with no traditional oligarchy or other alternative sources of political power, although this is perhaps less surprising given the large number of economic migrants to the province and their lack of other long-standing political or other loyalties. However, the importance of central government resources has, paradoxically, allowed the MPN to rally public opinion around resentment of central government interference, a 'federalist' position that has not implied support for the rights of other provinces or provincial parties.

12   Return to Democracy

Radical Raúl Alfonsín defeated Peronist Italo Luder by 50.5 per cent to 40.0 per cent in the 1983 presidential elections, although charisma, a clear electoral victory and democratic intentions were not enough to ensure a successful government. On the economic front, Alfonsín inherited a burgeoning foreign debt, a soaring budget deficit and an economy that had contracted by 15 per cent over the previous decade. However, the government reacted slowly from the time it took office in December 1983 until June 1985, when the Austral Plan was launched to reduce inflation and provide a tonic for the dyspeptic economy. By that time, much of the goodwill enjoyed by Alfonsín when he took office had evaporated, and what remained was insufficient to persuade Argentines of the need to make sacrifices for the greater good of a long-term improvement in the economy. Even the feel-good factor involved in winning the 1986 World Cup, which consolidated team captain Diego Armando Maradona as a national idol, provided only a minimal bounce for Alfonsín's sliding approval ratings. The government also failed to show great vigour in defending the Austral Plan; more populist economic measures prior to the 1987 mid-term elections represented the end of the ailing Austral Plan, and by 1989 the country was in a hyperinflationary crisis. (The new unit of currency introduced, the austral, was initially worth US $ 1, falling to 14 to the US dollar early in 1989 and reaching some 17,000 by the time of the May elections.) Proposals to begin a privatization process were too little, too late, and an attempt to move the national capital from

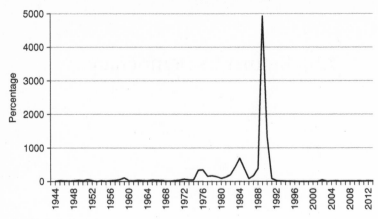

Graph 2. Inflation

Buenos Aires to the southern city of Viedma, in order to reduce the
degree of centralization in Buenos Aires, foundered on apathy and the
economic crisis, which left no funds for a costly transfer of national
government to a city lacking the necessary infrastructure for that purpose. At the same time, efforts to reduce unemployment led to a costly
rise in public employees, and declining purchasing power contributed
to 13 general strikes during Alfonsín's term.

On the political front, Alfonsín's most notable success was the
creation of the CONADEP, the findings of which were used as the
basis of a landmark trial of the nine former junta members who had
governed Argentina during the dirty war of the 1970s and early 1980s.
While the trial, which ended in prison terms for several of the former
junta members, represented a watershed internationally, at home it
opened the floodgates for an interminable series of prosecutions of
former military repressors (the mere estimate of 30,000 disappearances
gives an idea of the number of repressors who participated in the 'Dirty
War'). The impossibility of trying all of the guilty, and pressure from
restive armed forces pushing for an end to the trials, led Alfonsín to
present the Full Stop law in December 1986, giving a cut-off date for
charges to be brought against military and police officers.

The spate of cases brought in the short span of time allowed was far
more than the government or armed forces had expected, provoking
the first of a series of uprisings, led by army Colonel Aldo Rico during

Figure 15. President Raúl Alfonsín receives the report of the National Commission on Disappeared Persons (CONADEP) from Ernesto Sabato (courtesy of the archive, *Diario La Nación*)

Easter week of 1987. Although Alfonsín claimed not to have negotiated with the rebels, in June 1987 the Due Obedience law exempted from trial all officers who could claim to have been following superior orders in carrying out the repression – and, incidentally, made it clear that the government's firmness with the armed forces was at an end. Alfonsín was to face two more military uprisings, one led by Rico at the Monte Caseros military base in Corrientes (although he was in theory in detention at the time), and one led by Colonel Mohamed Alí Seineldin – a hero of the Falklands/Malvinas war and a right-wing Catholic – at the Villa Martelli base in Buenos Aires in December 1988. All three uprisings were known as the *carapintada* rebellions, as Rico, Seineldín and their followers covered their faces with camouflage paint before going into action.

As if this were not sufficient, in January 1989 a hitherto unknown left-wing group, the *Movimiento Todos por la Patria* (All for the Motherland Movement, MTP), led by former ERP militant Enrique Gorriarán Merlo (also responsible for the assassination of former Nicaraguan dictator Anastasio Somoza in Paraguay in 1980), attacked the La Tablada military barracks in Buenos Aires. The attack was apparently carried out in the belief that the act would help to prevent a military coup that the MTP thought imminent. The 25-hour-long siege produced dozens of deaths among both the attackers (some of whom disappeared or were killed after detention) and military personnel (mainly conscripts), and caused panic in a country which had lived through a decade of extremist violence in the 1970s and feared a replay of the previous debacle. Although this was palpably not the case, the surge of violence by both the Left and members of the army made it appear that control had slipped from Alfonsín's grasp. Closer to the May elections, violence of a different kind, arising from the hyperinflation and the desperation of individuals whose salaries no longer had any purchasing power, also received considerable media attention, as mobs sacked supermarkets and chaos appeared to be looming yet again.

The *carapintada* rebellions, in particular the Villa Martelli events which occurred only five months before the national elections, were to benefit the Peronist campaign by showing up the weakness of the Radical government in the face of military unrest. This was not entirely fortuitous. Carlos Menem's Interior Minister, Julio Mera Figueroa (former leader of the Peronist Youth and operator of Vicente Saadi), would note later that the *carapintadas* had been to Menem what the Montoneros had been to Perón, that is, a mechanism to achieve power which, once in power, was no longer useful and had to be eliminated.[1] By the time of the December 1990 *carapintada* rebellion, which Menem sent tanks to crush, he had no reason to seek to maintain ties with such a difficult ally, and every reason to break them.

Both the Peronists and UCR saw their share of the vote drop in the 1985 legislative elections, with provincial parties becoming the main beneficiaries of the general disillusionment with the two main parties, although it was the UCR which was primarily undermined by this shift: the ruling party saw its majority reduced in Congress, with many provincial representatives more inclined to support the Peronists in opposition to the government. The Peronists would again increase their vote in the 1987 legislative elections, rising to some 42 per cent of the national vote and reaching a congressional majority, while the number of UCR provincial governorships fell from seven in 1983 to two – Córdoba and Río Negro – that year. That rise in power, after the party's 1983 debacle, was to spell disaster for many of Alfonsín's initiatives, relentlessly blocked by the opposition in Congress. An attempt to prepare a constitutional reform, which would have created the post of prime minister and reduced the power of the president, was scuppered by the Peronists (not least because it proposed to allow immediate re-election of the president, a move which potentially benefited Alfonsín and would have extended the Peronists' period in the political hinterland).[2]

Financial incentives from the debilitated government were used to guarantee at least passive Peronist support in Congress for initiatives such as annual budgets or the new federal revenue-sharing agreement adopted in 1988, although these undermined the weak economic position of the state. Catamarca and La Rioja, governed by the Saadi family and by Menem, respectively, were especially favoured by these incentives. For example, while Catamarca, with 0.7 per cent of the national population, had received 1.96 per cent of total federal shared revenues under the military government, it received 2.83 per cent in 1986 and 3.06 per cent in 1987. In the case of La Rioja, with 0.6 per cent of the population, federal revenues rose from 1.7 per cent to 2.51 per cent and 2.9 per cent of the total for the same years. In the case of Catamarca, federal funds accounted for up to 89 per cent of total provincial resources, and additional ad hoc contributions, such as national treasury contributions aimed at covering provincial deficits, reached 724 per cent of Catamarca's total revenues (both provincial and national) in 1986.

The new law on federal revenue sharing, Law 23.548, adopted in 1988, was the first in history which did not apply any scientific criteria to determine the percentages of federal funding fixed for each province, but which instead gave higher percentages to provinces whose governors had weight at the national level. Likewise, the new electoral law adopted in 1983 had greatly increased

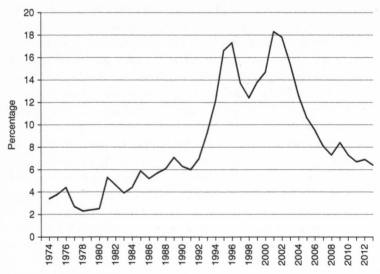

Graph 3. Unemployment

the congressional representation of small provinces, most of which were Peronist-governed, implying that they had more legislative votes which required more incentives to those provinces. While this was officially designed to strengthen the historically neglected provinces, in fact it gave them increased leverage to virtually blackmail the national government to finance heavy spending on public-sector employment which would conceal real unemployment levels – and, incidentally, increase the vote for the provincial rather than the national government.[3]

MENEM PRESIDENTE

The nomination of Carlos Saúl Menem as the Peronist candidate for the May 1989 elections represented an apparent return to classical Peronism: while long-time party apparatchiks like Italo Luder and Antonio Cafiero had considerable experience and respectability, they were uncharismatic and unlikely to stir passions. Menem, while mocked in Buenos Aires for his provincial air and affectation of imitating nineteenth-century *caudillo* Facundo Quiroga, was first and foremost a charismatic figure, and one who was dynamic, giving his followers something to follow. Ideology played a minimal role in his political make-up: Menem, like Perón himself, had little difficulty in attracting support from people to both the Left and the Right, being totally prepared to include any useful segment within his coalition and being blessed with the ability to make his listener believe that he was in agreement with him.

Menem's ascendant political career was boosted by the aftermath of the dictatorship, which had reduced political activism to a considerable extent (not least through the physical elimination of political activists). Thereafter, the lack of political dynamism of the country as a whole was closer to the level of La Rioja and Catamarca, the provinces where Menem flourished and where the PRN had found a satisfactory model for the passive and traditional society it wanted for Argentina. Menem was also favoured by the economic crisis afflicting the last months of the Alfonsín government (a crisis, it might be added, encouraged by the Peronist opposition in Congress), which made it unlikely that the UCR would win the 1989 elections, and by the UCR's eventual choice of candidate. Eduardo Angeloz, the oleaginous governor of Córdoba, would later be forced to resign the governorship and be tried on a series of corruption charges (of which he was acquitted). Apart from his limited popular appeal, Angeloz did not even have the wholehearted support of his own party, being in conflict with Alfonsín and thus with the party factions which remained loyal to the president.

The reality which Peronism had faced in 1983, with its tradition of following a vertical leadership structure (and indeed a single leader), coupled with the losses it suffered during the dictatorship, was that it had no real leadership. Its principal figures, such as Saadi or Cafiero, were politicians who had moved at a secondary level, but who were not popular political leaders. The fact that the UCR had also lost the leadership of Balbín in the same period was less relevant, given that the party had already survived its first important leader, Hipólito Yrigoyen, by 50 years and that its platform had changed relatively little since that time. Menem stepped into the Peronist vacuum, making it clear that a talent for leadership was more important for success than political coherence or long experience, as Perón himself had demonstrated years earlier. Like Perón, Menem was able to represent the desires of significant sectors of the population, although these had changed over the years and now focused on economic stability. That

Menem was, in appearance, the anti-Perón in terms of personal style and political preferences was irrelevant.

THE 1989 ELECTIONS

The Menem campaign for the 1989 elections was solidly populist in style, as was his vice-presidential candidate, Eduardo Duhalde, mayor of the Peronist district of Lomas de Zamora in Greater Buenos Aires. Duhalde had been the only significant provincial Peronist leader who had refused to back Cafiero's candidacy, and was rewarded with the vice-presidential slot, not least because he attracted votes in a province where Menem had less support (in particular in the Greater Buenos Aires area). Although Duhalde never tired of noting that he was 'Peronist, not Menemist', an attitude for which Menem never forgave him, he became an integral part of the Federal League which supported the candidacy of the provincial *caudillo*. (Duhalde would step down as vice-president in 1991 to become governor of Buenos Aires province.) Menem paraded through much of the country on horseback, dressed in a traditional poncho and his trademark flowing hair and sideburns, and his campaign promises focused on two chimeras: a productive revolution and an across-the-board salary rise, although it was never stated how these two difficult aims would be achieved and the prevailing economic crisis reversed. His campaign slogans also centred on the messianic, with words such as 'Follow me, I won't defraud you', emblazoned across his smiling photos.

Menem's campaign easily obliterated those of his more lacklustre rivals, Eduardo Angeloz, seeking to distance himself from the collapsing Alfonsín government, and Alvaro Alsogaray, an elderly former army engineer. Alsogaray's right-wing UCeDe party focused on neo-liberal, University of Chicago free-market economics that would unequivocally spell tight belts and austerity for the bulk of the population, an unattractive prospect even for those who knew at heart that some type of economic shock would be necessary to put an end to expensive populist and statist policies and to try to stimulate growth. Despite this, Menem's flamboyant style and his more outré public statements (for instance, his frequent claim that he kept the published works of Socrates at his bedside, despite the fact that Socrates was not generally known to have published) gave many *porteños* a certain hope that he could not possibly become president, as he continued to be seen as a figure of ridicule (and increasingly, fear) by many people with a more sophisticated cultural level and a limited knowledge of the inner workings of politics.

In the 14 May 1989 elections, Carlos Menem won with 47 per cent of the vote, only 7 per cent more than the votes received by Italo Luder in 1983, despite all the brouhaha surrounding his campaign. Angeloz received 37 per cent of the vote, while Alsogaray predictably received only 6 per cent. The election of Menem sent a shiver through much of the more sober part of Argentine society, as well as international political circles, given his carefully cultivated image of a semi-savage demagogue bent on running wild with populist economic policy. However, Menem promptly surprised many observers (and most of his voters) by forming an alliance with Alsogaray, and becoming more papist than the Pope in economic orthodoxy. He also made public an alliance with most of the country's principal business leaders, a class which had previously been considered the enemy of Peronism (the traditional Peronist march refers to Perón as 'combating capital', a position to be reversed by Menem).

This was the sector, together with the UCeDe, responsible for many cabinet appointments. For example, Menem's first two economy ministers, one of whom died a week after assuming office, came from the giant trading company Bunge & Born, one of the most traditional Argentine mega-companies, and held up by Perón for over a generation as an example of the worst kind of cruel exploiter. The election of Menem and his success in office, in addition to his own personal popularity and political talent, was strongly tied to the shrewdness of the leaders of some of the country's largest business interests, including oil company Perez Companc, cement giant Loma Negra and Bunge & Born. This led them to realize that only a Peronist could successfully implement the type of neo-liberal economic policies they wanted, which would turn traditional Peronist policies on their head and provoke the political lynching of any non-Peronist who attempted it. Menem was a man with charisma and unlimited ambition, and without significant convictions or scruples as to how to fulfil that ambition.

Runaway inflation and a pervasive sense that the economy could disappear into a black hole overnight forced Alfonsín to hand over the reins of power five months ahead of schedule, on 8 July 1989. Menem, not slow to accept the challenge, demonstrated that he had learned from Alfonsín's error of delaying painful decisions and began to act rapidly and in a manner completely at odds with his earlier rhetoric. Incorporating into his government members of the UCeDe and Harvard economists (who rubbed elbows with figures brought from La Rioja due to their established loyalty), within 18 months of assuming office Menem had carried out a sweeping range of reforms. These included the privatization of airline Aerolineas Argentinas and of telephone company ENTEL. (The latter was placed under the authority of Alsogaray's daughter, María Julia, who would later become a perennial Menem functionary and one of the principal targets of corruption charges later in his administration.)

The government also opened the oil market and announced that oil company YPF and other state companies would be privatized. Further projects included a reduction in the number of state employees; the construction of a foreign policy based on closer ties with the United Kingdom and 'carnal relations' with the USA; the destruction of the vestiges of opposition coming from the surprised trade union movement; and the fixing of the US dollar exchange rate at 10,000 australes. In April 1991, Economy Minister Domingo Cavallo would launch the so-called Convertibility Plan, again replacing the national currency with another, the peso, and making it legally convertible to the US dollar at a rate of one to one. This move, which limited the money supply to the equivalent of dollar reserves and virtually eliminated fears of a new inflationary epidemic and the crash of the national currency against the dollar, caused a sharp upsurge in confidence, which in itself helped to stabilize the economy (albeit reducing competitiveness by overvaluing the currency). It made Cavallo the most popular figure in the government, to the extent that it was believed that convertibility depended on his continuity in government, rather than that of Menem. (When Cavallo resigned in July 1996 following repeated clashes with Menem, despite apocalyptic warnings that the end of convertibility was at hand, economic policy went unchanged and convertibility continued its course.)

MENEM IN POWER

Menem, supposedly representing the most hard-core and retrograde element of Peronist populism, rapidly abandoned his anti-imperialist rhetoric and promises of a swingeing salary increase, in favour of wholeheartedly courting the USA and embracing market economy orthodoxy. This included privatizing state companies which had been the base built up by Perón in the 1940s. However, all of this is not as surprising as it might appear. Menem's greatest resemblance to Perón lay in his lack of ideology, his pragmatism and the willingness to opt for the most convenient position at any given time, as well as a complete lack of shame over declaring one position and immediately adopting its opposite. That his party should have followed him in this is also unsurprising: the Peronist movement (not uniquely) preferred success to principles on the whole, and the new neo-liberal mode was visibly a shorter road to success than adherence to traditional Peronist discourse. At the same time, the party, for all its infighting, remained accustomed to following the leader, and a leader who is dynamic and successful is easier to follow.

The fact that Menem's policies should have appeared to be the mirror image of 'true' Peronism reflected the fact that some 40 years had passed, and that the world in which they moved was not the same. Perón's contemporaries in Europe were nationalizing companies and establishing state welfare systems in the 1940s, and less-developed countries were establishing a non-aligned position or seeking benefits from the US–Soviet conflict. By the late 1980s and early 1990s, Europe was also privatizing, reducing the state and opting for the free market (Menem could be said to have followed the policies of Reagan and Thatcher a decade later), while the fall of the Soviet Union meant that the only superpower left with which good relations could generate benefits was the USA. Both Perón and Menem were sufficiently pragmatic (or sufficiently unscrupulous, which is often much the same) to follow the policies which appeared at the time to be likely to succeed, and neither would have remained doggedly loyal to those policies had he been governing at a different moment in history.

Unlike the rising economy enjoyed by Perón in the early 1940s, Argentina in the 1990s was suffering from a 'revolution of falling expectations'. In particular, the high unemployment that became a fixture from the late 1970s was a problem Perón had never had to face. Exhausted by hyperinflation and increasing poverty, its greatest desire was stability at any price. This was the 'revolution' headed by Menem. Although, like Perón, Menem failed to make a permanent change in the socio-economic structure which would maintain those gains, for nearly a decade his government was seen as the guarantor of a stability which, if it did not imply growth or improved future prospects, at least allowed the weary householder to calculate his spending for the month with the certainty that prices would not have quadrupled before the month was out. Also, like Perón, his policies favoured a rise in consumerism – not to say conspicuous consumption – as lower inflation and a favourable exchange rate allowed a rise in foreign travel, inexpensive consumer imports and the purchase of consumer durables on credit.

The Menem government was successful in reducing inflation to almost zero and stabilizing the economy, as well as attracting foreign investments through privatization and other mechanisms, generating what international publications were pleased to call a miracle in the early 1990s. Privatization of public services such as telephones, gas, electricity, subways and trains produced undoubted improvements in service: new telephone lines, which had previously taken up to a decade to install, were now obtainable within weeks. However, concession contracts imposed few limits on the new operators, allowing prices to soar – despite virtual zero inflation, tariffs were set in dollars and indexed to US inflation – and monopoly conditions to continue. For example, although telephone company ENTEL was converted into two companies on privatization, Telefónica de Argentina and Telecom, the former held a monopoly in the south of the country and the latter in the north, meaning that until full deregulation in November 2000, there was no more real competition than before. A similar division was made in the Buenos Aires electricity company SEGBA, which gave successor companies Edesur and Edenor a monopoly in their respective districts. As in the case of Perón's often-criticized nationalizations, however, it must be borne in mind that Argentina was not in a privileged position to dictate privatization conditions, given inefficiency and disinvestment in many state companies.

Unemployment, which had been kept low over the years through inflated public-sector payrolls and the enormous staff kept on by state companies, soared to over 18 per cent by 1998. This was due both to the reduction in employees at privatized companies and to downsizing at other private companies, which argued that high taxes and employee costs reduced their competitiveness (already reduced in times of a strong US dollar due to the currency peg). Surveys by both private consultants and the state statistics bureau showed that poverty increased, despite greater economic stability, with a rising number living below the poverty line and an ever-increasing imbalance in the distribution of wealth.[4] Moreover, corruption in high office, always commonplace in Argentina, became so blatant as to disgust many observers hardened by a lifelong experience of corruption, especially in relation to privatization and the funds arising therefrom.[5]

ARMS, DRUGS AND ORGANIZED CRIME

Corruption allegations were also a permanent companion of Menem's most intimate circle, making the problem even more blatant. His reconciliation with his temperamental wife, Zulema Yoma, who had aspirations to imitate Evita as first lady, was short-lived, and the country was treated to the spectacle of the first lady being turfed out of the presidential residence by the security forces in 1990. Despite this public rupture, Menem remained close to his former in-laws, whose influence and financing had been of crucial importance to his career, although it became increasingly detrimental in public relations terms. The Yoma family's leather tanning business had hundreds of millions of dollars in unpaid and unpayable debts with state banks by the late 1990s, as a result of loans made without the normal guarantees. In a well-known scandal which broke at the beginning of 1991, 'Swiftgate', Menem's brother-in-law Emir Yoma reportedly pressured the directors of meat packer Swift Armor in Argentina for a hefty bribe in exchange for being granted licences. The amount of the bribe provoked a protest to the US Embassy, which leaked the information. In March of that year, sister-in-law Amira Yoma, at the time Menem's private secretary, was accused, together with her husband, of laundering narco dollars brought into the country in her diplomatically immune suitcases.

Another even more alarming case linked to Menem's closest family was the death of his son, Carlos Facundo, in a helicopter crash in March 1995, shortly before the May presidential elections. Although early versions indicated that Junior, as he was known, had flown too low and had become enmeshed in power cables, the rumour that the helicopter had been shot down gathered increasing strength. Initial investigations supposedly indicated that there were bullet holes in the

Figure 16. President Carlos Menem, 5 August 1997 (courtesy of the archive, *Diario La Nación*)

craft, although the metal parts which included the holes were to go missing, and the structure of the aircraft was sold off for scrap metal despite forming part of a judicial investigation. Junior himself had allegedly told his mother that he might be killed at any time, purportedly at risk due to his closeness to the inner circle and the knowledge he had picked up relating to mafia activities including arms, drugs and money laundering being carried out close to the president's office.[6] Whatever the facts, one of the most alarming aspects of the case was the very fact that the unpunished assassination of the president's son could be widely believed as a real possibility.

Another individual widely believed to have influence in the government, at least due to his financial backing, was the controversial businessman Alfredo Yabran, charitably characterized as a postal tycoon with major interests in security transport and private postal services. Less charitable reports characterized him more disturbingly: 'super-minister' Domingo Cavallo denounced Yabran as a mafioso with strong influence in the government after his resignation in July 1996. Yabran gained particular notoriety in January 1997, after a grisly murder which captured public attention. José Luis Cabezas, a photo journalist who had published photos of Yabran, was kidnapped and murdered by former security personnel linked to the businessman.

Yabran himself was widely reported to have threatened Cabezas after the unauthorized photos of the magnate, who preferred total anonymity, were published in the weekly magazine *Noticias*.[7]

Yabran, who protested his innocence, visited the Casa Rosada in an effort to curtail the media pressure to which he was subsequently subjected, an apparent demonstration that his influence with the executive went beyond that of the ordinary citizen, or even the ordinary corporate tycoon. In May 1998, he committed suicide. Although this case (in which Yabran's former chief of security was eventually convicted of Cabezas' death) was less clearly linked to wrongdoing within the government itself, it represented another element in the widely accepted perception that the Menem government was mixed up in illicit and dangerous activities.

Other sinister events were also believed to be linked – albeit less visibly – to Menem and his shadowy relationships, including the 1992 bombing of the Israeli Embassy and the 1994 bombing of the AMIA Jewish community centre, in which 85 people died and which was alleged to have involved Hizbollah and Islamic Jihad, as well as members of the Buenos Aires provincial police. The failure to advance in investigations, and a series of irregularities in the judicial process, were attributed to a Menem-backed cover-up of Iranian participation, which a Justice Ministry investigation in 2004 later linked to 'questions relating to the obscure financing of his electoral campaign'. While the accusations are open to question, they revived concerns over institutional deficiencies and corruption as threats to security.

Another decision by Menem which was widely believed to be linked to personal cupidity, given that there was no widespread popular demand for such a move, was the announcement in December 1990 of a blanket pardon for the former military leaders convicted of human rights violations. The pardon also included those not yet tried, and members of the Montoneros and other armed opposition groups jailed for their activities during that period. However, the fact that the pardons came only three weeks after the final *carapintada* rebellion at the beginning of December 1990, ruthlessly put down but still involving former members of the Menemist 'family', also raised the suspicion that here was a deal similar to that struck by Alfonsín when the Due Obedience Law appeared shortly after the Holy Week rebellion three years earlier.

THE MENEM IMAGE

After the spectacularly populist nature of the 'Follow me, I won't defraud you' campaign in 1989, all that remained of populism in the Menem government was symbolic rather than economic in nature. In late 1989 he had the mortal remains of nineteenth-century *caudillo* Juan Manuel de Rosas returned to Argentina from England, where they had rested for over a century. However, this type of gesture was used only to divert public attention from the pending devaluation imposed to try to halt spiralling inflation, and from the lack of visible economic recovery. The president remained flamboyant in his personal style, demonstrating a keen enthusiasm for receiving and being photographed with prominent visitors, including Princess Diana, Claudia Schiffer, Madonna, Alain Delon and the Rolling Stones. He also gave himself the luxury of playing a variety of sports, including football, basketball, golf and tennis with prominent professionals, as well as, in the latter two cases, with US presidents George Bush Senior and Bill Clinton. His personal style, in particular in tonsorial terms, varied over the years, with the flowing hair and sideburns giving way to a more bouffant style, then to a wig, when his own hair became less luxuriant and, finally, a more natural style which did not seriously attempt to conceal a bald pate. He openly visited a plastic surgery clinic in 1992 to have his face lifted and bags removed from under his eyes.

These rather jokey but harmless diversions did much to endear Menem to many, and suggested a shift in popular culture from that which had admired the more austere figure of Perón to the creation of a popular idol who made vulgarity and a touch of corruption a successful trademark. (The national admiration for the *chanta*, at any rate, remained unchanged.) At the same time, they did nothing to reduce his support among business sectors who were interested in the economic policy installed by his ministers, not in the president's personal affectations. Foreign policy based on embracing the imperialist powers formerly considered the enemy, and which involved forging a public friendship with both Bush Senior and Clinton, was also a success in place of the fiasco it might have been if the public had been unwilling to forgive the shift away from the Third Position. (That shift was so great as to cause the government to withdraw Argentina from the Non-Aligned Movement and to push for its inclusion as a non-regional associate of NATO.)

In fact, Menem put himself and Argentina on the front page of world newspapers and onto prime time news broadcasts, something which had rarely occurred in the past (except for negative coverage such as reports of a coup d'état or of the disappeared). This was sufficient for his policy to be seen as a success at home. So successful was he, in fact, at seducing foreign dignitaries that in 1998 he and his daughter Zulemita (acting as first lady since her parents' separation) visited the United Kingdom after a long chill since the Falklands/Malvinas war, and were received by the Royal Family at an official banquet at Buckingham Palace. This event was taken in Argentina as the culmination of a foreign policy which had brought Argentina back from isolation. The drop in inflation that allowed for a rise in economic security, and often conspicuous consumption for those who remained in employment, as well as the favourable exchange rate that permitted foreign travel, gave a boost to Argentine confidence that was mirrored in the construction of the new Puerto Madero district of Buenos Aires, an upscale neighbourhood of luxury flats, offices and restaurants on the site of the old port. The fact that other parts of both the capital and the rest of the country continued to deteriorate as infrastructure investment failed to make up for decades of neglect was less widely noted, although the increase in perceived citizen insecurity in the face of rising crime and expanding shantytowns was.

THE 1994 CONSTITUTION AND RE-ELECTION

Menem, despite his marital separation in 1989, followed Perón's line in frequently declaring himself a devotee and friend of the Catholic Church; he also followed Perón's lead in seeking a constitutional reform to allow for his immediate re-election. This came about through a bilateral agreement between Menem and Alfonsín, known as the Olivos Pact, reached in November 1993. This allowed for a guarantee that the clause prohibiting re-election would be removed in exchange for other concessions sought by Alfonsín (although the pact was repudiated by much of his party). This coup also represented a blow to the presidential hopes of Duhalde – considered the sure 1995 candidate – who found the ground he had carefully tended cut out from under his feet at a stroke, as had previous Buenos Aires governor Domingo

Mercante 45 years earlier. Relations between Duhalde and Menem, whose desire to remain in office indefinitely made him particularly suspicious of anyone with such obvious personal ambitions, worsened from their previous climate of fairly covert hostility to downright enmity.

Again, the need for constitutional reform was justified on the grounds of modernizing the constitution, although in practice the principal changes which emerged from the 1994 reform were immediate re-election of the president and elimination of the requirement that the president be a Roman Catholic. (The latter was seen as being included to favour the possible future aspirations of Menem's brother, Eduardo, the president of the Senate, who had remained a Muslim. However, it might also have implied that a divorce between Menem and his Muslim wife would not disqualify him from office by placing him in a borderline position vis-à-vis his membership of the Church.) Another significant alteration was that the president would hereafter be elected by direct vote, rather than by the Electoral College, a move which undercut the electoral importance of small provinces. Under the previous constitution, provinces had the same number of representatives in the Electoral College as they had in the Chamber of Deputies, and the 1983 electoral law had given the smallest provinces a number of representatives totally disproportionate to their population. Under that law, provinces were guaranteed a minimum of five representatives even where their population would not have guaranteed more than one. (As a result, for example, Catamarca had five representatives while Tucumán, with around five times the population, had nine.)

Despite high unemployment, constant fears over job security and rumours of widespread discontent, and possibly abetted by a sympathy vote related to the death of his son two months earlier, Menem won the May 1995 elections with over 50 per cent of the vote. Again, his result was helped by the candidates who stood against him. The UCR chose former Rio Negro governor Horacio Massaccessi, a lacklustre politician with a disastrous record as governor, who would subsequently be expelled from the party for corruption and who scraped up only 17 per cent of the national vote. These elections also saw the birth of a new opposition alliance, for the moment called the Frente Grande (later Frepaso), whose presidential and vice-presidential candidates were two former Peronists who had defected to the new party due to disagreements with the policies pursued by Menem. Former Mendoza governor José Octavio Bordón, who projected an image of modernity, progressiveness and efficiency, won the presidential nomination, while the vice-presidential candidate was Frente Grande founder Carlos 'Chacho' Alvarez, previously a Peronist deputy for Buenos Aires who had led a dissident faction in the Lower House.

Aided in part by a new image, and by a widespread weariness with the seamier side of the incumbent government, the Bordón–Alvarez ticket received some 30 per cent of the vote nationally, winning in the city of Buenos Aires. (Bordón, a sociology professor who had earlier passed from the Christian Democratic Party to Peronism before joining the Frente Grande in 1995, subsequently left that movement and resurfaced in the Peronist ranks in 1999 as education minister of Buenos Aires province.) Although this was a considerable achievement for a newly formed opposition movement (which enjoyed the lack of history and untarnished reputation of Peronism in its early days, as well as its combative appearance), the huge margin in favour of Menem made its impact relative.

Although Menem's charisma and personal popularity played a major role in his second electoral triumph, wider than the first, the vote also reflected both the perception that he was the undisputed leader of the pack and the continuing fear that his government was the only guarantee that convertibility would be maintained. This was not a minor factor: convertibility had done away with inflation and stabilized the volatile economy, facilitating savings and foreign travel for those who could afford it. Equally important, since its inception, most contracts – including housing rentals and bank loans – were denominated in dollars rather than in pesos, while wages remained in pesos. As such, a devaluation could imply mass bankruptcy. (Under the convertibility plan, most utilities bills, loans and rentals could be paid in pesos, always assuming these retained their parity with the dollar. However, while a rental contract of 400 dollars per month could be paid with 400 pesos at the time, a 10 per cent devaluation of the peso would mean that the rent would cost 440 pesos next month, without a commensurate rise in peso-denominated wages, while a major devaluation such as those experienced in the past could imply that rentals or loans could double or triple in pesos overnight, in order to make up the corresponding figure in US dollars.)

The paradox that a Peronist government should be considered by most of the middle and business classes to be the only guarantee of economic stability and the maintenance of free market policies was only half of the successful structure set up by Menem against all apparent odds. Not only was the party considered the only guarantor, but Menem was personally considered as the only politician able and trustworthy enough to maintain the system. In fact, Menem's potential competition within the party had been largely neutralized, for the time being at least.

From the early 1990s, many of the more prominent Peronist governors were virtual creations of Menem himself. Two of the more prominent and popular governors to assume office in 1991 had no political background at all but had been chosen by Menem due to their fame and the fact that their lack of political background was an asset at a time when the political class was largely discredited as corrupt and inefficient. Ramón 'Palito' Ortega had become a successful popular singer and film star in the 1960s and 1970s after starting out as a poor sugar cane cutter and shoe-shine boy from Tucumán, and later a successful Miami-based businessman. He returned to Argentina to become governor of his native province in 1991, with the full backing of Menem and the intervenor of Tucumán, Julio César Aráoz. In Santa Fe, former Formula One racing driver Carlos Reutemann, another former popular idol who had constructed a successful business career thereafter, was elected governor, and was generally credited with discharging that office capably and efficiently. Neither Reutemann nor Ortega represented in practice any real competition for Menem, their mentor.

Duhalde, another figure who had come to nationwide prominence at Menem's side, was to distance himself increasingly from Menem as governor of Buenos Aires. He was also to become increasingly mired in the difficulties of governing that province, which accounts for some 40 per cent of the national population. (It is popularly supposed that there is a sort of curse on the governorship of Buenos Aires, as no politician holding that important office has ever been a successful candidate for the presidency thereafter. Rather than a curse, this would appear to reflect the virtual impossibility of governing so vast, diverse and problematic a province effectively. It also reflects the widespread jealousy and dislike which Buenos Aires generates in the rest of the country, making residents of other provinces ill-disposed towards its governors.) Duhalde would also find himself obliged to adopt a more traditionally Peronist – that is, populist – image in order to distinguish himself from Menem, which automatically made him a dubious candidate for the millions seeking a continuation of the existing model.

In addition to carrying out an economic policy that represented the apparent inverse of his party's traditional line, Menem was also more than prepared to participate in the demystification of his party's founders. Although publicly remaining an adherent of Perón and Evita, Menem joined enthusiastically in the project to investigate their alleged links with Nazi war criminals, opening the national archives (although allegedly these were prudently cleansed beforehand[8]) and publicly promising support for the commission established for that purpose. This stance not only won him credit for being willing to expose past scandals in his movement, but also gave him the possibility of discrediting figures who by this time represented competition in the pantheon of great historical figures which he aimed to head. As Robert Potash, the Boston-based Argentina expert who presided over the commission, remarked at a press conference at the time, Menem was unlikely to make any effort to block the investigations, given that he had no interest whatsoever in avoiding the possible discrediting of Perón: his principal interest was to be greater than Perón.

THE QUEST FOR ETERNITY

The constitutional reform which had allowed for Menem's re-election in 1995 had reduced the presidential term of office from six to four years. It also included a transitory provision indicating that, if the incumbent who presided over the reform were re-elected in 1995, the term which ran from 1995 would be considered his second consecutive term and he would therefore not be allowed to stand for a new term in 1999. However, by 1998 Menem had already begun floating the argument that that transitory provision was unconstitutional. He contended that the term of office which had begun in 1995 should be considered the first, given that it was the first under the new constitution, thus paving the way for a new re-election bid in 1999. Although one federal judge ruled in favour of allowing Menem's candidacy, the bid foundered miserably in its attempts to find other significant sources of support. In some respects, Menem had been a victim of his own success: by this time, no political party questioned the basic tenets of the government's economic policy, and there was no question that any candidate would propose abandoning the convertibility plan for the Argentine peso. As such, Menem was no longer needed as a guarantor for the system.

At the same time, ten years in office had unquestionably taken their toll, with both the government and the faces fronting it largely exhausted and in need of replacement. Business was no longer convinced of the need to maintain Menem in the presidency, given that the economic system in place ran no greater risks under a new leader than under the existing one; moreover, the persistent and increasing rumours of widespread corruption had fatigued public opinion and made the international community eye Menem and his government somewhat askance. International lending agencies such as the IMF, which had showered largesse on Argentina and praised its economic policies, had begun to raise sharp criticism of its lack of fiscal discipline, uncontrolled spending, rising debt – which doubled from 62 billion dollars to 127 billion over the decade, as the inability to print money under convertibility did not lead to a corresponding cut in public spending – and the inefficient implementation of public works. Despite a brief recovery following a 1995–6 recession in the wake of Mexico's 'Tequila crisis', the economy returned to a stubborn recession from 1999 and refused to recover. In addition, a generation of political leaders – headed by Duhalde – who had waited patiently for their turn in the leading role were no longer prepared to allow Menem a further four years to consolidate his grip on power.

At the same time, Menem's second term saw a sharp rise in popular protests by those hard hit by his neo-liberal policies and the post-Tequila downturn. In particular, the newly unemployed following the privatization programme – notably former employees of YPF – began to protest through the use of roadblocks and became known as *piqueteros* (pickets). In many cases they gained broader support, notably in towns whose local economy depended heavily on YPF and consumption by its employees. The methodology used by the *piqueteros* became increasingly widespread, with 685 roadblocks recorded between 1993 and 1999, many of them by farmers and small businessmen as well as unemployed or impoverished workers.[9] Other forms of popular protest, such as the mass turning off of lights or telephones in response to tariff increases, also gained ground. In 1992, a competitor to the CGT, the *Central de los Trabajadores Argentinos* (CTA), was established primarily to represent the beleaguered state employees, and began to take strike action against the Menem government well before the CGT joined in half-heartedly later in the decade.

Although skirmishes between Menem and Duhalde in particular would continue for over a year in the run-up to the October 1999 elections, it was evident from early on that the president had lost much of his support for a third term, in particular as opinion polls began to suggest that he would lose the elections if a candidate. Brother Eduardo Menem, the Senate president, came out publicly against his candidacy, saying that it was unconstitutional and that a referendum could not be called for that purpose, leaving open little chance of a change. While Menem had received the support of most of the party machine and its principal figures for a third term, in mid-1998 Duhalde announced the calling of a plebiscite in Buenos Aires province on the question of a third term, and threatened to order his followers in Congress to support impeachment of any members of the Supreme Court who might eventually rule in favour of allowing a third term. This implied virtually certain loss for Menem, given that opinion polls indicated that he would lose the plebiscite – and in particular as Duhalde was the governor of the country's most populous province and therefore handled its huge development and social spending budgets at his own discretion.

Menem was also unsuccessful in persuading any of the more credible party figures to stand against Duhalde for the nomination in the longer term. Although Ortega, by this time social action minister, briefly announced his candidacy, backed by Menem, he quickly reached an agreement with Duhalde and announced that he would instead stand as Duhalde's vice-presidential candidate, thus avoiding a primary to choose the candidate. Reutemann rejected the possibility of standing for the presidency. Only Adolfo Rodríguez Saá, governor of San Luis, could be persuaded to challenge Duhalde for the nomination, but his lack of support in the rest of the country and perceptions of ineptitude and corruption made his candidacy a non-starter. In general, major party figures, if not openly declaring a break with Menem, began moving away from a figure and government whose corrupt image was worse than ever and whose level of popular approbation had slipped to disastrous levels.

This did not imply, however, that Menem did not use his still considerable pull both within and outside the party to undermine

Duhalde's candidacy, as well as undertake a number of last-minute government decisions and public statements designed to reduce his putative successor's vote. Among the extremely dirty tricks alleged, in addition to the death of José Luis Cabezas, Menem was rumoured to have had a hand in the September 1999 massacre in Villa Ramallo. Members of the Buenos Aires provincial police surrounding the local branch of the Banco Nación, where at least four bank robbers were holding bank personnel and others hostage, opened fire when they attempted to leave the building, killing two of the hostages, one of whom was shot at point-blank range when the confrontation was already over. The inability of the provincial police to handle the situation without producing a massacre, and the allegations that members of the force were involved in the attempted robbery, necessitating the killing of hostages who were also witnesses, wrought havoc in the Duhalde government and brought it to the brink of the abyss. Whether Menem in fact had any link to the Cabezas and Ramallo cases is virtually irrelevant: the fact that such a thing appeared credible and was widely believed to be true was as bad, and as effective, as if it were true.

Having been forced to abandon his aspirations for 1999, Menem immediately turned his attention to 2003, and was extremely conscious of the fact that his chances would be reduced if Duhalde were elected in 1999. If his government was a success, he would undoubtedly seek re-election (implying that Menem would have to wait until at least 2007, when he would be 76 years old), whereas if his government was a failure, the party would be unlikely to retain power in the next term. On the other hand, a win by the *Alianza* coalition of the UCR-Frepaso would increase his chances of a medium-term return. If the government was a failure (not an unreasonable prospect in the light of the huge budget deficit, high unemployment, debt levels and the lack of further state companies to privatize in order to reduce the shortfall), the public would be clamouring for a return to the glory days of Menem. On the other hand, even if the government was a success, he would be facing a much less popular and less charismatic figure than himself, and would be able to claim that his successor's government had been based on the reforms he himself had made.

13   Default and Disarray

Duhalde, who represented a more 'traditionally' populist aspect of Peronism than did Menem, was faced with trying to convince business interests that he had no intention of changing the economic model, but rather of giving it a more human face in order to include the excluded. This forced him to deviate from what was arguably his greatest strength as a campaigner, that of embodying the traditional populist politician. Although not charismatic or physically imposing, Duhalde excelled at connecting with some sectors, embracing men and women in shanty towns, riding horseback through rural areas, carrying a flag and surrounded by gauchos. The need to appear a serious candidate for oil companies, banks and the IMF forced Duhalde to leave behind these more colourful activities for the most part, converting him into merely another dull and not altogether credible politician in a dark suit. In other respects, both Duhalde and Ortega represented a completely different image from Menem – devoted family men, serious and sober politicians and much less charismatic figures, devoid of flamboyance due to Duhalde's suppression of his more histrionic aspects and to Ortega's naturally dry and inexpressive character. This change in image for the ruling party suggested that the attraction of Menem's playboy image was waning (as well as the fact that Menem himself was a one-off figure who could not successfully be imitated by others).

The opposition UCR and Frepaso parties maintained the same alliance they had established in Congress two years earlier, presenting a

presidential ticket consisting of UCR Senator Fernando de la Rua and
Frepaso leader Carlos 'Chacho' Alvarez, the former dissident Peronist
who had already been vice-presidential candidate in 1995. De la Rua,
a lawyer and long-standing career politician from the most conservative wing of the UCR, had been Balbín's vice-presidential candidate in
1973. A native of Córdoba, he had had a successful career in both the
Senate and the Lower House for Córdoba and the city of Buenos Aires,
but had a limited following elsewhere. His staid personality and lack
of presence made him all but invisible, but he conveyed the image
of an honest and hard-working professional politician. His campaign
played on his grey image: campaign spots promising improvements
in public administration and social spending were punctuated with
the phrase 'they say I'm boring', implying that dullness was equivalent to honesty. This was a far shrewder policy than attempting to
appear exciting, particularly as frivolity in politics seemed to have
gone out of fashion. At no time did De la Rua propose fundamental
changes to Menem's economic policy; like Duhalde, he proposed improvements to benefit the unemployed and the needy and to create
new opportunities, as well to fight corruption, but without touch-
ing either convertibility or the fundamental free market base of that
policy.

On 24 October 1999, after heavy but lacklustre campaigning, the
grey, decent and uncharismatic De la Rua dealt the Peronists their
second presidential defeat, both since the death of Perón. The surprise
on this occasion was that it was defeated after ten years of what was
generally viewed as successful government. Its defeat had much to do
with De la Rua's proposal of embracing its policies without embracing
its worst excesses, and of returning government to its supposed role
of efficient administration rather than show business. Duhalde was
unable to overcome the triple burden of the curse on Buenos Aires
governors, the implacable efforts of Menem to scupper his candidacy,
and of being publicly associated with Menem without being Menem
(and, indeed, of opposing part of what was considered successful about
Menem's government). He received a relatively respectable 37 per cent
of the votes cast and was forced to concede that his presidential aspirations had no real hope of materializing at present. Menem, from
the privileged position of not having been forced to compete, blamed
the defeat entirely on Duhalde, on the grounds that he had turned
against the Menem model.

The post-electoral period, which marked at least the temporary eclipse of Duhalde as a leading figure and Menem's temporary removal to the political wings, left a new political map and a new internal struggle within the party, with new figures benefiting from the results of the election. Carlos Ruckauf, a former member of Isabelita's cabinet who had served as Menem's vice-president in the 1995–9 term, maintaining extremely poor relations with the head of state, was elected governor of Buenos Aires province. Reutemann returned to the governorship of Santa Fe, and he and Ruckauf, together with the non-Menemist governor of Córdoba, José Manuel de la Sota, rapidly formed a virtual trinity of moderate Peronist governors who proposed to support the De la Rua government in exchange for the benefits that the position could offer. They were also united in their unwillingness to accept Menem's automatic domination of the party in the future – not least because his constant and seemingly not unrealistic claims that he would return to the presidency in 2003 would curtail the evident presidential aspirations of all three.

The loss of the 1999 presidential elections was a blow (though not an unexpected one) and caused a re-grouping of the party's principal forces, with both Menem and Duhalde losing power within its structure. However, the defeat was not seen in the apocalyptic terms of 1983, when it generated the doubt as to whether the party could survive its founder and whether indeed that election represented its death knell. Sixteen years later, it had become evident that it had sufficient flexibility and survival skills to maintain its position as one of Argentina's two main parties, and to generate a changing (not to say chameleonic) leadership able to attract significant voter support. That it should lose a national election was increasingly taken to be a normal occurrence in bipartisan politics, implying that if the UCR could win the elections in 1999, the Peronists could just as easily return in 2003.

At the same time, although the party lost the presidency, it maintained the majority of governorships (including the three largest provinces), as well as a Senate majority, implying that its ability to influence policy – and, possibly, to impede government, as had been the case under Alfonsín – remained significant, and that it continued to represent a substantial element of the Argentine population. In this respect, the Peronists had demonstrated both that the party was now capable of generating possible leaders and that it was still capable of serious infighting among those seeking leadership of what was still a highly verticalist structure where the winner takes virtually all, but faces sufficient competition to make it necessary to watch his back closely.

However, the after-effects of the economic policies followed in the Menem decade and De la Rua's failure to find alternatives to stimulate growth were to prove catastrophic. De la Rua's government quickly ran into trouble, not least because of the president's apparent indecisiveness and rumoured ill-health. In October 2000, only ten months after taking office, Vice-President Carlos 'Chacho' Alvarez resigned, following allegations that members of the government had bribed legislators to pass an unpopular labour reform. Despite having been elected on an anti-corruption platform, De la Rua refused to investigate the allegations, increasing the suspicion that corruption continued unchecked at high levels of government. The departure of Alvarez left the government without a vice-president – implying that the interim presidency would fall to the president of the majority-Peronist Senate whenever De la Rua was out of the country or otherwise unable to exercise his office – and incidentally spelled the end of the Frepaso influence in the *Alianza* government. The few Frepaso cabinet members were rapidly replaced by Radicals of the most conservative bent, implying that the government was no longer that which many voters had chosen. At the same time, De la Rua began to rely increasingly on a few close friends and advisers – including his son Antonio and his brother Jorge, who became justice minister – and became increasingly isolated from other strands of opinion.

The recession which had already begun in the later period of Menem's government proved intractable, further undermining the government's waning popularity. In March 2001, the orthodox Economy Minister Jose Luis Machinea (who had been Central Bank president at the time of the hyperinflation which brought down Alfonsín) resigned after failing to find a formula which would encourage growth and reduce rising unemployment. He was briefly succeeded by another Radical economist, the conservative defence minister, Ricardo López Murphy, although the latter's unpopular austerity measures, including cuts in public-sector wages, forced him to resign only a month later. With the economy adrift and little confidence that the government could resolve the worsening recession, De la Rua turned to

Menem's former super-minister, Domingo Cavallo, who in April 2001 became the third economy minister in a month.

Convinced, together with many others, that his mere presence would be sufficient to generate another economic miracle, Cavallo launched a series of unorthodox and increasingly desperate measures to stimulate growth, reducing taxes on exports and some productive sectors, only to reverse the reductions when it became apparent that tax collection was falling as a result of the recession and unemployment, making it impossible to finance public spending. A 'parallel' exchange rate, with the peso pegged to the average between the dollar and the euro, was introduced for exports, raising concerns that convertibility would be eliminated – despite the fact that, for Cavallo, the father of convertibility, this was the only economic policy he was not prepared to sacrifice. A series of new bond issues and IMF packages, including a 40 billion dollar 'financial armour plating' package, did little but increase the already soaring debt burden, while a 'mega-swap' of existing debt for new longer-term instruments also served primarily to increase the debt – to some 141 billion dollars – and the interest rates being paid. Finally, in July, Cavallo was driven to take the step already proposed by Lopez Murphy, who had been ousted as a result: public spending, including public-sector wages, was cut by 13 per cent in order to maintain a 'zero deficit' agreed with the IMF and to keep spending within the level of tax revenues. The threat remained pending that further cuts could follow if tax revenues were inadequate, which, in light of the increasingly recessive measures taken by the government, they were.

During this turbulent period of the De la Rua administration, the Peronists behaved largely as a fairly responsible and loyal opposition, seeking to avoid criticism that, as in the case of Alfonsín, it had made the president's life and government impossible. Menem himself had been a supporter of De la Rua, for the reasons cited in the previous chapter; the governors of the three largest provinces – Carlos Ruckauf of Buenos Aires, Jose Manuel de la Sota of Córdoba and Carlos Reutemann of Santa Fe – were all would-be presidential candidates who did not wish to appear to be rocking the ship of state, and made a public show of supporting De la Rua even as this became an increasingly unpopular position. At the same time, they managed to maintain a united front as the apparent power brokers of a future government, in favour of modernity and moderation and, incidentally, against a return of Menem to the fore.

Menem himself had successfully remained in the public eye following his retirement, in part through his highly publicized romance with a well-known Chilean journalist, the former Miss World Cecilia Bolocco, who had expressed her enthusiasm over the prospect of becoming Argentina's first lady in 2003. However, he remained low in the opinion polls, as the figure most widely blamed for the current crisis and for the high level of corruption which was drowning the country. Investigations into illegal arms trafficking to Croatia and Ecuador during his presidency led to his arrest by a federal judge in June 2001, shortly after his wedding, on charges of heading an 'illicit association' formed for the purpose of trafficking arms (other members of which allegedly included former brother-in-law Emir Yoma, former defence ministers Antonio Erman Gonzalez and Oscar Camilion, former army chief Martin Balza, former foreign minister Guido di Tella and – more tenuously – the once and future economy minister Domingo Cavallo). In light of his age, Menem was placed under house arrest, a popular move in a country increasingly impatient with the image of corruption he represented (in particular given that the wealth it had generated had not extended to the increasingly impoverished population at large). However, in November the charges were thrown out by a Supreme Court packed by Menem supporters, allegedly encouraged by De la Rua, and Menem was released.

The widespread rumour that De la Rua or members of his government had intervened in favour of Menem's release only served to increase public hostility towards the government and the political class as a whole. That animosity had already become clear in the October midterm elections, where some 42 per cent of the votes were blank or spoiled; in a number of districts these votes greatly exceeded the votes cast for any candidate. Even allowing for a high degree of voter wrath directed at both major parties, however, most winning candidates (blank votes aside) were Peronists, anti-government members of the Alianza or members of provincial or small left-wing parties. One of the most striking victories was chalked up by Eduardo Duhalde, who won the Senate race in Buenos Aires province with some 40 per cent of the vote, twice that of his nearest rival, former president Raul Alfonsín. While hardly a landslide, the election greatly increased Duhalde's weight within the party – particularly given that Menem had fallen on hard times, receiving virtually no explicit party support while under arrest.

By the end of November, the delicate situation was also complicated by the threat that the banking system was on the verge of collapse. Increasing instability and concerns that a devaluation was near had caused savers to withdraw 20 billion pesos (then equivalent to 20 billion dollars) from the banking system since the early part of the year, and capital flight increased as the elections, social protests and rising economic chaos took their toll. At the beginning of December, the government decreed a freeze on bank deposits to avert a continuing run on banks, placing a limit of 250 pesos per week on withdrawals. After lawsuits brought by angry depositors generated judicial rulings against the so-called *corralito*, Cavallo ordered banks to disregard rulings obliging them to return deposits. For those who remembered the intervention of banks in 1989, which led to the issuing of rapidly devalued 'Bonex' government bonds to replace confiscated deposits, it appeared obvious that their savings would again be confiscated by a government without other sources of revenue.

Reactions from outside the country also demonstrated that time had run out. After disregarding Argentina's failure to meet fiscal and growth targets for a number of years, the IMF announced the suspension of disbursement of a loan tranche due in December, on the grounds that the government had failed to meet the zero deficit goal and had taken no effective measures to control the collapsing economy. The tranche had been earmarked to meet interest payments due on the rising debt; in the absence of alternative sources of funds to meet the payment, Cavallo effectively confiscated funds from the private pension system he himself had established, obliging pension funds administrators to acquire a certainly unpayable government bond in exchange for their long-term deposits.

Within Argentina, the IMF was thereafter widely blamed for much of the crisis, although in this case the economic policies implemented were in fact designed by the government rather than imposed by the Fund, and indeed the IMF had expressed considerable scepticism over convertibility. If anything, it might be argued that the IMF was too lenient rather than too harsh, and that if it had suspended lending earlier a somewhat less painful debt restructuring might have resulted.[1]

The government's futile insistence on seeking to meet short-term payments on a debt it could not pay, while at the same time reducing salaries and pension payments and effectively stealing future pensions in order to cover its budgetary shortfall, inflamed popular anger. In particular, De la Rua's apparently greater interest in his bonsai garden than in the nation's problems, his seeming insensitivity to rising poverty and, above all, his insistence upon maintaining Cavallo in the economy ministry undermined any residual legitimacy. By mid-December, widespread looting of supermarkets was reported: although it was rumoured that these were encouraged by the Peronists and the Buenos Aires provincial police, there is no question that patience was at an end. Thereafter, protests spread from the looting of supermarkets in poor areas to demonstrations by angry middle-class protestors banging pots and pans and demanding the government's resignation. In this case, in particular, it was clear that the impetus came from the popular level and not from any political direction, although as protests progressed they were joined by trade unions, *piqueteros*, the poor and political groupings. It was also clear that the administration itself was woefully misguided in its reaction: on 19 December, De la Rua declared a state of siege to deal with the rising protests, many of which were concentrated under the windows of the Casa Rosada.

Following declaration of the state of siege, 30 people were killed by the police in various parts of the country, including looters driven either by desperation or by opportunism to break into supermarkets or other businesses. The death of unarmed demonstrators at the hands of the police represented the final nail in the coffin of De la Rua, whose coffin had already supported a surprising number. On 20 December, Cavallo's resignation was announced. This, however, was insufficient to save the situation; later the same day, De la Rua signed his own resignation and left the Casa Rosada by helicopter. The image shook those who remembered Isabelita's own departure 25 years earlier; in an effort to erase that image, De la Rua returned the following day to formalize his resignation – only then, as an afterthought, lifting the state of siege.

In the absence of a vice-president, De la Rua was replaced on an interim basis by the president of the Senate, the Peronist Ramon Puerta, a former governor of Misiones who made clear his intention of remaining only until a longer-term solution could be found. The question remained as to whether such a solution should involve an interim president to serve out the remainder of De la Rua's term, ending in December 2003, or a caretaker to call early elections. The latter option was disliked equally by Peronists and Radicals, neither of whom felt any certainty of winning, while the question of a president to serve the nearly two years remaining of the term was also vexed. Some Radicals considered that the presidency should go to a member of the ex-president's party, while the Peronists considered that, as the majority party in the Senate, they had the right to choose the interim leader. With infighting continuing over this question, a generally mistaken choice was made: instead of opting either for a caretaker government and early elections or for a credible figure who might have a chance of holding the presidency for two years, it was announced that San Luis governor Adolfo Rodríguez Saa had been chosen as interim president on 22 December; it was determined that he would hold the office for a three-month period, until new elections could be called.

Rodríguez Saa, whose national image had been linked as much to lurid revelations about his private life as to good government, moved immediately into the presidency with the air of a man who expected to remain there, generating fears that he would seek to stay in office rather than call early elections. He announced the creation of a third national currency – the *argentino* – to circulate alongside the peso and the range of national and provincial bonds which were already replacing legal tender in much of the country, and the long-awaited default on some 95 billion dollars in foreign debt, the largest sovereign default in history. At the same time, he proposed to scrap unpopular austerity measures such as public-sector wage and pension cuts. He also announced the incorporation into his cabinet of several former Menem cronies widely suspected of corruption, which did little to inspire confidence among the citizens who continued demonstrating against the government and the political class as a whole, demanding that 'they all go'. Moreover, his apparent intention of retaining the presidency generated suspicions among the party's more 'serious' candidates – Ruckauf, Reutemann and De la Sota in particular – who had backed his appointment on the grounds that he did not represent competition. One week after assuming office, having already lost his party's backing, Rodríguez Saa resigned.

On 2 January 2002, Senator Eduardo Duhalde was sworn in as interim president to serve out the remainder of De la Rua's term, with elections to be called in September 2003; Duhalde gave an undertaking that he would not stand as a candidate in those elections, but would rather seek to provide a stable transition. Unlike Rodríguez

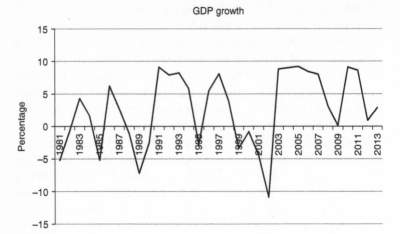

Graph 4. GDP

Saa, a figure from the second division of the party who received only a narrow mandate from the Legislative Assembly, Duhalde was chosen by 262 votes in favour (there were only 21 against and 18 abstentions), having negotiated the support of both the UCR and Frepaso, as well as the Peronists.

In the days after taking office, Duhalde confirmed the 'suspension' of debt payments announced by Rodríguez Saa, although pre-existing austerity measures were also maintained. However, Rodríguez Saa's other proposed policies, such as the *argentino*, were scrapped. On 4 January, Duhalde sent an emergency economic package to Congress, which both houses approved in a weekend session. The bill, designed by Economy Minister Jorge Remes Lenicov, included elimination of the convertibility plan and devaluation of the peso, at an official rate of 1.40 to the dollar. The banking controls imposed on 1 December were to be maintained for an unspecified period, with restrictions on access to salaries to be gradually eased, and dollar-denominated debts of up to 100,000 dollars were converted at the one-to-one rate.

Although Duhalde appeared on the face of it to be the most viable candidate for the role of interim president, given his comparative weight, experience in cross-party negotiations and apparent willingness to step aside after completing the difficult task of leading the transition, the intractable economy and his own vacillation quickly ended any expectation of rapidly stabilizing the crisis. Indeed, the crushing recession which had already lasted for nearly four years headed into outright depression, arguably the worst peacetime crisis since Weimar Germany. Poverty and unemployment soared, networks of citizens established systems of barter to compensate for a collapsed currency and lack of income and protests by the middle classes and unemployed (*piqueteros*) replaced trade union strikes; by their less organized and leaderless nature, these non-union protests were more difficult to resolve. However, the establishment of neighbourhood assemblies did little to substitute for government, and the coming together of middle- and lower-class interests in protests was short-lived. Workers occupied bankrupt factories in a series of well-publicized moves to keep production going through worker cooperatives (which would receive some funding from the hard-pressed government, although little was available). Economic policy focussed on the possibility of seeking new aid from the IMF. However, the Fund proved sceptical as to the government's commitment to reform, while the US government took the view that 'contagion' from the crisis would not spread to the rest of Latin America and that Argentina should therefore be left to resolve its own fate.

Economic policy thus veered between relatively populist measures and the orthodox practices demanded by the IMF, implying a series of about-faces which further undermined confidence. Faced with Fund disapproval of the use of an 'official' exchange rate, the government allowed the peso to float freely against the dollar, with the result that it quickly lost some 70 per cent of its value. Inflation began to rise sharply as a result, after years of price stability, as purchasing power sank and unemployment continued to rise. Although the devaluation was designed to increase the competitiveness of Argentine exports, in practice the impact on the domestic market was devastating, given that the export sector represented too small an element of GDP to balance the fall in domestic demand. This is not to say that the end of convertibility was an error – in fact, the currency board had long since become unviable in light of the heavily overvalued peso and the fact that dollar reserves were no longer sufficient to back money in circulation. However, in the light of the chaotic situation and lack of public and investor confidence in the political class, even valid reforms had become impossible to implement without generating an intolerable rise in social tensions.

Similarly, IMF talks centred on a sharp reduction in the budget deficit, in particular, a 60 per cent cut in provincial deficits. While valid from the point of view of economic theory, heavy spending cuts which reduce public employment – almost the only source of employment in some provinces – at a time when joblessness is at an all-time high are not politically or socially feasible. Although Duhalde announced a new 'social safety net' in April, providing monthly subsidies for unemployed heads of household (and administered by his wife, Hilda 'Chiche' Gonzalez de Duhalde, in charge of social welfare), the move did little either to reduce social deprivation or to lessen animosity towards state-imposed austerity measures. Those measures were to have few positive consequences, being too half-hearted to convince the IMF and too severe to be accepted by a population already falling into poverty, which ironically accused Duhalde of being too wedded to the neo-liberal policies of the IMF even as the IMF accused him of being too little committed to reform. However, although Remes Lenicov resigned, burned by the fallout from the crisis and the impact of his initial measures, in the second half of 2002 Duhalde and his new economy minister, Roberto Lavagna, began to succeed in stabilizing the battered economy. Nevertheless, GDP would contract by 10.9 per cent for the year and unemployment would exceed 20 per cent; the only good news, a record trade surplus, arose from the slump in demand and investment that virtually halted imports.

Notwithstanding some signs of relief on the economic front, in July 2002 Duhalde made a surprise announcement of early elections, moving the presidential contest up from September 2003 to April, with the winner to take office on 24 May. The announcement, which came despite his earlier promise to serve out De la Rua's term, was provoked by rising social tensions which peaked with the shooting dead of two protestors by police. The events brought back recent memories of the clashes that forced De la Rua from office, and undermined Duhalde's claim of 'legitimacy', based primarily on his supposed ability to reconcile disputes and avoid conflict. The inherent lack of electoral legitimacy of his government also encouraged protests, which he hoped early elections might resolve, although in practice he was also criticized alternatively for failing to call early elections immediately, and for failing to serve out the term for which Congress had appointed him. With the poverty rate soaring to over 50 per cent and the new phenomenon of *cartoneros* – individuals who searched rubbish for cardboard, scrap or other saleable items – firmly installed on the streets and in the public consciousness, and an unelected government ill-placed to negotiate with international lenders, arguably Duhalde had little choice but to seek such a solution. However, the difficulty of finding a credible candidate quickly became a new challenge.

This was not due to a shortage of volunteers. However, while former Radical Elisa Carrió of the centre-left *Alternativa por una República de Iguales* (ARI), virtually a successor to the fractured Frepaso, appeared to be the strongest non-Peronist contender (the Radicals having been badly damaged by the De la Rua debacle), the majority party itself proved unable to arrive at a consensus candidate. In order to avoid the possible proclamation of Menem as nominee, Duhalde as party president reached the decision to do without a primary, allowing an array of Peronist candidates to compete. The first to throw their hats in the ring were two former presidents, Menem and Rodríguez Saa, although both were unacceptable to Duhalde and anathema to broad swathes of public opinion, making a strong showing difficult. Duhalde's efforts to woo the popular centre-right governor of Santa Fe, Carlos Reutemann, failed to encourage the famously cautious former racing driver to announce a candidacy (perhaps prudently, given the chaotic situation still awaiting Duhalde's successor). A subsequent attempt by Duhalde to throw his backing behind Córdoba Governor José Manuel de la Sota, a respectable but colourless political figure perhaps too reminiscent of De la Rua, failed to push the governor's voting intentions even into double figures. Eventually, Duhalde settled on the candidacy of Santa Cruz Governor Néstor Kirchner, relatively little known at the national level, but with a reputation for efficient administration of the oil-rich province and a higher-profile spouse, the glamorous and outspoken Senator Cristina Fernández de Kirchner. The price of Duhalde's backing was the retention of members of his government in the new administration; thus, Lavagna would remain as economy minister and Daniel Scioli, the sports and tourism secretary, would become the vice-presidential nominee.

In the 27 April elections, three Peronist candidates – Menem, Kirchner and Rodríguez Saa – received a total of some 60 per cent of the votes, with former Radicals Elisa Carrió and Ricardo López Murphy gaining around 30 per cent (the official UCR candidate, Leopoldo Moreau, received just over 2 per cent of the votes, a historic worst for the party). However, with no candidate reaching the required threshold of 45 per cent, Argentina faced its first-ever presidential run-off between Menem, with some 24 per cent of the first-round vote, and Kirchner, with 22 per cent, only a week before the new president was to take office. Only three days before the run-off, and after days of speculation, Menem announced that he would not participate, leaving the strong impression that he had withdrawn in order to avoid what would certainly have been a heavy defeat; although Kirchner lacked strong national support, Menem faced strong hostility from many quarters after his decade in office, and his second-round vote would probably not have greatly exceeded his first-round result, implying a rout as the anti-Menem majority rallied around Kirchner. However, the decision (which brought accusations of cowardice and in effect terminated Menem's long and spectacular career) deprived Kirchner of a clear mandate, bringing him to office with little more than a fifth of the vote and raising questions over the legitimacy of this government as well.

Although little-known at the national level, Kirchner, born in Río Gallegos, Santa Cruz, in 1950, had a long experience of combative politics at the provincial level. Like his wife, a student at the University of La Plata in the 1970s, Kirchner had participated in radicalized sectors of the Peronist youth, although apparently not in any of its armed factions. Following the 1976 coup, they both returned to his native Santa Cruz, where the repression remained far less fierce than in Buenos Aires or Córdoba, and both dedicated themselves to law and politics. Much of their personal wealth sprang from this period, and allegedly from their success in foreclosing on mortgage debtors. After a spell as mayor of Río Gallegos, Kirchner became governor in 1991, a post he retained until he stood down to run for the presidency 12 years later. At the same time, Cristina backed his political project from a series of legislative seats, in the provincial legislature and thereafter in both houses of the national Congress. Buoyed by strong oil revenues, his government exercised substantial control over the province through high levels of public spending and the fact that much of the workforce was employed in the public sector. Payment by the national government of a debt arising from oil royalties led Kirchner to deposit the funds in Switzerland, provoking years of questions over the whereabouts and use of those provincial revenues.

On taking over the presidency in a disadvantaged position, Kirchner moved rapidly to cement his leadership, first focusing on changes to the Supreme Court (still dominated by judges known as Menem's 'automatic majority') and – perhaps surprisingly, given his lack of past form on the issue – on human rights, the purging of the armed forces command and the reopening of human rights trials.

His promises of an anti-corruption drive and the strengthening of institutions drew initial praise, although later perceptions that neither corruption nor institutions had improved, and indeed that the government had had limited success in the area of citizen security, would dent that image. He also broke with Duhalde, an unpopular figure, and for much of his presidency held the vice-president, Scioli, at bay. (Scioli, who as vice-president presided over the Senate, also had a number of sharp confrontations with Cristina, first as senator for Santa Cruz and then, from 2005, for Buenos Aires.)

Benefited by an improving economic environment – growth had picked up sharply in the first half of 2003 before he took office – Kirchner also succeeded in 2005 in negotiating a swap of defaulted debt that resulted in a write-down of two-thirds of the original debt. Much of that success was credited to Lavagna, although Kirchner's obsession with control over the economic portfolio and unwillingness to share the spotlight soon saw Lavagna replaced as economy minister. The cabinet was rapidly reduced to Kirchner intimates (including his sister Alicia, the social welfare minister) who rarely disagreed and who shared his inexperience of global politics in particular.

The 2005 midterm elections were characterized as a 'plebiscite' on the Kirchner government, and no expense was spared in boosting public spending, much of it purely political patronage by nature. With the Peronist party again split, Kirchner's *Frente para la Victoria* faction got more than 40 per cent of the total vote. Continuing strong growth – which averaged more than 8 per cent annually during Kirchner's term – ensured high levels of support, although in practice economic success was due more to favourable international conditions than to government policies, which were erratic at best and did little to encourage investment. A hostile stance towards the IMF, the USA and the United Kingdom in particular, and the renationalization of several privatized companies in foreign hands, was designed for internal consumption as a sign of independence, but led to increasing diplomatic isolation (not least since Kirchner had at best patchy relations with most of his regional neighbours, other than Venezuelan President Hugo Chavez), capital flight and investor wariness. This was most apparent in the hydrocarbons sector, where investment in natural gas – responsible for over 50 per cent of the energy matrix – fell in response to frozen tariffs and interventionism, causing proven reserves to fall by half during the 2000s, to only seven and a half years' supply by 2010.[2]

Despite Kirchner's public pro-poor stance, in practice many of his policies were directly designed to favour the middle classes, whose votes were more difficult to obtain, and who valued a return to greater consumption opportunities after the dark post-2001 period. In particular, the ongoing freeze on utilities tariffs benefited middle-class users of gas, telephones, electricity and public transport (the cost of liquid petroleum gas, used as fuel by poor households, rose by some 500 per cent during his term). In more general terms, his use of patronage in the depressed working-class districts around Greater Buenos Aires and in interior provinces, facilitated by strong growth and revenue flows, allowed him to gain at least temporary control over local power brokers and ensure both voter support and a supply of demonstrators at pro-government rallies (transported on government-supplied buses and often paid for their attendance). However, the freezing of tariffs and frequent shifts in policy towards investors tended to deter the capacity investments needed to sustain and increase the supply of energy and other goods and services, provoking increasing shortages as demand increased faster than supply. Moreover, the continuation of policies implemented as emergency measures by Duhalde at the height of the crisis – the use of subsidies for unemployed heads of household, the use of emergency economic decrees and the continuing freeze on tariffs – became increasingly difficult to justify in the face of strong growth, and opened opportunities for corruption and political manipulation.

At the same time, Kirchner's efforts to portray himself as a leftist prised open fissures within the party, which again began to divide into purportedly left-of-centre and right-of-centre blocs, highlighting the ideological vacuum at its heart as well as the difficulty of constructing coherent party structures when the largest political party continued to occupy, at least rhetorically, most of the political spectrum. Sharp clashes with other sectors of the party, a luxury Kirchner allowed himself when in command and in possession of strong fiscal flows, generated resentments within other strands of the party (as had been the case with Menem) that would harden into opposition as soon as Kirchner ceased to be perceived as an asset in the party's main goal of retaining power.

Serious underlying economic problems persisted despite the recovery. Unemployment remained high by historical levels, despite falling sharply from its 2002 peak, and poverty failed to return to pre-crisis levels. This situation repeated a pattern evident since the early 1970s at least: although poverty and unemployment always declined after peaking during a series of economic crises, they never returned to their previous level and structural poverty increased with each successive crisis. High levels of inflation remained a stubborn problem which attempts to impose price and export controls did little to remedy, while government intervention in the National Statistics Institute in early 2007 resulted only in blatant manipulation of inflation data that fooled no one. Moreover, under-reporting of inflation also led to under-reporting of poverty, given that the latter was calculated on the basis of the cost of living. By 2009 private estimates of poverty levels were more than double the official figures, an issue that became a cause of conflict between the government and the Church in particular as the administration reacted angrily to Church calls for greater social justice. According to the Catholic University, 17 per cent of the population was living in slum housing by 2010, in comparison with around 10 per cent in 2004.[3]

Among those who dismissed official inflation data were leaders of the CGT, whom Kirchner had attempted to co-opt on assuming office in order to create the institutionalized support base he lacked. Strikes and large pay awards began to increase, while efforts to co-opt *piquetero* groups carrying out protests and roadblocks also worked only in some cases, boosting animosities among rival groups. Moreover, Kirchner's persistently aggressive tactics towards the opposition, foreign investors, the media (he gave no press conferences during his term of office and frequently accused the press of seeking his downfall) and other sectors not seen as part of his power structure began to eat into popular support, as public opinion tired of the government's confrontational style and imperviousness to other strands of opinion. Frequent last-minute cancellations of foreign visits only cemented the view that the government was insular and inward-looking.

Nevertheless, with growth still strong, Kirchner came into the 2007 general elections with an almost unassailable position, not least given the continuing factionalism and incoherence that plagued most of the opposition. Despite a 60 per cent approval rating, in July Kirchner announced that he would not stand for re-election, instead backing his wife's candidacy. Apart from any other consideration, this appeared to be an attempt to avoid lame-duck status in a second term – unable to stand for a third consecutive term, the president would almost certainly have begun to lose power soon after re-election as the party began to look for a successor. However, the strategy of alternating in power with Cristina opened the possibility of numerous terms without running into this obstacle (and, according to the cynical, reduced the possibility of serious judicial investigations of corruption rumours). At the same time, despite her substantially different professional background, it proved difficult to avoid comparisons with Isabelita, also her husband's successor – while Kirchner's supporters could point to Cristina's far greater political experience, it was widely felt that she owed her candidacy to her husband's will. (Thus, somewhat paradoxically, the Peronist party has produced Argentina's only two women presidents to date, but in circumstances that could be viewed as inherently *machista*.)

Strong pre-election spending, a benign economic environment, an opposition in disarray and the use of government machinery to sustain her campaign made Cristina an inevitable winner. Following a desultory and ideologically vacuous campaign, in the October 2007 elections she received a first-round victory with some 45 per cent of the votes, well ahead of Elisa Carrió on 23 per cent and Roberto Lavagna on 17 per cent, but nevertheless a lower percentage than that received by Alfonsín, Menem or De la Rua in their respective victories. However, despite government policies that disproportionately favoured the middle classes, she performed relatively poorly in urban middle-class districts, losing to Carrió in the cities of Buenos Aires and Rosario and to Lavagna in Córdoba province. Ironically, much of her vote came from rural areas with which she would soon come into conflict.

Although Cristina's lack of executive experience was widely commented (as were concerns over her independence, or lack thereof, from her husband), her long legislative experience and greater interest in foreign affairs were taken as hopeful signs that some improvements might be made in Kirchner's less successful policy areas, with some strengthening of diplomatic relations and institutions. However, these hopes rapidly faded, as she reconfirmed virtually the whole of her husband's cabinet (a short-lived economy minister, Miguel Peirano, soon resigned on the grounds that he disagreed with economic policy, leading to the conviction that Kirchner continued to call the shots behind the scenes). Foreign policy also rapidly foundered, with tensions with the USA and Spain in particular on the increase. Immediately upon

Figure 17. Inauguration of President Cristina Fernández de Kirchner, 10 December 2007 (on the left, outgoing President Néstor Kirchner) (courtesy of the archive, *Diario La Nación*)

her inauguration, Cristina was moved to denounce a 'garbage' smear campaign from the USA, relating to investigations in Miami that alleged that she had received illegal campaign funding from the Chavez government in Venezuela. (The arrival in Buenos Aires of a Venezuelan businessman in August 2007, travelling on a plane chartered by Argentine state energy company Enarsa and in the company of members of the administration, had already attracted widespread comment when Customs officials in Buenos Aires found some 800,000 dollars in his suitcase; the businessman in question was subsequently seen in the Casa Rosada a few days later before leaving the country.) The president appeared to interpret the allegations as emanating from the US government rather than from an assistant US attorney. Relations with Spain were undermined by the government's renationalization of the airline Aerolíneas Argentinas, which led to claims of coercion of the company's Spanish owners. More generally, the failure to advance in talks to resolve the question of nearly 30 billion dollars in debt still in default (around 7 billion of it to the Paris Club) rapidly cooled hopes for a change of direction.

Cristina also soon clashed with her vice-president, former Mendoza Governor Julio Cobos, a Radical whose own party had turned against him when he accepted the candidacy. A so-called 'K Radical', Cobos attempted to adopt a more conciliatory posture than that taken by an increasingly shrill government. However, his relationship with the president finally broke down, and his own political capital rose sharply, following a debilitating 2008 strike by the agricultural sector over government policies including price controls, export freezes and, most significantly, a planned increase in export taxes on grains and oilseeds designed to sustain public spending that persistently rose faster than revenues. The strike, which achieved the unprecedented feat of uniting the country's four main agricultural organizations (which represented a range of large and small producers whose interests were often in conflict), also generated strong public support, despite the government's insistence on reverting to somewhat archaic Peronist terminology in referring to the farmers as oligarchs (or 'gorillas') and enemies of the people. (Despite claims that the Kirchners represented a 1970s brand of radicalism, in many respects they in fact harked back to the defensive and aggressively classist Peronism of the 1950s.) In July, a Senate vote on a government bill increasing export taxes was tied, forcing Cobos as vice-president to cast the deciding vote. His decision to vote against was wildly popular but led to violent tensions with the Kirchners and repeated calls for his resignation from government supporters. The vote represented the first sharp defeat experienced by the government, which had hitherto governed with little real opposition. The Kirchners' own approval ratings plummeted, from around 60 per cent at the end of 2007 to less than 20 per cent a year later.

Further moves to avoid spending cuts were no less dramatic, including the surprise October 2008 announcement that privatized pension funds administrators would be renationalized. The measure implied that social security contributions would be transferred to the state, often to be used to finance current spending, while pension funds themselves were increasingly used to invest either in state companies or in private companies where the government wished to increase its leverage. Although the measure was justified on the grounds of protecting pensions by returning them to state care, there was little question that it responded to political expediency – the government's desire for survival – rather than the common good. Indeed, privatization of pension funds had originally been justified as a means of removing them from state hands, following a series of virtual confiscations of pensions over the years, by Peronists, Radicals and military governments alike; public opinion widely viewed the move as merely another government grab that would drain the pension funds and leave contributors without their savings.

In this increasingly unfavourable environment, the government faced midterm elections in 2009 that threatened its majority in Congress (although in practice both Kirchner administrations had had heavy recourse to the use of emergency decrees, thus bypassing congressional control over many facets of policy, including public spending). With prospects declining, the government announced that the elections would be brought forward from October to June, and that Kirchner himself would head the government's list of candidates in Buenos Aires province. (He was seconded by Scioli, by now an unquestioned Kirchner loyalist and governor of the province.) The renewed insistence on casting the election as a plebiscite, and on focusing on the figure of Kirchner as its candidate, backfired badly: Kirchner and his *Frente para la Victoria* list lost in Buenos Aires province, coming second to a dissident Peronist list led by businessman Francisco de Narvaez. The government's lists came fourth in the cities of Buenos Aires and Córdoba, and even lost to the Radicals in the Kirchners' home province of Santa Cruz. As a result, although the *Frente para la Victoria* remained the single largest party in Congress, the government lost its majority in both houses to a range of opposition parties including the UCR (boosted somewhat in the polls by the public sorrow over the death of Raúl Alfonsín in April), dissident Peronists, Socialists, Carrio's new *Coalición Cívica* and other smaller groupings across the political spectrum.

Hopes that this outcome might force the government into a more conciliatory attitude towards the opposition appeared to be rapidly dashed, with the administration moving quickly to push through controversial legislation (including a media reform interpreted as an attempt to curb the opposition press) before the new Congress was sworn in. A new rise in the use of emergency decrees also appeared to be on the cards, although the opposition showed an increasing willingness to move to block this channel. A December 2009 decree ordering the use of some 6.6 billion dollars in Central Bank reserves to pay debt provoked strong defiance from the supposedly autonomous

Bank's president, Martín Redrado, and a concerted effort by the opposition to block the move through legislative and judicial means.
However, the diverse opposition also showed little sign of maintaining unity: Redrado was forced from his post and threats to reject his
replacement, Mercedes Marcó del Pont, proved largely rhetorical. Nevertheless, the president's allegation that both the courts and Congress
were trying to bring down her government, and her warning that
she would not automatically abide by their decisions, highlighted the
fundamental institutional weakness that continued to plague the political system, regardless of the government in power, and the threat
of a breakdown in governability.

With the 2011 presidential elections approaching, and the number of potential candidates mushrooming (both among opposition
parties and the so-called dissident Peronists opposed to the Kirchners), speculation increased as to which of the Kirchners would be
the government candidate – or indeed whether their continuing low
approval ratings might encourage them both to withdraw to Santa
Cruz. The overwhelming likelihood that Kirchner, now president of
the party, would stand in order to maintain the plan of alternating in
power, was generally welcomed by the opposition, given his greater
unpopularity and the difficulty he would face in obtaining the 40 per
cent of the vote needed to avoid a second round. However, Kirchner's sudden death of a heart attack in October 2010 put paid to the
strategy of alternating in the presidency and radically altered the political panorama. The opposition, which lacked cohesiveness and was
united only in its animosity to Kirchner, was thrown into disarray
while many dissident Peronists appeared less willing to challenge the
widow (whose own approval ratings received a sympathy boost) than
her divisive spouse.

Speculation also focussed on whether the president would maintain the policies apparently dictated by her husband, and indeed
whether she would succeed in holding her government coalition together. Despite adopting some more conciliatory positions – such
as reopening negotiations to pay off defaulted Paris Club debt and
inviting the IMF (virtually barred from Argentina after Kirchner
paid off the country's debt to the Fund, using Central Bank reserves, in 2005) to help devise a new national consumer price index – the fundamental policies of high public spending, patronage
and the use of decrees to circumvent Congress appeared to remain

in place. With Fernandez de Kirchner delaying any announcement as to whether she would stand for re-election, strong economic growth and the removal of the widely disliked Kirchner nevertheless made re-election suddenly more possible, and the position of the opposition substantially more uncertain. Despite Kirchner's brief stay at the centre of national politics, and shaky personal popularity, the Peronist phenomenon again repeated itself, with the political system defining itself largely in terms of whether it was for or against an individual who had centralised power in himself in the absence of stronger institutions or a more representative political class.

Although future developments in Argentina remain unpredictable, there are certain conclusions that can be drawn from events in recent years that point to a degree of continuity rather than change (although not necessarily stability). One of these is that the political will continues to be lacking to tackle the reforms needed to try to create a less dysfunctional and cyclical, and more equitable, economic system. Short-termism, personal gain and zero-sum attitudes remain paramount in political thinking, undermining any prospect of unpopular reforms that might bring long-term benefit but almost certainly short-term political cost. Moreover, it remains the case that reform is virtually impossible in a context in which periods of economic boom allow reform to be deferred, and periods of economic crisis render it politically unsustainable. Arguably, despite the discomfort involved in continuing boom-and-bust cycles, the experience that bust eventually turns into boom also allows for tolerance of the bad times that have been survived in the past.

Inflation has been, and continues to be, a case in point. Inflationary and hyperinflationary episodes have occurred regularly since at least the mid-twentieth century, causing periodic economic and political crises. However, with the exception of Cavallo's convertibility plan in the 1990s, following the hyperinflation of 1989, few attempts to contain it have proved effective (and, indeed, the fact that monetary discipline under convertibility was not matched by fiscal discipline led debt to spiral out of control, nearly doubling as a percentage of GDP during the lifetime of convertibility). Arguably, this has reflected a lack of vested interest in controlling it among the most politically powerful sectors: trade unions have successfully used inflation to raise wage demands (and wage-price spirals) and the government has effectively financed spending through inflated tax revenues and printing money, increasing the leverage obtained from political patronage and avoiding the blame for deciding unpopular spending cuts whose benefits would only be reaped by a future government. The apparent fudging of inflation data since 2007 points to a continuing problem with no palatable solution in sight.

At the same time, the difficulty of retaining political power remains chronic. The situation faced by the oligarchy following the rise of the Radicals, where they resorted to electoral fraud and obstructive use of their economic power when their ability to win office dissipated, is arguably being repeated in the two main political parties today. The number of citizens who identify themselves with either the UCR or the Peronists has fallen consistently since the return to democracy, and their captive voter base has dwindled. As such, the Peronists in particular have increasingly found it difficult to sustain support without 'chequebook' politics and the use of patronage (or economic coercion) to bring out the vote. This has made control over the state purse increasingly important and the risks of a lean fiscal position more acute: both voters and party bosses are increasingly fickle, and the representative capacity of the two main parties has diminished. The nebulous ideological character of both parties has doubtless played a role; while partly responsible for their longevity, the lack of clear policies and their replacement by sentiment or patronage has encouraged splits and factionalism rather than party discipline. However, in the absence of a new party with broad support – something that has often been predicted but has never materialized – their position at the centre of an increasingly vacuous political system will persist, although both may continue to find it easier to oppose initiatives than to innovate.

The other side of this coin is that, although voters are less identified with parties, they are also increasingly unwilling to accept without question the dictates of those parties, as witnessed by the events of 2001–2. This may prove a highly positive development – as, unquestionably, is the fact that even a crisis of the magnitude of 2001 did not provoke calls for military intervention from any quarter. However, these signs of greater political maturity have not corresponded with a rise in real political alternatives – brief sector alliances and calls to displace the entire political class cannot substitute for greater citizen responsibility and participation in the political process. With the political class widely discredited and politics viewed as an unsuitable profession by many, it will be difficult to remedy this. Moreover, the persistent tendency to view the past with nostalgia, or to debate past problems rather than look to the future, has done little to address structural problems and identify their causes and possibilities for change, cementing the tendency to repeat crises without adapting from a nostalgic past to an often difficult present and uncertain future.

NOTES

PREFACE

1 National Statistics Institute (INDEC), Complementary Survey of Indigenous Peoples, 2004–2005.
2 N. Shumway, *The Invention of Argentina*, p. 1–2.
3 J. B. Alberdi, quoted in E. Martínez Estrada, *X-Ray of the Pampa*, p. 226.
4 J. Brown, *A Brief History of Argentina*, xii; F. Luna, *Breve historia de los argentinos*, p. 262.
5 P. Lewis, *The Crisis of Argentine Capitalism*.
6 Quoted in D. Rock, *Argentina 1516–1982*, xxii.
7 J. Lynch, *San Martín*, 212, 211.
8 R. Crassweller, *Perón and the Enigmas of Argentina*.

INTRODUCTION

1 F. Luna, *Breve historia de los argentinos*, p. 17.
2 One of the few leaders who genuinely appears to have had little personal ambition, San Martín would retire to France after the disappointments suffered in the independence wars, and after handing over command of all independence forces to South America's other liberator, Simón Bolivar, in 1822. San Martín died in Boulogne in 1850.
3 F. Pigna, *Los mitos de la historia argentina 2*, p. 179.
4 Quoted ibid., p. 240.
5 Domingo F. Sarmiento, *Facundo*.

CHAPTER 1

1 See, e.g., D. Rock, *Argentina 1516–1982*, p. 132.
2 Ibid., p. 139.

CHAPTER 2

1 See, e.g., E. Adamovsky, *Historia de la clase media argentina*, 112–13.
2 See R. Munck, et al., *From Anarchism to Peronism*; M. Murmis and J.C. Portantiero, *Estudio sobre los orígenes del peronismo*.
3 Studies commissioned by the Roca government in the early years of the twentieth century discovered appalling living conditions in both rural areas and urban *conventillos*. See, e.g., F. Pigna, *Los mitos de la historia argentina 2*, p. 441–52.
4 See D. Rock, *Argentina 1516–1982*, p. 163.
5 Quoted in F. Pigna, *Los mitos de la historia argentina 3*, p. 31.

6   Quoted ibid., p. 31–2.
7   Quoted ibid., p. 19.
8   See E. Adamovsky, *Historia de la clase media argentina*, p. 111–12.
9   See, e.g., Rock, *Argentina 1516–1982*, R. Munck, et al., *From Anarchism to Peronism*.

CHAPTER 3

1   F. Pigna, *Los mitos de la historia argentina 3*, p. 214.
2   D. Rock, *Argentina 1516–1982*, p. 220.
3   Ibid., p. 233.
4   Murmis and Portantiero, *Estudio sobre los orígenes del peronismo*, p. 7.
5   See Munck, *From Anarchism to Peronism*; Murmis and Portantiero, ibid.
6   See Munck; Murmis and Portantiero; W. Little, 'The Popular Origins of Peronism'.
7   See Little, ibid.
8   R. Munck, *From Anarchism to Peronism*, p. 17–36.
9   Ibid., p. 38.
10 W. Little, 'The Popular Origins of Peronism'.
11 See, e.g., A. Fernández, *Sindicalismo e iglesia*; A.J. Soneira, *Las estrategias institucionales de la Iglesia Católica*; D.H. Levine, *Religion and Political Conflict in Latin America*; R. Gillespie, *Soldiers of Perón*, p. 64–5.
12 C. Mugica, *Peronismo y cristianismo*, p. 58.
13 R. Munck, *Argentina: From Anarchism to Peronism*, p. 47.
14 Murmis and Portantiero, *Estudio sobre los orígenes del peronismo*.
15 W. Little, 'The Popular Origins of Peronism'.
16 See Turner and Miguens, *Juan Perón and the Reshaping of Argentina*, p. 157.
17 See F. Luna, *Perón y su tiempo*; H. Gambini, *Historia del Peronismo*; Murmis and Portantiero, *Estudio sobre los orígenes del peronismo*.
18 F. Luna, ibid.; H. Gambini, ibid.; R. Munck, *From Anarchism to Peronism*.
19 F. Luna, ibid.
20 Turner and Miguens, *Juan Perón and the Reshaping of Argentina*, p. 55.

CHAPTER 4

1   See, e.g., T. Eloy Martínez, *Las memorias del general*.
2   Ibid.
3   T. Eloy Martínez, *Las memorias del general*, Ibid., p. 36.
4   In *Las memorias del General*, p. 99, Eloy Martínez cites a statement by the sister of Aurelia Tizón to this effect, saying that medical tests indicated that Aurelia was physically able to have children, although she also states that Aurelia refused to submit Perón to similar tests, in order to spare him any possible embarrassment.
5   A fuller account of this saga appears in Page, *Perón*, p. 51–2.
6   See R. Potash, *Perón y el GOU*.
7   While Perón has generated relatively few straight biographical works, possibly due to the nebulous nature of his personality, there are a number of biographies of Evita, notably N. Fraser and M. Navarro, *Eva Perón*; M. Navarro, *Evita*; and Alicia Dujovne Ortiz, *Eva Perón*, as well as Tomás Eloy Martínez' perspicacious novel, *Santa Evita*.
8   Interview with Raúl Suárez.
9   Interview with Raúl Suárez.

10 Recollections by Evita's contemporaries are cited in Dujovne and in Fraser and Navarro; interview with Raúl Suárez.

11 The newspaper *Ambito Financiero* was one of the few to give credence and considerable space to the story, although some television journalists would later see its sentimental and ratings value and begin interviewing Evita's supposed daughter.

12 The letter appears in M. Cichero, *Cartas peligrosas*, p. 25–7.

13 See, e.g., T. Eloy Martínez, *Las memorias del general*; Perón gives similar versions in various written works.

14 Interview with Raúl Suárez.

15 T. Eloy Martínez, *Las memorias del general.*, p. 49, 51.

CHAPTER 5

1 Domingo Mercante, quoted by Felix Luna, *El 45*, p. 57.

2 R. Potash, *Perón y el GOU*, Doc. 3.2.

3 See, e.g., R. Crassweller, *Perón and the Enigmas of Argentina*, p. 97–102.

4 J.D. Perón, *Diálogo entre Perón y las Fuerzas Armadas*, p. 53–4.

5 R. Potash, *Perón y el GOU*, Doc. 2.1, 101–103. This document is undated, but appears to date from early 1943.

6 *Criterio*, No. 797, 10 June 1943, 128.

7 See, e.g., A. Jauretche, *Política nacional y revisionismo histórico*, 118, 98.

8 See, e.g., U. Goñi, *The Real Odessa*.

9 Reference is made to this by both Felix Luna, *Perón y su tiempo*, and by Tomás Eloy Martínez, *Las memorias del general*.

10 J.D. Perón, *Diálogo entre Perón y las Fuerzas Armadas*, p. 26.

11 Quoted in L. Monzalvo, *Testigo de la primera hora del peronismo*, p. 79.

12 See R. Potash, *The Army and Politics in Argentina, 1928–1945*.

13 Quoted in Monzalvo, *Testigo de la primera hora del peronismo*, p. 79.

14 Ambassador Sir David Kelly to Sir Anthony Eden, telegram 178/13/44, dated 11 April 1944, in FO 118/728.

15 British Embassy, Monthly Report, February 1945, doc. 3/134/45, in FO 118/742.

16 R. Potash, *Perón y el GOU*, Doc. 3.2, 203.

17 E. Duarte de Perón, *Clases y Escritos Completos*, 64, 96.

18 G. Farrell, *Iglesia y Pueblo en Argentina*, p. 88.

19 J.O. Frigerio, 'El síndrome de la "Revolución Libertadora', 31.

CHAPTER 6

1 Estimates of participation were reported in *La Prensa* and the *Buenos Aires Herald* of 20 September 1945.

2 *Buenos Aires Herald*, 20 September 1945.

3 British Embassy Monthly Report, June 1945, doc. 6/134/45, in FO 118/742.

4 *Review of the River Plate*, 21 September 1945.

5 C. Reyes, *La farsa del peronismo*, 13.

6 Quoted in *La Nación*, 11 October 1945.

7 British Embassy Monthly Report, October 1945, doc. 11/134/45, in FO 118/742.

8 *La Prensa*, 18 October 1945.

9 Cited in F. Luna, *El 45*, 302; Turner and Miguens, *Juan Perón and the Reshaping of Argentina*, p. 151.

10 Quoted in L. Monzalvo, *Testigo de la primera hora del peronismo*, p. 192.
11 Ibid., p. 193.
12 F. Luna, *El 45*, p. 340–1; M. Navarro, 'Evita and the Crisis of 17 October 1945'.
13 E. Duarte de Perón, *Clases y Escritos Completos*, p. 144.
14 See, e.g., R. Crassweller, *Perón and the Enigmas of Argentina*, p. 159.
15 Quoted in J.D. Perón, *Peronist Doctrine*, p. 215.
16 R. Puiggrós, *El proletariado en la revolución nacional*, p. 104.
17 F. Luna, *El 45*, p. 44.
18 British Ambassador Sir David Kelly to the Foreign Office, communication 251/131/44, dated 12 June 1944, in FO 118/730.
19 E. Sabato, *El otro rostro del peronismo*, p. 41–3.
20 British Consulate, La Plata, Monthly Report; January 1946, in FO 118/749.
21 C. Reyes, *La farsa del peronismo*, p. 13.
22 US Department of State, *Consultation among the American Republics with Respect to the Argentine Situation*, p. 101, 6.

CHAPTER 7

1   The history of Cipriano Reyes is well described in F. Luna, *Perón y su tiempo*. Reyes eventually retired to La Plata to write poetry, and continued to give self-justifying interviews until well into his 80s, becoming one of the long-term survivors of the first period of Peronism. Reyes died in 2001 at the age of 95.
2   Interview with Father Hernán Benítez, 19 April 1991. Benítez, by this time a very elderly man, was not forthcoming on more than his own official version of events.
3   Interview with Dr. Emilio Mignone, 29 August 1990. Dr. Mignone was director of public instruction in Mercante's government until 1951.
4   A. Sampay, *Las Constituciones de la Nación Argentina* (1810–1972).
5   Quoted in R. Crassweller, *Perón and the Enigmas of Argentina*, p. 227.
6   Quoted in J.O. Frigerio, *El síndrome de la Revolución Libertadora*, p. 40.
7   E. Perón, *Clases y escritos completos*, 48; *La razon de mi vida*, p. 34.
8   J.D. Perón, *La comunidad organizada*, 51, p. 111.
9   J.D. Perón, *La comunidad organizada*, 79.
10 Quoted in J. Deiner, 'ATLAS', p. 177.
11 See, e.g., F. Luna, ibid.; A. Sampay, *Las Constituciones de la Nación Argentina*.
12 *Buenos Aires Herald*, 28 June 1947; US Department of State, Despatch from Vatican City, 1 July 1947, Microfilm 341, Reel 2:0311.
13 US Department of State, Despatch from Vatican City, 1 July 1947.
14 See T. Eloy Martínez, *Las memorias del general*. The post-war emigration of war criminals to Argentina and the Vatican's role in that process are well documented by Uki Goñi in *The Real Odessa*, although his assumption that this represented sincere Nazi convictions on Perón's part, rather than opportunism, is more questionable.
15 Ibid.
16 One of the most distinguished proponents of women's suffrage and women's rights in general was Alicia Moreau de Justo, the wife of socialist leader Juan B. Justo and one of the first woman to graduate from the University of Buenos Aires Faculty of Medicine, and a tireless rights campaigner for more than half a century. The images of Evita and of Alicia Moreau de Justo would be negatively contrasted by their respective supporters, although in fact both represented a positive image in that they were among the first Argentine women who offered an example of a woman assuming a public role and social responsibilities. Although a highly respected figure, however, the intellectual

Moreau had less resonance for the common woman than the figure of Evita, a working-class girl turned glamorous leading lady: working-class housewives dreamed of being Evita, not Alicia Moreau de Justo.

17 See N. Ferioli, *La Fundación Eva Perón*.
18 The scene is brilliantly evoked in Eloy Martínez' novelized work, *Santa Evita*.
19 Fraser and Navarro, *Eva Perón*.

CHAPTER 8

1 See, e.g., J. Page, *Perón*; F. Luna, *Perón y su tiempo*. Neither of these authors gives credence to the rumour that Perón was responsible for Duarte's death.
2 The question of oil and nationalism was a favourite theme of Radical Arturo Frondizi, president from 1958 to 1962, who published the book *Petróleo y nacionalismo* attacking Perón's sell-out of Argentina's oil interests.
3 P. Marsal, *Perón y la Iglesia*, 9. Pablo Marsal was the pseudonym used by a member of the Education Ministry, who has not been identified and who argues that Education Minister Armando Méndez San Martín was responsible for the Church–State conflict. It seems likely that Marsal was in fact a Father Gaynor, a former Inspector General of Religious Education and a Pallotine priest at San Patricio, Belgrano, who gave a number of statements to the US Embassy in an almost identical vein. See US State Department Confidential Files on Argentina, Microfilm 337, Reels 24–25 (25 March 1955).
4 Quoted in M. Lubertino Beltrán, *Perón y la Iglesia*, p. 79.
5 Quoted in G. Farrell, *Iglesia y Pueblo en Argentina*, p. 102–103.
6 Note of conversation between Perón and Ambassador Nufer, 21 June, 1955, US State Department Confidential Files on Argentina, Microfilm 337, Reel 28.
7 Confidential Despatch dated March 25th, 1955, ibid., Microfilm 337, Reel 24.
8 *Criterio* 1241, 11 August, 1955, 563–6.
9 Manifesto quoted in E. Ghirardi, *La Democracia Cristiana*, 87–8. The apparent desire to utilize not just political groups as a basis of political influence is similar to Peronism's identification of such groups as sources of political power. See, e.g., W. Little, 'The Argentine "Plan Político" of 1955'.
10 This translation appears in a despatch from the US Embassy dated 6 October 1954, US State Department Confidential Files on Argentina, Microfilm 342, Reel 21. A subsequent despatch, dated 3 November 1954, indicates that a government official who called on publisher Amérigo Barrios to enquire about the *Democracia* editorial was informed that it had been written by Perón himself.
11 US State Department Confidential Files on Argentina, Microfilm 342, Reel 21.
12 Despatch dated April 15th, 1955, ibid., Microfilm 337, Reel 24.
13 Interview with Dr Emilio Mignone.
14 Quoted in *La Nación*. 11 November 1954.
15 Ibid.
16 Eduardo Vuletich and Delia Parodi, quoted in *La Nación*, 26 November 1954.
17 Quoted in *La Nación*, 2 May 1955.
18 Memorandum from US Embassy dated 14 June 1955, US State Department, Microfilm 337, Reel 24. See also the statement of Vice-President Teisaire contained in the *Libro Negro de la Segunda Tiranía*, 210–14. Also noting that no flags were originally flying on 11 June, Teisaire states that the Argentine and Vatican flags raised by the crowd were in his possession and that the burned flag had been burned elsewhere, probably at Perón's instigation.
19 J.D. Perón, *La fuerza es el derecho de las bestias*, p. 89.
20 A report to the Foreign Office cites a rebel broadcast stating the aims of the uprising, and notes that 'it is significant that (the speaker) hardly mentioned

the Church question, which confirms my belief that this was not a primary cause of the revolt'. Despatch No. 96 dated 23 June 1955, in FO 118/845.

21 Despatch from British Embassy dated 21 June 1955, in FO 118/844.

22 *Libro Negro de la Segunda Tiranía*, 192–3, 213. Teisaire's statement quoted here indicates that the entire conflict was staged by Perón in order to enable him to expropriate the cathedral. As the *Libro Negro* was compiled by the government which overthrew Perón, for the express purpose of discrediting his government, such assertions cannot be assumed to be accurate.

23 Despatch dated 8 July 1955 from the British Embassy, in FO 118/846.

24 Purported minute of negotiations between the coup leaders and Perón, provided by a 'reliable source' to the British Embassy and appended to a despatch dated 22 June 1955, in FO 118/845.

25 E. Sabato, *El otro rostro del peronismo*, 43.

CHAPTER 9

1   See, e.g., *Libro Negro de la Segunda Tiranía*; R. Boizard, *Esa noche de Perón*.

2   See J. Page, *Perón*; T. Eloy Martínez, *Las memorias del general*; R. Crassweller, *Perón and the Enigmas of Argentina*; D. Sáenz and P. Manzanares, *Isabel: La razón de su vida*; M. Sáenz Quesada, *Isabel Perón*.

3   See, e.g., Sáenz Quesada, ibid., p. 39–54.

4   See D. James, *Resistance and Integration*; J.W. McGuire, *Peronism without Perón*

5   See *La Nación*, 6 September 2007.

6   J. Soneira, *Las estrategias institucionales de la Iglesia Católica*, 160–161.

7   D. James, *Resistance and Integration*, 39.

8   J. D. Perón, *La hora de los pueblos*, p. 172, 20.

9   Movimiento de Sacerdotes para el Tercer Mundo, *Nuestra opción por el peronismo*, p. 80–87.

10 Reproduced in Revista Así, 13 July 1971.

11 R. Gillespie, *Soldiers of Perón*.

CHAPTER 10

1   A good biography of Héctor Cámpora is contained in M. Bonasso, *El presidente que no fue*.

2   Quoted in D. James, *Resistance and Integration*, p. 184.

3   M. Andersen, *Dossier secreto*, p. 117–18.

4   See R. Gillespie, *Soldiers of Perón*.

5   Quoted in *La Gaceta*, 11 February 1975.

6   Quoted in *La Gaceta*, 22 February 1975.

7   *Informe Bicameral Investigadora de las Violaciones de Derechos Humanos en la Provincia de Tucumán*.

8   Quoted in *Página 12*, 10 February 1988.

9   Quoted in *La Gaceta*, 25 March 1976.

10 See CONADEP, *Nunca Más*.

11 See, e.g., I. Guest, *Behind the Disappearances*.

12 This is the argument put forward in James Neilson's excellent book *El fin de la quimera*.

CHAPTER 11

1   These definitions are used by, e.g., the World Bank and Argentina's Federal Investment Council. The low-density provinces, together with Mendoza, are major hydrocarbons producers; the eight underdeveloped provinces together had a combined gross provincial product that was less than that of any single advanced province, except Mendoza, in 1991.

2   See J. E. Supplee, 'Provincial Elites and the Economic Transformation of Mendoza, 1880–1914'; P.S. Martínez, *Historia de Mendoza*, p. 124–5, 139–40, 143–5; P. Lacoste, *Los 'gansos' de Mendoza*, p. 16–17, 96–7.

3   Quoted in Lacoste, p. 42.

4   R.A. Bazán, *El noroeste y la Argentina contemporánea*, p. 272–8.

5   R.A. Bazán, *El noroeste y la Argentina contemporánea*, p. 277.

6   Quoted in N. Morandini, *Catamarca*, p. 28.

7   In an apparent bid to distract public opinion, in late 1990 the preserved heart of nineteenth-century priest Fray Mamerto Esquiú was stolen from the cathedral, purportedly at Saadi's behest; popular rumour also widely held that Saadi was responsible for the 1987 desecration of Perón's tomb and the theft of his hands.

8   Quoted in S. Bandieri, et al., *Historia de Neuquén*, p. 292.

CHAPTER 12

1   See G. Cerruti, *El Jefe*, p. 356.

2   Figures from Dirección Nacional Electoral; see also Consejo para la Consolidación de la Democracia, *Reforma Constitucional. Dictamen preliminar*.

3   Ministerio de Economía, *Política para el cambio estructural en el sector público*, Tables 10, 19, 174, 184; INDEC, Censo Nacional 1980; provincial budgets 1984–1989; P. Pirez, *Coparticipación federal y descentralización del Estado*.

4   INDEC, *La pobreza en la Argentina; Encuesta permanente de hogares*.

5   See, e.g., H. Verbitsky, *Robo para la corona*.

6   O. Wornat, *Menem: la vida privada*.

7   See M. Bonasso, *Don Alfredo*.

8   See U. Goñi, *The Real Odessa*.

9   See E. Adamovsky, *Historia de la clase media argentina*, p. 446.

CHAPTER 13

1   See, e.g., M. Mussa, *Argentina y el FMI*.

2   According to the General Mosconi Argentine Energy Institute in a July 2010 report.

3   Quoted in *La Nación*, 21 July 2010.

BIBLIOGRAPHY

DOCUMENTS

Cartas del Venerable Episcopado Argentino al Excmo, Sr. Presidente Gral. Don Juan D. Perón y al Excmo. Sr Ministro de Educación Doctor Armando Méndez San Martín, de 16 de Marzo 1955. Biblioteca del Arzobispado de Buenos Aires.

Cartas Pastorales del Episcopado Argentino, 1943–1955 (reprinted in *Revista Criterio* and *Revista Eclesiástica del Arzobispado de Buenos Aires*).

Constitución de la Nación Argentina, Editorial Plus Ultra, Buenos Aires 1987 (6th edition).

Dirección Nacional Electoral, *Elecciones presidenciales, a gobernador y a diputados, resultados finales.*

Instituto Nacional de Estadística y Censos (INDEC), *Censo Nacional de Población y Vivienda 1980.*

Instituto Nacional de Estadística y Censos (INDEC), *Censo Nacional de Población y Vivienda 1991.*

Instituto Nacional de Estadística y Censos (INDEC), *Complementary Survey of Indigenous Peoples,* 2004–2005.

Instituto Nacional de Estadística y Censos (INDEC), *Encuesta permanente de hogares.*

Instituto Nacional de Estadística y Censos (INDEC), *La pobreza en la Argentina,* Buenos Aires November 1985.

Ministerio de Economía, Subsecretaría de Hacienda, *Presupuestos Provinciales.*

National Commission on Disappeared People (CONADEP), *Nunca Más,* Faber and Faber, London, 1986.

Poder Ejecutivo Nacional, Ministerio de Economía, *Política para el cambio estructural en el sector público,* Buenos Aires, 1989.

Poder Legislativo de Tucumán, *Informe de la Comisión Bicameral Investigadora de las Violaciones de los Derechos Humanos en la Provincia de Tucumán (1974–1983).*

Reports on the political situation in Argentina from the British Embassy, Buenos Aires, to the Foreign Office, 1944–6, 1953–5. Public Record Office, Kew, archives FO 118/728–49; FO 118/829–57.

Unión Democrática: pamphlets issued in the context of the 1945–6 election campaign. Author's personal archive.

US Department of State, Confidential Central Files on Argentina, 1945–1955, *Microfilm Collection*, London School of Economics, Microfilms 336, 337, 341, 342.

US Department of State, *Consultation among the American Republics with Respect to the Argentine Situation*, Washington, DC, February 1946.

BOOKS

Adamovsky, Ezequiel, *Historia de la clase media argentina*, Editorial Planeta, Buenos Aires, 2009.

Alexander, Robert Jackson, *The Perón Era*, Russell & Russell, New York, 1951.

Andersen, Martin Edwin, *Dossier Secreto*, Editorial Planeta, Buenos Aires, 1993.

Bandieri, S., Favaro, O., Morinelli, M., *Historia de Neuquén*, Editorial Plus Ultra, Buenos Aires 1993.

Barreiro, Hipólito, *Juancito Sosa: El indio que cambió la historia*, Avellaneda Tehuelche, Buenos Aires, 2000.

Bazán, Armando Raúl, *El Noroeste y la Argentina Contemporanea (1853–1992)*, Editorial Plus Ultra, Buenos Aires, 1992.

Benítez, Hernán, *La aristocracia frente a la revolución*, Copyright L.E. Benitez de Aldama, Buenos Aires, 1953.

Blustein, Paul, *And the Money Kept Rolling In (and Out)*, Public Affairs, New York, 2005.

Bonasso, Miguel, *El presidente que no fue*. Editorial Planeta, Buenos Aires, 1997.

Boizard, Ricardo, *Esa noche de Perón*, Ediciones Rex, Buenos Aires, 1955.

Brown, Jonathan C., *A Brief History of Argentina*, Facts on File, New York, 2003.

Campi, Daniel, (comp.) *Estudios sobre la historia de la industria azucarera Argentina*, Universidad Nacional de Jujuy, 1991.

Cerruti, Gabriela, *El Jefe: vida y obra de Carlos Saúl Menem*, Editorial Planeta, Buenos Aires, 1993.

Cichero, Marta, *Cartas peligrosas*, Editorial Planeta, Buenos Aires, 1992.

Crassweller, Robert, *Perón and the Enigmas of Argentina*, W.W. Norton & Co., New York, 1987.

Crenzel, Emilio Ariel, *El Tucumanazo (1969–1974)*, Centro Editor de América Latina, Buenos Aires, 1991.

Daiha, Alejandra, Haimovichi, Laura, *Menem y su entorno*, Puntosur, Buenos Aires, 1989.

Delich, Francisco José, *Tierra y conciencia campesina en Tucumán*, Ediciones Signos, Buenos Aires, 1970.

Duarte de Perón, Eva, *Clases y escritos completos 1946–1952, Tomo III*, Editorial Megafón, Buenos Aires, 1987.

Dujovne Ortiz, Alicia, *Eva Perón: La biografía*, Aguilar, Buenos Aires, 1995.

Eloy Martínez, Tomás, *Santa Evita*, Editorial Planeta, Buenos Aires, 1995.

Farrell, Gerardo, *Iglesia y pueblo en Argentina*, Editora Patria Grande, Buenos Aires, 1988 (3rd edition).

Ferioli, Néstor, *La Fundación Eva Perón*, Centro Editor de América Latina, Buenos Aires, 1990.

Fernández, Arturo, *Sindicalismo e Iglesia (1976–1987)*, Centro Editor de América Latina, Buenos Aires, 1990.

Filippo, Virgilio, *El plan quinquenal de Perón y los comunistas*, Editorial Lista Blanca, Buenos Aires, 1948.

Fraser, Nicholas and Navarro, Marysa, *Eva Perón*, W.W. Norton & Co., New York, 1980.

Frigerio, José Oscar, *El síndrome de la 'Revolución libertadora': la Iglesia contra el Justicialismo*, Centro Editor de América Latina, Buenos Aires, 1990.

Gambini, Hugo, *El peronismo y la Iglesia*, Centro Editor de América Latina, Buenos Aires, 1971.

——, *Historia del peronismo*, Editorial Planeta, Buenos Aires, 1999.

García de Loydi, Ludovico, *La Iglesia frente al peronismo*, Ediciones C.I.C., Buenos Aires 1956.

Garrone, Valeria and Rocha, Laura, *Néstor Kirchner*, Editorial Planeta, Buenos Aires, 2003.

Ghirardi, Enrique, *La Democracia Cristiana*, Centro Editor de América Latina, Buenos Aires, 1983.

Gillespie, Richard, *Soldiers of Perón: Argentina's Montoneros*, Oxford University Press, 1982.

Goñi, Uki, *The Real Odessa* (revised edition), Granta Books, London, 2003.

Hodges, Donald Clark, *Argentina 1943–1976: The National Revolution and Resistance*, University of New Mexico, 1976.

James, Daniel, *Resistance and Integration: Peronism and the Argentine Working Class 1946–1976*, Cambridge University Press, 1988.

Jauretche, Arturo, *Política nacional y revisionismo histórico*, A. Peña Lillo Editor, Buenos Aires, 1982 (6th edition).

Kennedy, Joseph John, *Catholicism, Nationalism and Democracy in Argentina*, University of Notre Dame Press, 1958.

Kirkpatrick, Jeane, *Leader and Vanguard in Mass Society: A Study of Peronist Argentina*, Cambridge, MA, 1971.

Josephs, Ray, *Argentine Diary: The Inside Story of the Coming of Fascism*, Random House, New York, 1944.

Lacoste, Pablo, *Los 'gansos' de Mendoza*, Centro Editor de América Latina, Buenos Aires 1991.

Lafiandra, F. (ed.), *Los panfletos: recopilación, comentario y notas*, Editorial Itinerarium, Buenos Aires, 1955 (2nd edition).

Levine, D. (ed.), *Religion and Political Conflict in Latin America*, University of North Carolina Press, 1986.

Sabato, Ernesto, *El otro rostro del peronismo*, Imprenta López, Buenos Aires, 1956 (2nd edition).

NEWSPAPERS AND PERIODICALS

Ambito Financiero, Buenos Aires, 1985–2000
Los Andes (Mendoza), 1976–2000
El Ancasti (Catamarca), 1988–91
Buenos Aires Herald, 1945, 1947, 1954, 1976–7, 1990–2000
Clarín (Buenos Aires), 1984–2010
El Cronista (Buenos Aires), 1984–8, 1995–2010
El Diario del Juicio, 1985
Democracia, Buenos Aires, July 1952
La Gaceta (Tucumán), 1976–2000
La Maga (Buenos Aires), 27 January 1993
La Nación, Buenos Aires, 1943–52, 1954–5, 1984–2010
New York Times, 1945–6
Noticias Gráficas, 22 November 1949
Página 12 (Buenos Aires), 1987–2010
La Prensa, Buenos Aires, 1945–6, 1955, 1984–99
The Review of the River Plate, 1943–6
Revista Así, Buenos Aires, August 1971
Revista Criterio, 1943–56
Revista de la Universidad de Buenos Aires, 1950–53
Revista Noticias, 1974, 1991
Rio Negro (Neuquén and Río Negro), 1976–88, 1993–2000
The Times of London, October 1945
La Unión (Catamarca), 1976–87

INTERVIEWS

Luis Iglesias Barbetto, interventor, Peronist Party of Catamarca.
Father Hernán Benítez, SJ, confessor to Eva Perón, rector of the University of Buenos Aires and spiritual adviser to the Eva Perón Foundation.
Msgr. Horacio Bózzoli, Archbishop of Tucumán.
Gen Antonio Domingo Bussi, former military and elected governor of Tucumán.
Dr. Ruben Chebaia, leader of UCR Tucumán, former mayor and gubernatorial candidate.
Dr. Osvaldo Cirnigliaro, PJ Tucumán, former secretary of planning and gubernatorial candidate.
Sen. Eduardo Córdoba, provincial senator PJ (Mendoza).
. Carlos De la Rosa, vice-governor PJ (Mendoza).
. Miguel Elías, former minister of economy of Tucumán.

López Echagüe, Hernán, *El otro*, Editorial Planeta, Buenos Aires, 1996.

Lubertino Beltrán, María José, *Perón y la Iglesia (1943–1955)*, Centro Editor de América Latina, Buenos Aires, 1987.

Luna, Félix, *Breve historia de los argentinos*, Editorial Planeta, Buenos Aires 2007 (44th edition).

——, *El 45*, Editorial Sudamericana, Buenos Aires, 1986.

——, *Perón y su tiempo*, Editorial Sudamericana, Buenos Aires, 1993 (2nd edition).

Lynch, John, *Argentine Dictator*, Oxford University Press, 1981.

——, *San Martín: Argentine Soldier, American Hero*, Yale University Press, 2009.

Mallimaci, Fortunato, *El catolicismo integral en la Argentina (1930–1946)*, Editorial Biblos, Buenos Aires, 1988.

Mansilla, César L., *Los partidos provinciales*, Centro Editor de América Latina, Buenos Aires, 1983.

Maronese, Leticia, Cafiero de Nazar, Ana, Waisman, Victor, *El voto peronista '83: perfil electoral y causas de la derrota*, El Cid Editor, Buenos Aires, 1985.

Marsal S., Pablo, *Perón y la Iglesia*, Ediciones Rex, Buenos Aires, 1955.

Martínez Estrada, Ezequiel, *X-Ray of the Pampa*, University of Texas Press, 1971.

McGuire, James W., *Peronism without Perón: Unions, Parties and Democracy in Argentina*, Stanford University Press, Stanford, CA, 1997.

Meinvielle, Julio, *Política Argentina 1949–1956*, Editorial Trafac, Buenos Aires, 1956.

Morandini, Norma, *Catamarca*, Editorial Planeta, Buenos Aires, 1991 (2nd edition).

Mugica, Carlos, *Peronismo y Cristianismo*, Editorial Merlin, Buenos Aires, 1973.

Murmis, Miguel and Portantiero, Juan Carlos, *Estudio sobre los origenes del peronismo*, Siglo XXI, Buenos Aires, 1971.

Munck, Ronaldo, et al., *Argentina: From Anarchism to Peronism*, Zed Books, London, 1987.

Mussa, Michael, *Argentina y el FMI: Del triunfo a la tragedia*, Editorial Planeta, Buenos Aires, 2002.

Navarro Gerassi, Marisa, *Evita*, Corregidor, Buenos Aires, 1981.

——, *Los nacionalistas*, Editorial Jorge Alvarez, Buenos Aires, 1969.

Neilson, James, *El fin de la quimera*, Emecé Editores, Buenos Aires, 1991.

Page, Joseph, *Perón*, Random House, New York, 1983.

Payró, Roberto J., *En las tierras de Inti*, EUDEBA, Buenos Aires, 1968 (3rd edition).

Pérez Gaudio, José Leopoldo, *Catolicismo y Peronismo*, Ediciones Corregidor, Buenos Aires, 1985.

Perón, Juan, *La comunidad organizada*, Editorial Pleamar, Buenos Aires, 1975.

——, *Conducción política*, Editorial Megafón, Buenos Aires, 1998.

——, *Peronist Doctrine*, Partido Peronista Consejo Superior Ejecutivo, Buenos Aires, 1952.

——, *Habla Perón*, Ediciones Realidad Política, Buenos Aires, 1984.

——, *La hora de los pueblos*, Editorial Norte, Buenos Aires, 1968.

——, *Manual del Peronista*, Ediciones Los Coihues, Buenos Aires, 1988.

——, *Libro Azul y Blanco*, Editorial Freeland, Buenos Aires, 1973.

——, *Política y estrategia: No ataco, critico*, Editorial Pleamar, Buenos Aires 1983.

——, *Diálogo entre Perón y las Fuerzas Armadas*, Editorial Jorge Mar, Buenos Aires, 1973.

Pigna, Felipe, *Los mitos de la historia argentina 2: De San Martín a 'el granero del mundo'*, Editorial Planeta, Buenos Aires 2009 (3rd edition).

——, *Los mitos de la historia argentina 3: De la ley Sáenz Peña a los albores del peronismo*, Editorial Planeta, Buenos Aires 2006.

Pírez, Pedro, *Coparticipación Federal y Descentralización del Estado*, Centro Editor de América Latina, Buenos Aires, 1986.

Poder Ejecutivo Nacional, *Libro Negro de la Segunda Tiranía*, Editorial Integración, Buenos Aires, 1958.

Potash, Robert (ed.), *Perón y el GOU*, Editorial Sudamericana, Buenos Aires, 1984.

—— (ed.), *The Army and Politics in Argentina 1928–1945 – Yrigoyen to Perón*, Stanford University Press, 1969.

—— (ed.), *The Army and Politics in Argentina 1945–1962 – Perón to Frondizi*, Athlone Press, London, 1980.

Puiggrós, Rodolfo, *El proletariado en la revolución nacional*, Editorial Sudestada, Buenos Aires, 1968.

Rock, David, *Argentina 1516–1982*, I.B. Tauris & Co., London, 1986.

Romero, José Luis, *A History of Argentine Political Thought*, Stanford University Press, 1963.

Sacerdotes para el Tercer Mundo – Capital Federal, *El pueblo, ¿Dónde está?* Buenos Aires, 1975.

Sacerdotes para el Tercer Mundo – Mendoza, *Nuestra Opción por el Peronismo*, Buenos Aires, 1972 (2nd edition).

Sáenz, Dalmiro and Manzanares, Pilar, *Isabel: La razón de su vida*, Editorial Sudamericana, Buenos Aires, 1998.

Sáenz Quesada, Maria, *Isabel Perón*, Editorial Planeta, Buenos Aires, 2003.

Sampay, A. (ed.), *Las Constituciones de la Nación Argentina (1810–1972)*, Editorial Universitaria de Buenos Aires, 1975.

Sarmiento, Domingo F., *Facundo: Or, Civilization and Barbarism*, Penguin Classics 1999.

Scobie, James R., *Argentina: a City and a Nation*, World Bank, 1971.

——, *Secondary Cities of Argentina. The Social History of Corrientes, Salta an Mendoza, 1850–1910*, Stanford University Press, Stanford, CA, 1988.

Seoné, María, *Todo o nada*, Editorial Planeta, Buenos Aires, 1992.

Shumway, Nicolas, *The Invention of Argentina*, University of Califor Press, 1991.

Soneira, Abelardo Jorge, *Las estrategias institucionales de la Iglesia Cat (1880–1976)*, Centro Editor de América Latina, Buenos Aires, 1989

Turner, Frederick C. and Miguens, José Enrique (eds), *Juan Perón an Reshaping of Argentina*, University of Pittsburgh Press, 1983.

Verbitsky, Horacio, *Robo para la Corona*, Editorial Planeta, Buenos 1992.

Walsh, R. *¿Quién mato a Rosendo?* Ediciones de la Flor, Buenos Aire (5th edition).

Wornat, Olga, *Menem: La vida privada*, Editorial Planeta, Bueno 1999.

Zicolillo, J., Montenegro, N, *Los Saadi: historia de un feudo – del 45 Soledad*, Editorial Legasa, Buenos Aires, 1991.

MEMOIRS

Amadeo, Mario, *Ayer, hoy, mañana*, Ediciones Gure, Buenos Air

Ara, Pedro, *El caso Eva Perón*, CVS Ediciones, Madrid, 1974.

Braden, Spruille, *Diplomats and Demagogues*, Arlington House, 1971.

Duarte, Erminda, *Mi hermana Evita*, Ediciones Centro de E Perón, Buenos Aires, 1972.

Duarte de Perón, Eva, *La razón de mi vida*, Ediciones Peuser, B 1951.

Eloy Martínez, Tomás, *Las memorias del general*, Editorial Pla Aires, 1996.

Kelly, Sir David V., *The Ruling Few*, Hollis and Carter, Lond edition).

Monzalvo, Luis, *Testigo de la primera hora del peronismo: r ferroviario*, Editorial Pleamar, Buenos Aires, 1974.

Pavón Pereyra, Enrique, *Perón tal como es*, Ediciones Ma Buenos Aires, 1973.

Perón, Juan, *Del poder al exilio*, Ediciones Sintesis, Buenos

——, *La fuerza es el derecho de las bestias*, Editorial Volv 1987.

——, *Yo, Juan Domingo Perón, Relato Autobiográfico*, (Tena, Luis Calvo, Esteban Peicovich (eds)). Editorial P 1976.

Reyes, Cipriano, *La farsa del peronismo*, Sudamerican 1987.

Dr. Carlos Eroles, historian.

Msgr. Gerardo Farrell, historian, Vicar General and Auxiliary Bishop of Morón.

Dr. Floreal Forni, sociologist, former member of Acción Católica.

Dr. José Alberto Furque, ex-federal deputy for Catamarca.

Msgr. Elmer Miani, Bishop of Catamarca.

Dr. Emilio F. Mignone, former member of Acción Católica, Director of Education for Buenos Aires province until 1951, director of CELS.

Sen. Alberto Montbrun, provincial senator UCR (Mendoza).

Msgr. Jaime de Nevares, Bishop Emeritus of Neuquén.

Msgr. Jerónimo Podestá, former bishop of Avellaneda.

Msgr. Cándido Rubiolo, Archbishop of Mendoza.

Father Sergio Schaub, Pallotine priest.

Dra Amalia Sesto de Leiva, Fiscal de Estado, Catamarca.

Father Fernando Storni, SJ, director of Centro de Investigaciones y Acción Social, Buenos Aires.

Dr. José Vitar, former PJ legislator, Tucumán.

ARTICLES

Cheresky, I., 'Sindicatos y fuerzas políticas en la Argentina preperonista (1930–43)', *Boletin de Estudios Latinoamericanos y del Caribe*, 31, December 1981.

Forni, F., 'Catolicismo y peronismo', *Unidos*, April 1987, December 1987, April 1988.

Frigerio, J.O., 'Perón y la Iglesia: historia de un conflicto inútil', *Todo es Historia*, October–November 1984.

Little, W., 'A Note on Political Incorporation: The Argentine *Plan Político* of 1955', *Journal of Latin American Studies*, vol. 14, no. 2, 455–64, 1982.

——, 'Electoral Aspects of Peronism, 1946–1954', *Journal of Interamerican Studies and World Affairs*, 15, 3 August 1973.

——, 'Party and State in Peronist Argentina 1945–1955', *Hispanic American Historical Review*, 53, November 1973.

——, 'The Popular Origins of Peronism', in Rock, D. (ed.), *Argentina in the 20th Century*, Duckworth & Co., London, 1975.

Machado, C. (ed.), 'Perón: estado y clase media' and '*Las clases medias argentinas*', in *Las Clases Sociales en América Latina: Documentos*, Montevideo, 1969.

Navarro, M., 'Evita and the Crisis of 17 October 1945: A Case Study of Peronist and Anti-Peronist Mythology', *Journal of Latin American Studies* vol. 12, no. 1, 1980.

Sidicaro, R., 'Consideraciones sociológicas sobre las relaciones entre el peronismo y la clase obrera en la Argentina 1943–1955', *Boletín de Estudios Latinoamericanos y del Caribe*, 31, December 1981.

UNPUBLISHED THESES

Deiner, J., 'ATLAS: A Labor Instrument of Argentine Expansionism under Perón', Ph.D. thesis, Rutgers University, 1969.

Hedges, J., 'Federal Relations and Provincial Politics in Argentina, 1976–1991', Ph.D. thesis, University of Liverpool, 1996.

Lizondo, M.A., 'The Impact of the Sugar Industry on the Middle Class of an Argentine City: San Miguel de Tucumán, 1869–1895', Ph.D. thesis, George Washington University, 1982.

Supplee, J.E., 'Provincial Elites and the Economic Transformation of Mendoza, 1880–1914', Ph.D. thesis, University of Texas at Austin, 1988.

INDEX

Acción Católica, 95, 129, 160, 161, 163
Acdel Vilas, Edgardo, 212–13, 232
Agosti, Orlando, 214
Agriculture, 15–16, 21–22, 26, 27–28, 124, 224, 228–9, 241; and Kirchner, 288
Alberdi, Juan B., 9, 12, 229
Alem, Leandro, 32–33
Alfonsín, Raúl, 218–19, 243, 245–50, 253–4, 259, 261, 274; and human rights, 246; death of, 289
Alianza Libertadora Nacional (ALN), 85–6, 165
Allende, Salvador, 204
Alonso, José, 182, 184, 192
Alvarez, Carlos 'Chacho', 263, 270, 272
Alvear, Marcelo T., 40–2, 47, 51, 225
Angeloz, Eduardo, 251, 252, 253
Antonio, Jorge, 179, 183
Ara, Pedro, 149, 150, 171
Aramburu, Pedro, 167, 170, 177, 182, 187, 188, 211, 213
Argentine Confederation, 7, 8, 14–15
Arias, Ricardo, 173
Avalos, Eduardo, 81, 99, 102
Austral Plan, 245
Avellaneda, Nicolás, 21–3, 229

Balbín, Ricardo, 121, 146, 147, 178, 195, 201, 205, 218, 270
Baring Brothers, 6, 31
Batista, Fulgencio, 176
Belgrano, Manuel, 5, 229
Benítez, Hernán, 139, 149
'Blue Book', 114
Bordabehere, Enzo, 50
Bordón, José O., 227, 263
Borges, Jorge Luis, 112

Borlenghi, Angel, 121, 161, 164, 165
Braden, Spruille, 113–4, 133
Bramuglia, Juan Atilio, 121
Buenos Aires, city of, 2, 3–6, 8–10, 14, 28–30, 36, 44, 53–4, 286
Buenos Aires, province of, 10, 16, 23, 47, 54, 181, 206, 252, 264, 267–8
Bussi, Antonio Domingo, 232–3

Castro, Fidel, 176
Cafiero, Antonio, 69, 163, 250
Caggiano, Cardinal Antonio, 138, 155
Cámpora, Héctor, 152, 179, 194, 195–6, 198–202, 215
Cantoni, Aldo and Federico, 36, 40, 44
Castillo, Ramón, 51–2, 81, 235
Carrió, Elisa, 281, 286, 289
Caseros, Battle of, 15
Catamarca, province of, 220, 221, 233–9, 249, 251
Catholic Church, 1, 8, 13, 55, 239, 262; and Juárez Celman, 31; and 1943 coup, 83–5; and 1946 election, 112–13; and Perón, 95–7, 128–9, 130–1, 154–67; and Christian Democrat Party, 157–9; and Peronist opposition, 189–92
Cavallo, Domingo, 217, 254, 258, 273, 274, 275, 276
Central de los Trabajadores Argentinos (CTA), 267
Cepeda, Battle of, 15
Chubut, province of, 15, 62
Cobos, Julio, 288
CONADEP (National Commission on the Disappearance of Persons), 212, 216, 246, 247
Concordancia, 47, 50–2, 60

Confederación General del Trabajo (CGT), 58–9, 93, 101, 103, 106, 115, 119, 160, 164, 177, 182, 186, 187, 199, 204, 230, 267, 285

Conquest of the Desert, 22–3, 229, 240

Constitution of 1853, 11–14; of 1949, 128–9, 133–5; of 1994, 261–2

Convertibility Plan, 254, 263, 270, 278, 291

Cooke, John William, 179

Córdoba, province of, 2, 15, 23, 36, 167, 187–8, 206, 286

Cordobazo, 187–8

Coup d'état of 1930, 45, 46; of 1943, 59–60, 81; of 1955, 163–4, 167–9; of 1962, 181; of 1966, 194; of 1976, 214–5

Debt, 6, 20, 31, 217, 273, 275, 283, 287, 290; 2001 default, 277–8

De la Rua, Fernando, 270, 280; presidency, 272–6; resignation, 276

Del Carril, Hugo, 112

De la Sota, José, 271, 273, 277, 281

De la Torre, Lisandro, 32, 50

Derqui, Santiago, 14

Dodero, Alberto, 126–7

Dorrego, Manuel, 7

Duarte, Juan, 73, 77, 136, 151–2

Duarte de Perón, Eva, *see* Perón, Eva

Duhalde, Eduardo, 252, 261–2, 264, 266, 267–8, 269–70, 271, 274; presidency, 277–81

Eichmann, Adolf, 137, 138

Ejército Revolucionario del Pueblo (ERP), 188, 194, 199, 206, 211, 212, 216, 231

Entre Ríos, province of, 6, 14, 15, 36

Espejo, José, 115, 120, 144, 152, 179

Eva Perón Foundation, 139–42, 152

Evita, *see* Perón, Eva

Ezeiza massacre, 200–1

Falklands/Malvinas conflict, 218

Farrell, Edelmiro, 82, 96, 102–3

Federalism, 11–12, 221–2; and federal intervention, 11, 13, 233, 237, 238–9

Fernández de Kirchner, Cristina, 281, 282, 283, 286–91

Figuerola, José, 121, 134

Firmenich, Mario, 187, 204, 211

Foreign trade, 4, 20, 21–2, 25–6, 37, 40–1, 47–8, 51

Fuerza de Orientación Radical de la Juventud Argentina (FORJA), 48, 85

Framini, Andrés, 181, 183

Franceschi, Gustavo, 84, 128

Franco, Francisco, 84, 136, 176

Frepaso, 262, 268, 273

Frondizi, Arturo, 147, 178, 179, 180–1, 193, 211, 237

Galtieri, Leopoldo, 218

Garay, Juan de, 2

Gardel, Carlos, 44

Gauchos, gauchesque literature, 19–20

Gay, Luis, 105, 111, 115, 118–20

General Confederation of Labour, *see Confederación General del Trabajo*

Grupo de Oficiales Unidos (GOU), 67, 81–3

Guevara, Ernesto 'Che', 176, 180, 186–7

Guido, José María, 181–2

Haya de la Torre, Víctor Raúl, 86–7

Human rights, 211–13, 215–17, 232, 246–8, 259

Ibarguren, Juana, 68–72

Imbert, Anibal, 77, 78

Illia, Arturo, 182–4

Immigration, 15–16, 19–20, 28–31, 54, 224, 229, 234, 241

Industry, 25–6, 28, 37, 40–1, 52–3; automotive, 41; import substitution, 52–3, 59, 124; mining, 233; oil, 41, 43, 223, 241–2

Inflation, 149, 245–6, 256, 285, 291–2

Instituto Argentino para la Promocion del Intercambio (IAPI), 122
Internal migration, 53–5, 56–7
International Monetary Fund (IMF), 266, 269, 273, 275, 279–80, 283, 290
Irigoyen, Bernardo de, 32
Isabelita, *see* Martínez de Perón, María Estela

Jauretche, Arturo, 48, 85
Juárez Celman, Miguel, 23, 30–2
Justicialismo (Partido Justicialista), 129–30
Justo, Agustín P., 47–50, 51
Justo, Juan B., 32, 47

Kelly, Guillermo Patricio, 85
Kirchner, Néstor, 238, 281, 282, 287, 289, 290; presidency, 282–86
Krieger Vasena, Adalberto, 186, 188

Lamarque, Libertad, 79–80
Lanusse, Alejandro, 188, 192–3, 194, 196
La Rioja, province of, 8, 9, 16, 249, 251
Lastiri, Raúl, 199
Lavagna, Roberto, 280, 281, 283, 286
Lavalle, Juan, 7
Law of Empheteusis, 6–7
Lencinas, Carlos Washington and José Néstor, 36, 40, 43, 225–6
Levingston, Roberto, 188
Liberating Revolution, 170–1
Liga Patriótica, 38–9
Liniers, Santiago, 4
Lonardi, Eduardo, 65, 167, 168, 170, 187, 189, 237
López, Estanislao, 8
López, Francisco Solano, 16
López Jordán, Ricardo, 16
López Murphy, Ricardo, 272, 273, 281
López Rega, José, 184–5, 193, 195, 198–9, 203, 204, 205, 207, 210–11, 212, 213
'Loyalty Day', *see* October 17, 1945

Luder, Italo, 213, 219, 245, 250, 252

Machinea, José Luis, 272
Magaldi, Agustín, 73, 74
Maradona, Diego Armando, 245
Marcó del Pont, Mercedes, 290
Martínez de Hoz, José, 217
Martínez de Perón, María Estela (Isabelita), 173–6, 183–4, 193, 195, 201, 202–5, 232; presidency, 210–14; coup against, 214–5
Massera, Emilio, 213, 214, 216, 217
Mendoza, province of, 2, 27, 36, 40, 43–4, 167, 184, 220, 221, 222–7
Menem, Carlos Saúl, 33, 227, 238, 248, 250–68, 270, 271, 281–2; presidency, 253–68; and corruption, 257–9, 274; privatizations, 254–6; and re-election, 265–8
Menéndez, Benjamín, 145, 187
Mercante, Domingo, 81, 90, 94, 115, 129, 134, 261–2
Miranda, Miguel, 121–2, 124
Mitre, Bartolomé, 9, 15–19, 21, 32
Montoneros, 188, 191, 192, 194, 199, 205, 207, 211, 213, 216, 248, 259
Monzalvo, Luis, 94, 105
Moreau de Justo, Alicia, 298
Moreno, Mariano, 5
Mosconi, Enrique, 41
Movimiento Popular Neuquino (MPN), 221, 240, 242–4
Movimiento Todos por la Patria (MTP), 248
Mussolini, Benito, 84, 88

National Reorganization Process (PRN), 215–6
Neuquén, province of, 220, 221, 239–44
Nicolini, Oscar, 77, 99, 135

October 17, 1945, 101–11, 230; Loyalty Day, 123
Onganía, Juan Carlos, 181, 231; and 1966 coup, 184, 189; presidency, 185–88, 190; overthrow, 188

Ongaro, Raimundo, 186
Ortega, Ramón 'Palito', 233, 264, 267, 269
Ortiz, Roberto, 50–1

Palacios, Alfredo, 149
Partido Autonomista Nacional (PAN), 17, 21, 23, 24, 32, 33
Partido Laborista, 111, 114, 118–9, 242
Patrón Costas, Robustiano, 52, 82, 235
Pavón, Battle of, 15
Pellegrini, Carlos, 32, 34
Peñaloza, Vicente 'Chacho', 16
Pérez Jiménez, Marcos, 175, 176
Perón, Eva Duarte de (Evita), 114, 117, 135–43; early life, 68–73; acting career, 73–7, 78–9; relationship with Perón, 77–80, 97; and military, 96–7, 143; and October 17, 105–6; marriage to Perón, 111; and Church, 130–1, 136–7, 155; 'Rainbow Tour', 126, 136–7; illness and death, 143–7, 148–51; vice-presidential bid, 143–5; and CGT, 14', 126, 136–7; illness and death, 143–7, 148–51; vice-presidential bid, 143–5; and CGT, 145; body of, 171–2, 193, 211, 213
Perón, Juan Domingo, 46, 186, 192–6, 226, 230, 236, 242, 243; role in 1930 coup, 13, 67–8, 98–9; early life, 61–3; military career, 63–7; first marriage, 63–4, 65; and fascism, 66; and GOU, 67, 81; and Evita, 77–80; and Nazis, 87–9, 137–8, 265; and trade unions, 52, 58–60, 89–94, 109–10; and Church, 95–7, 112–13, 130–1, 154–67; 1945 arrest, 99–101; and October 17, 101–4; and army, 107, 109–10, 111, 166; marriage to Evita, 111; 1946 election, 114–15; first Five-Year Plan, 121–5; and nationalizatons, 126–8; and 1951 elections, 143–7; second Five-Year Plan, 154, 155; and UES, 158; and

June 1955 coup attempt, 163–4; overthrow, 167–9; exile, 168, 173, 175–6; 'Operation Return', 182–3; 1973 re-election, 201–9; death, 208–9
Peronism, ideology, 85–7; and Nazism, 88; opposition to, 97, 98–101, 110, 113–15, 117, 118–21; Peronist Doctine, 129–32; 'Third Position', 132–3, 260; 'Organized Community', 131–2; proscription of, 176–84
Peter, José, 90, 92
Pinedo, Federico, 49, 51
Piqueteros, 266, 276, 285
Pius XII, 137
Privatization, 254–6

Quijano, Hortensio, 111, 145, 148
Quiroga, Facundo, 8, 9, 250

Railways, 18, 26, 27, 125, 126, 228, 230, 233
Ramírez, Pedro, 82
Rawson, Arturo, 82
Rebel Patagonia (*Patagonia Rebelde*), 38–9
Redrado, Martin, 290
Remes Lenicov, Jorge, 278, 280
Reutemann, Carlos, 264, 267, 271, 273, 277, 281
Revenue-sharing, 49–50, 249–50
Reyes, Cipriano, 93, 99, 100, 105, 111, 115, 118–19, 298
Rico, Aldo, 246–8
Rivadavia, Bernardino, 5–7, 9
Roca, Julio A., 13, 32, 33, 229, 240; and Conquest of the Desert, 22–3; presidency, 24–30
Roca-Runciman Treaty, 47–8
Rodrigo, Celestino, 213
Rodríguez Saa, Adolfo, 267, 277, 281
Rojas, Isaac, 168, 176
Rosas, Juan Manuel de, 7–10, 49, 260
Rucci, José, 194, 205, 207
Ruckauf, Carlos, 271, 273, 277

Saadi, Ramón, 235, 237, 301

Saadi, Vicente, 218, 234, 236–8, 249
Saavedra Lamas, Carlos, 50
Sabato, Ernesto, 110, 169
Sáenz Peña, Luis, 33
Sáenz Peña, Roque, 35, 36
Sáenz Peña law, 35
Salta, province of, 17
San Juan, province of, 17–18, 36, 40, 44, 77, 167
San Martín, José de, 5–6, 222
Santa Cruz, province of, 39, 62, 282
Santiago del Estero, province of, 2, 36, 236
Sarmiento, Domingo F., 9, 12, 17–21
Sapag family, 221, 239–40, 241, 242–4
Scalabrini Ortiz, Raúl, 48, 85
Scioli, Daniel, 281, 283, 289
Seineldín, Mohamed Alí, 247–8
Sociedad Rural (Rural Society), 22, 98, 113
Solano Lima, Vicente, 182, 195, 202
Solis, Juan de, 2
Standard Oil, 41, 43, 153
Stroessner, Alfredo, 173

Tacuara, 187
Tamborini, José, 111, 114
Tejedor, Carlos, 21, 23
Tizón, Aurelia, 63–5, 296
Trade Unions (see also CGT), 38, 39, 41, 54–9, 90–4, 184, 186, 187, 267
Tragic Week (Semana Trágica), 38–9
Triple A (Argentine Anti-Communist Alliance), 198, 201, 211
Trujillo, Rafael, 176

Tucumán, province of, 2, 5, 13, 27, 186, 211–13, 220, 221, 227–31, 236, 264

Unión Cívica Radical (UCR), 32–4, 36, 47, 134, 178, 226, 269; antipersonalistas, 40, 42, 47; UCRI, 178, 181, 182; UCRP, 178, 181, 182
Unión Democrática, 111–13
Unión Industrial Argentina (UIA), 54, 99
Unión de Estudiantes Secundarios (UES), 158, 160
United Provinces, 6–7, 10
Uriburu, José Felix, 46–7
Urquiza, Justo José de, 10, 11, 14, 15

Valle, Juan José, 172–3, 188
Vandor, Augusto Timoteo, 179, 191, 182, 183, 184, 186, 188, 206, 207
Vargas, Getulio, 86, 153
Videla, Jorge R., 214
Vuletich, Eduardo, 161

War of the Triple Alliance, 16–17, 22–3

Yabran, Alfredo, 258–9
Yacimientos Petrolíferos Fiscales (YPF), 41, 43, 153, 223, 241–2, 254, 266
Yrigoyen, Hipólito, 13, 21, 33–4; presidency, 36–40; second presidency, 42–6; and Lencinas, 36, 40, 43, 225; coup against, 45–6; death, 45